YOUR
LABRADOR
RETRIEVER
PUPPY

MONTH by MONTH

TERRY ALBERT, DEB ELDREDGE, DVM, and DON and BARB IRONSIDE

△
ALPHA
A member of Penguin Random House LLC

ALPHA BOOKS

Published by Penguin Random House LLC

Penguin Random House LLC, 375 Hudson Street, New York, New York 10014, USA • Penguin Random House (Canada), 320 Front Street West, Suite 1400, Toronto, Ontario M5V 3B6, Canada • Penguin Books Ltd., 80 Strand, London WC2R 0RL, England • Penguin Ireland, 25 St. Stephen's Green, Dublin 2, Ireland (a division of Penguin Books Ltd.) • Penguin Random House (Australia), 707 Collins St, Docklands, Victoria 3008, Australia • Penguin Random House India Pvt. Ltd., 3rd Floor Mindmill Corporate Tower, Plot No. 24A, Sector 16A, Film City, Noida, UP 201 301, India • Penguin Random House (NZ), 67 Apollo Drive, Rosedale, North Shore, Auckland 1311, New Zealand • Penguin Books (South Africa) (Pty.) Ltd., 24 Sturdee Avenue, Rosebank, Johannesburg 2196, South Africa • Penguin Books Ltd., Registered Offices: 80 Strand, London WC2R 0RL, England

007-190021-December2012

International Standard Book Number: 978-1-61564-221-2
Library of Congress Catalog Card Number: 2012941777

17   16   15   10   9   8

Interpretation of the printing code: The rightmost number of the first series of numbers is the year of the book's printing; the rightmost number of the second series of numbers is the number of the book's printing. For example, a printing code of 12-1 shows that the first printing occurred in 2012.

Printed in the United States of America

Note: This publication contains the opinions and ideas of its authors. It is intended to provide helpful and informative material on the subject matter covered. It is sold with the understanding that the authors and publisher are not engaged in rendering professional services in the book. If the reader requires personal assistance or advice, a competent professional should be consulted.

The authors and publisher specifically disclaim any responsibility for any liability, loss, or risk, personal or otherwise, which is incurred as a consequence, directly or indirectly, of the use and application of any of the contents of this book.

Most Alpha books are available at special quantity discounts for bulk purchases for sales promotions, premiums, fund-raising, or educational use. Special books, or book excerpts, can also be created to fit specific needs. For details, write: Special Markets, Alpha Books, 375 Hudson Street, New York, NY 10014.

Publisher: *Mike Sanders*

Executive Managing Editor: *Billy Fields*

Development Editors: *Mark Reddin and Christy Wagner*

Senior Production Editor: *Janette Lynn*

Copy Editor: *Jan Zoya*

Cover and Book Designer: *Kurt Owens*

Indexer: *Heather McNeill*

Layout: *Ayanna Lacey*

Proofreader: *Laura Caddell*

Contents at a Glance

This book is dedicated to my friend and mentor, Liz Palika. Thank you so much for your friendship and inspiration over the 25 years we've known each other.

Appendixes

Contents

Month 10: Transition 231

Month 11: Putting Your Lab to Work 259

Month 12 (and Beyond): Your Lab Grows Up   293

Introduction

Over 20 years ago, an 8-week-old yellow Labrador Retriever puppy named Tank came into my life. I had only owned one dog, a Sheltie, up until then, and I had no idea at the time that this puppy and the Labrador breed would become so special to me.

During our years together, we enjoyed obedience competition, hunting tests, and agility. He accompanied me as I rode my horse on miles of logging roads through the woods, and he went to work with me each day when I became a dog trainer. Then I volunteered for Labrador rescue and found out that every Lab I met was just as fun-loving and smart as my Tank.

He was a challenging dog, a combination of field and show breeding. He was intense and focused; he did nothing halfway but threw himself into every adventure full force—I had to hurry to keep up! I never learned so much, made so many wonderful friends, or had so much fun as those years I spent with Tank, my first Labrador Retriever. Since then, more wonderful Labs have shared my home, and they have been equally devoted, fun, and cherished.

In This Book

Each chapter in this book covers a month of your Lab puppy's development. You learn what you can expect from your pup and how to deal with each stage of growth. It's easy to be overwhelmed by the challenges of raising a Lab puppy, and I hope this book helps you through the first 12 months of this big adventure!

First you find out what goes on at the breeder's and how her care affects the future of your puppy. You get tips on choosing the right breeder and puppy for your family. You also learn how to prepare for his arrival and make him comfortable in his new home.

The following chapters explain the various aspects, month by month, of your puppy's physical development, health care, nutritional needs, grooming, socialization, behavior, and training. And we end each chapter with a special section dedicated to building your friendship with your new Labrador Retriever puppy—because after all, isn't that one of the most important things?

Although no two Lab puppies mature at exactly the same rate, the process is the same. If your pup grows faster or slower, it doesn't necessarily mean something is wrong. He'll catch up or slow down and turn out wonderfully normal.

The Extras

You'll find extra information sprinkled throughout the book that help you raise your Lab puppy. Here's what to look for:

> ### DOG TALK

These are definitions of terms you may not understand or haven't heard before. They're also included in the glossary at the back of the book.

> ### HAPPY PUPPY

Turn to these sidebars for ideas to help you raise a happy and content puppy.

> ### TIPS AND TAILS

In these sidebars, you find hints and advice to help you with various puppy-raising challenges.

Acknowledgments

It takes a village to raise a Lab, and it took a village to help me write this book. Special thanks to my advisers, Barb and Don Ironside and Deb Eldredge, DVM, who offered valuable input and carefully reviewed every word. Also thank you to the many breeders, trainers, and other experts who shared their knowledge and experience with me: Susan Eberhardt; Pat Hastings; Pat Schaap; Sarbit Singh, DVM; Heather Luis; Nina Mann; Melanie Montiero; Lorna O'Connor of CCI; Fran Scarinci; Christine Rinaldi; Cary Saunders; and Nancy Shahan-Wall. —Terry

Trademarks

All terms mentioned in this book that are known to be or are suspected of being trademarks or service marks have been appropriately capitalized. Alpha Books and Penguin Random House LLC cannot attest to the accuracy of this information. Use of a term in this book should not be regarded as affecting the validity of any trademark or service mark.

4-H Program	Benadryl
Advantage	Boy Scouts of America

Canine Good Citizen

CGC (Canine Good Citizen program)

Dawn

Fleabusters

Frontline

Galileo Bone (Nylabone)

Girl Scouts of America

Kong

Kwik Stop

Missing Link whole food supplement

Planet Dog Orbee-Tuff

Rescue Remedy

Scrabble

Simple Green

Styrofoam

Thundershirt

Vetwrap

Vicks VapoRub

Months 1 & 2

The Littermate

Months 1 & 2	Month 3
Breeder starts socialization	

Littermates and mother teach appropriate canine behavior

Rapid growth

Welcome to the first 2 months of your Labrador Retriever puppy's life! Even before your Lab puppy is born, hundreds of outside factors influence her future health and happiness. In this chapter, we follow a litter's physical and mental development from birth through the first 8 weeks.

You learn how the mother dog's health care, nutrition, and temperament affect her puppies. You also discover that the breeder plays a crucial role before, during, and after whelping. The breeder also starts socializing the puppies before they go to their new homes.

Physical Development

A Lab puppy is totally dependent on her mother during the first 2 weeks of life, when she's unaware of anything in her world except food and the warmth of her mom and littermates. But by the time she's 8 weeks old, she'll have gone through several important developmental stages and be independent enough to leave the litter and move on to her new home.

At Birth

Lab puppies average 12 to 20 ounces at birth. Their weight depends on how many puppies are in the litter, with bigger litters producing smaller puppies. Weight can also vary from puppy to puppy within the litter.

The average litter size for Labs is 8 to 10 puppies, although it can range from a single puppy to as many as 16. With a large litter, the breeder spends more time ensuring everyone gets a turn to nurse. The breeder also may have to supplement the mother's milk with hand-feeding.

As each pup is born, the mother severs the umbilical cord and removes the amniotic sac that surrounds each individual puppy. At birth, puppies have an incomplete nervous system and don't move spontaneously on their own, so it's up to Mom to get them started. She licks them to make them breathe, stimulate blood circulation, and prompt them to eliminate.

The breeder supervises the birthing process and removes the sac if Mom is busy with other puppies. She also cleans and ties off the stump where the umbilical cord was attached. She then puts an ID collar of sorts on each pup, usually rickrack or ribbon. Each collar is a different color so the breeder can keep track of each puppy and his or her development.

For at least the first 2 weeks, the *whelping box* is kept in a quiet, private place. Mom doesn't want other dogs around and won't welcome canine intruders. Too much commotion is stressful for her and her puppies, and she'll burn precious calories fussing and protecting her babies. She'll eventually calm down as she gets used to her duties. After the puppies' eyes open, the whelping box can be moved to a more stimulating environment so the pups can start getting used to household sights and sounds.

When first born, some Lab puppies have ridges in their coat that look like corduroy fabric, or like someone ran a comb though their fur. This is from being squished together in the uterus and goes away almost immediately. Some breeders think it is a predictor of a thick, healthy coat later in life.

When the puppies are 3 or 4 days old, their blood is capable of clotting, and some breeders will have their veterinarian remove the front *dewclaws*. This used to be standard procedure for Lab puppies, but it's not necessary and is now seldom practiced. Some people feel removing the dewclaws is important for hunting dogs because the dewclaws get snagged and torn in the brush while they're working. Others feel that dogs use their dewclaws for holding onto things (such as when they're chewing on something) and for climbing.

DOG TALK

The **whelping box** is a large nesting area where the mother gives birth to her puppies. There's often a ledge around the sides, so Mom won't accidentally crush a puppy against the wall. The **dewclaw** is a vestigial toe and toenail partway up each of a dog's front legs. It serves no obvious purpose.

The period between birth and 2 weeks is called the neonatal period. Puppies sleep 90 percent of this time and eat the remaining 10 percent. They're born with a sucking/

rooting reflex so they can nurse; this is more pronounced when they are 24 to 48 hours old. But by 4 days old, this reflex disappears, and they nurse on their own.

At birth, a puppy has an underdeveloped, primitive sense of touch, smell, and orientation to objects. She can't see, hear, or move away from stimuli yet; if something hurts, she'll squeal and wiggle in distress. By 2 days old, the puppies are able to move on their own toward Mom and compete for a place to nurse. The breeder places a surface such as fleece in the whelping box so the pups can dig in their feet, which helps them get around.

A newborn's eyes and ears are closed. The eyes may blink as a reflex, but she can't see yet because the retina isn't fully developed. She sleeps with her head tucked to her chest. During the first week, the puppies move a lot in their sleep—kicking, whimpering, and jerking as they start to exercise their muscles. By 6 to 10 days of age, their sleep is quieter and their waking time is more active.

At 8 to 10 days, the puppies should be double their birth weight. By 7 to 8 days, a Lab's front legs can support her weight. Within a day or two, her rear limbs are able to support her pelvis. She'll start to stand and be walking by 10 to 12 days.

A Lab pup's eyes and ears open at about the same time as she begins walking. At 10 to 14 days, her eyelids open. She can't see anything but shadows at this point, and blinking is still a reflex rather than voluntary reaction. At the same time, her ear canals open, she starts to hear, and she'll startle at noise.

Weeks 2 and 3

Days 14 to 21 mark what's called the transitional period. During this time, the puppies' senses and motor skills are still poorly developed, but they are able to explore more of their surroundings. A sure sign of good neurological development at this time is, when set down, a puppy extends her back legs in anticipation of reaching the ground.

The mother is now producing peak amounts of milk. The pups are growing fast in these last days prior to *weaning*. Their suckling is strong and well developed. The puppies weigh approximately 2½ to 3 pounds and gain about 1 pound during this week.

> **DOG TALK**
>
> **Weaning** is the process of gradually changing a puppy's diet from mother's milk to solid food.

Mom continues to clean up after her puppies until they're 3 or 4 weeks old and then the breeder takes over. By keeping their potty area clean, the breeder starts the housetraining process. At about 18 days, the pups move to a corner of the whelping box to relieve themselves. By 21 days, they have established a group elimination area. The breeder enlarges their living area to take advantage of the fact that the puppies do not want to sleep and play in their own waste. She may add a wire pen so the pups can leave the whelping box to play, but they're still too young to have the run of a large room.

Around 19 to 21 days, a pup responds to light by moving her head away or blinking. Her hearing also continues to develop, and she'll startle to loud noises. Her sight also improves, and she becomes more mobile.

When the puppies are 3 weeks old, the socialization period begins and lasts until approximately 12 weeks. During this time, positive and negative experiences will affect her behavior for the rest of her life. The breeder introduces a variety of household sights and sounds, like the television, dishwasher, vacuum cleaner, and radio.

The puppies also start interacting with each other. They experience a dramatic increase in motor development as they start to chew and explore their surroundings.

Weeks 4 to 6

During this period, the central nervous system continues to mature. Even that cute little wagging tail indicates neuromuscular development.

The puppies start to look less like baby rats and more like dogs. At 4 weeks, a Lab pup is a pudgy little lump that doesn't appear to even have legs and weighs roughly 6 or 7 pounds. By 6 weeks, she's found those legs and is making good use of them. Labs grow dramatically during this period, and their puppy coats get longer and thicker.

The pups can now orient to sounds and sights around them. The optic nerves mature by 28 days, so the puppies can see more than just shadows. Shapes begin to have meaning. By 30 days, they start to recognize familiar sounds. The ears are fully open at 35 days (5 weeks), and the pups no longer startle to noise as they did when their ears first opened.

At 3½ to 4 weeks, their teeth start to come in, and the pups are able to chew semi-solid food for the first time. Now is the time Mom starts to wean her litter, and the breeder introduces puppy food.

Often the breeder starts feeding the litter outside. The pups naturally wander away from the eating area after the meal to relieve themselves. This helps them learn a routine of eating, eliminating outside, and coming inside. Many litters are well on their way to being housetrained before they go to their new homes.

By 4 weeks, puppies need to start eliminating on different surfaces. If a puppy is encouraged to potty on grass, dirt, concrete, and gravel now, she'll be willing to go on various surfaces throughout her life (for example, if she is boarded in a concrete kennel run). Both males and females now squat when they relieve themselves.

A host of new behaviors start when a Lab puppy discovers she has teeth. She now has the tools she'll use to explore her world, and everything that fits in her mouth is fair game. She'll chew dog beds, towels, chair legs, anything that moves … and anything that doesn't. She'll carry things around, and tug on your pants leg.

Her interactions with her littermates change dramatically, too. Puppies follow each other around play-fighting, guarding their toys, and growling. She'll compete for food and guard it from the others. She'll shake her head while holding a toy. She'll start to understand how her jaw pressure affects others, learning the critical skill of bite inhibition. Play-biting leads to discipline by her littermates as well as her mother, but it teaches her to communicate without injuring. The mother also disciplines her puppies if they bite her too hard while nursing, which speeds up the weaning process.

Individual puppies can now be taken away from their mom and littermates for short breaks so they get used to being separated. This helps a puppy feel less frightened when she leaves her family to go to her new home.

Weeks 6 to 8

By this time, a litter of Labs is a lot of fun. They start to gang up on each other, wrestle, sniff each other's faces and butts, and learn to recognize each other. Puppies begin actively hunting and playing. They can be seen pouncing on bugs and butterflies, and they also begin play-mounting each other.

At 6 weeks, a Lab puppy weighs 10 or 11 pounds, with males being heavier.

The puppy's vision is not yet completely developed, but as the retina matures, she can follow objects with her eyes and respond to light. She can recognize shapes, so this is a good time to start exposing her to other animals, like cats, rabbits, and birds. At this point, it's enough for the pup to get acquainted with the sight, sounds, and smells of another animal. Too much interaction isn't safe for either species.

It's also an excellent time to introduce people of various sizes and shapes. A hat or umbrella dramatically changes what the puppy sees, even on the same person she just met. Research has shown that a puppy who has met a large variety of people, places, and things when very young accepts new and unusual things much more easily throughout her life.

By 8 weeks, a puppy is mature enough to learn and remember new things, and this is an excellent time to start training, especially housetraining. At 10 to 12 pounds, she's also getting a bit hefty to carry around, but until she's had all her inoculations, the breeder carries her whenever she leaves home. You should continue this practice when she arrives at your home.

> ### HAPPY PUPPY
>
> Here's an easy way to carry your Lab puppy: with her facing sideways, scoop under her front legs from the side with one arm, and over her rear with the other. Steady her hind end as you lift by holding up her legs while you hold the front of her body slightly higher. Hold her against your body so she feels secure and isn't likely to wiggle free.

Lab puppies are too heavy for small children to carry, so don't let them drag her around by her armpits or collar. At home, she should happily follow her new friends. Until she is able to walk nicely on a leash, let Mom and Dad carry the pup.

Health

A diligent breeder does her best to produce healthy Labradors. Even before the mother is bred, the breeder takes steps to prevent health problems in future puppies. When the puppies arrive, she monitors both the mother and the litter to ensure they all thrive and remain healthy.

Health Clearances the Parents Should Have

Careful pretesting for inheritable defects helps ensure your puppy will live a long and healthy life. In some cases, an affected dog never shows symptoms but is still a carrier of the genes that can pass along the defect. If two carriers are bred to each other, a percentage of the puppies will develop the disorder.

The breeder should have her veterinarian conduct the following tests before the dogs are bred:

Brucellosis: This is a bacterial disease causing reproductive problems in both male and female dogs. Therefore, both parents should be tested before breeding. Brucellosis causes stillborn puppies, or pups who die within a few days of birth. Affected breeding dogs should be spayed or neutered.

Hip dysplasia: Hip dysplasia is a crippling disease that affects many Labs. Symptoms often don't appear until a dog is older, when arthritis begins to affect her movement. At 2 years old, a Lab's hips are mature enough to be x-rayed to identify the condition. The x-rays are sent to the Orthopedic Foundation for Animals (OFA) or PennHIP for grading. The dog's hips are rated from excellent to severely dysplastic. The hip grades of Excellent, Good, and Fair are within normal limits. Dogs with no problems are listed as Normal.

Elbow dysplasia: Like hip dysplasia, elbow dysplasia affects many Labs and can also be identified through x-rays when a dog reaches 2 years old. OFA only grades affected dogs, designating Grade I through III, to explain the level of degenerative joint disease associated with elbow dysplasia.

Progressive retinal atrophy (PRA): PRA is an incurable disease that causes blindness in Labs. PRA often has late onset in Labs, at about 5 to 8 years, which is well past the first time a dog is usually bred. Once widespread, in recent years, a genetic test has been developed to identify PRA-affected dogs. The test can be done at any age. Results are registered with the Canine Eye Registration Foundation (CERF). Some breeders state that their puppies are "clear (normal) by parentage." This means that two clear parents were bred to each other, and the puppies couldn't have inherited the gene.

Retinal dysplasia: The abnormal development in the eye's retina, currently there is no genetic test available to identify it, so breeders have their dogs' eyes tested annually and register the results with CERF. While examining the eyes, the veterinary ophthalmologist also checks for cataracts.

Tricuspid-valve dysplasia: This causes congestive heart failure. Dogs are tested at 1 year old by a veterinary cardiologist who listens for a heart murmur or other abnormalities. If the cardiologist has any doubts, he recommends a Doppler reading to confirm the condition. Some breeders have the Doppler reading done for all their breeding dogs automatically to eliminate any doubt. Results are registered with the OFA.

Centronuclear myopathy (CNM): CNM is an inherited condition that results in weak muscles and causes the dog to have difficulty walking. A genetic test identifies the disease and is administered at 1 year old. All breeding dogs should be tested. The testing facility provides a certificate saying whether the dog is clear (normal), a carrier, or affected.

Exercise-induced collapse: This is an inherited condition some young Labs (about 1 year old) have that causes them to appear rubber-legged, have difficulty walking, or even collapse after a short period of strenuous exercise. A genetic test is available for the disease, and the testing facility provides a certificate saying whether the dog is clear (normal), a carrier, or affected.

Many Labs don't show symptoms of a genetically inherited problem until they are adults. In Month 12, we go into further detail about these conditions and their effect on an adult dog's long-term health.

The Mother Dog's Care

Well before the puppies are born, the mother dog needs extra food and care. Her health directly affects that of her brood. She needs to be in optimum physical condition when her litter is born.

Mom won't want to leave the nest when she's getting ready to whelp and the first day after giving birth, but she needs to eat because the puppies need nutrition. Producing milk for a large litter of puppies uses up a tremendous amount of energy. The breeder feeds her in the whelping box every 4 or 5 hours so she produces enough milk for her litter. The breeder also takes the mother out for a short walk several times a day so she can relieve herself and have a break.

The mother gets most of the breeder's attention during the first few days. A vet examines the *bitch* within 24 hours after whelping to be sure there are no retained placentas or unborn puppies. He also examines her milk to be sure it looks healthy and safe for the pups.

DOG TALK

A female dog is called a **bitch,** and the mother of the litter is referred to as the *dam*. A male is called a *dog,* and the father of the litter is the *sire*.

The breeder cleans the bitch's nipples and mammary glands after each nursing session. This keeps bacteria from causing her pups to get sick and also protects Mom from mastitis and other problems.

The breeder takes Mom's temperature daily to be sure she isn't developing any delivery-related complications. One problem that can arise is pyometra, a uterine infection. If it's a small litter, Mom can have too much milk, which is very painful and can cause mastitis, an infection of the mammary glands. The breeder also watches for signs of metritis, a bacterial uterine infection that can develop immediately after giving birth. Eclampsia, another post-whelping ailment, is caused by a calcium deficiency.

An unhealthy mother can pass infection to her litter, and the veterinarian can't give the bitch most antibiotics because she would pass a toxic dose to her puppies through her milk. If necessary, the puppies have to be removed from their mother and hand-fed.

> ### TIPS AND TAILS
>
> When you visit the litter, the bitch may not appear as healthy or pretty as you expected. After her puppies are weaned, the mother dog "blows coat" and for several weeks, sheds so much of both her undercoat and outer coat that patches of skin might even show. Her tail appears more like a whip than a typical Lab tail. Even if she was in excellent shape when the pups were born, she's undergone extreme physical and hormonal changes during pregnancy and nursing. Her coat suffers as her milk dries up, her mammary glands shrink back to normal size, her hormones stabilize, and her body gradually returns to its original condition.

Breeder Vigilance

Although individual breeders may handle some of the details differently, they play a significant role in the care of the bitch and her litter. The breeder's first priority during whelping is to assist with delivery. She cleans and stimulates a puppy if Mom is busy with the others. She also ensures the pups start nursing. If there's a lengthy delay between puppies, she may have to transport Mom to the vet for a caesarean (surgical) delivery.

After whelping, the breeder cleans the whelping box and continues to clean it daily while the pups are growing. If bacteria and waste are allowed to accumulate, the health of the puppies and their mother is jeopardized.

The bitch goes through tremendous emotional and physical stress during the early weeks. Even the nicest female can get a little testy. To avoid upsetting her, the breeder keeps visitors and commotion to a minimum. Overhandling the puppies also upsets the dam, and an upset mother could kill or injure her brood.

Observing the mother and her litter, the breeder watches to be sure Mom bonds with her puppies and is caring for them. She checks daily to see everyone—Mom and the puppies—have bright clear eyes, their noses don't run, and there are no other signs of disease.

The breeder weighs each puppy daily so she can verify they are all gaining weight and getting enough food. They should double their weight in the first week. If they aren't, the breeder must figure out if mother doesn't have enough milk, if she has an infection, or if something else is going on.

One of the biggest health risks for newborns is exposure to parvovirus. The virus lasts in the environment for a year or more, and a person or an animal can pick it up on their feet simply by walking in the grass. To protect the litter, the breeder takes precautions when anyone enters the house. Family and guests are asked to take off their shoes before coming indoors. Visitors are asked to wear clean clothes and wash their hands when they arrive. These measures are continued until the pups have all left for their new homes.

When Puppy Problems Occur

If a puppy is fussy, she's usually cold, hungry, or in pain. The breeder needs to figure out what might be the problem because it could be a life-threatening situation.

Too cold: Newborn puppies have very little fat, and their blood vessels are not developed enough to retain heat on their own. Therefore, keeping the litter warm is the highest priority during the first weeks. Nestling with Mother and their littermates keeps the pups warm, and the breeder often provides a heat lamp. If Mom leaves the nest for even a few minutes, the temperature starts to drop, and the puppy's metabolism slows. If this goes on too long, the pup becomes weak and can't nurse or digest her food. By 2 weeks old, the puppies can better regulate their temperature and don't have to sleep in a pile to keep warm.

Navel infection: The bitch severs the umbilical cord with her teeth, but if she cuts too close, the pup's navel area can get infected. The breeder cleans and disinfects the navel and applies an antibiotic ointment.

Fading puppy syndrome: A seemingly healthy puppy may fail to gain weight and gradually fade, acting listless and losing interest in nursing. If the breeder can identify the cause, she can take steps to save the puppy. Some causes are cold temperatures, not getting enough milk, or birth defects. If the mother was in poor health when the pups were born, she may not be able to produce enough healthy milk, which often contributes to this problem.

Swimmer puppy: A puppy who doesn't stand up by 10 days old and start walking soon after is called a "swimmer." Her legs will splay out sideways, and she'll use a pedaling motion to propel herself around on her tummy. The condition is more likely to affect large or overweight Lab puppies and may be caused by delayed development or muscle weakness. If allowed to continue, the puppy's rib cage flattens out and the condition becomes permanent. The breeder must step in and get the puppy up on her feet several times a day. Putting the pup on carpet or other rough surface gives her traction. With help, most puppies make a complete recovery.

Hernia: A small bump in the navel or groin area indicates a hernia. A veterinarian will identify the cause and decide if it needs attention. Many hernias close on their own in a few weeks or months. If not, it can be repaired when the dog is spayed or neutered.

Nutrition

Before she whelps and while nursing, the mother dog needs extra food and water to produce adequate milk. As the pups grow, she needs still more calories and fat—up to three times her usual amount by the third week. Some breeders feed the mothers high-performance or puppy food to provide extra nutrition. If the mother's diet is still inadequate, her coat will look poor and she'll lose weight. She may get uncontrollable diarrhea and become dehydrated.

The mother needs a constant supply of fresh water. The moisture supplied in mother's milk is just as important as its nutritional content. Both the bitch and her pups can get dehydrated quickly. If she doesn't get enough water, she can't produce enough milk for the puppies. Young puppies process a lot of water through their systems because they need to maintain blood volume and stay hydrated.

By the fourth week, the puppies are ready to wean. At this time, the mother gradually reduces her food intake and her milk starts to dry up.

Mother's Milk

Mother's milk, especially during the first 24 hours after birth, is critical to protecting her puppies from disease. When born, the puppies' immune systems are not yet fully developed. If the mother has been vaccinated regularly, her first milk, called colostrum, contains *antibodies* that provide *passive immunity* from diseases like parvovirus and distemper. Breeders sometimes have their bitch tested to determine the amount of antibodies in her system before she is bred. The more she has, the more she can pass on to her pups. A healthy mother with a strong immune system passes enough antibodies in those first 18 hours to protect the puppies until they can develop their own.

Puppies are only able to absorb maternal antibodies during the first 12 to 18 hours of life, so it's essential that they nurse as soon as possible after birth. After that, the mother's milk cannot provide any further protection.

The mother's milk changes as the puppies grow. It supplies all their nutritional needs up until 4 weeks of age, and the milk's energy content increases steadily as puppies become more active. The fat level in the milk also increases dramatically and then gradually decreases by weaning time. Calcium content increases up until 4 weeks.

Supplementation

Supplements like vitamins and minerals aren't necessary if the mother is fed a complete food. In fact, excess nutrients throw off the balance and causes problems. The veterinarian helps the breeder decide what, if any, supplements are needed. Some breeders feed their bitch yogurt or cottage cheese to keep up her calcium levels, especially if she has a large litter.

If she's not producing enough milk, the pups must be supplemented with a homemade or commercially made milk replacer. The breeder feeds the babies every 3 hours with an eyedropper, or uses a baby bottle if they are older than 2 weeks old.

Weaning

Weaning starts naturally, initiated by the mother when the puppies are 3½ to 4 weeks old. If the bitch doesn't have enough milk, weaning can start earlier. When the puppies' teeth start coming in, they hurt the mother when the pups nurse, so she lets them nurse less often. She begins to spend less time in the nest. She'll stand while they nurse and leave when she's tired.

Weaning takes 1½ to 2 weeks. The process starts gradually, and the puppies continue to nurse during the transition. For the first week, they get one meal a day made of puppy food and water, blended until it's almost liquid. The breeder may have them lick the food off the end of her finger to help them understand what to do. The puppies make a terrific mess, lapping it up and stepping in their gruel. A few days later, the breeder increases to two meals a day. By 5½ weeks, the pups are fully weaned. Some moms let the pups nurse occasionally until they leave for their new homes.

By 6 weeks, the puppy teeth have fully erupted, and the litter is able to chew dry food for the first time. Their food no longer needs to be runny and wet.

Grooming

Even the tiniest puppies need some grooming to keep them clean and healthy. Their mother starts the process, and the breeder helps out when the puppies are a few weeks old.

Initial Grooming

Mom grooms the litter during the first weeks. Besides keeping them clean, licking stimulates them so they will eliminate. She also keeps the whelping box clean. By the time the pups are 4 weeks old, she no longer needs to lick them; they can eliminate on their own.

During weaning (4 to 6 weeks), the breeder cleans puppy faces with a wet rag as they finish each meal because the watery gruel can cause puppy acne. Acne in puppies is a surface skin infection, which, if not treated, can spread to the mother when the pup continues to nurse.

Toenails

Sharp puppy toenails hurt Mom, and scratches can cause her teats to get infected. Therefore, the breeder starts clipping the puppies' toenails at 4 or 5 weeks. She only needs to trim the front toenails to protect the mother. The rear nails give the puppy traction for walking.

By the time the puppy comes to you, she's already used to the clipping procedure.

Social Skills

It's never too early to start a Lab puppy's social education. These early experiences prepare her for the many new people and things she will encounter when she leaves the comfort of the whelping box.

Socialization Starts at 3 Weeks

When a pup's eyes and ears are open and she is able to stand and walk, she's a sponge ready to soak up everything she can in her exciting new world. Her experiences—both positive and negative—for the next 9 or 10 weeks will permanently shape her social and psychological development. Breeders and new owners take advantage of this limited window of opportunity to introduce their puppies to hundreds of people, places, and things.

Socialization will be well under way by the time you bring home your puppy. Invest time during these pivotal weeks of your Lab's development, and you'll reap the rewards for the next 12 to 15 years. Well-socialized puppies grow up to be dogs who learn faster, can adapt to new situations with less stress, are confident, and are less likely to develop behavior problems.

> ### TIPS AND TAILS
>
> Scientific researchers have tried to explain how much of a puppy's personality depends on inherited traits, and how much is due to her environment. By environment, they mean her early socialization and training—things you can control to a great extent. The conclusion was that about 35 percent of a pup's personality traits, such as shyness, dominance, and other factors, are inherited. This leaves 65 percent of her adult personality to be shaped by her environment, including you, the breeder, and her experiences.

Inadequate socialization during this period results in an adult dog who is fearful, possibly aggressive, and avoids contact with animals and people. An unsocialized dog will likely be turned out in the backyard to live alone, where she will become increasingly wild and poorly behaved. It's a sad scenario that happens all too often.

Puppies Discover Their World

Before 8 weeks of age, a Lab puppy has no fear; she approaches anything and anyone. Next month, she'll be less confident and feels much more vulnerable and hesitant. But for now, mildly frightening experiences are unlikely to permanently affect her personality.

In the 1980s, Pat Schaap, an expert dog trainer, developed "The Rule of Sevens" for socializing a puppy. With her permission, we offer them here:

By the time a puppy is 7 weeks old, he/she should have …

- 🐾 Been on 7 different types of surfaces: carpet, concrete, wood, vinyl, gravel, dirt, wood chips, etc.
- 🐾 Played with 7 different types of objects: big balls, small balls, soft fabric toys, fuzzy toys, squeaky toys, paper or cardboard items, metal item, sticks, hose pieces, etc.

- Been in 7 different locations: front yard, back yard, basement, kitchen, car, garage, laundry room, bathroom, crate, etc.

- Met and played with 7 new people: children, older adults, someone with a cane or walking stick, someone in a wheelchair, or walker, etc.

- Been exposed to 7 challenges: climb on a box, climb off a box, go through a tunnel, climb steps, go down steps, climb over obstacles, play hide and seek, go in and out of a doorway, run around a fence, etc.

- Eaten from 7 different containers: metal, plastic, cardboard, glass, china, pie plate, frying pan, etc.

- Eaten in 7 different locations: crate, yard, kitchen, basement, laundry room, living room, bathroom, etc.

These early experiences should be repeated and built upon constantly throughout the socialization period and throughout your Lab's life.

> ### HAPPY PUPPY
>
> The socialization period from 3 to 12 weeks of age is the most critical period in a puppy's life. What your puppy learns during this time largely determines if she is outgoing, happy, and confident, or shy, aggressive, and wild when she's an adult. Although later training and socialization might improve her behavior, it can't completely erase the effects of this early learning period.

Puppy Testing

By the time the puppies are 7 weeks old, you may have met the litter several times and are wondering how to choose which pup is right for you. Many breeders use puppy testing to help evaluate a litter. The breeder knows the pups well, and testing is a structured way she can evaluate the differences between puppies. It's not a pass-fail test; she simply observes the puppies' reactions to different situations while getting an idea of how each pup will react as he or she grows. Puppy testing is usually done at 7 or 8 weeks, before the pups leave for their new homes, before they have been influenced by training, and before the first fear period.

Many different tests have been developed by an assortment of scientists and behaviorists over the past several decades. Clarice Rutherford, a scientist and long-time owner of Labrador Retrievers, and Dr. David Neal, a veterinarian, first published a puppy test in 1981. As far back as the 1950s, scientists Scott and Fuller were evaluating how the early weeks of a puppy's life affect her lifelong personality.

You could ask the breeder if she does puppy testing and if so, if you may watch a session. She knows her bloodlines, has tested other litters, and can compare them to how previous puppies matured. One test doesn't deliver an ironclad verdict on a puppy's temperament; the troublemaker may be tired today, and the shy one might have just woken up from a nap. The breeder knows this.

The tester looks at three major areas of interest:

🐾 How the pup interacts with the tester

🐾 If the pup seems willing to please

🐾 How quickly she forgives when the tester does something she doesn't like

By looking at the total picture of her responses, an experienced tester can come to some conclusions about the pup's personality at this point in her life. There isn't a one-word description of a pup. She is not always dominant, submissive, or frightened. Keep an open mind.

The tester puts each puppy through a series of short manipulations. To test her willingness to be handled, he restrains her, holds her up off the ground, and gently pinches between her toes. Other tests check her social attraction to people. He asks her to come from a few feet away and then follow him. Sensitivity tests explore how she reacts to loud noises, moving objects, and petting.

After observing the test, talk to the breeder about the puppy's overall reactions. Is she over the top, jumping on the tester, always active and hyper? Does she resist handling? Is she enthusiastic, outgoing, and eager to please? Is she quiet and thoughtful but willing to participate? Is she shy and fearful? Is she independent and aloof?

What do each of these personality traits mean for you? The breeder will help you look at each puppy's behavior to help you select the puppy who will best fit with your expectations, experience, and lifestyle.

Behavior

A puppy's mother and littermates begin teaching her how to successfully interact with others in her world. What she learns in the first 8 weeks of her life establishes a foundation you can build on when she comes to live with you.

Mom Is First Teacher

A well-behaved, calm mom raises well-behaved, calm puppies. If she is fearful, stressed, or aggressive, she teaches her puppies to react in the same way. She may be somewhat agitated and protective when her puppies are first born, but her instincts soon settle down and her temperament returns to normal.

As soon as weaning starts, Mom also starts to wean them from her constant attention. She spends less time with them, and they no longer depend solely on her for food. When out in the yard, she watches over them as they start to explore, and they discover they don't need her nearby every second.

She gently but firmly disciplines them when they jump on her or bite her ears—this is their first lesson in dog manners from Mom as she teaches them the doggie version of "No." Her growl and bark when she "yells" at her puppies sounds ferocious but is all for show. Often another "auntie" dog goes along with the pups, and they learn that another dog will discipline them, too, if they get out of line.

A puppy learns to appease Mom if she gets annoyed. The pup rolls on her back and shows her belly in submission. She may even release a little urine. The scent reminds the mother dog, "See, I'm just a baby. I'm sorry." This skill comes in handy when Puppy tries her antics on older or unknown dogs as she grows.

Littermates as Teachers

Puppies practice the skills they'll use as adults by playing with their littermates. They learn to hunt, pounce, chase, and get along peacefully with each other. The pups teach each other how rough they may play and how hard they're allowed to bite. Bite inhibition is one of the most critical skills a puppy needs to learn, and she needs to learn it from her peers.

A puppy who is in a single-puppy litter or is removed from the litter too soon may never learn her dog manners. Her mother and her human family can help make up the difference, but it's no substitute for learning from her siblings.

Your Lab Puppy Comes Home

Month 2	Month 3	Month 4
	Socialization at home with new owner and other pets	
	Fear imprint period	
	Begin house and crate training	
	Rapid growth	
	1st DHPP vaccines	

Your Lab puppy has gotten a good start in life from his mother, littermates, and breeder. Now, at 8 to 12 weeks old, it's time for him to meet his new family.

In this chapter, we share the information you need to select the best puppy for your family, prepare for his arrival, and navigate his first few weeks in your home. You learn the ins and outs of puppy-proofing your home, vaccines, health care, feeding, grooming, socializing, and the first steps of training.

Choosing Your Puppy

Before you decide on a breeder or visit a litter of pups, make some choices about the dog who will be part of your family for the next 10 to 14 years. You may have already given some thought to the type of Lab you want. This section offers information that will expand your knowledge and help you make educated decisions when you visit breeders.

Labrador Characteristics

Labrador Retrievers have distinct characteristics, including color. Labs can be yellow, black, or chocolate, and all three colors can appear in the same litter.

Yellow Labs can vary from almost white to a deep fox-red color. Most have black pigment around their eyes, around their mouths, and on their noses. Some have brown pigment, and still others have pink. The pink coloring is called Dudley, and, although it disqualifies the dog from showing in conformation, it has no effect on his health or ability to be a wonderful pet. As your Lab grows up, his black nose may become what's called a "snow nose," where small patches fade to pink. Again this has no health consequences.

There's no such thing as a "golden Lab." There are Golden Retrievers and Labrador Retrievers, but they are not related. Some service dog breeders purposely breed the two together, and the result would be a Golden-Lab—a mixed-breed dog. But a purebred Labrador is referred to as yellow, not gold.

Black Labs have a thick, glossy, solid black coat and usually have black noses, black eye rims, black lips, and dark brown eyes. If you see a Lab with light eyes—brown or yellow—that's just a variation and does not signify blindness or other problems.

Chocolate Labs range from light brown to deep chocolate. Their eyes might be brown, gold, or yellow. The nose, eye rims, and around the mouth should also be chocolate, although you'll often see dogs with pink coloring. When you pick out your puppy, he'll still have his puppy coat, which may be lighter. His feet and face will be his true color, which appears when he sheds his puppy coat in a few months.

You may have heard the old wives' tale that chocolate Labs are more hyperactive. In reality, there's no difference in the personality of any particular color.

Labs are often described as either "English style" or "American style." These descriptions refer to their size and build, rather than where they come from. "Show" versus "field" is a better description. The English/show style is a shorter, heavier dog with a blocky head. These are the dogs you see at dog shows. The American/field style is usually taller, finer boned, and has a less-dense coat. These dogs are bred primarily as hunting dogs and have more energy. Most Labs fall somewhere in between the two extremes. And *all* Labs are energetic and active.

There's minimal difference between the sexes. Dogs are individuals, and sex has little impact on their personalities. Owners report that males are more affectionate and bond better with you, while females are more aloof and independent. Males also sometimes mature more slowly than females.

If you're looking to get more than one Lab, it's not generally a good idea to get two puppies from the same litter. They'll often bond with each other more than their human family, and one will usually be more shy and reserved, relying on his sibling for cues. Two dogs from the same litter—especially females—may not get along because their personalities are too similar. Get your second dog from a litter with different parents, and wait at least 6 months before doing so. Then your puppy will bond to you, not his playmate.

What's Important to You?

When you've decided on a sex and color for your puppy, your next decision is whether you want a show or field type. If you plan to hunt with your Labrador, find breeders whose dogs have proven hunting ability. Ask if they hunt with their dogs, if they've obtained hunting titles, and if they've sold puppies to hunting homes. You can also ask for references. Many show dogs also hunt, and their breeders compete in hunting tests to ensure their dogs are still able to do what they were bred to do.

If you plan to compete in obedience, agility, or other dog sports, take this into consideration. Field dogs often have an intense drive to work and make excellent competitors. Again, ask breeders if their dogs have competed successfully in these venues.

Registration Papers and Contracts

When you purchase a puppy, you'll encounter some unfamiliar terms and confusing paperwork. Don't feel overwhelmed; this is typical of what all breeders provide. Here are the meanings of some items you'll be dealing with:

Contract: The contract between the breeder and a puppy buyer states the conditions of purchase. For example, the dog may not be bred, the breeder retains co-ownership, or the dog must be returned to the breeder if the owner can no longer keep him at some later date.

AKC: This is the American Kennel Club, the main registry in the United States for purebred dogs. The AKC is a nonprofit organization.

Registration papers: Your puppy's breeder will provide AKC papers naming the sire and dam, date of birth, and other information. You fill in the name you choose for your dog, and submit the papers to the AKC to register your puppy.

Limited registration: Most pet puppies are sold on a limited registration, which means if the dog eventually produces puppies, they cannot be registered. The dog is still eligible to compete in most performance events, though. Some breeders convert the registration to full status when the dog reaches 2 years old and the owner provides records of favorable health checks for hips, elbows, and eyes.

> ### TIPS AND TAILS
>
> Are registration papers important? Papers are no guarantee your puppy is a certain quality or the parents were health-tested. But papers do give you the sire's and dam's names, and you can research their pedigree with the AKC. Without papers, you have no guarantee your dog is a purebred Lab. The breeder may also not be careful to breed healthy, correct-looking dogs; follow any code of ethics; or offer any kind of guarantees.

Let the Breeder Help

If you're not sure how to choose a puppy, your breeder can help you pick out the right puppy for your family. She has lived with the litter every day for 2 months, and she knows their personalities. By the time the puppies are 10 days old, individual puppies are more active as they try to be the first to nurse, while others hang back and need some help. The pups have been interacting since they were just a few weeks old, and the breeder knows who's the bossiest, who loves everyone, and who is the quietest. She's been watching their activity level, their dominance during play, and who makes the most eye contact with people.

When you interview breeders, tell them what activities you plan to do with your Lab. When the breeder knows what you have in mind, she can pick out the best matching pup for your family. She'll give the more active puppies to owners who want to hunt or compete in agility, for example. If you plan to do therapy visits with your Lab, she'll pick a more laid-back, people-oriented pup.

When you first talk to a breeder about buying a Lab puppy, know that a responsible breeder might ask you to complete a questionnaire and interview to be sure you would be a good fit for one of her puppies. You all want the same thing: the right puppy in a home he will stay in for his entire life and grow up happy and loved.

At the same time, you want to ask some questions and make some observations of your own:

🐾 Are the puppies raised in a clean environment?

🐾 Are they well socialized?

🐾 Are the other dogs in the breeder's house clean and well cared for?

🐾 Do the other dogs seem to have good temperaments?

🐾 Does the breeder offer copies of all clearances for the sire and dam?

🐾 Does the breeder offer a written contract and/or guarantee?

🐾 What does the breeder do with her dogs besides breed them? Are they performance dogs, show dogs, hunting dogs, etc., or is the breeder just breeding to make money?

The breeder should be happy to answer your questions. If she's not, move on to the next breeder on your list.

Lab Puppy Personalities

Lab puppies, even those in the same litter, exhibit entirely different personalities. You can't label a pup with absolute certainty, but here are some characteristics you might see:

The **tank** bowls over his littermates, eats first, grabs the toy firs' attention. His intense drive makes him a good prospect for hunti or performance sports. This same dog can be bull-headed and hard to time owner. Teaching self-control from the time he is young helps channel his the-top personality.

The **social butterfly** is the life of the party and will keep you laughing. He's happy, enthusiastic, confident, and ready for anything, although he might be a little rambunctious and easily distracted. He's still a really fun dog and perfect for an active family with older children.

Mr. Sensible is also happy and enthusiastic, but he's a little more low-key. Whatever you want to do, he's fine with that. He's affectionate, willing and eager to please you, but has a calmer disposition than his "butterfly" littermate.

The aristocrat, often a female, is also affectionate but can be aloof and independent when she chooses. She may seem to learn slower, but don't let her fool you. She is thoughtful and methodical about everything she does.

The quiet one might have been raised outside in a kennel, and he may not have had much socialization. Very few Lab puppies are shy or fearful, but when one is hesitant to join playtime or seems a little skittish, a conscientious breeder steps in and helps the puppy, who soon catches up to his littermates. Patience and confidence-building exercises can make this dog a loving and devoted pet. He might not be a good choice for a family with small children who might overwhelm him or for a first-time dog owner, however.

Preparing for Your Lab Puppy

It's fun to shop for your new puppy while you're waiting for him to arrive. In this section, we give you a shopping list of the supplies you need to keep your pup healthy and safe.

Bowls: Stainless-steel bowls with rubber nonslip bottoms are easier to sterilize and last longer than other types of bowls. Labs eat fast, and your puppy will push the bowl around the floor in his rush to gulp his dinner. Lab pups are notorious chewers, and plastic bowls get teeth marks that make them harder to clean. Ceramic bowls are pretty, but a bouncing Lab puppy can break even the heaviest crockery.

Collar and leash: Pick a collar that fits around his neck but has enough holes so you can loosen it as he grows. A flat nylon or leather collar is the only type of collar you need. When you put it on, you should be able to fit two fingers between the collar and his neck. Be sure it isn't so loose he can pull out of it. Tighten the collar enough so it rides closer to his ears, not down by his shoulders.

One option is an adjustable martingale collar that slips over his head and tightens only when he pulls on the leash. There is no buckle. If he decides he doesn't want to go where you're going, he can't back out of a martingale collar. Don't leave a martingale collar on an unattended puppy, however; he could get caught in something and strangle.

Select a matching nylon leash, or get something made of leather or cotton rope that's easier on your hands. A 6-foot leash is helpful while your pup is learning how to walk nicely at your side. When he's older and taller, a 4-foot leash is long enough, and you won't get tangled up in the extra length. Stay away from adjustable-length leads for now. That'll just teach your puppy to pull, and you don't want that.

When taking your puppy on a walk, you may opt to use a head halter in addition to a traditional collar. This style goes over the nose and behind his ears like a horse's halter, which makes it easier to control a pup who pulls. Some have a clip that attaches to the pup's regular collar so if the puppy rubs it off, he's still attached to the leash. Your puppy will still be able to open his mouth to eat and drink while wearing a head halter.

TIPS AND TAILS

Lab puppies can be really destructive. They see leashes, collars, bowls, crates, and beds as toys, and they can quickly demolish everything in their path. Choose sturdy, relatively chew-proof supplies, and be diligent about keeping them out of your inquisitive pup's reach. Provide him with plenty of things he's allowed to play with and chew instead.

Crate: From the very beginning, your puppy should spend some time in his crate. It's his safe haven from the world, a place he will enjoy throughout his life. The crate is also an essential housetraining tool. Choose a crate that's bigger than your pup, but not so big he can soil in it and sleep at the other end. Some crates come with a divider you can remove as your puppy grows.

Crates come in a variety of styles. Your puppy will feel safe and surrounded in a plastic crate, which simulates a den. Some of the flimsy plastic crates aren't strong enough to hold a rambunctious Lab puppy, so get a heavy-duty one. Many plastic crates are airline approved, so if you're going to travel, this is the one you need. Check with the airline for confirmation that the crate you choose is acceptable.

Then there are wire crates. There are different advantages to this type of crate. Your puppy can see out and feel like he's part of the action, even when he's confined. A wire crate often has a side door and an end door, so you can rearrange it to suit your room. If the pup won't settle down, spread a towel or blanket over the crate to block his view. Wire crates allow air to circulate, which is important in hot weather. They fold down flat and are easier to store than the plastic crates, too. If you opt for a wire crate, we recommend you get one made of heavy-gauge wire that will resist the efforts of a strong Lab puppy.

Mesh or fabric crates are best for adult dogs who are already crate trained.

> ### HAPPY PUPPY
>
> Consider buying two crates: a plastic one to keep in the bedroom for sleeping and a wire one for in the family room where he can spend time with you without getting underfoot.

Rubber curry: These brushes come in several shapes, including round, oval, or rectangular. The curry fits in the palm of your hand and has rubber bumps on the other side. It loosens your pup's undercoat before you brush him.

Slicker brush: A slicker brush has short metal pins on a rectangular rubber backing. This is the brush you'll use the most. It gets out all that loose undercoat when your Lab starts shedding. You'll also use this one for quick touch-ups when he rolls in dirt or leaves.

Shedding blade or tool: A shedding blade is a metal piece about 12 inches long that's serrated on one edge, with rubber handles at each end. It quickly skims loose hair off your dog's coat. (Find these at a horse supply store.) Or you can buy a shedding tool such as the Furminator, which pulls out gobs of loose hair and undercoat during the heavy shedding seasons.

Toenail clippers: The breeder started the toenail-clipping process for you, and 8 weeks old is not too young to trim a puppy's toenails. The best clippers are guillotine-style that squeeze and cut off the end of the nail. Be sure to get extra blades, because dull blades tear the nails. An alternative tool is a *grinder*. The grinder has a sandpaper-covered tip that grinds down the nail instead of clipping.

Toothbrush/toothpaste: No time like the present to teach your pup to enjoy having his teeth brushed. Get either a toothbrush or a fingertip brush and toothpaste formulated especially for dogs. Human toothpaste makes dogs and puppies sick.

Pet gates: When he's not in his crate, you'll still want to confine your puppy so you can prevent housetraining accidents and chewing. Pet gates come in sizes that block doorways or even large spaces between rooms. You can buy inexpensive plastic, fancy metal, and or furniture-quality wood gates. Some styles mount permanently with screws, while others are pressure-mounted so you can remove them when your puppy grows up. Deluxe models have a pass-through gate so you don't have to take them down every time you want to walk through the doorway.

Ex pen/playpen: A folding wire exercise pen gives your puppy some room to move around while still confined. If he's acclimated to it when he's little, he'll respect the pen when he's bigger. Use the ex pen when you leave him alone and while you're at work. The pens are available in heights from 24 to 48 inches; get a tall one so he's not tempted to climb out.

Puppy toys: Anything that comes apart is not a good toy for a Labrador, because he can swallow pieces and that could cause a bowel obstruction. Most toys made especially for puppies just aren't strong enough for Labs. Get larger toys, even for the youngest pup. Heavy-duty rubber bones are best.

> **HAPPY PUPPY**

If your puppy doesn't show an interest in his chew toys at first, coat the toy in chicken broth or smear on a few dabs of peanut butter. That'll get his attention!

Born to retrieve, Labs always have something in their mouths. Yours will constantly bring his toys to you, and his favorites are probably stuffed animals. If you get stuffed toys, pick them up when you aren't able to supervise. A toy made especially for dogs shouldn't have buttons or pieces that come off easily, but he'll still do his best to pull out the stuffing or squeaky and eat it.

Balls awaken your puppy's retrieving instinct, so they're always a favorite. But be sure to get sturdy ones that are too big to get stuck in his mouth. Other fun toys include plastic water bottles—1 gallon or liter size. They're noisy, fun, and disposable. Knotted rope toys are fine until they start to fall apart, so replace them as needed. Rawhide chews soften as the puppy chews and can break apart. They also can cause an obstruction or upset tummy, so monitor your pup's activity with them.

Toys that dispense food entertain your pup while you're away. Get several, and leave a different one in his ex pen each day. Stock up on toys like the heavy-duty Kong you can stuff with kibble and peanut butter and freeze.

> **TIPS AND TAILS**

Test all toys while you're home with your puppy before you give him something and leave for work. Labradors are chewing maniacs and can destroy almost anything.

If Puppy has the house strewn with toys, he'll have a hard time learning what's okay and what's not okay to chew. Set up a toy box, and let him pick out his favorite of the moment. Switch toys out regularly so they seem new and exciting.

Bed: Finally, be sure to provide your new addition with a bed. An inexpensive bed is fine until your pup grows up a bit. An old throw rug or beach towel keeps him just as cozy as a $100 plush bed. And just a heads-up: he'll probably destroy several beds between now and the time he's an adult.

Puppy-Proof Your House

Anything that can hurt a human baby can hurt your puppy, too. Puppies don't have hands, so yours is going to explore his new world with his mouth. Anything he can sink his teeth into is fair game, and it's your job to be sure he stays safe. That means puppy-proofing your home.

Start by getting down on the floor for a puppy's-eye view of your home. You might be surprised what you find under the couch. Puppy-proofing is an ongoing project, so remember that within a month, he'll be able to reach things that are out of reach right now.

> **TIPS AND TAILS**
>
> Have your children help you puppy-proof the house and yard. The kids will enjoy the task of finding things that might hurt the new puppy and helping you put them away.

Remove dangling objects. While you're on the floor checking for stray objects, remove or reposition dangling drapery or window blind cords, tablecloths, and houseplants. It's not unheard of for a pup to strangle on a drapery cord.

Also, tie up electrical cords out of reach, or encase them in a cord-keeper. PVC pipe is one way to encase the wires. A puppy who chews through a cord can be electrocuted and even killed. Cover electrical outlets, too.

Remote controls and telephones have your scent concentrated on them, so your pup will gravitate toward these toy-size items. Don't leave them out on the coffee table. In fact, take everything off the coffee table for the next year.

Move breakable knick-knacks out of reach of puppy teeth, and later, Labrador tails. A Lab's tail can wipe out an entire shelf of figurines with one swipe.

Paperclips, pens, buttons, jewelry, and other tiny bits that fall out of your pockets or off the dresser are very attractive to puppies—and very dangerous. Be vigilant about picking up anything your pup might find interesting. Look under the bed and dresser, under the coffee table, and under any other place that's your puppy's eye level.

Now is also the time to teach your kids to pick up their clothes. If they don't, they'll learn this lesson the hard way the first time Puppy carries underwear into the living room in front of company. Shoes and socks are heavy with your scent and, therefore, most appealing. Many a Lab puppy has had emergency surgery after swallowing a sock.

Wastebaskets provide an open invitation to a curious Lab. Purchase cans with hard-to-remove lids, or put the trash bin in a latched cabinet.

Take chemicals and cleaners out of bottom cupboards in the kitchen, bathroom, and garage. Use childproof latches to keep Pup out of mischief. Sharp puppy teeth can cause a can of deodorant to explode. Put medications and cosmetics out of reach, too.

Foods such as chocolate, onions, yeast dough, and coffee are dangerous for dogs so be sure to keep these well out of his reach. (See Appendix D for a complete list of foods and other household hazards to keep away from your dog.)

Close toilet lids so your puppy doesn't fall in and drown (yes, really) or drink toxic cleaners.

Screen off fireplaces or wood-burning stoves. An exercise pen works well for this purpose. Put the wood somewhere he can't get to it. A Lab of any age *will* chew wood!

> ### TIPS AND TAILS
>
> During the holidays, block his access to the Christmas tree with an ex pen or other fence. Ingested tinsel or ornaments can cut his insides or cause a fatal blockage.

Identify poisonous houseplants, and remove them. It only takes a leaf or two of some plants to kill your beloved Lab. (See Appendix C for a list of poisonous plants to keep out of your pup's reach.)

Puppy-Proof Your Yard

Even if your puppy won't be spending a lot of time out in the yard, it still needs to be puppy-proofed in case you ever need to let him out. As with the inside of your house, you need to be sure the outside of your house and yard are safe for your Lab.

If your yard is fenced in (and it should be), check your fence for loose boards, holes, or any place you can see daylight through or under. The slightest hint of an escape route will tempt him to dig. Be sure the tension wires at the bottom of chain-link fencing are securely fastened. Don't forget to look behind bushes and sheds, too.

Block small spaces where a pup might get stuck, like between the garage and a fence or shed, for example. Be sure to recheck regularly. You never know what he might do out there.

Your barbecue grill, drip pan, and the accompanying cooking tools are full of wonderful food smells. Put them out of reach after use. Patio chair pads should also be stowed away when you're not using them.

Build a temporary fence around the pool, hot tub, or pond, if you have these water areas. Block access to decks and balconies to prevent your puppy from falling off.

Store garden and pool chemicals in a puppy-proof cabinet. Don't use snail or rodent bait in your yard. Both are especially attractive to dogs. Likewise, keep fertilizers, pesticides, and herbicides out of his reach and consider limiting their use on your yard. These might not seem especially toxic to you or your children, but your puppy is low to the ground and his entire body is exposed to concentrated doses. Keep your pup out of the yard for at least 48 hours after you treat it.

Antifreeze can also kill quickly. Dogs are attracted to its sweet taste, and your Lab puppy will have no trouble getting under the car to lap it up. Motor oil and radiator fluid are also hazards. Check under the car often, and wipe drips up immediately.

Ice-melting products contain assorted chloride compounds, and even a small amount can be lethal for dogs. Your puppy may ingest it if he licks his paws after playing outside. Buy pet-safe products; they are identified on the label.

Bulbs and some outdoor plants, like oleander for example, are poisonous (see Appendix C for a complete list). Cocoa mulch contains the same deadly ingredient as chocolate—theobromine—and a small amount can quickly kill a puppy. Compost bins should be off-limits to your puppy as well. Fermenting materials produce molds and bacteria that are toxic when eaten.

Watch your Lab puppy extra carefully the first few weeks when he's outside your home. He'll surely show you something you have missed picking up or putting away.

Your Pup's Professional Staff

It's easy to feel overwhelmed with a new puppy, especially if you're a first-time dog owner. But you're not alone. You have a staff of helpful professionals available to help you.

Your first and most important adviser is your veterinarian. If you don't already have one, ask your friends, especially fellow Lab owners, if they have a vet they like. If your breeder lives close, she can suggest someone. Local trainers or kennel staff may also be able to recommend a clinic. You can also check with your state's veterinary medical association for a listing of local vets. The American Animal Hospital Association (AAHA) also has a list of members at healthypet.com.

Schedule a visit to the clinic to meet the veterinarians and staff and make some observations while you're there:

🐾 Is the clinic clean and neat?

🐾 Does the staff seem friendly and willing to answer your questions?

🐾 Do you like the vet's bedside manner?

🐾 What are the doctors' specialties and education?

🐾 Do they treat many Labs?

🐾 What kinds of Lab health problems have they treated?

🐾 Are the hours convenient?

🐾 Where do they refer you if there's an emergency during off-hours?

Also on your list should be a dog trainer. Although your Lab won't start puppy kindergarten for a few weeks, start asking around now for a good trainer who offers puppy classes. Try to find an instructor who has experience training Labradors. Different breeds learn at different rates, and methods that work on a Sheltie, for example, may not be successful with a Lab.

Ask if you can watch a class, and make some notes on what you see:

🐾 Do the puppies seem happy and safe?

🐾 Do students get enough individual attention?

🐾 Are they having fun?

🐾 Are their questions answered?

🐾 Does the trainer offer more advanced classes for when your puppy is older?

🐾 Does the trainer use positive methods?

Puppies should *not* be wearing chain collars or be trained with any kind of force. Ask the trainer what clubs or professional associations, like the Association of Pet Dog Trainers (APDT), she belongs to. Although obedience instructors aren't legally required to be certified in any way, you want to know yours is keeping up with knowledge and advances in the field.

You could also have a pet sitter come to your home mid-day while you're at work so your puppy can get his lunch and a potty break. This helps him housetrain much faster. When you interview the pet sitter, ask for references and proof of liability and property damage insurance. Ask about her experience with puppies and if she is a member of any professional organizations.

Development

A Lab puppy goes through dramatic physical and mental changes during the first few months of life. As he grows into his feet and adds pounds to his frame, his brain also develops, so his ability to concentrate and learn improves at the same time.

Physical Development

At 8 weeks old, your Lab puppy is starting a growth spurt that will continue until he's about 6 months old, when it slows down dramatically. That roly-poly little butterball you brought home will probably weigh between 10 and 12 pounds. By the time he reaches 12 weeks of age, his weight could double. That's an increase of 2 or 3 pounds a week! He'll alternate with being clumsy and sure-footed as his legs start to grow. The little squirt who can barely keep up will soon be galloping ahead and running circles around you.

His sight and hearing ability are now fully functioning, as is his brain. At this stage, different Labs can vary by a week or more in their growth level, so if yours lags behind, don't worry too much.

Mental Development

Although puppy is physically advancing, he's still emotionally immature. He's capable of learning, but his attention span is very short. He'll need his lessons broken up into tiny steps and reinforced by plenty of praise. He'll retain anything he learns during this period, good or bad, throughout his life.

Health

Start your Lab pup out right with proper health care. Like human babies, puppies need extra attention during their first year. The initial health records from the breeder will help you set up a schedule with your veterinarian for future exams, vaccines, and parasite prevention.

Your Puppy's Health Records

In your puppy's going-home packet, the breeder should provide a complete health history. This includes dates the pup was wormed, the brand name of the wormer, dates of the first vaccines, and which specific vaccines were administered.

She should also provide the CERF certificate (see Months 1 and 2), showing when the puppy's eyes were examined and what the results were. If the puppies were treated for giardia or other parasites, that should be noted as well.

A copy of the sire and dam's health clearances, explained in the previous chapter, should also be included. You might also receive photos of the parents and each of their pedigrees.

> ### TIPS AND TAILS
>
> Your breeder might give you a bag of the food your puppy has been eating, a familiar toy, and a piece of blanket or T-shirt the puppies have been sleeping on. Put the latter in with your puppy the first few nights so he's comforted by their scent. Along with your sales contract, receipt, and AKC registration form, she might also give you articles and information on Labradors and puppy-raising. Go over each item with the breeder before you leave so you're comfortable you understand what you're signing and how to use the information she provides.

Diseases, Vaccinations, and Schedule

The breeder will have given your puppy his first in a series of immunizations. It covers distemper, hepatitis, parvovirus, and parainfluenza (DHPP), the basic core vaccines every dog should have. He's too young for the rabies vaccine right now.

You may not hear about these ailments very often, but that's because most dog owners vaccinate their dogs. Ask any shelter worker, and they'll tell you disease occasionally breaks out in their shelter. Unfortunately, they have to euthanize an entire population of shelter dogs to contain an outbreak. Needless to say, these diseases are pretty serious.

A viral infection, distemper causes upper-respiratory symptoms such as runny nose and fever. As it progresses, the puppy suffers from vomiting, diarrhea, pneumonia, and neurological problems. Once it causes bleeding in the intestinal tract, it's quickly fatal. Distemper is transmitted through saliva, urine, feces, and airborne droplets such as a sneeze, and your puppy can get it from another dog or a wild animal like a fox, ferret, raccoon, or skunk. It most commonly occurs in puppies 9 to 12 weeks old. Regular cleaning with detergents and disinfectants destroys the virus.

Canine hepatitis, caused by an adenovirus, was originally transmitted to dogs from foxes, and today it's common wherever dogs, foxes, or coyotes exist, and is spread by direct contact with an infected animal. The puppy will have a fever and enlarged lymph nodes on the head and neck. He may die within a day or two from internal hemorrhaging, liver disease, and swelling in the brain. Hepatitis comes on very quickly in puppies 6 to 10 weeks old, and there is no cure. It's harder to eradicate from the environment because it's resistant to detergents and disinfectants.

> ### TIPS AND TAILS
>
> You may be confused when you see your puppy's vaccine records. DHPP is sometimes designated DAPP. If *H* stands for hepatitis and *A* stands for adenovirus, what disease was your puppy vaccinated for? Hepatitis is caused by the canine adenovirus type 1 (CAV-1), so the two terms are sometimes used interchangeably. To confuse matters more, there's an adenovirus type 2, which is part of the kennel cough or bordetella, group of diseases, which are much less serious.

Part of the kennel cough syndrome, the main symptoms of the parainfluenza virus are a dry cough and runny nose. If not treated, it can lead to secondary pneumonia and death.

Parvovirus is a relatively recent canine disease, first striking in the late 1970s and now found throughout the world. Parvo also affects coyotes. It is one of the most highly resistant viruses and can survive in the environment for five months or longer. The symptoms include bloody, foul-smelling diarrhea, fever, and depression, and your veterinarian will test a stool sample to confirm the diagnosis. Parvo is treated with intravenous fluids and medications to control vomiting and diarrhea. The disease is most severe in puppies 6 to 14 weeks old, and many die even with expensive veterinary care. Chlorine bleach is the only effective disinfectant.

There are many other noncore vaccines available for dogs. Rather than overload your puppy's immune system right now, discuss them with your vet and decide together if and when your puppy should receive them. Some optional vaccines include bordetella (kennel cough), Lyme disease, coronavirus, leptospirosis, and rattlesnake vaccine. We go into more detail about these in later chapters.

Your puppy will not be fully protected until he has had several booster shots. The vaccine at six to eight weeks old primed his system to develop antibodies now that the ones provided through his mother's milk longer protect him. Boosters are given at 3- or 4-week intervals up to a total of 3, for example 6, 10, and 14 weeks, or 8, 12, and 16 weeks. The last one is administered at about 14 to 16 weeks of age and then a booster is given 1 year later. After the 16-week vaccine, it's safe for him to venture out in public.

Protect your puppy from infection by limiting his contact with the outside world until he is fully immunized.

Your Puppy's First Veterinary Appointment

Within a week of bringing your Lab puppy home, take him for his first vet visit. Bring along some treats, and make it a fun experience. What he learns now about the vet's office determines how he views it for the rest of his life.

Carry him into the vet's office, and don't let him explore on the floor. Although the office looks clean, your puppy is especially susceptible to illness at this age.

Bring the breeder-supplied health records with you to your first appointment. The veterinarian will recommend a schedule for future deworming and vaccines based on those records.

The doctor will do a complete physical exam. She'll listen to your puppy's heart and lungs, look in his ears, examine his mouth for abnormalities, check for a hernia on his belly, and make note of his weight and overall physical condition.

Dealing with Parasites

Roundworm, hookworm, and whipworm are intestinal parasites that grow and reproduce in a puppy's body. He may show no symptoms, or you may see the worms in his stool. Weight loss, a dry dull coat, diarrhea, or potbelly are also indicators he may have worms.

All three types of worms can be transmitted when the puppy accidentally eats, licks, or walks on contaminated soil and then licks his feet. Roundworms especially can be passed from the mother to her puppies.

If your puppy has worms, it doesn't mean the breeder did something wrong. Most vets assume all young pups have worms and will advise a deworming now and again in two weeks. Even though the breeder wormed the pups, it doesn't kill all the worms. The first worming kills adult worms, but it doesn't kill the larvae. The second worming kills the worms that have developed since the last worming. It may take several treatments over a period of weeks to eliminate all of them.

If your puppy is having diarrhea, the vet might opt to test a stool sample to check for giardia and coccidia, two other parasites that sometimes affect puppies (and adult dogs). Your pup can ingest these single-celled parasites from infected water or soil, or from contact with an infected puppy's feces. Both can also be transmitted to humans. Medication quickly kills the parasites.

Some topical flea-control products are made specifically for puppies. Ask your veterinarian what to use, so your pup doesn't get a toxic dose. Some orally administered flea-control products also prevent heartworm and other types of worm infestations and are available by prescription only.

Nutrition

Feeding your new Lab is more involved than just setting down a bowl of kibble once or twice a day. Choose a food with the nutrients a puppy needs to develop strong muscles, organs, and bones. By feeding him quality food and developing good feeding habits when he's a puppy, you'll help ensure his future good health.

Your Lab Puppy's Nutritional Needs

Dog-food manufacturers want you to feed your pup puppy food for a year or more, but Lab puppies don't need excess nutrients to grow and thrive. In fact, many breeders recommend you buy one bag of puppy food and switch to adult food as soon as that's gone.

Puppy foods encourage overly fast growth, which can cause orthopedic problems later in life. They contain the same basic nutrients as adult food, but in slightly different amounts. A healthy, balanced diet includes protein, carbohydrates, fat, minerals, vitamins, and water. For puppies, manufacturers sometimes add additional protein, fat, vitamins, and minerals.

Dog-food ingredients are subject to regulation by the Association of American Feed Control Officials (AAFCO). AAFCO establishes the minimum and maximum percentages of each nutrient that must be present in order to declare the food "healthy and balanced." AAFCO also approves labeling "for puppies" or "for all life stages." But they don't regulate what exact ingredients should make up the foods, and that's where it gets tricky to select a food for your Labrador.

The quality of the ingredients is the most important factor in selecting a brand. Low-quality ingredients can affect your dog's digestion and behavior. Read the dog food label, and choose a food that's higher in meat protein and fat and lower in grain carbohydrates. (Ingredients are listed in order according to volume.) Dogs are meat eaters and don't do well on a vegetarian diet.

Your pup needs protein. Protein contains amino acids that help build his healthy bones, muscles, skin, and hair. The best protein sources are meat, fish, and poultry. Less-expensive protein sources come from plants, like wheat or corn gluten, and are harder for your puppy to digest.

Puppy and dog food labels should name the meat source (beef, lamb, or chicken). If you see meat meal, that's a good, concentrated source of protein. Meat by-products are made up of the less-desirable parts of the animal, such as the feathers or feet. Choose a food that has a specific meat source as the first ingredient, such as lamb or lamb meal.

Also important, carbohydrates provide sugars (glucose), starches, and dietary fiber. Simple carbohydrates, such as fruit, absorb easily into the body. Complex carbs like whole grains, potatoes, peas, and beans also provide fiber and starches to help your puppy's digestion. Additional starches are sometimes added to dry food during manufacturing to help the kibble retain its shape and texture.

Whole grains are a healthy source of carbohydrates. Refined grains such as white rice and white flour are stripped of their most important nutrients—B vitamins, dietary fiber, and iron. They add calories but not much nutrition. Some "empty" carbohydrates, such as cellulose or peanut hulls, are used as fillers and aid in forming a solid stool. They have no nutritional benefit. They also are harder to digest and sometimes cause excess gas.

Recent scientific studies have suggested that excess cereal carbohydrates cause hyperactivity in dogs, and that's the *last* thing a Labrador retriever needs.

Fat provides energy and essential fatty acids, and helps the body absorb fat-soluble vitamins A, D, E, and K. Fats add flavor and texture to dry food and are sprayed onto the food after cooking. The essential fatty acids help lubricate your puppy's joints and keep his coat shiny and healthy, while the calories in fat give him energy to grow.

Your pup needs certain vitamins and minerals, too. Vitamins are crucial to cell functioning. The fat-soluble vitamins (A, D, E, and K) are stored in the liver, and excess cannot be eliminated. Excess water-soluble vitamins (C and assorted B vitamins) are eliminated in the urine. If food becomes rancid, the vitamins are destroyed, so manufacturers add antioxidants to extend the shelf life and prevent spoilage.

Minerals build healthy bones and teeth. Dog-food companies used to add a lot of calcium to their puppy formulas to aid growing bones, but this practice has changed because excess calcium can cause your Lab to grow too fast and develop overly large bones with less density, making them brittle and easily broken. Large-breed puppy formulas have less calcium than small-breed foods for this reason. Calcium in the right amount is necessary because it works with phosphorus to aid functions such as muscle contraction.

Some additional minerals important to your puppy's overall body functioning are zinc, iodine, selenium, and copper.

If you're feeding a "complete and balanced" puppy food made with meat and other high-quality ingredients, you shouldn't have to add any vitamins, minerals, or other supplements to your puppy's diet. In fact, doing so can do more harm than good. So opt for a good-quality food, and discuss any nutrition concerns you may have with your veterinarian before supplementing.

Make Changes Slowly

The breeder will probably send home a small bag of the brand of kibble your puppy has been eating. If you're going to continue with this brand, that's fine. If you decide to change brands, make the change *gradually* to avoid upsetting his tummy.

Start by mixing ½ of the new food with ¾ of the old food for several days. If your pup seems to tolerate it well—with no diarrhea—you can up the amount of the new food by mixing the new and old food ½ and ½ for a week. For the next week, mix ¾ of the new food with ½ of the old. Eventually, you should be able to eliminate the old food completely with no problems.

How Much to Feed?

Lab puppies are notorious for being overweight. And fat puppies grow up to be fat adult dogs. You should be able to feel your puppy's ribs, even when he is only eight weeks old.

There's no hard-and-fast rule about how much to feed your pup this month. Most breeders recommend about 2 cups per day.

Whatever you do, don't blindly follow the recommendations on the bag of puppy food, which are usually way too high.

Proper Feeding Practices

This month, feed your puppy three meals a day if at all possible. He will survive if you're working and he only gets fed twice, but he will get pretty hungry.

When feeding, select a spot where your puppy can eat undisturbed, possibly in his crate. Feed him in the same place every meal. Put his food down and leave it for 10 to 15 minutes. If he hasn't eaten, pick it up until the next mealtime. Because you know when he has eaten, you also know when he needs to go out, and that helps with housetraining. He'll also look up to his people as the providers of food—an important motivator when you start training.

Your pup doesn't need any table scraps or other goodies to make his food tasty. In fact, giving him scraps only teaches him to turn up his nose at plain kibble. Practice good feeding habits now to avoid a beggar later on.

All-Important Water

Last but certainly not least is water. Water is the most essential nutrient. The lack of other nutrients causes illness, but your puppy cannot survive without water.

It's especially easy for puppies to get dehydrated, so keep plenty of water available to your puppy. Be sure to change it every day because fresh water encourages him to drink.

> ### TIPS AND TAILS
>
> The breeder adds water to your pup's food as she's weaning him, but after he's completely weaned, you don't need to add water to his food.

Grooming

It may seem unnecessary to groom your Lab puppy when he's only eight weeks old, but if he learns to tolerate grooming now, he'll be easier to groom throughout his life. And you'll be glad you took the time once you see how much an adult Lab sheds!

Instead of looking at grooming as a chore, make it fun, and an opportunity for you and your pup to spend time together.

Treat Him Kindly

Puppies need to feel secure. They've had close contact with their littermates and mom, and now they're all alone in the world except for you. Take advantage of his need to cuddle, and teach him to enjoy handling at the same time. You'll need to clean his ears, trim his toenails, brush his teeth, and investigate injuries throughout his life, so you want him comfortable being touched anywhere on his body.

Remember, your pup is learning good and bad things during this time, so be sure your grooming and touching are always good. Never drag your puppy by the collar.

If you need to make him go somewhere, pick him up until you've taught him to walk on a leash. And never swat him with a newspaper or rub his nose in an accident. You aren't teaching him anything except to be afraid of you. You shouldn't have to use any harsh discipline on your puppy. After all, he doesn't even know the rules yet.

> **HAPPY PUPPY**
>
> Every time you handle your puppy, show him that being touched is a good thing. He'll look forward to your attention.

Massage Your Puppy

Gentle massage is a loving way for your puppy to get used to handling and grooming. Always keep it fun and positive, with lots of treats. He doesn't understand what you're saying yet, so your tone of voice is important. A soothing voice helps him calm down and relax. Massage him in short sessions when he's naturally tired and ready for his nap, and you'll soon have a sleeping pup.

Sit down on the floor with your legs out in front of you. Roll him on his back or side. He'll struggle as you hold him, so reward him when he stops wiggling, even for a second, by giving him a treat and letting him get up. Let him move around a little between tries. If he's not happy to come back to you, you've pushed him too far. Remember that he doesn't have much of an attention span yet.

By the third time you put him on his back, he'll start to figure out what you want and calm down faster. After a few sessions, he'll relax quickly.

A firm touch is less likely to tickle, so keep that in mind as you slowly pet his body and legs and rub your fingers between his toes. Work with his paws until you can hold each one in your hand without a struggle. Gently stroke his ears from base to tip, and turn each ear inside out. Stroke his tail from the base to the end and pull your hand off the tip as if the tail was longer than it is. (Suddenly stopping at the end of his tail feels jarring to him.) Massage his mouth, and lift his lip and massage his gums with your fingertip. Let him fall asleep if he wants to.

Introduce the Brush

When he readily allows you to hold onto a paw without snatching it away, introduce the brush and other grooming tools. At this point, you aren't trying to do a complete grooming job; you just want him to see the tools, feel them on his body, and get lots of praise for allowing you to touch him with them.

Let him investigate each tool for a minute or so while you praise him and hand out treats. Let him feel the sensation of each tool on his body for a second, and immediately praise him and take it away.

Gradually work up to brushing his tummy, chest, neck, and legs. Do this several times a week.

Trim His Toenails

In another session, reintroduce the toenail clippers. Although the breeder probably trimmed his toenails, he was so young he may not remember anymore. He needs a refresher course because he's in a new home with new people.

Stroke his leg with the clippers while you hold his foot and let him investigate this strange object. Tap lightly on his toenail, and give him a treat when he doesn't pull back. Do this for all four feet and each toenail. Break it into several sessions, or take play breaks in between feet or toes. Stop when he's done something right. If you have to, back up a bit in the process. Quitting is his reward for doing the right thing.

Once he accepts tapping on his toenails, trim off a tiny piece of one toenail. Praise him while you cut, and immediately give him a treat and release him. The point is not to actually shorten his nails, but to get him used to the feeling of the pressure from the clippers. If he can't tolerate that, just close the clippers for a second on his nail and release without cutting.

Watch out for the quick. This is a blood-filled vein that runs down the middle of each nail. If you accidentally cut the quick, it will hurt and bleed, and your pup will *not* want you to do it again! Black and chocolate Lab puppies have dark toenails, and you won't be able to see the quick through the nail. Yellow Labs often have white nails, and you can see the quick. The more often you trim his toenails, the farther back the quick will recede and the less likely you are to nick it. Always err on the side of caution and cut back less than $\frac{1}{32}$ inch.

If you cut the quick, hold your fingertip tightly over the end of the nail until the pressure stops any bleeding. Apply a product called Kwik-Stop or run a bar of soap across the tip of his nail to help the blood clot.

Social Skills

Labs are naturally happy and outgoing, but they need proper socialization when they're young to ensure they mature into well-adjusted adults. Systematically introduce your puppy to the creatures and experiences he'll encounter throughout his lifetime. By starting when he's young and carefully controlling his interactions, you'll prevent future behavior and temperament problems.

The Labrador Temperament

Originally, the Labrador Retriever was developed as a hunting dog. Why is this important to you? Because the same characteristics that make a Lab a good hunting dog also make him an excellent family dog.

He has to cooperate with the hunter, be ready to obey, and be eager to please. Intense and focused on the job at hand, Labs have a strong work ethic and great perseverance, while at the same time they're able to wait quietly for hours in a duck blind between retrieves.

For you, he is ready to play at a moment's notice or lies quietly at your feet for the evening. He'll work for you at whatever task you send his way for no more payment than the chance to be with you. Not independent like a Bloodhound or a guarding breed, Labs are all about their people. Lousy watchdogs, yours might tell you someone is at the front door, but he has no desire to scare anyone away. His sense of humor keeps you entertained, and his happy-go-lucky attitude lasts his lifetime.

Fear-Imprint Period

Lab puppies are naturally curious and interested in everything around them. But between 8 and 12 weeks, most puppies go through a phase where they're more likely to be significantly affected by a scary experience. A traumatic encounter during this *fear-imprint stage* could spoil his attitude toward that thing for the rest of his life. Most pups won't experience anything overly frightening at this age, but it's worth taking precautions to avoid unnecessary scares. This is a bad time to discipline him severely, yell at him, or force him to approach something he finds scary.

> **DOG TALK**

The **fear imprint stage** lasts for several weeks and usually starts soon after you bring your puppy home. He may remember overwhelming or frightening incidents that occur during this time for the rest of his life and always react to them with fear.

When something traumatic happens, it's hard to know how the puppy looks at it. For example, an 8-week-old pup, just entering the fear imprint period, is badly startled when someone drops a bowl of apples behind him. This could cause a lifetime phobia, but what exactly the puppy may become afraid of is difficult to predict. It could be objects hovering over his head, things coming up behind him, apples, bowls, or some other factor the pup focused on during the incident.

In spite of the risks, he still needs to be socialized. Allow your worried pup to approach a scary person or thing in his own time. Try not to overwhelm the puppy or accidentally reward his fearful behavior. If you overreact, he might decide there really is something to be frightened about. Or he could conclude he's being praised for acting scared, and he'll act frightened to get attention from you. Sometimes Labs are *too* smart.

If he barks or makes a big fuss when he sees something, try to ignore it and praise him when he calms down. Remember, praise desired behavior, ignore unwanted reactions or frightened behavior, and just keep patiently working with him. Continue to present experiences he was familiar with before this period, and introduce him to new things. In about 2 weeks, he'll regain his confidence.

There's a balance between overprotecting and overwhelming your puppy. With that in mind, it's time to start the socialization process in earnest.

Socialization Basics

During the 8- to 12-week period, your Lab puppy learns easily, and what he learns, he'll remember for his lifetime—good and bad. Your goal over the next few weeks is to introduce him to a multitude of positive experiences.

Socialization is not a one-time thing. You need to expose him to new things every day. If you bring your Lab home at 8 weeks of age and he never sees another dog, person, or place until he's 16 weeks old or older, he won't develop into the outgoing confident dog he has the potential to be. An unsocialized puppy can become excessively fearful or aggressive, not typical Labrador traits at all.

The breeder started socialization when your puppy was just a few weeks old (see the Rule of Sevens in Month 1). Now it's your turn to continue his efforts. Remember that because your pup hasn't yet completed his vaccines, this isn't the time to take him to the park or out in public. But there are many things you can do to socialize your pup.

Invite assorted people to your home one at a time or in small groups. Your Lab needs to meet people who are tall, short, fat, thin, old, and very young. He should see hats, coats, uniforms, umbrellas, and wheelchairs. When Puppy approaches someone new, praise him for being brave. For example, a guest could get down on the floor, toss a treat, and speak in a happy voice to encourage him and then ignore him while he works up his courage and decides to investigate.

If your puppy is fearful, start with the new person at a distance so Puppy can get used to him before getting too close. Act like the stranger is no big deal. Talk in a normal tone of voice, and shake hands or touch the person's shoulder so your puppy understands that you think the scary person is just fine. Give your pup the opportunity to interact with everyone while they give him treats and pet him. Do this several times a week until he is at least 16 weeks old.

> ### TIPS AND TAILS
>
> Include your mail carrier in the socialization process. After all, he or she will arrive on your doorstep every day for the rest of your dog's life. Provide a box of biscuits and ask him to offer one to your puppy every time he delivers the mail.

Although your Lab saw many things at the breeder's home, those same things may seem new to him in at your house. Continue to expose your puppy to various surfaces: asphalt, gravel, concrete, grass, snow, dirt, and puddles. When he has a chance to interact with his environment, he's more likely to remember it, so feed or play with him on each material.

Accustom him to different locations, too, such as the bathroom, the living room, the garage, the patio, his crate, and your car. You can safely take him to homes that have no pets if you carry him to and from the house. Visit the vet's office for a pet-and-treat session.

Introduce your Lab to assorted sounds, like the lawnmower, televisions, the dishwasher, music, thunder, yelling, kids, sirens, motorcycles, gunshots (if you're going to hunt), and other loud noises. Start with the sounds far away, and slowly move closer, or record loud sounds and play them back while gradually increasing the volume. Remember that at this age, you want him to have positive experiences, not terrify him to the point where he'll be emotionally scarred for life. If your puppy seems worried, adjust the exposure accordingly.

Set up some physical challenges for him, and let him figure out each item for himself. Set up an obstacle course in the back yard. Have him climb steps, go through a tunnel, play in a cardboard box, climb over and under obstacles, and walk up a ramp or small teeter-totter. Lay a board across several bricks and teach him to walk on it.

By allowing him to figure out new things for himself, you're helping him build confidence and problem-solving skills. When he reacts in a calm and happy manner, praise him. You are there to provide a comfort zone for him, and he needs to know all is going well. You're also there to protect him from overwhelming situations and remove him when something is just too much for him.

Also remember that you are quite large in relationship to your Lab puppy. If you greet your puppy by bending over him, you block his view of everything else in the world—a terrifying thing to a puppy. Think of how uncomfortable you are when a large person gets in your personal space and hovers over you—you want to move away. No wonder a puppy is sometimes afraid of new people.

Make introductions easier on your puppy by inviting everyone to get down on the floor at his level. Pet him by scratching his chest rather than patting him on top of the head. A hand looming over him will cause him to shy away, but the palm of your hand, down low and reaching in his direction, isn't so scary.

Your Lab Puppy and Children

Labs and children were made to be together. If you don't have kids, borrow some and have a puppy party. Puppies need to learn how to interact with children, and equally as important, children need to learn how to properly interact with puppies.

Start by inviting over just one well-behaved child at a time. For the initial introductions, keep the sessions short, calm, and controlled so your puppy doesn't get overtired or overwhelmed.

Some children don't know how to play with a puppy. Avoid tug-of-war and teasing games. Teach the kids to give the puppy a treat for looking at them when they say his new name. Help them teach the pup to sit or learn a trick like "shake." Play "puppy-come" games, where everyone sits in a circle, each one calls the puppy in turn, and rewards him with a treat. Have the child brush the puppy, hold his leash, hug him lightly, pet him, or toss a toy a few feet away.

TIPS AND TAILS

Never leave your puppy alone with children. It's up to you to protect him while you supervise and direct the activities.

As more kids visit, there might be lots of yelling and running around. You want your pup to get used to the commotion, but all this activity encourages him to join in. Children often run and scream, waving their arms and batting at the puppy when he jumps on them. To him, this is an invitation to play.

Teach kids to "be a tree" when Puppy gets too excited and starts nipping or pulling on their clothes. Have the child fold her arms across her chest, stand perfectly still, and not look at the puppy. When your pup quits leaping, quietly praise him and have everyone stay settled for a few minutes. Distract him with a toy or chewy and put him on a leash to prevent him from jumping and nipping again.

Watch your puppy's reactions as he plays with children, and remove him if he seems overwhelmed. Puppies tire quickly. After a short play session, he can snuggle while he falls asleep in a child's lap.

Introducing Other Family Pets

If you have other dogs in the house and they're over 6 months old, choose a neutral territory, possibly at a friend's house, for them to meet your puppy so they won't see him as an invader. Introduce each dog one at a time, loosely holding the leash. A tight leash makes the adult dog feel restrained and like he can't get away, which makes him more likely to lash out at the puppy.

Also, don't leave your pup alone with the big dogs. They need supervision for several weeks until everyone is comfortable and the puppy has figured out his place in the hierarchy (see the "Socialize to Calm Adult Dogs" section in Month 4).

If you have a cat, know that the cat takes much longer to get used to your pup than the puppy to her. A cat's first instinct is to run, and a puppy's is to chase—what fun! It may take a few weeks for things to settle down. Be sure your cat has a place up high where she can get away from the puppy. Baby gates can block Puppy's access to the cat's territory, for example.

Let them smell each other through a closed door, and take the puppy on a leashed tour of the cat's favorite room. Let the cat leave when she wants to. At night, when the pup is in his crate in your room, Kitty will get used to his smell and learn the pup can't get to her. Whenever the cat is around for the first week or two, leash the pup so he can't chase her. When he gets too close, Kitty will hiss and swat him. They may become great friends, or they may just tolerate each other.

Small pocket pets like birds and hamsters and caged animals like snakes are safest in their cages when a young Lab is on the scene. He can get used to their presence from his crate. Don't try to introduce them nose to nose; you're the one that's likely to come away with wounds. If you don't make a big deal of it, they won't either, and everyone can peacefully coexist without interacting. Keep doors to the pet rooms shut when you're not able to supervise, so a curious puppy doesn't knock over a cage or aquarium.

TIPS AND TAILS

Prevent your puppy from leaping on or otherwise interacting too much with other animals. A bird can peck or bite and a cat will scratch and hiss at a strange, overactive puppy. Besides the risk of injury to either animal, you want this to be a positive experience for your pup. His first exposure to other species should be from a distance or otherwise controlled.

Introducing Other Puppies

Contact with other puppies is important. Puppies teach each other acceptable dog manners. If one plays too rough or bites, the other one disciplines him or quits playing. You may be able to set up play dates with your pup's littermates, or your veterinarian may have other puppies in his practice he can refer to you.

Limit your puppy's contact with other dogs, both puppies and adults, unless they're completely vaccinated and show no signs of illness. Wait at least until after the second set of vaccines before you set up a puppy playtime.

Behavior

Perfectly normal puppy activities might test your sanity if you're not used to having a puppy in your home. Plan ahead for a few inconveniences and challenges during the first few weeks.

Sleeping Through the Night

At night, put Puppy in his crate by your bed, and expect to get up and take him out once or twice. His little bladder can't hold it more than a couple hours. By 10 to 12 weeks, he should be able to sleep through the night.

Pick up all the water an hour or two before bedtime so he doesn't tank up right before he goes to sleep. And give him one last break outside before you put him in his crate for the night.

Curiosity—Not Just for Cats

Without constant supervision, unwanted behaviors become habits and are much harder to eliminate later. As your Lab pup gains confidence, he'll start to explore his world more and more. If left to his own devices, he'll discover that digging is fun and chewing keeps him entertained. These are normal doggie behaviors, but not something you want to encourage! That same curiosity leads Puppy into every nook and cranny, searching for more exciting things to eat and play with, exposing him to things that could hurt him.

Be sure to always supervise your pup when he's out of his crate, and you'll both be better off.

When Your Puppy Starts Biting

As Puppy starts exploring, he uses his teeth like babies use their hands. He tastes everything. He doesn't know his own strength, so he tests to see what happens when he bites hard or tugs. It's never okay for him to use his mouth on a person. Teach him bite inhibition from the first day you bring him home. His littermates started the job, and you can continue teaching him using the methods his fellow puppies used.

When Puppy starts nipping at your arms or clothes, yelp loudly like another puppy would. This tells him you are displeased. Fold your arms and turn away from him. Abruptly leave the room. Ignore him. Game over. He'll get the message after a few tries.

When you see him consider biting but then think better of it, praise him. Redirect his attention to a toy or acceptable chewy. If he's too wound up to quit, put him in his crate for a 3-minute time-out. If family and friends are consistent in their reactions, he'll quickly learn to keep his teeth to himself.

Training

At 8 weeks, your puppy is capable of learning specific lessons and connecting his actions with certain words. Teaching good habits now prevents bad habits from developing. It is much easier to stop problem behaviors before they become a habit than to change them when he's a teenager.

Training Techniques

Positive training methods make learning fun. Your pup's attention span is limited right now, so keep sessions short—no more than 5 minutes. Remember, he doesn't understand what you're saying to him right now, but your body language and tone of voice communicate your meaning. Always reward him for doing something right. Lure him with treats, or shape him into position and reward him. Add the command name once he understands what you're asking him to do.

There's no need for harsh corrections with a puppy this young. Instead, interrupt him and redirect his energy to something else.

A Family United

An 8-week-old puppy needs to feel safe and secure in order to grow up confident and well adjusted. He must be comfortable that he understands the rules of the house and that everyone reacts the same to his behavior.

Everyone in the household needs to agree on the dog rules. Lab puppies are cute and cuddly, but will you want him on the couch when he's an adult? Will he have access to every room? Where will his preferred elimination spot be? Where will he eat? Does everyone agree not to let him jump up on people? If you are inconsistent in enforcing the rules, your puppy will be confused and you'll wonder why he isn't learning anything. Decide on the rules together, and enforce them equally.

Agree on the words you'll use for different commands. Does "Down" mean "lie down" or "get off me"? Do you call him by saying "Come" or "Here"? Too many names for the same action only confuse him.

Agree on discipline, too. Rather than drag the pup by his collar, hang a few leashes around the house so anyone can easily hook him up to control his behavior. Agree that you all will ignore bad behavior or distract him rather than hit or yell.

Prioritize Housetraining

Start housetraining the first day you bring your new puppy home. Your Lab will need to go potty as soon as he wakes up, right after eating or drinking, and after a play session. He'll need to go almost hourly the first week. By 12 weeks, he should be able to last an hour and a half.

Keep him close and supervise him during this time, or put him in his crate. Don't allow him to make a mistake. When you take him out, go to the spot you want him to use and he'll probably pee immediately. Don't play or entertain him. Just stand there and wait. Be sure to praise him to the skies when he goes, and offer a treat. He'll quickly learn that peeing outside produces treats. If he doesn't go immediately, put him back in his crate for 20 minutes and try again. When he performs, give him some supervised freedom indoors before confining him again.

It's worth repeating: you must go outdoors with your puppy and praise him when he eliminates so he'll know he's done the right thing. If you just put him outside, how will you know he's done his business?

Housetraining often takes longer in winter, when it's cold and snowy outside. You don't want to go out and stand in the cold, and Puppy doesn't want to get his feet and tummy wet. Dig out a snow-free area, or erect a small shelter over his potty spot so you both won't mind so much.

When you leave your pup at home alone, set up his ex pen with his crate (door open or removed), water, and a spot to relieve himself. He'll select a corner of the pen to use. Encourage him with a piece of turf, a piddle pad, or even a doggie litter box in that spot. The best solution is to use the same surface he is expected to use outside. He'll quickly make the connection.

If he has an accident in the house, you have to try to catch him in the act and interrupt him. Make a loud noise, scoop him up, and take him straight outdoors. Wait with him while he finishes going, and praise him. If you don't see the accident happen indoors, clean it up and forget about it. He'll have no idea what you're mad about if you scold him at that point.

> **TIPS AND TAILS**

Your pup will jump up against the wire pen you've set up to confine him, and if he doesn't stop now, he'll learn to knock it over. Never pick him up when he's jumping; ignore him until he puts his feet on the floor. Rattle the pen until he backs down and then praise him. Don't pet him while he's on his hind legs, either. That's just rewarding him for pushing on the pen. This method also works when he's jumping against a pet gate.

Crate Training

The crate is a training tool for you and a safe haven for your puppy. Don't use it as a punishment, and don't confine your pup in it for more than a few hours.

To introduce the crate, toss in a treat and let the puppy go in and get it. Do this a few times throughout the day, leaving the crate open so he can explore it on his own. At mealtime, place his dinner inside the crate with the door open. After a few meals, close the door while he eats.

He may whine and cry a little the first few times you close the door. Wait until he settles down and then reward him by letting him out. If you let him out because he doesn't like it, he learns that making a fuss gets him what he wants.

At bedtime, place the crate next to your bed. Give him a chewy toy, place the blanket the breeder gave you (with his mother's smell on it) in the crate, put him in, and close the door. You might not get much sleep the first night!

Practice putting the puppy in his crate for a few minutes while you read or watch TV nearby. Give him a chewy filled with treats, and let him see you leave the room and return a few times. He'll soon be comfortable and settle down for a good chew and a nap. Save the best chew toys for crate time, so he looks forward to it. And always wait until the puppy is quiet before you let him out.

Limit Freedom

For the next few months, your pup is too young to have the responsibility of the entire house and yard. With no one there to instruct him, he learns bad habits like digging in the wastebasket and chewing. He could also get hurt.

Indoors, use pet gates to block his access to other rooms. If he's scolded for having an accident in the house, he'll just go to another room. You can't see him, and he doesn't get in trouble, so in his mind it must be okay. He's figured out that peeing in front of you is bad, and out of your sight is fine. Housetraining will progress faster if you keep him in the same room with you.

If you have to leave him outside for a while, put him in his ex pen. He'll get to enjoy the great outdoors without the hazards.

Teach "Come"

As we've mentioned, "Come" is an easy command to train and lots of fun for you and your Lab. The way to get a lifelong reliable recall is to start training early. Always call him for a positive reason. Take advantage of his willing nature; he'll probably race to you as soon as you call. If good things happen every time he responds, he'll always be happy to come to you. If you're going to do something he won't like, you go get him.

To introduce "Come," put your puppy on a leash. Get down on your puppy's eye level a few feet away and open your arms wide. In a high, happy voice, say, "Come!" or "Come here!" Reward him with praise, play, and treats when he responds. Cheer him on as soon as he looks your way. If he doesn't come, encourage him with a little tug on the leash and reel him in.

Practice from just a few feet away at first. Later, hook him to a longer lead, like clothesline rope, so you can enforce the recall. Then start over in a new place from close up again, gradually working farther away.

Have family and friends call your pup, too. Play games where one person calls him and then another. Keep it short, and quit before he gets tired.

> ### TIPS AND TAILS
>
> Here's a helpful training tool: put a few pieces of kibble in a small food storage container, and shake it when you call your puppy. He'll soon learn that the shaker means treats. You can even shake it from another room, and he'll come running. Make several shakers, and set them around the house so you can find and use them easily.

You and Your Puppy

During the first few weeks, you're both learning about each other. He's learning even if you aren't actively teaching. He's figuring out his name, who's who, what makes you happy, what not to do, and what his new routine is. You're starting to recognize when he needs to go out and when he's tired, hungry, frightened, or wants to play. You're all settling into your new life together.

Name Your New Lab Puppy

Your Lab will have two names, a call name and a registered name. His call name is the one you use every day. His registered name is the one on his AKC papers. The two don't have to be similar at all.

The best call names for your pup are ones he'll easily recognize and have an upbeat, happy sound to them. Names of one or two syllables are short and snappy. If you make his call name too long, you'll undoubtedly shorten it to a nickname. For instance, Frederico will soon become Freddy, and Francesca, Franny.

Don't choose a name like Flo, which sounds too much like "no." Think about what the name will sound like when you call him from across the park. Will you be embarrassed? Will Puppy recognize what you said?

The AKC registered name is limited to 36 characters, including spaces. For an extra fee, the name can have up to 50 characters. With the breeder's permission, the kennel name can precede the puppy's name, as in, for example, Windy Acres Coming Storm (call name Stormy). Sometimes the sire or dam's name is first on the registration: Samantha's Chocolate Surprise (call name Cocoa). It's up to you. Windy Acres Coming Storm could have Louie as his call name, or something else totally unrelated to his registration.

What to Expect During the First Week

Today is the big day. The breeder has done her job, and now that wonderful ball of fur is delivered into your arms, ready or not. Here's what to expect the first few days.

Your puppy might fall asleep in your arms on the way home. Take him outside as soon as you arrive so he can relieve himself in his designated spot. Once the smell is there, it will remind him to go in that place again. Let him explore around outside for a few minutes—supervised, of course.

Once you're sure he's emptied his bladder and bowels, bring him inside and let him explore the main room where you spend most of your time. If he has an accident, ignore it. He will be too confused to remember anything you try to teach him at this point.

Let your Lab tell you what he wants to do next. He may approach you for attention. If so, get down on the floor with him for quiet introductions, sniffing and maybe a few treats. He may fall asleep immediately. Puppies need a lot of sleep and tire quickly. But every puppy is different.

On the first day, let him get to know your family; visitors can meet him later. After a few days, he'll recognize individual family members. It's everyone's job to make him feel welcome and safe. Don't overwhelm him with lots of noise or roughhousing. As he starts to feel safe, he'll watch what you're doing and start to follow you. He'll be excited to see you and begin to learn his name.

Be sure his basic needs for food, water, and sleep are met. Take him out hourly for potty breaks. Be patient with accidents and chewing.

> ## HAPPY PUPPY
>
> Lab puppies are naturally happy and outgoing. During this period of his life, playing is fun *and* instructive. This isn't the time to be serious about anything. Make training a game, and he'll learn fast and remember forever. Even a pup who makes a mistake can be corrected in a positive way by distracting and redirecting him to an acceptable behavior. A full tummy, a soft toy, and a warm bed all make for a *very* happy puppy.

Practice Patience

A Lab puppy doesn't learn everything on the first try. It takes at least three repetitions for him to start getting the idea, and you may have to start all over tomorrow. He will make mistakes, have accidents, chew something, and whine in his crate. Remember, he's just a baby. Keep training and forgive him. He's learning how to learn. He wants desperately to please you; he just needs time to figure out right from wrong.

When you run out of patience, let another family member take over for a while or put him in his ex pen or crate. If you lose your temper, he'll be frightened and see you as unpredictable.

Manage your puppy's environment. Even though you have puppy-proofed your house and yard, he still requires direction, supervision, and confinement. Keep temptation out of reach, and prevent trouble before it occurs.

The Importance of a Routine

A puppy starts to feel safe and secure when he knows what's expected of him and when he'll be fed, walked, put to bed, and left alone. Set up a daily schedule with fixed times for every activity, and stick to it as much as possible. Try to keep weekends the same as weekdays. If you get up at 6 A.M. on weekdays, he'll quickly learn to anticipate getting up at that same time on weekends.

Many people take a few days off from work when they get their new pup. Don't shower him with attention for four days and then suddenly go off and leave him on the fifth day. Introduce his schedule immediately. A young puppy sleeps as much as 16 to 18 hours out of every 24, so he needs a lot of rest and quiet time, even when you're home.

Month 3 > Month 4 > Month 5

Socialization at home with new owner and other pets		
	Teething begins—heavy chewing period	
	Enroll in puppy class	
Rapid growth		Switch to adult food
	2nd DHPP vaccines	3rd DHPP and rabies vaccines

During Month 4, your puppy looks to you for everything. She follows you anywhere and is eager and happy. The period from 12 to 16 weeks, or 3 to 4 months, is a lot of fun for your family and your puppy. You continue socialization and training and take her to puppy class. Her focus is more social than studious, but lessons set the foundation for future learning and good behavior.

This month is also a challenge as your joyful toddler becomes more active. Overenthusiastic about everything, she acts first and thinks later. She starts teething, and her entire world changes as she gnaws on anything that might comfort her sore mouth.

Keep in touch with your breeder, and call her when you have questions about your puppy's development. You may be worrying about something entirely normal, but you won't know unless you can ask an expert. Plus, she'll enjoy hearing about your lab's progress.

Physical Development

You'll notice big changes in your Lab puppy this month. She loses her roly-poly physique as her legs get longer in proportion to her body. She also begins teething, as mentioned earlier, and this means chewing.

Size and Weight

A 12-week-old puppy weighs somewhere between 20 and 25 pounds—roughly double what her weight was at 8 weeks. She'll gain another 10 or more pounds this month. By 16 weeks, she'll be half or more of her adult height and weight.

With Labs, it's hard to accurately predict specific height and weight because there are so many variations within the breed. Assess her body condition (see Appendix B), and work with your vet to estimate what your dog's weight should be.

Teething

By 16 weeks, your puppy is losing her baby teeth, and the adult teeth are pushing through her gums. First her incisors, the small front teeth on the upper and lower jaw, start to come in. Females usually start teething earlier than males.

As with human babies, the process is painful, but instead of fussing and crying, she'll chew to relieve the pain. Hide your most precious possessions, shoes, handbags, and the remote control. She doesn't target these items with evil intention. They smell like you, and that comforts her. When you catch her chewing on your golf shoes, trade them for an approved chew toy. You may see some blood on her toys, but that's normal.

Provide your pup a variety of safe and varied chew toys, and keep them handy because you'll be negotiating plenty of trades. Rotate the toys so she has just a few at a time. Then they'll seem as new and exciting when you offer them.

Don't yell and chase her when you catch her chewing. She'll think her beloved owner has suddenly lost her mind, and she'll be afraid of you. She'll hide with her prize next time, and you'll have trouble getting it away from her.

Frozen bones, cold carrots, ice cubes, or stuffed frozen Kong toys feel good on her sore gums and keep her occupied for longer periods. Keep in mind that frozen treats will make a mess, so confine her when you give her these gum soothers, or give them to her outside. You can rub her gums with a teething product like Orajel or use a natural remedy like chamomile. Know that on occasion, she might not feel like eating—that's normal. And she might not want her mouth touched. Remember, her mouth hurts right now. Soak her food in a few tablespoons of water so it won't be painful to chew.

Your puppy may get bad breath, have soft stools, or be a bit lethargic during teething. All of this is normal, but if you are concerned, consult with your veterinarian to rule out infection or other problems.

Health

At this stage of your Lab puppy's life there are some new concerns worthy of your attention. The most important things to watch for this month are signs that your puppy has eaten something she shouldn't. Because she's teething, revisit your puppy-proofing efforts (covered in Month 3) and supervise her carefully. When you can't watch her, confine her.

When to Take Your Lab Puppy to the Vet

As you and your Lab puppy get acquainted, you may wonder when a case of puppy diarrhea or vomiting means it's time to head to the vet. What might be a minor condition in an adult Lab can quickly become critical in a puppy, so watch your puppy, and if signs of illness continue for more than a few hours, contact your veterinarian.

The following things warrant a trip to the veterinarian including booster vaccines and those nasty parasites you'll want to keep away from your pup.

Diarrhea or vomiting: A puppy can get an upset tummy from eating too much or too fast. She may have swallowed a piece of stick in the yard or eaten too much grass. If her feces contain blood or mucous, this may be a sign of parvovirus. Vomiting is also a symptom of poisoning. If your puppy is staggering or shaking, *take her to the vet immediately.*

Refusing food or water: A puppy can get *dehydrated* quickly, so offer your Lab plenty of water. If she doesn't want to drink, offer ice cubes. They'll provide the moisture she needs but not make her queasy. Gnawing on the ice cubes also gives her something else to think about other than how she feels.

> ### DOG TALK
>
> **Dehydration** is an excessive loss of body fluids, especially water. Overheating and illness are common causes. To check for dehydration, lift your puppy's skin along her back. If she's well hydrated, it should make a tent shape and drop immediately back into place. If the skin remains standing up in a ridge, she's dehydrated. Also check her gums; they should be moist, not dry.

While other breeds may skip a meal, this is especially unusual for a Lab puppy. If meal skipping is accompanied by lethargy or listlessness, it could indicate something is seriously wrong. When she feels like eating again, start off slowly, feeding her a bland food like cooked plain skinless chicken and steamed rice or cottage cheese. When she feels better, gradually switch her back to her regular food.

If she doesn't feel better within 12 hours, call your vet. Your puppy may have a blockage caused by something she ate, such as socks, gravel, sticks, or bones.

Sudden changes in activity level: Beyond just a tired puppy taking a nap, is your pup lethargic, dull-eyed, and uninterested in her surroundings? Or is she frantic and hyperactive? Sudden changes like this might be a sign of fever, disease, or something as minor as a thorn in her foot.

Signs of pain or injury: Is she limping, whining, or crying when you touch her? Does she bite or snap at you? She might be trying to tell you where it hurts.

Breathing problems: If she is gagging, wheezing, or suddenly appears unable to breathe, this could be an emergency. She may have something stuck in her throat or might have been stung by a bee.

Fever: A puppy's temperature, taken rectally, is usually between 100°F and 102.5°F. Her nose is normally moist and wet, but it may be dry and warm if she has a fever. However, feeling your puppy's nose is not a foolproof way to detect a fever. Use a digital thermometer to get an accurate reading.

TIPS AND TAILS

To take your puppy's temperature, use a rectal thermometer lightly coated with petroleum jelly. Keep her occupied at the front end with treats. Hold up her tail and gently put the thermometer into her rectum about 1 inch. Hold it there for 2 minutes or until it beeps (if you have a digital model). Call your veterinarian if it reads over 103°F.

Urine or bladder problems: Is an almost-housetrained pup suddenly having frequent accidents? Is there blood in her urine or is it a dark color? Is she straining to go? This could be a urinary tract or kidney infection.

Constipation: Straining to eliminate may mean your pup isn't drinking enough water. Offer her canned food; it contains more moisture than dry food and helps get things moving. She also may have eaten something that caused a blockage. Sometimes, a puppy appears to be straining when she actually has diarrhea, so try to get an accurate read on what's happening.

Eye or nose discharge: She may have inhaled a foxtail or have something in her eye. It could also be a sign of upper-respiratory illness.

Unusual odor from mouth or ears: She could have a broken tooth that's infected or some decayed food stuck in her teeth. She also may have an ear infection or ear mites.

The veterinarian will want to know when the symptoms began and how the puppy has been acting. For digestive issues, you may be asked to bring in a stool sample.

Labrador Retriever Myopathy

Centronuclear myopathy is an inherited disease in Labradors that may show symptoms this month. A DNA test identifies this degenerative muscle disease, and your puppy's parents should have been tested for it.

Symptoms become apparent at 3 or 4 months. You'll first notice that your puppy's gait is odd and that she bunny-hops with her rear legs instead of running normally. The symptoms are worse when she is cold, stressed, or overexcited. She may start to look bony and have muscle wasting around the head and shoulders. She may hold her head down and tucked against her chest.

The disease doesn't progress beyond 6 to 8 months of age, and although your Lab can recover and be a good pet, she won't be as active as most Labs. See your vet for an accurate diagnosis.

Booster Vaccines

Three or four weeks after your Lab's first vaccines, you should visit the veterinarian for her second DHPP vaccine. Each booster continues to build her immunity by stimulating the production of antibodies that protect her from disease. At 12 weeks, she's not completely protected yet.

The final vaccine, at 14 to 16 weeks, completes the series, and she can start visiting the outside world. At 16 weeks, or 4 months, your veterinarian gives your pup her first rabies vaccine, which is effective for 1 year. Your pup needs a booster for both DHPP and rabies 1 year later.

The core vaccines all dogs should have—distemper, hepatitis, parvovirus, and parainfluenza—all have a low risk of side effects. But you should be aware of the symptoms in case your dog has a reaction. They can occur minutes, hours, or days later and can last from a few minutes to hours.

At the site of the injection, bad reactions include pain, swelling, hair loss, inflammation, abscess, or intense itching. A reaction to nasal or oral vaccines could include ulceration in the nose or mouth, eye discharge, or coughing.

The most severe vaccine reaction in dogs is anaphylactic shock, which is an extreme allergic response. Symptoms include difficulty breathing, swelling, low blood pressure, and weakness.

A mild allergic reaction can be treated with an antihistamine, but consult with your vet before administering any over-the-counter drug so you don't overdose or give your Lab anything toxic.

External Parasites

Gone are the days when you had to constantly spray, dip, and bathe your dog in toxic pesticides to get rid of fleas and ticks. For the most part, you can control or eliminate these pests with over-the-counter products. However, some situations do require a visit to the vet.

Here's how to check your pup for these nasty critters:

Fleas: Roll your puppy over on her back, and you may see fleas scrambling across her tummy to hide. Often you'll just see flea "dirt." The black specs are flea droppings, and the white specs are their eggs.

Ticks: Ticks feed on your dog's blood (as do fleas). A tick embeds its head in your dog's skin and can remain attached for several days, filling up with blood. A full tick looks like a grape hanging off your puppy's body.

Both fleas and ticks can quickly get out of hand if you don't protect your puppy. Ticks can transmit serious diseases to your dog—and you—such as Rocky Mountain spotted fever, erlichia, and Lyme disease. Ticks also have a toxin in their salivary glands that can cause a condition called tick paralysis, which causes a dog's hind legs and ultimately her entire body to become progressively weaker.

A puppy who has been bitten by a flea or tick may become lethargic, have a nasal discharge, or exhibit joint pain and lameness. If these symptoms occur, take her to your vet to test for parasite-borne diseases. Your pup may also have an allergic reaction to flea saliva and develop a skin infection that requires treatment.

Topical preventives like Advantage or Frontline are applied between the shoulder blades and partway down the spine so your puppy can't lick or scratch off the medicine. Many brands are even still effective after your Lab swims or has a bath. The dose is in proportion to your dog's weight, and most are approved for puppies, but read the label carefully. The product distributes through your pup's coat and oil glands in the skin without being absorbed completely into the body. Most products are effective for 30 days, and fleas or ticks are usually killed within 12 to 48 hours. A bonus: they don't have to bite your puppy to be killed, as with some preventives.

Sometimes a dog will have an allergic reaction to a topical product, with symptoms including itching, redness, or swelling. If your pup exhibits these symptoms, bathe her with a dish detergent such as Dawn that will remove the product without harming her.

Oral flea and tick preventives are often combined with heartworm pills in a single dose. Administered once a month, they offer continuous protection for your puppy. Some brands also kill lice and other types of worms like roundworm, hookworm, and whipworm. An additional advantage to oral products is that they don't leave a greasy residue on your dog's coat or cause skin irritation.

You'll find flea dirt not only on your pup, but also in her bed, her crate, and anywhere else she's been. Fleas jump off the dog and hide in the carpet until another warm host walks by. You haven't eliminated all the fleas around you just by treating your puppy. You'll have to treat other dogs, the cats, your yard, and your house to completely get rid of fleas. Nontoxic borax-based products and services like Fleabusters that dehydrate and kill fleas are available to treat your house and yard.

Ticks are common in the woods and in fields of tall grass. They like to hide several feet off the ground along hiking paths, waiting for an unsuspecting victim—you or your puppy—to latch onto. The more remote and overgrown an area, the more likely you and your Lab are to come home with a few hitchhikers, so stick to open trails as much as possible.

When you get back to your car, go over your dog thoroughly so you can remove the ticks before they attach to your puppy and start to feed. Rub her hair against the direction it lies so you can see down to her skin. A black spec no bigger than a pencil point can be a tick. Ticks look for warm spots, so pay special attention to your dog's "armpits," in the folds of her neck, her groin, and her ears.

At home, go over your puppy with a flea comb to remove any hangers-on. Just because you remove a tick doesn't mean it won't hop right back on, and ticks have a hard shell that's hard to crush. To be sure it's gone for good, douse the tick in alcohol or insecticide.

Once a tick is attached and feeding, it's much harder to remove. Use tweezers or a specially made tick-puller. Grasp the tick as close to your pup's skin as possible. Slowly pull the tick from your dog's body. The head breaks off easily, and you don't want to leave it embedded where it can cause an infection. Resist the temptation to crush an engorged tick; it's filled with blood that will explode everywhere. After you've removed and killed the tick, clean your puppy's skin and dab on some antibiotic ointment.

Fleas and ticks are common on rats, mice, rabbits, deer, and coyotes, so there are plenty of opportunities for your puppy to be re-infested. Even if your Lab doesn't currently have fleas or ticks, consistent use of flea and tick control products will protect her.

Nutrition

A growing puppy needs plenty of food, but what she eats is also important. While you ensure she's getting enough, be careful that she's also eating the right kinds of foods, and not learning any bad habits, like begging.

Appetite and Growth Spurts

Your puppy needs more food this month to keep up with her growth—up to about 4 cups a day. She'll probably eat as much as you give her, so don't think she's still hungry just because she's wolfing down her food. Increase her food in small amounts—maybe ¼ cup at a time—to match her growth, not her appetite.

Don't forget, you're using a lot of treats for training, too, and that adds to her total calorie count. Use part of her daily kibble ration as training treats.

Table Scraps

The eating habits you teach your Lab puppy now are established for life. If she has to compete with other dogs for her food, she'll learn to gulp down her meals. If you feed her from the table while you eat dinner, you're creating a lifelong beggar. Set up a feeding routine now, and stick to it.

Feed your Lab at the same times every day. If she knows when mealtime is, she won't pester you throughout the day. If you feed her just before you sit down for your dinner, she'll be full and not so anxious to join you (then again, it seems Labs are *never* full …). After she's eaten, that's it—no seconds. Don't let those big sad "Oh please, I'm starving!" puppy eyes fool you.

If you absolutely have to give her something from the table, wait until you're done and then put it in her food dish. If you toss a couple scraps on the floor while you're scraping dishes, you'll have a pest for life.

If it's too late, and you already have a beggar on your hands, put her in another room, put her in her crate, or tie her to something until you're finished eating.

Feeding tables scraps can be dangerous to your dog. "Give the poor dog a bone" is one of the worst things you can do, especially if it's a cooked bone. Cooked bones are dry and brittle. They can break apart easily and puncture your puppy's esophagus, stomach, or intestines. Poultry bones are smaller and more dangerous than beef. Large pieces of bone can cause an intestinal blockage. Raw bones are safer, but raw poultry bones are still risky.

People who feed their dog a raw diet often grind the raw bones to minimize danger.

Holiday leftovers are especially hazardous for dogs. Greasy turkey (and the bones) tossed in the trash is just too tempting for a curious puppy or adult Lab to resist. Besides the danger bones present, fatty foods can cause pancreatitis, a potentially fatal inflammation. Severe vomiting, diarrhea, dehydration, and lethargy are symptoms of pancreatitis, and your puppy will require several days of hospitalization—if she survives.

Grooming

You're lucky. Labs are hardy, wash-and-wear dogs who shed dirt easily and require minimal maintenance. But they still need some regular grooming to keep them in good condition and ensure they're in good health. With routine grooming, your puppy will look and feel better, and you'll catch small health problems before they become big issues. Best of all, you'll enjoy time together.

Labs' Grooming Needs

A Lab needs a good brushing about once a week, but she rarely needs bathing because her thick, double coat is water- and dirt-repellant. She'll shed heavily twice a year, in the fall and spring, and her coat will need more attention during this time.

A weekly grooming routine should include the following:

🐾 Brush coat

🐾 Clip toenails

🐾 Check ears and clean if necessary

🐾 Brush teeth

In Month 3, you introduced your pup to some grooming tools and started teaching her to enjoy being groomed. This month, you continue grooming … in spite of her protests. An active Lab puppy is in no mood to sit still, and she'll wiggle, bite, and play puppy games to get out of being groomed. Take her for a long walk or vigorous play session just before it's time to groom so she'll be tired and sit still for you. Give her a toy stuffed with peanut better or biscuits, and let her gnaw on that while you work on her.

Reward her for sitting still, and break grooming into little pieces between treats. For example, trim one toenail, give her a treat, and brush her for a minute. Then trim another toenail and treat. Stop after a few minutes, and do some more a half hour later.

Include a health check as part of your routine. Here's what to look for:

Skin: Check for lumps and bumps, cuts, and scratches. Carefully examine under her legs against her body where ticks and grass seedlings might stick to her.

Feet: Examine her paw pads to be sure they're not raw or cracked. Look for thorns or other foreign objects embedded between her toes or in her paw pads. Check her toenails to see if there are any broken or infected nails that need attention.

Mouth: Check to see if her gums are red or sore, especially while she's teething. Look for broken teeth or objects stuck between her teeth, and look for lumps or cuts on the roof of her mouth and under her tongue. Be sure her gums are bright and pink.

Eyes: See that her eyes are clear and bright, not cloudy or with mucous in the corners. Be sure no grass or other irritants are in her eyes.

Ears: Wipe out her outer ear with a damp cloth or cotton ball, and look to see if there's discoloration or debris down in the ear. Smell her ears; a bad smell means an ear infection.

If you look your puppy over carefully on a regular basis, you'll recognize immediately when she's injured or ill. When she's used to being checked over, she'll also be more likely to let you examine her when she's not feeling well.

Setting Up a Grooming Schedule

Pick one afternoon or evening once a week, and spend some quality time with your Lab puppy cuddling and grooming. Place a beach towel or old sheet in front of the TV, and combine grooming time with your favorite sitcom. Set out your tools: brush, flea comb, toothbrush and toothpaste, toenail clippers, Kwik Stop, and treats. By the time you're ready, Puppy will be ready, too, because she knows what's up.

Once a week may not be enough. If you're an especially tidy housekeeper, you'll soon realize that Labs shed a lot, and the more often you brush her, the less often you'll have to vacuum. Two or even three brushings a week may be necessary. During shedding season, you may want to take the grooming party outside, because you'll have more hair to deal with.

Other grooming chores, like teeth and toenails, may only need attention once a week or every two weeks.

Social Skills

Your last opportunity to have a significant impact on your puppy's personality is between 12 to 16 weeks. This month ends the first critical period of socialization. Continue the lessons you started last month by exposing her to more people, sounds, smells, and textures.

Socialize to Calm Adult Dogs

If you have another dog in your household, you've seen her interact with your puppy. But one canine friend does not make a socialized puppy. Your Lab needs to meet dogs of different breeds and sizes while she's young. One-on-one encounters are safer.

Choose your puppy's companions carefully. The only adult dogs your puppy should meet now are well-socialized and tolerant dogs of both sexes. A puppy needs older dogs to teach her lessons you and other puppies can't teach. Adult dogs generally forgive a pup or discipline her lightly for her transgressions during the first few months. It's better that your puppy learn her doggie manners now, when no one is likely to hurt her.

When she meets an adult dog, your puppy will use the same appeasement behaviors she offered her mother back in the litter. She'll approach the adult with a low-slung "I'm-a-little-puppy" wiggle and her tail tucked between her legs. Then she'll roll over and offer her tummy for a sniff. She may release a little urine so the adult dog can tell how old the puppy is. By doing this, your puppy is communicating that she's not challenging the older dog and that she's not sexually mature yet. She may also lick the adult's muzzle or lift one paw toward her, both submissive behaviors she learned when just a few weeks old.

A pup who doesn't offer submission when she approaches an adult may be chastised. Most dogs will tolerate a baby until she steps out of bounds. Leaping on the adult, walking over her, yanking on her tail or ears, chasing, pouncing—all play behaviors—are fine until the grownup has had enough.

Another favorite puppy ploy is to try to steal a bone or toy from the adult dog. You'll see the grownup purposely put the bone just out of reach and watch the puppy approach it. When the puppy attempts to take the item, the adult will come to her feet with a bark and reclaim her rightful ownership.

An adult dog uses varying degrees of discipline. She may growl, give a severe look, air snap, or even give a short sharp bark—all low-level corrections. After one or two incidents, most puppies understand. Some pups, however, are oblivious to the message, and the adult will ramp up her response. She'll roar like a lion, chase away the pup, or stand over the puppy and plant a paw on her body. All this sounds very ferocious, but no one gets hurt.

> **TIPS AND TAILS**
>
> When introducing your puppy to an adult dog, try to stay out of the action and let nature take its course as long as possible. Don't discipline the older dog; she's just establishing the dog rules, and your puppy needs to learn this valuable lesson.

Monitor the behavior of both dogs to ensure a safe encounter. If your puppy is persistently obnoxious, step in and stop her. Give the older dog a break before she loses all patience. If the older dog is standing over the puppy with her hackles up, stiff tail, and ears forward, or is chasing the puppy, this might be a sign of an overactive prey drive. Stop it before instinct takes over and your pup gets hurt.

Meanwhile, don't make excuses for your Lab puppy, either. "She's just a baby. She doesn't know any better," isn't going to teach her a thing. And if you step in and rescue her, she'll learn she can be a brat with no consequences.

Socialize to Many People and Things

Get creative this month. The fear-imprint period is over, and your Lab pup is more responsive and outgoing. Invite the cheerleading team to come over in uniform, a football player in uniform, kids wearing backpacks, and other people in unusual clothes.

Let her investigate your wet umbrella when you come in. Then pick it up and hold it over your head and shake the water off onto her. Let her walk over a metal grate or figure out a pile of rocks. Although her vaccines are almost done, she doesn't have full immunity, so limit her exposure to public places.

> **HAPPY PUPPY**
>
> Have a family contest to see who can up with the most interesting new thing to introduce to your puppy.

It might seem obvious, but if you pet a puppy in different ways, you get different reactions. The way you pet her can even cause her to mouth or bite at you.

Stroke her in the same direction her hair grows. Rubbing against the growth may be uncomfortable and make her move away from you.

 Scratch her chest rather than reach for her head. An incoming hand is the perfect target for an excited, mouthy Lab puppy, and a shy pup will cower at a hand looming over her.

🐾 Pet fast if you want her to get excited (she will probably start to mouth you); stroke slowly if you want her to calm down.

🐾 Stop before your puppy decides she's had enough. Always leave her wanting more.

When your puppy meets new people, she may offer her belly and release some urine, just as she did when meeting adult dogs. This is normal canine behavior, and Labs almost always outgrow it. An especially submissive Lab may continue to urinate even when she no longer rolls over on her back to greet someone.

To prevent submissive urination from becoming a habit, avoid situations that cause her to urinate. Let her approach people rather than allowing them to loom over her or corner her. It seems like no big deal to you, but from the puppy's viewpoint, this new person might as well be King Kong.

Also, don't punish your puppy. This just frightens her more. You want to build her confidence, not punish her for what's a purely physical reaction.

That said, don't comfort her, either. Your sympathy and worried voice may have the opposite effect of what you intended and convince her there was good reason to be afraid.

Behavior

Your Lab's personality will really start to shine this month. She'll gain confidence as she has successful experiences, and she'll enthusiastically tackle new challenges. While she wants to stick close to you, she also wants to check out the world. She takes her cues from you when she's unsure, and fearlessly follows you everywhere.

Enjoy it now and take advantage of her devotion, because next month she'll be a preteen and ready to take over the world.

Prevent Separation Anxiety

While we all wish our dogs could be with us all day every day, it's not possible, and our puppies need to learn to spend time alone. A dog who can never be left at home without destroying the house may be suffering from separation anxiety. Teach your Lab to feel safe and comfortable alone while she's still a puppy, even if you're home all day. Your life or job situation may change someday, and you're heading off future trauma by teaching this lesson when she is young.

Confine your puppy in her crate or pen when you're gone. she's not yet mature enough to have the run of an entire house or yard. What you may think is separation anxiety may really be simple puppy mischief. When you're not there to supervise, she's free to indulge her curiosity and entertain herself in doggie ways. She knows she can't dump the trash and eat the kitty litter in front of you, but when you're gone, she makes her own rules.

Teach your puppy not to rely on your constant attention every minute you're at home. Set up her crate or pen, wherever she can stay when you're gone, and practice leaving her in it for short rests during the day. She'll learn to feel safe there, chewing on her toy and listening to household noises. She'll also realize that being in her pen doesn't always mean she's going to be left for long periods.

Deafening quiet could unnerve your puppy, so when you leave, turn on the radio or television so the house still has signs of activities she'd hear when you're home. Background noise also blocks out scary sounds from outdoors, so she isn't reacting to unknown terrors.

HAPPY PUPPY

Exercise your puppy before you leave her alone at home. Take her for a walk, practice obedience, or play a game. Then give her a chance to settle down and relax so she won't still be excited when you put her in her pen.

She'll quickly learn that the rustle of keys, you picking up your briefcase or purse, getting your jacket out of the closet, or picking up your books all mean one awful thing: you're going and she's staying. While you're teaching her to spend time alone, occasionally go through your leaving routine without leaving. Pick everything up, fiddle with it, and put it back down and go back to what you were doing.

Don't make a fuss over your puppy when you come and go. Put her in her pen and do something else for a few minutes before you leave. Then just leave. Big good-byes and petting just rev her up and upset her. When you come home, ignore her while you put down your things and get settled. Then greet her calmly and let her outside for a break.

Mouthing and Overexcitement

Puppies learn by playing, and her over-the-top behavior this month includes plenty of chasing, pouncing, biting, and mounting. We talked about puppy biting in Month 3, but now your Lab is constantly grabbing and biting everything she sees. As you walk through the house with a puppy attached to your ankle, you'll be wondering what on earth you can do to get her to stop this.

Labs are an oral breed. They're genetically wired to use their mouths. The behavior goes back to what they were bred for: carrying a bird back to the hunter. A good hunting dog has a soft mouth, but a Lab should never put her teeth on her people. Don't allow puppy-biting to continue—a 60-pound piranha is not what you signed up for when you got a Lab.

Mouthing and overexcited behavior go hand in hand. Here are some tips to minimize both:

🐾 Pet her body first, not her head. Your hand reaching toward her face is an easy target. Pet slowly using long strokes on her body and head.

🐾 Don't roughhouse. Your hands darting at her encourage mouthing. Rough handling of her head, even in fun, also invites her to play bite.

🐾 Be sure she's getting enough exercise and sleep. A wound-up or tired puppy is more likely to jump and bite.

🐾 Schedule play dates with other vaccinated puppies. They will discipline her if she bites too hard or plays too rough.

🐾 Stop the game if she won't quit mouthing. Step in and stop the action when she plays too rough with the kids or other puppies.

🐾 When she's really excited, use less body language and a quiet voice. Calm her with some quiet massage and petting. Offer a chew toy after she calms down, not before, or she'll think it's a reward for all her frenzied activity.

🐾 If she's too wound up to accept handling, let her drag a leash so you can lead her away from an overactive situation to a place where she will calm down.

🐾 Teach her to bring you a toy when she's overexcited or mouthing you. Make a big deal out of it. She'll quickly learn to go get her toy whenever she's excited.

🐾 Give her a short time-out in her crate or pen.

Vocal Discovery

You'll wake up one morning this month and realize your puppy has discovered she can do things with her voice. Barking at the cat makes the cat run, barking at other puppies makes them play, and barking at the mailman makes him go away. This is about the time many Lab owners throw up their hands and enroll in puppy classes.

It starts when she barks excitedly and you respond. Next thing you know, she's standing in front of you barking for attention. And it works, doesn't it? If only to shut her up, you immediately take action. This rewards the behavior, and before long, you have a chronic barker.

If you don't accidentally reward her for barking, she'll eventually grow out of this stage. When she's barking for attention or just getting too wound up, put her in her crate for a time-out.

Don't let her out until she's quiet. Don't talk to her, either. It might take 5 minutes or as long as a half hour. If you give in and release her, she decides that if she barks long enough, there's a chance you'll let her out. She'll keep trying until she hits the jackpot.

Training

At 12 to 16 weeks, it's the time to teach your puppy specific behaviors. She needs to learn vital skills by the time she's 5 months old; if you don't start until then, she'll be too distracted by adolescence to learn much. The commands you teach her now build a framework for later training and communication.

The puppy is focused on you right now and an eager student. She's realized that watching and listening to you produces good things. She's able to connect your words to her actions and remember what worked for her yesterday. And whether or not you're teaching, she's certainly learning.

When teaching your puppy something new, work with her in a quiet place with no outside interference: no TV, video games, or other household activities. You want her to focus on you. When she learns a behavior, you can teach her to respond in spite of distractions.

Puppy Class

You're doing everything right for your Lab puppy. She's meeting new people every week, you've started training, and her housetraining is going well. Even so, puppy class, often called puppy kindergarten, is an essential part of her education and social development. The window of time where this can benefit her the most is closing fast.

You started searching for a trainer when you first got your puppy. (See Months 1 and 2 for tips on selecting a puppy trainer.) Now it's time to finalize your decision and enroll.

(See Months 1 and 2 for tips on selecting a puppy trainer.)

> ### HAPPY PUPPY
>
> Approach training as a game. Your puppy's attention span is still short, and she'll learn faster if she's having fun. If she's really active, train after she's had a short play session, when the edge is off and she can concentrate better. Adjust your methods to her personality and mood.

You might be worried about enrolling in a training class knowing your puppy isn't yet fully immunized. But at some point, the risk of inadequate socialization is greater than the risk of disease. If you select the school carefully, her chances of getting sick are less likely. Choose a facility that's clean and well maintained. Check out the health requirements for all dogs entering the premises, including for other classes. All dogs should be vaccinated, and no unknown dogs are allowed. Some facilities rent their space on weekends for dog clubs and competitions; does this one? What are the health requirements for dogs who attend these events? Do they clean and disinfect thoroughly afterward?

Most classes accept puppies from 10 weeks up to 4 months old. Expect to see a mix of old and young, big and small. Unless your puppy is very young, Labs are usually at the bigger end of the scale. The instructor separates the pups if the big ones are overwhelming the little/younger ones. You don't want a sensitive puppy to be overwhelmed and frightened or the bully rewarded for pushing other puppies around. Puppy class is for developing social skills and confidence, not destroying them.

Don't be offended if your bundle of joy is singled out. Any pup who plays too roughly should be removed and introduced slowly to just one or two puppies at a time. That's a lesson she needs to learn, and that's why you're at class.

Classes are a combination of playtime and lessons. All-play-all-the-time gets the puppies too fired up. Your Lab puppy learns the difference between active playtime and when she has to settle down or pay attention. Her reward for calming down is to go back and play some more. She's handled, trained, and corrected by new people. Equally important is the opportunity to play and learn her dog manners and bite inhibition with other puppies.

The instructor will set up play equipment that presents new and fun challenges you don't have at home, like agility equipment. While observing you with your pup in class, the instructor will be able to identify potential problems and help you explore solutions. The instructor will also help the entire family get involved with the puppy's lessons.

Puppy classes are as much about training you as training your puppy. You learn how to teach your puppy, properly reward her, and introduce her to basic obedience exercises like sit, down, and come. You learn how to shape her behavior to manage play biting, jumping up, and chewing. You also practice social skills like meeting new people and animals and learn how to handle situations when she's afraid. You play new games with your puppy that both teach and build your bond with her. And you can ask your instructor questions when you get stuck on a problem.

Many puppy class instructors follow the American Kennel Club S.T.A.R. (Socialization, Training, Activity, and Responsibility) Puppy Program. The 6-week course ends with a quiz for both owners and puppies. Owners also make a Responsible Dog Owner's Pledge to accept responsibility for the care and training of their puppy. For more information, visit the AKC at akc.org/starpuppy.

Teach "Sit" and "Down"

A practical command, "Sit" is also easy to teach. It's a command you will use over and over again. For example, tell your Lab to sit before you put her food down, so you can attach her leash, to greet people, for a vet exam, or before you go through a door. The first thing she'll learn is to sit for a treat. Many people teach their puppy to sit for her dinner as early as at 8 weeks.

Let's review the steps for "Sit." Your pup doesn't need to be on a leash unless you have trouble keeping her attention.

With Puppy standing, hold a treat just above and in front of her head. She'll look up to reach for it. Don't hold it so high she tries to jump up and take it. Slowly move your hand backward toward her tail, keeping it just above or in front of her nose. She'll naturally rock back and sit when you lean into her. Immediately feed her the treat and praise her while her rear is still touching the ground.

Say "Okay!" and let her get up. She'll soon learn that "Okay!" means she's finished and can move.

> ### TIPS AND TAILS

If you have trouble getting her to sit, have her stand with her back near a wall or piece of furniture. Then she can't back up because she has nowhere to go.

Repeat this three or four times, and you'll find she starts to sit as soon as you lift your hand. You're teaching her the hand signal for "Sit" before she's even learned the word.

When she reliably sits for you, add the word "Sit" just before she actually sits. Don't say "Sit down"; save "Down" for another behavior. Pretty soon she'll associate the word with the action.

When she understands the word "Sit," ask her to sit without the hand signal or lure. Produce the treat and praise as soon as she responds. If it doesn't work, she doesn't understand yet, so go back and work some more on the first steps.

At first, let her up as soon as she gets her treat. Once she's responding well, wait for a second or two before you release her with "Okay." Don't stare at her; that will make her uncertain and she'll stand up. Work up to a few seconds before you release her. Then alternate with some immediate releases and sometimes letting her sit for a few seconds. You'll see her fidget and think about getting up. Try to release her while it's still your idea, not hers.

When her sit is consistent, ask for it in other rooms and outside, with you facing her, and with you at her side. Always praise her warmly, even if you don't have a treat. Pretty soon she'll sit whenever you look at her!

Invite everyone in your household to tell her to sit. Hand out treats, and have your guests tell her to sit before she greets them.

"Down" is an easier position for a puppy to hold when she has to stay in one place for more than a few seconds. "Down" is useful when you're out in public, standing and talking to someone, waiting in the vet's waiting room, when you groom her, and when you need her to settle for a period of time. While a dog can hold a sit for a minute or two, she can be trained to stay in the down position for 30 minutes or more.

"Down" is a little harder to teach, for several reasons. Your little wigglewort will want to play instead of letting you manipulate her into a down. Down is a submissive position, and she may not want to accept your control. If you've been practicing handling her, she'll learn the down much more quickly.

Let's review the steps for "Down." Starting out on a slippery floor will make the process easier.

With your pup sitting, hold a treat in front of your puppy's nose and slowly lower it to the floor. When your hand gets to the floor, pull the treat slowly away while pressing gently between her shoulder blades. If she lowers her body to the ground, great!

Watch her elbows. As soon as they touch the ground, feed her the treat, praise her, say "Okay," and let her up.

Some dogs will feel the pressure of your hand and immediately push back—a natural opposition reflex. If your puppy does that, you'll need a different approach. Instead of pressing between her shoulder blades, scoop your arm under her front legs and pull them forward, lowering her body to the ground.

> ### TIPS AND TAILS
>
> Training your Lab isn't a one-person job. Take advantage of your family's interest in your new puppy to involve everyone in training and socialization. When you play and train together, you all learn how to deal with her, get the results you want, and be consistent in what you teach. As an added bonus, your pup will respond and bond with all of you.

Another method to teach "Down" is to sit on the floor and bend one knee with your foot on the floor. Lure your pup under your leg with a treat. She'll have put her front end down to reach under and get the treat. As soon as her elbows touch the floor, give her a treat, praise her, and release her. Lure her farther each time until her entire body is down before you give her the treat.

Whatever method you use, you may have to scoop under her rear legs to settle her back end. Sometimes she'll get stuck with her rear up in the air. Help her understand that all of her needs to be on the floor.

As you did with the sit, practice numerous times over several sessions. Then start practicing in different places and on different surfaces. Your puppy will test you and try to get out of getting down by rolling over, wiggling, and biting at your hands. Have patience! Don't give her a treat until her elbows and back legs are on the floor.

When she anticipates what you're asking, she'll get down as soon as you start to shape her into position. You'll be able to touch her less and less. Pretty soon, the motion you use—luring her nose down with a treat and pulling it out in front of her—turns into a hand signal, and you can add the command "Down" as she starts to comply. Always follow through and be sure she goes all the way down.

Up until now, you've been on the floor with your puppy, and that's the picture she has in her mind of the exercise. She won't understand what you're asking if you stand up and tell her "Down." Gradually work with her until you can stand up on your knees and then stand completely up and she'll still comply. Don't bend down toward her when you give the command; stay upright. Bending over her is an invitation to get up and come to you.

Once she can do both a sit and a down in response to a verbal command, play a game with her—push-ups. Ask for a sit, a down, a sit, and a down, alternating several times. She'll pop up into a sit and throw herself down. She'll anticipate the next command, and you can make her wait until you tell her. She's learning to listen and respond quickly—and you're both having a lot of fun.

Talk to your puppy as you train her. Your Lab responds to your body language and tone of voice more than she hears the words you say. How do *you* give *your* dog an obedience instruction?

Some people (usually women) politely ask their dog to comply. "Puppy, sit?" She hears she's not sure about it and she worries. Another approach: baby talk, which tells her it's playtime. Either way, she gets confused.

Many men, on the other hand, take the words *obedience command* seriously. They stand up stiff and straight in an authoritative pose, and bark out a gruff "Sit!" Their harsh tone and overpowering body language make the puppy think she's done something wrong. About this time, the owner thinks her dog is a sissy, and the puppy decides her owner is a tyrant.

Tell your dog once, say it firmly, expect her to comply, and reward her with happy body language and warm and loving praise. You're not just teaching an obedience command here; you're building a relationship of mutual respect and trust.

Introduce Leash Walking

Until now, you've been carrying your Lab puppy out in public, and she happily follows you around at home. But she's getting heavy, and it's time for her to learn to walk nicely at your side. In this section, we learn leash walking.

Break the following steps into short sessions. At the beginning of each session, start with something she knows well before you move on to new things.

To begin, take your hungry puppy to a confined area with no distractions. Hook the leash to her flat collar (no chain collars, no harnesses). Let her drag the leash around, get tangled, and figure out how to untangle herself. Let her step on it and get stuck. She'll figure out to move her feet or give to the pressure of the leash to relieve the pull on her neck.

You can stand, kneel, or sit on the ground. Hold one end of the leash steady, and put just enough pressure on it that she feels it. Every action provokes a reaction, and her first instinct when she feels the pressure is to pull away from it. She may struggle, flip over, bite at the leash, and throw a full-fledged tantrum. Be a statue, and let her figure it out. Don't say anything.

Continue to hold firmly, but don't pull her. The instant she gives the tiniest bit to the pressure and the leash slackens, release the leash, praise her, and give her a treat. If you loosen the pressure before she gives to it, she learns that struggling makes it go away. You want her to learn that calmly moving *toward you* makes the pressure stop.

Pick up the leash again and repeat. After a few tries, she'll realize that if she gives in to the pressure, you'll give her a treat. She's teaching herself what leash pressure is and how to make it stop. Set her up for success. Make it easy for her, and don't move on to the next step too quickly.

Stand up and step backward, keeping light, steady pressure on the leash. Wait quietly until she leans toward you or takes a step in your direction. Don't look directly at her. Some puppies are intimidated by your gaze and afraid to move forward. Don't go to her; she is learning to come to you.

Encourage her with praise when she even thinks about moving forward. You'll be able to tell. If she comes all the way to you, great! That's where you want her. Give her some extra loving every time she comes to you. If she balks, just keep the steady pressure on until she gives in and complies. She's confused, and you may have moved on before she really understood what you wanted. Practice backward steps until you both can move two or three steps without pressure.

Now turn so you're sideways and a step ahead of her. Because you're no longer facing her, it presents a different picture, and she'll be confused at first. Repeat the previous steps in this position. Pay careful attention to the feel of the pressure on the leash. Without looking, you can tell if she's giving to the slight pull.

Stand with your puppy at your left side with the leash in your hands. The clip should hang loosely from her neck. Take one step forward with your left foot and tighten the leash slightly as you do so. If your puppy moves with you, give her a treat, praise her, and have a party! She did just what she was supposed to do! If she balks, stop and wait until she gives in to the pressure and then quietly treat, praise, and take another step.

TIPS AND TAILS

When you want your dog to walk with you, always start out with your left foot. That's a visual signal down at her eye level that it's time to move. When you want her to stay in place, step off with your right foot.

Work up to taking several steps before you stop and praise her. If she pulls against the leash, just stop briefly and try again. This trial-and-error method keeps her thinking. As she understands what works and what doesn't, she'll catch on.

At this point, just before you take your first step, add your command word: "Let's go," "Walk," "Heel," or whatever you decide to use. One word of caution, though: "Heel" is a precise position used in obedience competition where a dog is at your left side, her ear lines up with the seam of your pants, and she is looking at you. You may want to teach a variation of "Heel" later to use when you take her out in public or if you plan to compete with your dog. If so, save "Heel" for later. For now, you're just teaching her to walk nicely at your side with no pressure on the leash, a much looser position.

Don't add steps too quickly; you want her to be successful. When she starts getting pretty good at leash walking, you can add variations to make it fun for both of you. Take several steps, turn in the opposite direction, and invite her to catch up. Go fast, go slow, turn left, turn right, and walk in a circle. Always encourage her, praise her, and give her treats when she's by your side or catches up. She needs lots of feedback.

By now, she's walking well in the living room, but that's not the real world. Practice in the backyard, the driveway, and in other places so she *generalizes* the concept of walking on a leash.

DOG TALK

A puppy **generalizes** a lesson when she learns that a particular command means the same thing in many different places and situations. For example, "Sit" means "rear end on the floor" in the living room, driveway, garage, yard, and at puppy class. She also learns "Sit" means sit when someone else uses the word, even when the person is standing, sitting, or across the room.

When she's walking nicely in a few places, add a mild distraction, like a family member walking at a distance. Remember to keep this practice short—just a few minutes.

If you begin to lose the puppy's attention, try to get it back quickly. As soon as her attention to you wanders, make noise, change directions, skip, or pull a squeaky toy out of your pocket. She'll hurry to catch up and find out what she missed. Be more interesting than that distraction could ever be, and always praise and reward her when her attention is back on you. Gradually add other distractions as she gets the hang of the game, such as a ball, a cat, a child on a bike, or a car going by.

Natural distractions, like a good smell or a leaf, will always tempt your canine buddy. If you stop and wait while she sniffs, she's teaching *you* the rules of the walk. If you decide to let her sniff, give her permission before she gets to the item. Give it a name, like "Go sniff." Practice calling her back to continue walking, and praise her when she responds. She'll soon learn.

Housetraining Progress

By the end of this month, your Lab puppy should be almost, if not completely, housetrained. She should easily sleep through the night in her crate without needing to go out. If this isn't happening, first be sure she doesn't have a urinary tract infection. Have your vet check a urine sample.

If she's healthy and still having accidents, review the housetraining process outlined in Month 3, and tighten up your supervision. Labs are relatively easy to housetrain compared to other breeds.

The main cause of delayed housetraining is that owners stop going outside with their puppy each time she needs a break, and she hasn't really learned why she's out there. They let her out and give her a treat when she comes back in. They don't know if she's eliminated or not, and the puppy thinks she's being rewarded for coming in, so she doesn't take her time and get the job done.

If she's having accidents in the house, keep her in the same room on a leash, next to you. Do you recognize the signals that she needs to go out? If you're busy and can't watch her, put her in her crate. Every time she pees in the house, she's essentially being rewarded for her behavior. The smell remains, and it becomes harder for her to understand why she can't go there again.

Plan ahead. Keep track of when she eliminates, and a pattern will emerge. Anticipate those times, and take her out before she asks. If she doesn't go, confine her in her crate for 30 minutes and try again. These methods should help you catch up on her housetraining and quickly make a difference.

Handling Your Lab Puppy's Collar

When your Lab gets too heavy to pick up, you may be tempted—especially when she's been into some especially aggravating mischief—to take her by the collar and drag her outside or to her crate. Think again. It only takes once or twice for this action to create a hand-shy dog who avoids being caught—or worse, may snap at you to get away from punishment.

The alternative? Keep leashes hanging on every doorknob so you can hook her up and escort her. A puppy who hangs back and resists being dragged will usually happily follow you on a leash. Or grab a few treats and show them to your pup. She'll quickly stop and follow you. If she doesn't want to go out, let her see you put the treats just outside the door and close it. The same method works with her crate. Put the treat in her crate, and shut the door with her outside. Pretty soon she'll want to go where the treats are, and she'll be happy to comply with your wishes. You have just successfully distracted her from her misbehavior and turned it into a learning opportunity.

Still, your puppy needs to allow you to take her by the collar without protesting. Someday, your 60-pound Lab will crash out the gate or front door, and you need to know you can grab her in an emergency without getting into a wrestling match. By that time, she'll be much stronger than you, and you might not win.

You've been working on handling your pup. Now it's time to focus on this specific lesson. Take hold of her collar, and offer her a piece of kibble. If she shies away, start by reaching for other parts of her body where she enjoys being touched. Do this many times. When she's comfortable with you touching her collar, wrap your hand around it for a few seconds and release. Every once in a while—not often and not more than once per session—grab the collar quickly. You don't want this to turn into a hand-biting game. She'll learn you aren't coming at her to hit her.

Everyone in the family should practice this skill with your puppy so she trusts all of you.

You and Your Puppy

You love your new puppy and want to keep her safe, so select safe toys and supervise while she plays with them. Even though she's still just a baby, try not to overprotect her. As you play and get to know each other, you'll learn to read canine body language and communicate better with her.

Choosing Safe Toys

Your Lab will destroy toys no other puppy on earth could dismantle. Remember, Labs are mouth-oriented, and chewing is an important part of their play. If you don't provide chew toys, she'll make her own—usually your designer shoes or the coffee table leg.

There's no magical list of safe toys. The best way to know for sure is to test them on your pup. For a Lab, choose heavy-duty chewies that are larger than you might think a puppy needs.

Toys fall into several categories:

🐾 **Toys she can tear apart:** Many toys are fine as long as you're there to take them away when they start to fall apart.

🐾 **Toys she can have when you leave her alone:** Super-tough indestructible toys (you'll soon learn which ones these are) will last several months before they break.

🐾 **Real bones and chewies:** These are made of natural substances, and you can offer them to her while she's young if you supervise carefully.

Stuffed animals with squeakers inside may be shredded in minutes, or they may last days. Knotted ropes, tough fabric toys, Planet Dog Orbee-Tuff toys, tennis balls, and other items may be safe now, but as she grows and her mouth gets stronger and bigger, she'll easily shred or swallow them.

> **TIPS AND TAILS**

Never give your puppy a toy she can get completely in her mouth, especially a round ball. If she swallows it, it can block her airway or lodge in her stomach and cause an obstruction.

A Galileo Bone is a super-tough version of the Nylabone and is almost indestructible. These are usually safe to leave with your pup when you're not home. Hard rubber toys like a Kong—that you can stuff with treats and freeze—last for several months. A frozen, stuffed Kong also eases her teething pain. As with other toys, check her Kong for cracks or missing chips of rubber. When she's started to break it up, throw it away.

Real bones and chewies (as opposed to rubber or nylon) are made from real animal parts, which is fine for a puppy, but most of these products are unsafe for an adult Lab. Many varieties are available, including marrowbones, stuffed bones, smoked or filet mignon–flavored bones. Check to be sure they don't cause diarrhea and that there are no bits and pieces in her stool. Be vigilant. A Lab puppy's strong jaws can break off sharp chunks that she'll then swallow. Pieces can lodge in her intestines and cause a life-threatening blockage that requires surgery. A small chunk could lodge in her windpipe. A sharp sliver might perforate her intestine.

Here are some examples of real chews:

Rawhide bones, made of cowhide (leather) are not digestible, which means a puppy's body cannot break down the material and pass it through her system and eliminate it. Rawhides soften as your puppy chews, and she can tear off a large piece and swallow it.

Bully sticks are made of beef muscle and are digestible. Your puppy will get hours of entertainment from a bully stick, but take it away when it gets small enough to lodge in her mouth or swallow.

Stuffed bones are made from femur bones and are cut, cleaned, sterilized, and filled with peanut butter or meat-flavored mixture (not necessarily real meat). The stuffing may have additives and chemicals. The outside will splinter after a certain amount of chewing, so take them away when they reach this point.

Cooked bones, as mentioned earlier, are never safe for any dog. Cooking dries out the bones, making them splinter easily. Your puppy will swallow chips or sharp pieces, and those could hurt her insides.

Pig snouts are made of flesh, not bone, and are more easily digested by your puppy.

> **TIPS AND TAILS**

Choose products made in America wherever possible. Many imported chew bones are processed with chemicals that are dangerous to your puppy.

Overprotecting Your Puppy

There's a fine line between protecting your puppy and *overprotecting* her. Allow your pup to figure out new things for herself as much as possible. She doesn't have much experience yet, so she'll try things and get stuck. If she's cautious, let her take her time.

For example, if she climbs into a cardboard box tipped on its side and it falls over, there's no door. Resist the temptation to rescue her. Let her poke around and try different things. Unless she collapses in blind panic, she'll eventually climb out or knock the box over. Then you can throw toys in the box to encourage her to continue exploring what the box will do. Will the flaps hit her as she crawls out? Does the bottom break out if she bats at it?

A puppy who is allowed to experiment grows up self-confident and eager to try new things. She develops problem-solving abilities and learns to think for herself. If you're too overprotective, she grows up shy and fearful, expecting you to step in and save her from every situation. This learned helplessness is hard to undo once she grows up. Her dependence on you will lead to separation anxiety and other unwanted behaviors.

Of course, you'll want to protect her from a charging dog or horde of unruly children. But whenever possible, let her learn about her world in her own way.

How Canines Communicate

Dogs have three primary ways of communicating with each other:

- 🐾 Body language
- 🐾 Voice
- 🐾 Smell

They'll try to communicate with you the same way, so learn how to read your puppy and what she's telling you. Look at the total dog, her posture, her arousal level, and what may be triggering her response.

Some behaviors are obvious, and it won't take you long to recognize them. A play bow and bouncing around, for example, are signs of a happy puppy who is ready to interact with you.

A wagging tail is pretty obvious, too … or is it? It can mean many things. If she holds her tail high and stiff, she's excited or curious. She may be wagging her tail furiously while she barks at a stranger. A slowly wagging tail may mean she's uncertain. A tucked tail indicates fear or submission.

Her ears also tell a story. If they're forward and alert, she's interested, happy, or paying attention. If she folds her ears back and down, she may be worried, frightened, or submissive.

Even her mouth helps indicate her state of mind. A drooling puppy or one licking her lips might be stressed. If she's trying to lick your face, that's a submissive gesture she used with her mother. What may sometimes look like a snarl will actually be a smile.

The hair along her spine may stand up (known as piloerection) when she is overly excited or meeting a new dog.

You'll quickly learn the different tones of your Lab puppy's bark. There are the "someone's-here-and-I'm-upset" bark as well as the "I'm-happy-you're-home" bark. Other variations include "I want something," "I need to go out," and "Ouch."

A whimpering puppy could mean she wants something or is in pain. She may also yelp in pain or because she wants your attention.

A growling pup might be playing with a buddy or threatening a tennis ball. Most growly Lab puppies are just trying out their vocabulary during play.

> **TIPS AND TAILS**
>
> If you have a truly aggressive puppy who growls as a threat and follows it up with a warning snap or bite, get help from a qualified behaviorist *now*.

Our noses don't give us even a thousandth of the information a puppy picks up when she smells something. Puppies smell another dog's urine, feces, anal glands, tail glands, and more. All this gives them information about another's identity, age, and sexual status. They can tell if their friend Rover peed on this bush yesterday or if a rabbit was in the backyard overnight. We can't compete, but we can realize that dogs need to sniff to get vital information about what's going on around them.

The Importance of Play

When you brought your puppy home, you removed her from her entire social group: her mom and her littermates. She needs you to be her playmate now. She needs to run, chase, wrestle, bark, and explore. She's spending hours alone while you're at work, and she's raring to go when you walk through the door at night. Fifteen minutes of play here and there is hardly adequate in her eyes.

Now you know why she endlessly drops a toy at your feet, chases and nips at your pant legs, pesters your other pets, and just generally gets into mischief. She needs to play!

Toys and chewies help occupy her time, but she needs time with people and other animals, not just to teach her social skills, but because, like any living being, she gets lonely.

Balance Teaching, Guidance, and Play

You're probably thinking right now that owning a Lab puppy is a lot of work. In some ways it is because you're adding another family member who needs education, discipline, and love to grow into a socially acceptable adult.

But don't lose sight of why you got your puppy. While you teach her new things, play with her, and redirect her misbehavior, remember she's just a baby and she's not purposely trying to get into trouble. She's trying to figure out the world around her, and she can only do that by trial and error. She'll learn faster through fun and play than by punishment and isolation. And you'll both have a lot of fun while you navigate these first memorable months together.

Month 4 >	Month 5	> Month 6
	Socialization in public	
	Teething begins—heavy chewing period	
	Ready for basic commands	
	Switch to adult food	
	3rd DHPP and rabies vaccines	

A Lab puppy goes through dramatic growth and changes between 4 and 5 months of age (weeks 16 through 20). He's not quite a teenager, but he's not a baby, either. In this month, we talk about physical changes like teething, growth, and how to monitor your puppy's health. By now, he has completed his vaccines, and you can take him out in public to continue and expand his socialization.

His behavior is rapidly changing as he grows and gains confidence. You'll see him exert his independence, and he'll test your limits to see what the rules are and what he can get away with. You have a good foundation in place to guide you both through this headstrong month, and your consistent training and guidance will prevent behavioral problems before they become entrenched habits. Your priorities right now are exercise, teaching, and plenty of chew toys.

Your Lab is ready for a license, microchip, and ID tags. And of course, your active puppy will give your entire family hours of laughs and fun.

Physical Development

Think of your puppy as a preteen right now. Some physical characteristics are permanent, but his awkward proportions and teething pain are, thankfully, temporary.

Paws and Legs

During this month, your Lab pup's body grows rapidly and at different rates. He'll look out of proportion and clumsy because he's growing from the outside in. His paws, nose, ears, and tail will be too big, almost adult size. Eventually his torso will start to lengthen and his legs will gradually catch up. He'll reach approximately 60 percent of his adult height during this month.

He'll reach about half of his adult weight during this month, too. A male who will eventually weigh 65 to 80 pounds weighs about 32 to 36 pounds at 4 months. A 24-inch-tall adult male is about 14 inches at the shoulders during Month 5. A female who will weigh 55 to 70 pounds at adulthood weighs roughly 26 to 35 pounds and is about 11 or 12 inches tall at the shoulders. These are estimates based on a dog who will fall within the breed standard when mature. Your dog may be larger; most Labs are not smaller than the standard.

His brain is developing, too, and by 5 months old, he'll have a maturity level similar to what you'd expect in a 10-year-old child. He's still very much a puppy, approaching puberty. He'll be very active and always a step ahead of you this month, much to his delight.

Teething Continues

This month, the adult molars along the sides of his mouth start to come in. His canine teeth—his two upper and two lower fangs in the front—follow. His teeth won't finish emerging to their maximum height until he's 10 to 12 months old. That means he'll continue to chew voraciously during the next few months to ease his teething pain.

Except for the canines, the adult teeth come in behind the puppy teeth. If his puppy teeth aren't loose and falling out by 6 months, have your vet examine his mouth. If the puppy teeth don't fall out soon enough, the emerging adult teeth can come in crooked and cause bite problems.

Twizzles, Zippers, and Other Characteristics

You may think all Labs look alike, but many have identifying characteristics that set them apart from their fellow pups. For example, according to the AKC Labrador *breed standard,* a Lab may have a small white spot, no bigger than a quarter, on the chest.

> **DOG TALK**
>
> The **breed standard** is a description of the ideal Labrador Retriever as developed by the Labrador Retriever Club, Inc., which is the parent club of the breed in the American Kennel Club (AKC). The standard specifies guidelines for size, color, structure, and temperament.

In Newfoundland, where the Labrador originated in the 1700s, there were two types of water dogs, a Lesser Newfoundland and Greater Newfoundland, and both had some white on their bodies. The Lesser Newfoundland became the Labrador, and the other became the large Newfoundland breed we know today. Today, both breeds occasionally still have a white spot on the chest.

Many Labs develop a "twizzle" at the end of their tails at around 4 or 5 months. A Lab's thick coat wraps itself around the tail, and an inch or so will continue off the end in a twist of hair. Breeders often consider this a sign that he will have a healthy "correct" coat when he matures. The twizzle stays with the Lab all his life.

Does your Lab puppy have a "zipper" between his eyes? This is a little ridge of standing-up hair that runs down his forehead between his eyes. It's easier to see in a black or chocolate dog. There's nothing wrong with this little quirk, and many owners point to their dog's zipper with pride.

Some Labs have what's called a "Bolo mark" on their feet. Named after the famous black Lab Dual Ch. Banchory Bolo (1915–1927), a Bolo mark is a small white patch on the bottom of a dog's feet behind the pads. This peculiar marking has survived through generations of Labs descended from this one dog.

A "splash" Labrador puppy is a rare surprise in an otherwise normal litter. Picture a yellow dog with a black spot on his side, or a black lab with a yellow patch somewhere. This genetic mix-up can range from the tiniest speck to large splashes of color.

Another variation occurs when a puppy is born with tan "points"—markings over the eyes, chest, and legs. This is a throwback to Gordon setters who were bred to Labs in England during the early years of the breed. Brindle markings (black broken stripes on a brown background) appear very rarely on the legs and chest of a black dog, and you may not notice them until he's several months old.

Whatever your Lab puppy looks like—black, yellow, chocolate, or totally mismarked—he'll still be a great pet or hunting dog.

> **TIPS AND TAILS**

A white spot on the chest and Bolo marks are acceptable under the breed standard; other markings are disqualifications for a show dog.

Health

Vaccines and heartworm prevention are priorities for your puppy during his fifth month. Once vaccines are completed, he can safely venture out in public.

As you travel with your pup, you might find he gets carsick, so spend some time acclimating him to the car to prevent tummy upsets.

Finishing Puppy Vaccines

If you didn't finish your Lab's vaccines last month, be sure to schedule a vet visit this month to get his last DHPP booster. The series should be complete by 16 weeks of age.

He also gets his first rabies vaccine during Month 5.

Considering Additional Vaccines

After your pup has completed his core vaccines, discuss additional vaccines with your veterinarian so you can decide together when and if your puppy needs them. Noncore vaccines should be administered based on your geographic location, lifestyle, and risk of the disease. Consider the environment your Lab will be exposed to—outdoors, hunting, contact with other animals, tick-infested areas, etc. Regional considerations come into play, too, for example, if you live in an area with rattlesnakes.

Here are some other vaccines to discuss with your Lab's vet:

Bordetella: Commonly called kennel cough, bordetella is a group of upper-respiratory bacteria that causes coughing, sneezing, and other symptoms similar to the common cold in humans. Kennel cough is highly contagious and spreads from dog to dog quickly. Healthy adult dogs recover quickly, but in puppies it can progress to pneumonia. There are several strains of kennel cough, and the vaccine doesn't protect against all of them.

The vaccine is given either intranasally or by injection and is required by boarding kennels and dog daycares. To be effective, a booster should be administered a week before exposure to other dogs. If you're going to board your puppy, he should receive the vaccine at least a week before going to the kennel and a booster every 6 to 12 months.

Coronavirus: This disease can be quite severe in puppies, especially if he has other infections as well. The virus is transmitted by contact with infected oral and fecal secretions. Once a dog is infected, the disease is shed in his stool for several months. The puppy may have no symptoms at all or have diarrhea, which can cause dehydration. Coronavirus is rarely fatal and responds well to treatment, so vaccination is not usually recommended.

Giardia: If you camp, hike, or hunt with your Lab, you might consider this vaccine. Along with coccidia, giardia is a single-celled protozoa that the dog ingests through infected water or soil. Puppies kept in dirty living situations often get giardia or coccidia. Adult dogs who hunt or spend a lot of time outdoors in the woods or near water may be reinfected over and over. The main symptom is watery or mucousy diarrhea. The vaccine doesn't protect against infection, but it does prevent the dog from shedding the protozoa. Giardia is a *zoonotic* disease, which means humans can also be affected. It's inexpensive and easy to treat, so most people do not choose to vaccinate for giardia.

> **DOG TALK**

A **zoonotic disease** is transmissible from one species to another, for example, from dogs to humans.

Lyme disease: Transmitted by a bite from a tick, Lyme disease is one of several tick-borne diseases. If your dog spends time in the woods or if ticks are common in your area, discuss this vaccine with your veterinarian. It doesn't protect against other tick-borne diseases, though. The initial vaccine is two doses, 2 to 4 weeks apart, followed by an annual booster at the start of tick season, which may vary depending on where you live.

Leptospirosis: Dogs should receive this vaccine only if you live in an area where there have been known cases of the disease. Leptospirosis is a bacterial disease transmitted by skin contact with the urine of infected animals, primarily rats and mice. It can also contaminate streams, rivers, and lakes, where a dog might ingest it. Two doses are recommended, 2 to 4 weeks apart, along with an annual booster. Leptospirosis is also a zoonotic disease and is transmissible to humans.

Rattlesnake venom: This vaccine protects against Western Diamondback rattlesnake venom. It also provides some protection against the Eastern Diamondback rattlesnake. If you live in an area where these snakes are common, the recommendation is two doses, one month apart, and a yearly booster.

Tetanus: This vaccine is not often recommended because dogs have a natural resistance to infection from the bacteria. It's commonly found in soil contaminated by horse and cow manure, and it enters the body through an open wound.

Heartworms and Preventatives

Heartworm is caused by a parasitic worm and is transmitted to your dog by mosquitoes. Formerly confined to the Southeast, today it affects dogs throughout the United States.

The mosquito bites an infected dog and ingests the heartworm larvae in that dog's blood. The mosquito moves on to your dog and injects the larvae into your dog, where they migrate to the bloodstream. There they grow into mature heartworms that attack the pulmonary arteries, which lead from the lungs to the heart. As the worms reproduce, the body tries to fight them off and sometimes has an allergic reaction to the worms.

You can prevent heartworm infestation in your puppy by administering a monthly prescription preventive that kills the immature larvae before they have a chance to grow or reproduce. The preventative medication can be started anytime after 8 weeks of age and well before mosquito season begins in your region.

Once a puppy reaches 6 months old, your veterinarian will need to do a heartworm blood test before beginning the medication. Your Lab will require an annual retest. Some people discontinue the preventative during the winter months, so a retest is required before you restart in the spring.

Symptoms of heartworm include coughing, weight loss, vomiting blood, and ultimately heart failure and death. Treatment of heartworm is long and hard on your dog. Arsenic is used to kill the worms, and the dog must be strictly confined. Too much exercise will cause a large mass of worms to go into the lungs and cause serious complications. The worms die slowly over a period of 4 to 6 weeks and are passed into the lungs where the dog's immune system destroys them. Once that step is complete, the dog is treated with another medication to kill the surviving larvae. A heartworm test at the end of treatment confirms that the parasites are completely gone.

As you see, prevention is the best choice for dealing with the threat of heartworm.

Giving Your Puppy a Pill

Labs, especially puppies, will eat anything, so you may never have a problem giving yours a pill. Hide it in a dab of peanut butter, liver sausage, cheese, or canned food, and you're done … you hope.

Some Labs are masters at eating around the pill and spitting it out. In this case, you'll need to be more assertive. If you've been doing handling exercises with your puppy, he's used to you looking at his teeth and touching his face, so you're halfway there.

From behind, put your hand over his muzzle and your thumb and middle fingers behind his large canine teeth on either side. Squeeze in his lips. Pry open his mouth with your other hand, push the pill to the back of his tongue and down his throat, and close his mouth. Hold his mouth closed, and stroke his throat with your finger until he swallows. Give him a spoonful of canned food, cheese, or other special treat so he'll keep swallowing and you can be sure the pill is down.

Your vet can sell you an inexpensive pill gun, a long syringe that holds a pill on the end. Coat the pill with butter so it goes down easily, stick the plunger in the back of your pup's mouth, and inject the pill.

Carsickness

Labs love nothing better than a car ride, but all that excitement can be too much, and suddenly … he's carsick. A puppy's ears and sense of balance aren't mature yet, so he's more likely to get sick than an adult dog. Once he's gotten carsick, he dreads riding in the car and it's likely to happen again. Typical signs he's getting sick include yawning, panting, whining, drooling, and eventually retching and vomiting.

To help prevent carsickness, confine him in a crate so he can't wander around the car or look out the windows, which contributes to nausea. Cover the crate so he can't see out, and be sure to anchor it so it doesn't fall over when you go around a corner. Or put him on a harness and attach it to a seatbelt so he faces forward.

> **TIPS AND TAILS**
>
> An airbag is dangerous to puppies, so disable it or put him in the back seat (like you would a human baby).

Lower a couple windows about an inch to equalize the air pressure in the car. Give your Lab a toy he loves when you put him in the car. Call it his special "car-ride" toy, so he makes positive associations with car rides.

Ginger is a natural treatment for nausea, so a gingersnap cookie may help settle his stomach. Or open a capsule of ginger and pour the granules onto some food or a bit of yogurt. Limit his food and water an hour before travel.

If nothing seems to work, talk to your veterinarian about motion sickness medication for your Lab.

If your puppy has developed a phobia against riding in the car, retrain him to think of it as a fun experience. Stop taking him on long car rides for a couple of weeks. Instead, take him on short trips to fun places. If every car ride takes him to the vet or boarding kennel, no wonder he doesn't want to go.

Feed him treats or meals in the car. If he won't get in, start by feeding him next to the car, and work up to a treat on the running board, a treat on the car floor, and one on the seat. Don't start the engine or go anywhere; just let him get used to the idea that the car isn't a bad thing.

Start the car and turn it off immediately while he's in the crate or back seat. Sit in the car with the engine running for a minute or two while he eats, and shut it off and quit.

Gradually progress to where you drive to the end of the driveway, down to the corner, and around the block. Your goal is a series of short, pleasant trips without your puppy getting sick.

Nutrition

Your Lab puppy's appetite may fluctuate this month because his growth is uneven—one day his legs are longer, the next his feet are growing, and then nothing may change for a week. Teething pain also contributes to his occasional lack of appetite. This is normal and nothing to worry about, unless you see symptoms of illness.

Your Puppy's Weight

There is no hard-and-fast rule about how much a Lab should weigh at any given age because their size varies so much within the breed. A shorter, stocky Lab looks heavier even if he's the right weight. A taller, lanky Lab puppy has finer bones and looks lighter overall. A taller puppy does not necessarily need more food. If you hear or read that his weight should fall somewhere between 26 and 35 pounds, that's not very specific, so you really need to look at your dog's body and condition to assess his weight.

Even though a young puppy gets a lot of exercise, he can still eat too much and get fat. An overweight puppy has a higher risk for injury because his bones aren't strong enough yet to carry the extra pounds. If you can't feel his ribs or see that his tummy has a little tuckup behind his rib cage (see Appendix B), cut back on his food. Give him a little more in the morning and less at night, so he'll have extra calories to get him through his active day.

If his coat is shiny, his eyes are clear, and his body feels and looks good, you're feeding him the right amount. If his coat is dingy, his eyes are runny, or his tummy looks bloated all the time (not just after he's eaten), he may have worms and need another round of deworming treatment.

Switching to Adult Food

If you haven't switched to adult food yet, now is the time. As you did when you brought him home and changed brands of food, make the switch gradually. Mix ¼ of the adult food in with his puppy food for several days. Then go to ½ and ½ for a few days. Complete the switch after a week or so.

Now is also the time to switch your Lab puppy to two meals a day. Start by gradually cutting back the amount of his midday meal and adding it to his other two meals. Right now he's eating more than he will as an adult, about 4 cups a day. Usually the recommended amounts on the dog food bags are too much food for a Lab.

Most dogs don't do the work they were bred for, and a pet Lab doesn't necessarily need food designated specifically for Labrador retrievers.

Paying Attention to the Feces

A puppy's bowel movements provide important clues about his health. Examine a fresh stool for an accurate assessment. Feces should be formed and solid, not runny or extremely dry. Blood or mucous may be signs of illness, a sudden change of food, or a result of eating something he shouldn't. A very black stool may have blood in it.

Look, too, for foreign objects: grass, gravel, fabric, or bits of plastic from a toy or bone. Freshly deposited feces may contain live worms if he's infested.

While you're changing your pup to adult food, check his feces for loose stools or diarrhea. Cut back on the new food, or slow down the transition if he has loose stools.

Keep an eye on your puppy's stool volume, too. A large amount of stool could mean your puppy isn't absorbing his food well. Dogs who have a small stool volume are using their food to its maximum potential.

Grooming

While your Lab puppy doesn't need endless grooming, he requires light brushing year round and regular grooming sessions during shedding season. His ears also need regular attention so you can catch problems before they become chronic.

A Labrador's Coat

Labs are born with a short, thick double coat. The harsh outer coat has natural oils that repel dirt and water—perfect for a hunting retriever and an added bonus for the pet owner. (However, his coat should never feel oily or greasy.) The soft undercoat protects your puppy from extreme cold and heat.

Labs shed lightly year round and heavily twice a year—spring and fall. (Females also shed heavily about 10 to 12 weeks after their heat cycle, about the same time they would be blowing [shedding] coat if they were weaning a litter of puppies.) The undercoat starts to shed first, followed by the outer coat. You may have to brush your pup daily during shedding season. Frequent brushing speeds up the shedding process, and the sooner the old coat comes out, the sooner the new coat grows in.

> **TIPS AND TAILS**
>
> Although it's tempting when he's in full shedding mode, you should never shave your Lab. He'll continue to shed anyway as the new hair grows in, and you've taken away his protection from hot sun and winter cold.

Lab hair is not like other breeds, whose shedding hair gathers into fluffy puffs and wafts across your hardwood floors. A Lab's hair is short and straight. It weaves into the carpet fibers, blankets, and woven furniture fabrics. It's hard to remove, even with a vacuum cleaner. Brush your Lab regularly to cut down on your household cleaning chores.

Brushing Your Lab

Frequent brushing distributes the natural oils in your Lab's coat and keeps it healthy and shiny (not as obvious in a yellow Lab). Brushing also removes a lot of dirt that gets down in the undercoat. If brushed often and thoroughly, your Lab may never need a bath.

If the weather is nice, you'll save yourself a lot of housework if you brush him outside. In spring, the birds will thank you because they'll use the fur for soft nesting material.

You've been teaching your puppy to tolerate and even enjoy grooming, so getting him used to brushing shouldn't be much of a problem. Start with the rubber curry, and massage his skin in circles—this brings the loose hair to the surface. Follow with the slicker brush. Start at his rear end, and work your way forward, brushing in the same direction the coat grows, away from your pup's head. A slicker can scratch his skin, so don't use too much pressure. And don't forget the feathers on his rear legs. Even his tail needs attention.

Lift a section of hair with the back of one hand while you brush with the other so you can get close to the skin and remove more hair. Then use the slicker to brush *against* the direction the coat grows to loosen more undercoat. (This is the one time you brush against the grain.) His coat is heaviest under his throat and along his shoulders, so pay extra attention to these areas. Once finished, a shedding blade is especially effective on the outer coat, raking off loose hair that's still embedded in the coat.

By now you're covered in dog hair, but you haven't gotten it all yet. An undercoat rake or a medium-tooth metal comb pulls out mountains of undercoat. Start again at the rear, and work your way forward. By taking this extra step, you may be able to brush less often.

Use a damp cloth on his face and outer ears rather than a brush. When you're completely finished brushing, run the wet cloth over his entire body to pick up stray hairs and remove static electricity or dandruff. A fabric softener sheet also removes static in dry weather.

Labs shouldn't have doggy odor. If yours does, check his ears for a problem. If his coat is dry and he has dandruff, he could have a skin condition or allergies. If you've left soap in his coat after a bath, it could also cause irritation, so be sure to rinse well.

Cleaning His Ears

Labs are notorious for getting ear infections. Your puppy's ears lie flat against his head, limiting airflow and trapping moisture and debris inside. Labs are also prone to allergies, which cause redness and inflammation in the ear area.

Wipe out his ears every week so he is used to the procedure and will be more tolerant if he needs treatment. And after he swims, hunts, or runs outdoors in tall grass, check his ears for dirt, grass seeds, ticks, and moisture and dry and wipe out his ears thoroughly.

Using a barely damp soft cloth or paper towel wrapped around the end of your finger, hold the ear leather (flap) up and away and wipe the ear from the inside to the outer edge. Clean out nooks and crannies with a cloth covering your little finger. This is all he should need on a regular basis. Cleaning too often removes the protective layer of wax that protects his inner ear.

If his ears are especially dirty, use a cotton swab on a stick to gently clean the ear canal. If your puppy doesn't cooperate, this may take two people. Again, hold the ear leather up. Turn the swab in one direction as you put it in, and hold it in the same direction as you reverse out of the ear. This way you won't redeposit the dirt. Don't go too deeply because you don't want to damage the eardrum. Also, if your puppy thrashes around, you don't want to poke into the inner ear.

If something gets down in the ear canal, it can cause an infection. If you see reddish-brown gunk or his ears smell bad, it could be a yeast infection caused by water, an infection caused by a foreign object, or even ear mites.

A Lab with an ear problem will shake his head, hold his head at an odd angle, scratch at his ears, and even whimper as he tries to ease his discomfort. He may be unwilling to let you touch his ears. Visit the vet for an accurate diagnosis and treatment plan.

TIPS AND TAILS

If your Lab has chronic ear problems, your vet might recommend medication or regular cleaning with an ear wash product. Squirt the ointment into the ear, and massage the base of the ear where it meets the jaw line. This pushes the medication deeper into the ear canal. Your Lab will immediately shake his head, which distributes the ointment in the outer ear. If you use an ear wash, thoroughly dry his ears after cleaning.

Social Skills

Finally your Lab is able to go out and meet the world. He can accompany you on walks, to the park, family activities, and other outings.

As bold and confident as he is at home, he's now on unfamiliar turf, so he may be uncertain at first. But that'll change as you meet new friends.

The Jolly Routine

Actions speak louder than words. When your puppy is uncertain or frightened, show him by your behavior that there's nothing to be afraid of.

Select an item that makes your puppy wag his tail when he sees it—a ball, squeaky toy, stuffed animal, or other small toy. When you notice something you know will scare him, like a large truck driving by, pull out the toy. If possible, before he can even react to the scary thing, act happy, play with the toy, and pretend you're having a wonderful time. Expect your puppy to be confused, but keep going.

After a minute or two, put away the toy and ignore him. In about 5 minutes, pull out the toy again and repeat your excitement. You'll know your routine has started to ease his fears when he wags his tail as soon you produce the toy.

You may not have time to head off his fear, but this is a good starting point to distract him from what frightens him. It may take up to 6 weeks of repetition to change his attitude about whatever scares him, but those few weeks hardly compare to a lifetime of fearlessness.

Socializing to Strangers

When you are out in public with your puppy, you are his protector. Well-meaning strangers will charge up with their hands out to say hello. Children will crash toward him with a toy and throw their arms around his neck. As you try to keep people from overwhelming him, they'll respond: "It's okay, I *love* dogs!" It's not about them; it's about your Lab, and after a few of these bulldozer encounters, a pup will hide in fear or take off in the opposite direction when someone approaches him. Worse, he may feel cornered and snap.

Don't let that happen. Turn into a linebacker, and bodyblock all comers. Don't be afraid of being rude. After all, you wouldn't let them charge at your children, would you? If you do your job, your puppy won't feel he has to defend himself from others.

Hold your hand up to stop the person. If your puppy seems happy and ready to interact, let him approach the person first. Have the person stop, stand sideways to him (which is less imposing), and even crouch down so he'll feel safe. Use your jolly routine so your puppy understands everything is safe.

A dog who grows up fearful of strangers will think he has to take manners into his own jaws when danger approaches. He'll bark aggressively and even bite to protect himself—or you—when someone comes up to you.

Let him watch the person and decide for himself if he wants to say hi. If your Lab isn't comfortable, respect his wishes and don't force him. Put a serious look on your face and explain he is "in training." Hand the person a treat and invite them to toss it in his direction and move on.

Socializing to Children

At home or in public, your Lab will meet children of all ages and, you hope, love them immediately. Tell children to "ask the puppy" if he would like to meet them. If your puppy says no, ask them to respect his feelings today because he may be tired.

How do you know if your puppy isn't in the mood to play? He will hide behind you, crouch down, avoid looking at the kids, or move away.

If he's ready to say hi, put two fingers through his collar to keep him from jumping on the child. Have the child stand quietly and speak nicely to the puppy, not in a high, squeaky, excited voice. Let your pup choose to approach the child. Have kids pet him on his chest or his back where he won't dive for their fingers. Let them put a treat on the ground for him to eat.

Going for a Walk

Enjoy daily walks, when your pup can experience new sights, sounds, and smells, but remember he's still a puppy and will tire easily. Plan to walk about 10 minutes per month of age. So if he's 4 months old, a 40-minute walk will tire him out.

Don't worry about how far you get on your walks. There's so much to experience. You may not get very far while he meets people, sniffs, and explores.

Walk your Lab on a 4- or 6-foot leash. A long line or retractable leash won't give you enough control, and he could easily pull it out of your hands if he gets frightened and runs. Don't let him off leash in parks, on trails, or at the beach unless you're in a fully fenced enclosure.

A walk is the perfect time for your puppy to practice sit, down, walking politely, and paying attention to you. Don't let him pull ahead, or he'll learn to drag you all his life.

He may balk at new things like a mailbox, parking lot flags, or a motorcycle zooming by. He may bark at cars or kids on skateboards. If he sees a street vendor dressed like a pizza and tossing around an advertising sign, don't be surprised if he spooks. He'll think he's encountered an alien. Wouldn't you?

The world is full of exciting new smells and sounds. He'll encounter trash in the gutter and gum on the sidewalk. He'll know where the nearest restaurant is and quickly recognize the scent of other dogs. Busy traffic will smell like burning rubber; honking horns and police sirens will startle him. Let him investigate for himself without comforting him, and use the jolly routine to help him gain confidence.

There are a few places you shouldn't take him yet. Street fairs and festivals have hundreds of people jammed together, loud music, food smells, and traffic. Remember, his eye level is around your knees, so all these unfamiliar things coming at him from above his head can be terrifying. Work up to crowded situations slowly. Don't take him to fourth of July celebrations or anywhere fireworks are being used.

Dog Parks

Visits to the dog park can do more harm than good. You have no way of knowing if the dogs there are vaccinated or trained. Many owners chat with each other and ignore their dogs, allowing them to bully other dogs unmonitored. Dogs squabble over toys, and fights break out. There's no "lifeguard" on duty enforcing rules or asking owners to remove rude or aggressive dogs. You alone are your dog's protector.

At peak periods, usually early evenings and weekends, the dog park is crowded and play can easily get out of control as the dogs become overstimulated. A normal dog will quickly be overwhelmed, much less a quiet or shy puppy. Decide if your puppy is ready for this kind of interaction. Consider taking him on quiet weekday mornings when the park isn't so busy, especially when he is young and it is new to him. If you see other dogs are playing rough or aggressively, leave.

Wherever you are, be a responsible dog owner. Clean up after your puppy. Carry pickup bags, and either deposit them in nearby trash cans or take them home with you. In some jurisdictions, you can be cited if you're caught leaving your dog's droppings.

Behavior

Your young Lab's behavior changes dramatically this month as he asserts his independence and explodes with endless puppy energy. Prepare yourself with consistent puppy management techniques and a sense of humor so you'll get through this fun and challenging period with your sanity intact.

Your Shadow Disappears

While your puppy is busy physically growing this month, his mind is equally busy absorbing everything it can. He'll have endless energy and very little self-control. He's easily distracted and will use any excuse to ignore you. During this period of creative obedience, he'll tease you by coming close and taking off or grabbing toys and playing keep-away. Busy, busy, busy! However will you get him under control?

Be sure your Lab puppy gets plenty of exercise, training, and mental stimulation this month. While it seems harder to get his attention, keep working on handling and control exercises. You can demand more from him; he's not an infant anymore.

If he's not listening to you, let him drag a leash when you're there to supervise. You'll be able to pick up the leash and get his attention to enforce your instructions.

Keep Your Lab on Leash

When you two are away from the house, *never* let your Lab puppy off leash. This rule also applies to walks in the woods or open fields. At this age, he is impulsive, distracted, and prone to developing selective hearing—in other words, he ignores you. Make liberal use of the "Sit" command to get his attention back on you while you're on walks.

HAPPY PUPPY

You'll know it when you see it. Suddenly your calm, well-behaved Lab will cut loose and take off around the yard or house (or both) for no apparent reason. Lab lovers have named it butt-tucking because he goes so fast his rear looks like it's in front of his chest. This zooming is pure puppy exuberance, so let him run and burn off some steam. Zooming is a better activity for outdoors where random items in his path—like furniture and children—won't interrupt his fun. Labs never seem to grow up, so be prepared for lifelong zoomies!

our Lab is still teething, and he's certainly still chewing this month.
provide him with sturdy chew toys. As he gets bigger, some of the old
toys a.. ..es may no longer be safe, so monitor what he's got in his mouth and
remove the unsafe toys. When his adult teeth are in, he'll continue to chew to ease his
gum and mouth discomfort. And because he's a Lab, it's safe to assume he'll chew like
a puppy for the rest of his life.

With that in mind, monitor his behavior and redirect him to appropriate chewies.
Don't give him household items like old shoes. He'll have trouble telling which ones
are his to chew and which ones he should leave alone.

Take steps to ensure he can't chew certain things. For example, don't put a bed in
his crate if he's a chewer. Keep clothes picked up and shoes put away. Close bedroom
doors. Use a bitter spray product (available at pet-supply stores) on items you don't
want him to chew; the bitter spray makes it taste bad. If you don't have bitter spray,
you could also use mouthwash or red pepper sauce mixed with water.

If you find he's chewed something, put him in another room so he doesn't see you
clean up the mess. If he watches you, he'll be fascinated that you're paying so much
attention to what he's done, and he'll do it again for you.

Corrections

By now, your puppy has an idea of right versus wrong in many situations, but during
this rebellious phase, you'll have more trouble getting his attention. Commonsense
discipline has its place while you're raising your Lab. It's not necessary to yell or hit
your puppy. Instead, use a sharp phrase like "Ack" or "Psssst" to interrupt what he's
doing, immediately praise him for stopping, and redirect him to something else like a
sit or walking away.

> **TIPS AND TAILS**
>
> Don't use his name when disciplining your puppy. If he hears "[Name],
> no!" he'll eventually think his name is a correction, and you don't want
> that.

You might wonder why we didn't suggest you use "No" to interrupt your Lab.
"No" often turns into "No, no, no, no, NO!" and when you get excited, your puppy
just hears you making a bunch of noise. You don't sound calm or in charge, and your
puppy will ignore you until you get to the last angry "No!"

He Won't Outgrow Bad Behavior

"He's just a puppy" is an excuse that isn't going to work much longer. If there are no consequences when he misbehaves, he doesn't know his behavior is unacceptable. Any bad habits he's forming now will be much harder to deal with when adolescence is in full swing next month. A habit takes much longer to *break* than to *make*.

Sure, you're tempted to let him get away with unacceptable behavior like jumping on you once in a while because it's tiring to supervise him constantly. But by doing this, you're inadvertently rewarding the behavior. When he gets away with it sometimes, he'll try it again and again. On the other hand, if he *never* gets rewarded for jumping, he'll eventually quit trying.

The entire family needs to be consistent with discipline and training. When one person in the family allows your Lab puppy on the couch and someone else doesn't, he soon figures it out and will jump on the couch when the enforcer isn't around.

Stick to your guns, and enforce all the rules, all the time. Make liberal use of the crate for short time-outs when you can't watch him. Loving discipline, plenty of exercise, and readily available chew toys will help you and your puppy negotiate this stage.

Training

Scientists call this age the "avoidance period." Your Lab puppy is no longer hanging on your every word. There's so much to see and do in the world, and he wants to do all of it *right now*.

This month, break his lessons into small steps so you can keep his attention and better his chances for success. Train thoroughly, and practice a lot this month. Labs aren't an overly emotional or sensitive breed, so you can be patient but firm.

Keep training fun, or he'll lose interest. A few 1-minute training sessions throughout the day have a bigger impact on him than one 10-minute session, and he'll learn to incorporate these short lessons into everyday life.

What's in a Name?

Does your Lab know his name? How do you use it? Your dog's name should be a wonderful word that he happily responds to. Think about whether he knows or responds to his name. If he doesn't, here's an exercise you can try to teach him.

Load up your pocket with treats, and take him out in the backyard or for a walk. Let him get distracted, sniffing at the grass or another mildly interesting scent. Say his name once without a loud or urgent tone in your voice. Does he turn and look at you? If so, give him a treat and have a happy dance. Or does he ignore you?

Generally when you say a person's name, you expect him to look at you, and you then tell him what's on your mind. You wouldn't say his name and then ignore him. Often that's exactly what we do to our dogs. Or when he doesn't respond immediately, we say his name several times. He may think his name is Rover, Rover, Rover. The more we chatter, the less he listens.

If your puppy isn't listening, practice getting his attention and rewarding him when he responds to his name. His name is not a command. If you mean "Come," then say, "Rover, come!" not just "Rover!" And never use his name as punishment.

How many names does your puppy have? Is there a "Roverdoofusgoofus" name when he's being a darling little puppy, and a silly "Sadie-adie-adie" name for when he's into mischief? Or a firm "Rover-Johnson-come-here-right-now" name when he misbehaves? All these names could further confuse him.

Don't waste the power of your puppy's name. If you say his name, have a reason and give him something to do. You need to be worth leaving that luscious scent behind.

Reinforcing Household Rules

As adolescence approaches, your preteen Lab will test the rules again and again, and you'll wonder where all his training went. The more consistent you are in enforcing household rules now, the more control you'll have in the coming months. In fact, if he hasn't mastered some basic obedience by the end of this month, he will only get more difficult to train.

Sit, down, and walking on a leash should be your priorities, and you should use them often. Have him sit before you feed him, or have him lie down by your chair when you're watching TV. Your puppy may be pushy now, poking you to be petted, but have him earn his attention by asking him to sit first.

If your Lab is misbehaving, let him drag a 6-foot leash in the house. When you pick up the leash and lead him away from misbehavior, he doesn't get rewarded with playtime. If you grab him when he has something in his mouth, you've rewarded him by touching him and interacting. He'll think it's a great game, and to him, negative attention is better than no attention at all.

If he's not allowed on the couch, he will try it this month. Rather than pull him off, pick up the leash and hold it with steady pressure, like you did when you were teaching him to walk on leash. He should respond to the pressure and get off the couch. Reward him with praise when he does.

Your puppy needs to learn "inside rules," particularly to settle down in the house. You can use his ex-pen to confine him temporarily, or if he's really rambunctious, he could benefit from a tie-down. Either way, he can be within eyesight of his family while still enjoying some freedom. Loop his leash over a doorknob and shut the door, or put a large eye screw in the wall and attach his leash to that. A chain leash is excellent for this because he can't chew it. Otherwise, spray the leash with bitter spray or mouthwash. He now has limited mobility and should settle down and relax. Give him a chew toy to occupy him. Be sure he can move around a little but isn't able to eat the wall.

HAPPY PUPPY

Children in your house need to follow inside rules, too. Don't let them play wild chase games with the puppy indoors. He won't understand that he has to settle down unless everyone is consistent.

Cutting Back on Treats

When you first teach your puppy a new command, you reward him with a treat every time he does the right thing. But you don't want to carry food in your pocket for the rest of your life. So how do you make your Lab comply?

Praise him with a word, like "Good!" along with the treat every time he complies. Gradually he'll associate the word with the treat and recognize you are pleased. Always use an upbeat happy tone of voice when saying "Good!" He reads your tone and body language more than what you say.

As he gets used to being rewarded with "Good!" gradually cut back on treats. First, hide the treats in your pocket and don't pull one out until he sits or whatever you're asking him to do. A treat is not a bribe; it is a reward. Always praise him, but occasionally skip the treat, so he never knows when he'll get one. Don't use a pattern because he'll quickly figure it out. If you give a treat every third time, he'll pick up on that, and the other two times, he won't respond nearly as enthusiastically. Mix it up so he doesn't know what to expect.

Think of yourself as a slot machine. If you played the slots and got $1 back every time you played, it would get pretty boring. But if once in a while, just often enough to keep you playing, you won $50, and just once won $1,000, you'd be playing all night on the chance you'd get another big win. Same with your puppy. Occasionally, give him a jackpot of a handful of extra tasty treats he doesn't usually get. This motivates him to keep playing the obedience game so he can get the jackpot again. Labs *love* this.

If you fade the use of treats too fast, he may lose interest. Labs are so food-motivated that he may hold out. If that happens, back up a little and give him them more often.

Remember that when you're teaching a new skill, give your puppy a treat and praise every time he does something right. Don't reduce the frequency until you're sure he understands the exercise.

Introducing "Sit-Stay"

Before you teach the stay, your Lab puppy should always sit promptly when you give the "Sit" command.

There are two components to "Stay." One is time, and the other is distance. You can't work on both at the same time because he'll get confused. Start with lengthening the time he stays. Then work on distance, cutting back the time to almost nothing. Once he stays when you walk away from him, you can start building time back into the exercise.

As always with a puppy, your body language helps him stay. Have him sit at your left side on a loose leash. Step off with your right foot, and pivot in front of him, several inches away. If you crowd him, he's more likely to stand up. If he stays sitting, great! Praise him, give him a treat, pivot back into position at his right side, and release him by touching him and saying "Okay." Practice pivoting into position and back without letting him stand. Do this a few times until he's used to it, and take a short break.

If he has trouble staying as you pivot, put your finger against his muzzle as you turn. It should be just enough to stop him.

You've been giving him a treat as soon as he sat. Now pivot in front of him and wait a few beats. He may look confused. If he makes eye contact, smile at him and say nothing. Too much eye contact will intimidate him and make him stand up. Gradually work up the time he sits to about 15 seconds. This takes a lot of concentration, and he's probably sitting there worried he's supposed to be doing something. Intersperse a few instant releases, so the length of time he's sitting varies.

If he stands up before you can release him, put him back in the original position and try another, shorter stay. Don't restart where he came to you; go back to the start. Don't say anything, just put him back in the sit. Keep practicing until you can get a 30-second stay. Incorporate a short "stay" into your walks and at other times of the day to reinforce his training.

Next, add the hand signal and command word. Before you pivot in front of him, put the palm of your hand in front of him nose and say "Stay."

When he's consistently holding his stay, it's time to throw in some variations. This time when you pivot, step farther away, about a foot. He may try to get up and move closer to you. He'll be watching you intently, waiting for a signal it's okay to move. As soon as you so much as twitch, he'll try to stand up. Before he's all the way up, lean into him, and he should sit back down. Your body language pushes him back into the sit.

Don't repeat the word "Stay" over and over. Don't stare into his eyes. Relax your posture, as if to tell him, "We aren't going anywhere." Quietly praise him during the stay.

TIPS AND TAILS

To release your Lab from the stay, always go back to him and touch him. You want him to relax and wait patiently. Otherwise, as soon as you step toward him he'll think he's finished and stand up. Praise him quietly, walk back to him, praise him again, and touch him as you say "Okay" to release him. Don't ever call him to you from a stay, or he'll be anxiously watching for a command.

Practice variations on the stay where you're up close and farther away and for various lengths of time. When working well at 1 foot away for 30 seconds, try standing farther back, about 18 inches. As you step backward, he may think you want him to come with you, so be sure to keep the leash slack. Say "Ack" and lean toward him if he starts to get up. Go back to him, and release him immediately if he stays in the sit. If he doesn't, put him back in position and don't step so far next time. Mix it up with some stays where you're right in front of him again. Each time he's successful, touch and release him. Quit when you're ahead, when he has just done something right.

It will probably take you a full month to get a steady 1-minute sit-stay from 4 feet away. Doing something, like sit or down, is an action concept. Not doing anything, like stay, is a little harder for him to understand.

Introducing "Down-Stay"

Once he grasps the idea of "sit-stay," "down-stay" is much easier for him to learn. Teach him the down in small increments, as you did the sit-stay. First add time and then reduce the time and add distance. When he stays better with you at a distance, rebuild the time.

Teach him to relax while he's down. If he's lying in a sphinx position, up on both haunches, he's ready to spring into action, so you'll teach him to roll on one hip. Watch him when he's resting and figure out which hip he usually chooses.

Assume you're facing him and he usually rolls to his right hip. Put him in a down, hold a treat in your right hand, and push the treat back toward his left hip. As he follows your hand, he'll roll onto his right hip. If he doesn't get it, you can put pressure on the left hip with one hand to help him. When he gets the idea, have him roll onto his hip every time he does the down. Making this an automatic part of the "down" command helps you both be more successful with the stay.

The hand signal for the down-stay is the same as for the sit-stay. Put your open palm in front of his face as you give the command "Stay." Stand up straight, and pivot in front of him. If you bend over him or look him in the eyes, he'll get right up. Stand relaxed with your weight on one hip. He needs to see that nothing is going to happen, so he can relax. If he fidgets, say "Ack" but don't go back to him unless he gets up. When he's still, go back and release him. If he gets up, put him back in place and start over a little closer to him.

Your puppy will try to creep toward you. When he moves forward, correct him with your voice. He'll stop, and a few seconds later, he'll creep forward again. He's inching his way to you. Labs love this little game. When he creeps, go back to him without a word, stand him up, take him back to the starting point, and put him back in his down-stay. If you have to, put a piece of tape on the floor to remind yourself where you started.

When his stay is solid for about 30 seconds and 2 feet away, add a small variation. Fidget a little, and shift your weight slightly. He needs to learn to stay even if you move. He's not to get up, no matter what you do, until you release him.

Introducing Stairs

Your puppy needs to learn to climb and descend stairs. If he doesn't learn this skill as a puppy, he will probably be afraid to try stairs when he's an adult. Before you've worked with him on the stairs, use baby gates at the top and bottom of stairways to keep your puppy safe. And it will be less stressful for you both if you start teaching him about stairs at home without outside distractions.

One or two stairs isn't nearly as frightening as a full staircase, so start by teaching your pup to go up and down one or two steps, preferably carpeted stairs, which are easier for him to negotiate without slipping. Once he's mastered a few carpeted stairs, you can work on a full-length staircase or take him out in public to try it.

Your goal is to keep your Lab from racing up and down the stairs. As a small puppy, he could be badly hurt or even killed if he tumbles head over heels. When he's an adult, you both could take a dangerous spill. Visualize the stairs as a place of calmness and serenity, where he climbs and descends one step at a time at a leisurely pace.

Start with a hungry puppy on his leash and a pocket full of really tasty treats, like cheese or chicken. You might want to do this at mealtime and use his kibble. Kneel on the floor next to the foot of the stairs. Lift up his front paws, place them on the bottom stair, give him a treat, and let him go. After a few tries, he'll put his feet up on his own when you lure him with the treat.

After a few repetitions, move the treat farther up and back toward the second stair so your Lab has to lift his rear feet onto the stair to get to the treat. When he gets one foot up, praise him and feed him. When he gets completely on a stair, praise him quietly and have him stand or sit there for a second. This is not a game of speed.

As you gradually add stairs, have him stop on a stair and sit or lie down for a treat. This keeps it from becoming a race to the top (or bottom). To make it more fun, set a treat on each stair and let him sniff his way up. As he goes down, have him stop and sit often for a treat.

When he's familiar with one set of stairs, introduce him to new locations. The first few times you may have to start over until he discovers that most stairs are alike.

If you have open stairs with no vertical backs, like those going to the basement or to a second-floor apartment, have him practice climbing and descending those stairs, too, because they'll look entirely different to him and seem much scarier. They're also more dangerous for your pup. If he gets in a hurry, he could slip, his leg could slide through the opening, and he could break a leg or tear a muscle. Practice these stairs as if he's never seen a staircase before, so he understands how to go up and down safely.

Teaching a Flawless Recall

Remembering how you started his training, calling your puppy should always result in a reward for him. Up until this month, he probably joyously came when you called and followed you everywhere. Now you're seeing a suddenly independent puppy, and he may ignore you completely, or at least until it suits him.

Someday there will be an emergency when he needs to stop what he's doing and come to you before he heads into traffic after the neighbor's cat. To be ready for this, practice the recall when lots of distractions, like other dogs, cars, people, rabbits, and good smells, are around to compete for his attention.

> ### TIPS AND TAILS
>
> In your Lab's mind, "Come" from 20 feet away is very different from "Come" from 6 feet away. Don't call him to you if you can't enforce the command. He'll learn that he doesn't have to respond, and you'll just be background noise.

Start teaching him at home and then move on to the great outdoors when he understands the command. Attach a long line to his collar—30 feet of lightweight string or clothesline works well. These materials are light enough that he doesn't have the weight of a leash to remind him he's under your control. Take him to an enclosed area and let him wander.

When he's 10 to 15 feet away, call him to you. Use your best happy voice. As soon as he looks at you, jump up and down excitedly and encourage him to come to you to see what you're going on about. Reel him in with the line if he doesn't come immediately. Praise him, play with him, and give him treats but then let him go back to what he was doing. He'll learn that coming to you doesn't necessarily end his fun. Don't be a pest; just call him once or twice each 5-minute session. If you have trouble getting him attention, rattle your treat shaker.

Add distractions as part of this training. This is where the kids can have some fun. They can play catch or dance around to get him interested. As soon as you call, they freeze and won't look at the puppy. As he gets good at the game, they can continue distracting him while you call. Take turns holding the line so he'll come to everyone in the family.

Practice with the long line at parks and other places you regularly take him so he'll learn that the rules are the same everywhere. Have him check in occasionally, reward him, and let him return to play.

Teaching him to come when called is not a one-day project. Practice often and in many places.

Catching Your Pup

There will come a day when your Lab gets away from you and refuses to come; he's just having too much fun. Picture the recall as he may see it. You're at the park, and he's running and playing. He sees you take out the leash, a sure signal the party's over. Behind you, he sees the car, another sign that it's time to go home. Forget it, he's not coming.

You're angry and frustrated, but don't let it show. Who wants to come to someone who is yelling and screaming at them? He'll tuck his tail and take off. Here are some methods to help you catch him; these also work while you're training him on the long line:

- As he approaches you, stand sideways to him. A full frontal greeting is intimidating and may cause him to back away from you.

- Crouch down to his eye level, open your arms wide, and happily call him. When your body language is saying happy things, he is more likely to respond.

- Change the picture he sees. Don't get the leash out until you have your hands on him. Or never put it away, but keep it hanging around your neck or from your back pocket.

- Don't call him with your car or the exit gate right behind you in his line of sight. Stand where it looks like this is just another "checking-in" recall.

- Carry a squeaky toy or ball, and let him see you playing with it. Toss it in the air, juggle it, and dance around like you're having a great time. All that fun is hard to resist.

- Fall down on the ground face first. Make a big drama of it, and he'll wonder what's up and come running. He'll be licking your ears and climbing on you in no time.

- Turn around, yell to him, and run away from him. He's likely to give chase.

You've finally got him leashed up, and you want tell him what a bad dog he is for not obeying. Don't. The last thing he did was come to you, and he thinks any punishment or reward is for that. You can't punish him for something he did 5 minutes ago because he won't make the connection. Praise him, tell him he's a wonderful dog, and take him home for more recall practice.

You and Your Puppy

You'll be having a lot of fun with your puppy this month, but he also needs some attention and guidance to keep your friendship on the right track.

Now that your puppy is going out in public, he needs to wear identification in case he gets lost. His busy antics may frustrate you at times, so prepare yourself with items like food-dispensing toys that will occupy him when you need a break. The kids also need guidance to develop a good relationship with their new puppy.

Getting Him an ID Tag, License, and Microchip

Identification is your puppy's ticket home if he gets lost. When your Lab reaches 4 months, he has had his rabies vaccine, and most communities require that he be licensed. An ID tag includes your personal contact information, and a license has the animal control jurisdiction's info. In addition, if you haven't already, now is the time to microchip your puppy and register the number.

The well-dressed Labrador should always wear his ID tag. His tag should include your name and phone number, including the area code. Consider putting your cell and home phone numbers on the tag so if someone finds your puppy, you can be contacted even when you're out of town. If the sound of jingling tags bothers you, order a collar with your phone number printed on it, or a pouch that holds all the tags quietly and attaches to the collar. You can also purchase tags that slip onto the collar and lie flat against it. Flat tags are less likely to catch on something and get lost.

> ### TIPS AND TAILS
>
> The lettering on plastic ID tags wears down quickly, and as the plastic ages, it also breaks easily. Engraved metal lasts much longer. Be sure the tag has a heavy ring or S-hook. Put each tag on a separate ring so if one is lost, the others are still attached.

There are many good reasons to license your dog. All 50 states have dog licensing laws. Anyone who finds your dog will be more willing to handle him if they know his rabies status. If your dog bites someone, his vaccine record is on file. Animal Control will notify you and hold your dog longer than they will an unlicensed dog if they have a license on file. Some jurisdictions also give your dog a free ride home. Penalties for having an unlicensed dog are much higher than the cost of the original license, so take the time to get your pup licensed.

Either city or county agencies issue the license. You will submit his rabies vaccine certificate with the license application. Your vet might even send it in for you.

If your Lab loses his collar, a microchip provides lifetime identification he can't lose. The chip, the size of a piece of rice, is encased in biocompatible glass to prevent infection and is injected between your pup's shoulder blades. The chip operates on a radio frequency, is not a tracking device, and doesn't require a power source to be activated. When someone runs a scanner over your dog, it reads the chip like a UPC code on an item at the grocery store.

Once the chip is implanted, you pay a nominal one-time fee for lifetime registration with a national registry, such as the American Kennel Club Companion Animal Recovery Program (akccar.org), American Veterinary Identification Devices (avidid.com), or HomeAgain (public.homeagain.com). The chip number is registered with a national database where it can be traced back to you. The microchip manufacturer can provide this service, or there are other national registries. Most registries provide a collar tag so whoever finds your dog knows to have the dog scanned. Shelters, veterinarians, and rescue groups usually have their own scanners. If your dog is lost, contact the registry immediately. Most have a 24/7 telephone hotline.

TIPS AND TAILS

A microchip does *not* include your personal information, just a number. If you don't register your Lab's microchip, the shelter can't find you and the chip is useless. Before you register the chip, find out what registry your local shelter uses. Many people designate their veterinarian or breeder as the secondary contact.

Numerous manufactures make microchips, and in recent years, universal scanners have been developed that can read most brands and frequencies. These scanners are labeled ISO compliant by the International Organization for Standardization. Be sure the chip you purchase is compatible with ISO scanners. Over 160 countries follow these standards, and dogs have been reunited with their owners from around the world. Some countries require a microchip before you can import a dog.

Shelters usually scan the dog all over because some microchips migrate elsewhere in the body, like down his shoulder or leg, for example. Newer chips have a small hook that anchors the chip and layers of connective tissue grow over it to hold it in place. Have your dog scanned during his yearly health checkup to be sure the chip is still in place and active.

A GPS system (called A-GPS for assisted global positioning system) for dogs has recently been developed. A small tracking device is attached to the dog's collar and interacts with satellite and cell phone towers to follow the dog's movements. You'll receive an email or text message if your dog leaves the designated safe area you've set up. This state-of-the-art technology is fairly expensive—to the tune of several hundred dollars—but it provides you with extra peace of mind.

Frustrated Owner = Confused Puppy

A new Lab puppy can be a shock to the household, especially if your last dog was very old and you've forgotten what it's like to have a puppy. Or maybe this is your first dog, and you had no idea he was going to be this active or destructive. When the cute factor wears thin—usually right after he chews up the couch pillow or committed some similar crime—what can you do?

Remember, he's a puppy, and Lab puppies are especially active. What he's doing—barking, chewing, biting, digging—are all normal puppy behaviors, and he hasn't developed much, if any, self-control yet.

A tired puppy is a good puppy. Playtime, especially with you, solves a lot of puppy problems. Mental as well as physical exercise tires out your puppy.

Puppies learn by doing, and this month he is testing his limits. If he doesn't try things, he doesn't learn. If you never have to say no, how will he know the rules?

One correction doesn't mean lesson learned. He's a baby, and he'll forget. Be patient and consistent, and keep teaching.

When you get angry, your puppy is confused and sees you as unpredictable. He may not understand why you are so upset; he just knows to get out of your way. When his behavior is too much, put him in his crate with a chew toy, hand him off to someone else, or go for a walk by yourself.

Don't give up—get help. Before you get completely frustrated, talk to your veterinarian, puppy class instructor, or someone who can see what your puppy is doing and offer constructive suggestions. What works for one puppy might not work for yours, and there's more than one way to approach any problem.

HAPPY PUPPY

It's bedtime and you're tired, but your puppy won't settle down. What to do? Consider soft music with a low pulsing beat that simulates his mother's heartbeat. You can buy CDs and videos specially made to comfort and quiet your dog.

Food-Dispensing Toys

The way to a Lab puppy's heart is through his stomach. Food-dispensing toys entertain your puppy and keep him from wolfing down his food. Many kinds are available; hard plastic is best for Labs. The dispensers come in various shapes: balls, cubes, etc. Look for one he can't chew up.

Put his kibble in the toy. Add one piece at the opening so it falls out right away and he gets rewarded. Your puppy will soon be batting and rolling the toy all over to make more food come out. This is a noisy toy if he's on a hard floor. Separate him from other dogs, because bigger dogs will take it away—sometimes aggressively—because food is involved.

Another type of food-dispensing toy is an interactive puzzle. The best-known puzzles are made by Nina Ottenson. They're graded by difficulty, and some are made specifically for puppies. Your puppy has to manipulate the puzzle by stepping on a piece, picking it up, rocking it, or pushing it to get to the food prize.

You can make your own version of a food puzzle at home. Put kibble or treats in each cup of a cupcake tin. Place a tennis ball over each cup, and let your puppy figure out how to remove the ball and get to the treat. Don't be surprised if he figures out pretty quickly that he can dump the entire tin by stepping on it!

Puppy and Kids: Building the Friendship

The bloom is off the rose, and your puppy isn't brand new anymore. How do you keep the kids involved and build the relationship between puppy and child?

When other children come over, tell your kids that your puppy is a baby and can't speak for himself, so it's their job to recognize signals the puppy is tired or doesn't want to play. Explain to them that when your puppy turns his back, avoids eye contact, won't come to them, or tries to leave, that the puppy is tired and ready for his nap. A child will proudly assume the role of protector.

It's important for you to teach your puppy to respect your kids. A toddler or elementary school–age child will dislike a puppy who jumps up or knocks them down. The child may try to tell the pup what to do, and your puppy doesn't listen.

This little person isn't much bigger than the pup, and your Lab may see him as a littermate. Help your children use their own body language to stop the pup from jumping on them. Put the puppy on leash, and have the kids practice getting him to calm down by standing up straight and still, not looking at him, folding their arms, and ending the game.

Ensure that your puppy responds when the kids say "Sit" or "Down." Let your child reward the puppy while you hold the leash and enforce commands.

> ### TIPS AND TAILS
>
> Snap a second leash on your puppy so both you and your child are attached to him. Then, when he doesn't listen, you can help your child get him to respond.

It's also important to teach your kids to respect your puppy. Establish rules for the children's interactions with the puppy. The puppy will match his energy level to them, and everyone will stay safe. Point out that they wouldn't like it if the puppy did these things to them, and that they need to respect the puppy's feelings, too.

Here are some rules to establish with your kids and your puppy:

❧ No jumping on or falling on the dog.

❧ No kicking, hitting, or throwing things at the puppy. When toys become weapons, take them away.

❧ No teasing the puppy and enticing him to chase.

❧ Don't sit on the puppy or wrap your arms tightly around his neck or head.

❧ Leave the puppy alone when he's in his crate; no poking fingers in the crate and no teasing.

❧ Leave Puppy alone when he's eating.

A child may become jealous of the attention your puppy gets when guests visit your home. Children may also get jealous of each other if the puppy spends more time with their siblings or with Mom and Dad.

To avoid this, involve the children in the puppy's training. They can take turns giving commands, praising, holding the leash, and providing distractions. Help them teach the puppy tricks, like "Shake," that they can demonstrate when people visit. Move the puppy's crate into different rooms every few nights so he spends time with everyone. You could also have your child prepare the puppy's meal and give it to him. Your child should have the puppy sit before he puts down the bowl.

You can't expect an elementary school–age child to take complete responsibility for the care of a puppy. In fact, if it becomes a required chore, he may resent the puppy. But one very important job, like putting down his food dish, will help him bond with the puppy and also feel a sense of accomplishment.

You can also encourage harmony between kid and puppy by encouraging your kids to play games with your Lab puppy. Hide and seek is one option. Have one child restrain the puppy while another child hides. Have the hidden child call the puppy. When he finds him, switch sides.

Find the treat is another fun game. Let the puppy watch the child hide a treat in plain sight. Release him and praise him for finding it. Gradually hide treats in harder places or out of the room so he has to look harder. You don't want him digging up the couch looking for a treat, however, so establish some guidelines with the kids about good hiding places.

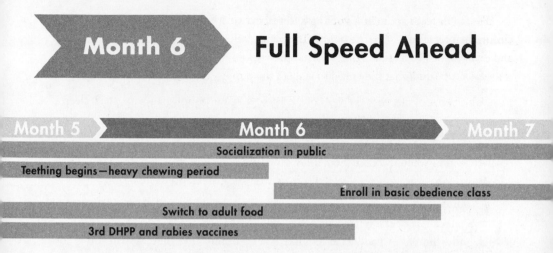

Month 5 > Month 6 > Month 7

Socialization in public

Teething begins—heavy chewing period

Enroll in basic obedience class

Switch to adult food

3rd DHPP and rabies vaccines

During months 5 and 6, your Lab puppy finishes her huge growth spurt, and her body starts to balance out. She has endless energy but not much common sense, so you'll spend time this month reviewing her training. Consider this a keep-her-busy month. Socialization is an ongoing process, so continue to introduce her to more places, people, and things.

Your Lab puppy is prone to injuries at this age—some of which lead to physical problems later in life—so we help you prepare your first-aid kit and get ready for emergencies. If it's fall or springtime, you may be experiencing her first major shedding season, so we also share some methods to cope with all that dog hair.

Physical Development

Although your Lab is looking more like a dog, she's still very much a puppy at heart, as you'll see in her behaviors this month. You'll also notice that the amount of sleep she needs is changing as she matures.

Looking Less Like a Puppy

A puppy grows rapidly during the first 6 months. At this point, she can look mature and well balanced, or she can still be all legs and tail. She has reached about 75 percent of her adult height but only about 60 percent of her adult weight. At 5½ months, a male puppy who will be within the standard at adulthood—22½ to 24½ inches tall at the shoulder—will be 17 to 19 inches and 39 to 48 pounds. A female who will mature to 21½ to 23½ inches will now be 16 to 18 inches tall and 33 to 42 pounds. This is just an estimate, and some puppies will be taller but may not weigh much more yet.

Her adult teeth are in and starting to set permanently in her jaws, so the chewing continues.

All About Sleep

A newborn puppy sleeps 90 percent of the time. As your puppy grows up, she'll sleep less, but still as much as 13 hours a day when she is an adult.

Just like a teenage human, an adolescent dog sleeps more, especially during growth spurts, when she's using up energy to build bone and muscles. And considering her high activity level all day, no wonder she's tired at the end of it.

An adult dog's sleep is different. She'll wake up more often, and about 25 percent of her sleep can be characterized as "active," where she seems to be dreaming. She'll twitch and whimper or paddle her legs likes she's running after that last ball you threw for her.

If your Lab lives indoors and doesn't get much activity, she may sleep more than an active dog. She'll adjust her sleep time so she can be active when you're home and make up for lost sleep when you're at work or sleeping yourself. Some dogs cope with extreme stress by sleeping more.

> ### TIPS AND TAILS
>
> Yawning doesn't necessarily mean your Lab is tired; it's also a stress response.

Your dog has an internal clock, and a Lab will *never* sleep through breakfast. In fact, you can be sure she'll wake you up at precisely the same time every morning. This quickly becomes a habit when you respond positively by getting up and feeding her. So much for sleeping in on Saturdays!

Scientists theorize that because a dog's brain is similar to a human's in some structural aspects, dogs do dream. Stanley Coren, PhD, FRSC, noted that a dog enters the dream phase about 20 minutes after falling asleep, and evidence has shown that she dreams about daily activities. The dog's breathing becomes shallow and irregular, and her eyes move behind her eyelids, just like the dream phase in human sleep. Watch your own puppy for signs she's dreaming.

Health

An active young Lab is more likely to be injured than be ill at this stage in her life. Reckless and uncoordinated, blasting into adventure with no thought to her own safety, your Lab puppy is her own worst enemy. She's also getting taller, and she may be able to reach objects on high shelves that were previously out of her reach.

It's essential that you learn to recognize and react to accidents, illnesses, and especially emergencies. Assemble a doggie first-aid kit, or combine it with your family's first-aid kit, because many of the items are the same (more on this in the later "Assembling Your Doggie First-Aid Kit" section). Being prepared gives you peace of mind and the ability to act when the unthinkable happens.

Getting to Know Your Puppy's Vitals

During an emergency, you'll need to assess your Lab's vital signs. For reference, you need to know what her normal heart and breathing rates are, and what her gums normally look like.

To check your puppy's breathing rate, lay her on her right side and let her rest quietly. As you watch her chest rise and fall, count the number of breaths in a 15-second period. Multiply that by 4, and you have the number of breaths per minute. The normal rate is 10 to 30 breaths per minute for an adult and 15 to 40 breaths for a young puppy. At 6 months, her breathing rate will be about the same as an adult's. The breathing rate is also influenced by the temperature of her surroundings and her activity level.

To check her heart rate, again lay her on her right side. Bend her left leg until her elbow touches her chest, and put your right hand on her body where her left elbow meets her chest. You should feel her heart beating. Count the beats for 15 seconds, and multiply that number by 4. Normal for a puppy up to 1 year old is 120 to 160 beats per minute.

Next, look at her gums (mucous membranes). When she's healthy, her gums are pink and wet. Dark red, blue, brown, or very pale gums indicate she's not getting enough oxygen into her blood.

Also check her capillary refill time. Firmly touch her outer gum with your finger and release. The gum should be white where you touched it. Watch the white fingerprint turn back to pink; it should take no more than 2 seconds. Too fast or too slow indicates a problem with her blood circulation.

Your Lab puppy's normal temperature is between 100.2°F and 102.8°F. See Month 4 for instructions on how to take your dog's temperature.

Once you understand what's normal for your Lab, you'll be able to accurately assess her condition in an emergency.

What Is an Emergency?

An emergency is any situation where you must take action immediately to prevent further injury or death. In some situations, you can treat a problem or observe your Lab for a while before contacting the vet. For example, if your puppy has stopped eating, you have some time to look at options. If your puppy can't breathe or seems to be choking, there's no time to lose, and you must respond without delay.

Potential emergencies include the following:

- 🐾 **Trauma:** hit by a car, or fallen from a building
- 🐾 **Difficulty breathing or choking:** she is gasping for air, pawing at her mouth, panicked, or her gums are turning blue or white
- 🐾 **Seizures:** long or short duration, or multiple seizures
- 🐾 **Excessive bleeding:** spurting blood, prolonged bleeding you can't stop by applying direct pressure
- 🐾 **Deep cuts:** exposed bones or organs
- 🐾 **Snake bite:** bite marks on your puppy's skin, swelling, bleeding from the bite, trembling or drooling, difficulty breathing, signs of shock
- 🐾 **Burns:** blisters, swollen reddened skin, loss of skin and hair
- 🐾 **Suspected poisoning:** vomiting or diarrhea; trembling or twitching; seizure; abnormal gum color; heavy drooling or foaming from the mouth; burns on the lips, tongue, or mouth; bleeding from mouth, nose, ears, or anus
- 🐾 **Broken bone:** pain, swelling, lameness, bone protruding from skin, limb held in abnormal position
- 🐾 **Heat stroke:** panting heavily, bright red gum color (may turn blue or gray in later stages), body temperature above 104°F, difficulty walking, collapse
- 🐾 **Bloat** (mostly adult dogs): drooling, retching, attempting to vomit, unable to defecate, pacing and restless, distended abdomen, signs of shock

Calm, Assess, Call, and CPR

When you've identified an emergency, you need to stay calm, assess the situation, call the vet if necessary, and administer CPR (Cardio Pulmonary Resuscitation) if required.

It's worth repeating: *stay calm*. Panic can make people do crazy things, and you can't help your dog if you get hurt, too. If she's been hit by a car, for example, you don't want to run out into the road unless it's safe to do so. So stop and take a deep breath.

First be sure you can approach your puppy safely. A frightened, injured dog, even your own, may bite. Speak calmly and reassuringly to her. Don't make any sudden movements that might cause her to bolt in fear. Use submissive body language: stand or crouch sideways to her, and don't look her directly in the eye.

To restrain your puppy, put the snap end of a leash through the loop for your hand and make a noose. Drop the noose over your puppy's head, and tighten it without touching her.

Muzzle your dog by taking a long piece of gauze from your first-aid kit and wrapping it around her muzzle, crisscrossing under her lower jaw and tying it behind her neck. You can also use a belt or other piece of fabric to do this.

> ### TIPS AND TAILS

Shock occurs when not enough blood and oxygen flow to the internal organs. Shock is common after serious injuries, especially if there's been major blood loss. Symptoms of early shock include increased heart rate, pounding pulse, and red gums. Middle stages of shock are indicated by low body temperature, weak and rapid pulse, pale gums, and a woozy and weakened animal. Slow breathing and heart rate, weak or no pulse, depression, unconsciousness, and cardiac arrest can indicate late stages of shock, which leads to death.

Next, assess the situation. Do a visual survey of the scene. Check your dog's posture, look for blood or vomit, listen to her breathing, and look to see if there are any obvious signs of what caused the injury, such as poison or a snake. Then check her airway, breathing, and circulation—the ABCs of first aid.

Assuming you can touch her, does your puppy have an open airway? Check her mouth and throat for obstructions, and clear any if you can, using tweezers or forceps from your emergency kit.

Is she breathing? Look at the rise and fall of her chest. If you aren't sure, put your cheek against the front of her nose to feel or listen for her breathing. If she is, move on to the next step. A dog can be unconscious and still be breathing.

If she's not breathing, start rescue breathing immediately.

Does she have circulation, meaning a pulse or heartbeat? As discussed earlier, lay your dog on her right side, slightly bend her left leg until her elbow touches her chest, and put your right hand on her body where the left elbow meets her chest. Can you feel her heart beating? To check for a pulse, use two fingers on one of three places: high inside either rear leg about halfway between the front and back of the leg where you feel a slight recess, on the underside of either front paw just above the middle pad, or on the underside of either hind paw just above the middle pad.

If there is no heartbeat or pulse, start chest compressions immediately.

If you're alone, call for help or call the veterinary hospital before you start rescue breathing or CPR. If it's after regular hours, call the emergency animal hospital nearest you. If you have someone with you, let them call while you start CPR. Your advance call enables the hospital to be ready to help as soon as you arrive.

The veterinarian will want to know a few things:

🐾 Is the puppy breathing? Describe.

🐾 Has she vomited or passed any stool or foreign objects?

🐾 What's her pulse?

🐾 What color are her gums?

🐾 Is the puppy bleeding? How much? Where is the blood coming from?

🐾 What's her temperature?

🐾 Has anyone administered CPR?

The veterinarian may ask additional questions and give you instructions to help you care for your dog until you can get her to the clinic.

Next, administer CPR rescue breathing or chest compressions if your puppy has no pulse and isn't breathing. This life-saving procedure keeps oxygen in your puppy's system until help arrives. Continue CPR until she regains consciousness or you arrive at the vet's office.

It's essential that you first be certain your dog is actually unconscious. Never perform CPR on a dog who has a heartbeat or is breathing. Try to rouse her by gently shaking her body and talking to her. If that doesn't work, continue with CPR.

First, check her airway: Tilt her head back to align with her neck to open up her airway. Pull her tongue forward, and remove any foreign objects.

Administer rescue breathing: Close her mouth tightly, and wrap one hand around her muzzle to keep it closed. Take a deep breath, and put your mouth over her nose, sealing her nostrils. Exhale firmly while watching for her chest to expand.

Remove your mouth, take another deep breath, and repeat four or five times, allowing her chest to return to normal after each breath. Give about 20 breaths per minute. Continue until she revives or you arrive at the vet.

Perform chest compressions: If your dog still isn't breathing after the first four or five rescue breaths, check again for a pulse or heartbeat. If she has none, her heart has stopped and you need to immediately begin compressions.

With your dog still lying on her right side, position yourself so you face her. Locate her heart (explained earlier). Straighten your arms and cup one hand over the other. Begin rapid, firm compressions, strong enough that your puppy's chest moves about 1 inch. For an adult dog, the chest should move 1 to 3 inches. After five compressions, give one rescue breath and check for a pulse. If she still has no pulse, continue the series of five compressions and one rescue breath until she revives or you get to the vet.

When your puppy is breathing and has a heartbeat, transport her to the veterinary hospital as soon as possible. Ideally, have someone else drive while you concentrate on your puppy.

Assembling Your Doggie First-Aid Kit

A pet first-aid kit enables you to respond quickly when your dog needs help. You can buy premade kits for pets or humans and add additional items you might need. Label your kit or storage container clearly, and keep it where you can get to it quickly, possibly in your car. Or keep several first-aid kits in strategic places.

A basic first-aid kit should include the following:

- ❧ Your veterinarian's contact info and the nearest emergency vet hospital contact info
- ❧ A copy of your dog's health records
- ❧ A muzzle to fit your dog or a long strip of gauze (30 to 36 inches)
- ❧ Antihistamine (Benadryl or equivalent) to treat an allergic reaction (Discuss the correct dose with your vet based on your Lab's weight. Remember that the dosage will change as she grows.)
- ❧ Tweezers, needle-nose pliers, forceps, or hemostat, for removing foreign objects from the mouth or throat
- ❧ Saline eye wash for flushing irritants from a dog's eye
- ❧ Mild grease-cutting dish soap (like Dawn) for removing sticky or caustic substances from your dog's coat

🐾 Rubber gloves or latex gloves

🐾 A rectal thermometer and petroleum jelly

🐾 Hand sanitizer

🐾 Antiseptic solution

🐾 Antibiotic ointment

🐾 Elastic bandages

🐾 Veterinary wrap (such as Vetwrap) to hold bandages in place

🐾 Blunt-nose and pointed scissors

🐾 Sanitary pads to bandage a bleeding wound

🐾 Nonstick bandages

🐾 Various sizes and shapes of gauze pads to clean and protect wounds

🐾 A flashlight

🐾 A first-aid book (You can also get a pet first-aid app for your smartphones for less than $5. See Appendix E.)

You may want to keep a leash, several towels, and a blanket in your car or with your first-aid kit. A leash can be used to restrain your puppy or as a muzzle. Use towels to clean up blood or vomit. A blanket can be used as a stretcher or to keep your puppy warm.

> ### TIPS AND TAILS
>
> Something else to keep in your doggie first-aid kit is the number for the ASPCA Animal Poison Control Hotline: 888-426-4435. Veterinarians are on call 24 hours a day, 7 days a week. You will be charged a small consultation fee. Be sure to gather as much information as possible about the poison before you call.

Pet First-Aid Classes

The Red Cross and many private trainers offer pet first-aid courses that cover both dogs and cats. Classes last around 4 hours and provide training that prepares you to effectively care for your pet in an emergency situation.

You learn how to handle an injured dog, assess her condition, and safely transport her to the vet. You also learn what to do in specific situations like a broken bone, heatstroke, snakebite, or excessive bleeding. The course also trains you to do a modified Heimlich maneuver on a choking animal.

One of the key benefits of pet first-aid classes is that you get hands-on practice in bandaging, splinting, and CPR using the CPR dummies. The Red Cross program also includes a book and DVD you keep with your first-aid kit for reference. The book covers common injuries and emergency illnesses and reviews all the instruction you received in the class.

Check with the Red Cross, your veterinarian, or local dog trainers for pet first-aid courses in your area.

Nutrition

Speed eating and food guarding cause ongoing health and behavior issues if not prevented. Also in this section, you learn how to choose healthy treats for your Lab puppy.

Dealing with Speed Eaters

At 6 months, your Lab puppy undoubtedly eats like she hasn't seen a bowl of food for weeks. It starts when she's with her littermates and has to compete for a spot to nurse, and the behavior continues at the puppy pan when she begins to eat solid food. Labs, more than any other breed, elevate speed eating to a fine art. But it can cause problems.

A dog who drills through her dinner also inhales too much air, which causes gas and discomfort. She finishes eating long before her stomach has a chance to tell her she's full, so she'll still want more. Then she runs outside and gulps down a bowl of water. This adds up to a tummy ache, and as she ages, this puts her at risk for bloat, a potentially fatal condition.

Here are some suggestions to slow down your speed eater:

- ❧ Don't make her compete for her food. If other dogs are in the house, feed everyone in separate rooms so they don't feel their food is threatened.
- ❧ Add water to her food and let it soak. The food expands in the bowl and not in her stomach, so she'll feel full faster.
- ❧ Don't use a bowl. Toss her food on the floor and let her scavenge and eat one kibble at a time. Be sure to do this on a clean, hard surface like a concrete patio or kitchen floor. A typical Lab will eat gravel, dirt, seeds, and anything else in her path.

❧ Put a large rock in the dish. She has to eat around it, which slows her down. Use a rock that's too big for her to put in her mouth.

❧ Break her meal into small portions, giving her just ¼ cup at a time.

> ### TIPS AND TAILS

Usually a temporary problem, a sudden diet change can cause an upset tummy with resulting gas and diarrhea. Your puppy could also have eaten something in the yard that didn't agree with her. Flatulence alone doesn't usually indicate a serious health problem, but if you're worried, talk to your vet. If the problem continues and there's no medical cause, examine the ingredients list on the dog-food label. Certain ingredients may cause excessive flatulence. If your puppy's food has soy, beans, or cellulose listed in the ingredients, you might want to see if a different food solves the problem. Remember to switch foods gradually, because that in itself can cause gas.

Preventing Food Guarding

Your Lab puppy should feel comfortable when anyone in the family reaches into her bowl, touches her while she's eating, or takes away her food bowl. At the same time, you want to be sure she won't bite you if you need to pick up the bowl. It's always easier to prevent a problem rather than fix one, so it's important you teach your Lab to welcome your presence while she's eating.

Do this exercise once or twice a week, or once every couple days. Don't make a pest of yourself, or she won't be happy to see you coming.

Divide her meal into four or five portions. Give her one portion and then sit nearby on the floor, ignoring her. When she's done, pick up the bowl and put more food in it. She'll learn that having you near her food is a good thing because more food is on the way.

Each time you add food, add one special goodie, like a bite of cheese or hot dog. Not only does she get more food, but that food is *great!* She's starting to enjoy this game. Or reach into the bowl while she's eating and add a treat. Touch the bowl while you add treats, or pick up the bowl, add a treat, and give it back to her.

Touch your puppy's collar while you put a treat in her bowl or pick it up. Hold her collar for a second or two, put the bowl back down, and add the treats.

Be sure you teach your kids the feeding game. Once they understand what you're teaching your puppy, they'll enjoy helping.

Your puppy needs to feel secure enough that she doesn't have to watch out for flying objects and can eat her meal in relative peace. This is not the time for a toddler to spill a cup of milk on the dog or for cheerleading practice next to her dish. Be sure everyone in the family leaves her reasonably alone when she eats. You want to be able to approach her and her bowl, but you don't want the entire family bugging her to a point where she feels the need to protect herself or her food.

Choosing Treats

Just as you would check the ingredients in a dog food, look at what's in the treats you purchase for your pup. Treats should account for no more than 5 to 10 percent of her total daily intake of food. Cut back on kibble if she's getting a lot of goodies.

Treats also may be high in fat, salt, and sugar to add flavor. The added salt will make your dog drink more. Select treats that are the same brand and ingredients as your dog food—or better yet, use part of her daily food ration for treats.

Soft or semi-soft treats often have added dyes and fillers. Just because something looks like a piece of bacon or beef doesn't mean that's what it is. Binding agents are also often added to make the treat stick together and look like a chunk of meat. Some "bones" are made with vegetables and cornstarch and may break apart quickly in a Lab's iron jaws.

Most treats are not intended as a complete, nutritionally balanced food, and this will be noted on the package. A junk-food dog treat can upset your puppy's nutritional balance, especially if she gets too many.

As an alternative to a constant barrage of commercially made treats, use bits of raw carrot or cooked plain chicken. Cheese cubes are also good in small amounts, but too much of a dairy product can cause diarrhea.

Just because you have a big dog (or at least she will be soon) doesn't mean she needs a 4-inch-long dog biscuit every time she gets a treat. Break them up, or buy small biscuits.

Grooming

Labs are usually very clean … when they stay out of mischief. She'll need an occasional bath, so learn how to go about it in this section. And because Labs do shed, it's important that you learn to take some preventive measure to deal with all that dog hair.

Bathing Your Lab Puppy

Labs rarely need baths. You can probably get by with only bathing her once a year, during the summer, if that often. Too many baths strip her coat of protective oils and make it dry and dull. In hot weather, you can bathe her outside—an added plus.

That said, if her shedding really bothers you, a bath will reduce the hair she loses. Brush her thoroughly before the bath, massage her coat while you bathe her, blow-dry her coat to remove more loose hair, and then brush her thoroughly again.

Confine your Lab in a big tub (a horse water trough works great) or on a leash so she'll stay in one place. Ask a helper to restrain her while you bathe her. If the tub is slippery, put a bath mat in the bottom. Use cool to room temperature water to wash your Lab. Hot water will dry out her skin, and although cold water won't bother her, you shouldn't use ice-cold water, either.

You don't have to give her a complete bath the first time you introduce her to the tub. The idea is for her to enjoy a short, fun experience, not necessarily get her clean! Have your helper offer treats throughout the process.

Let her sniff the hose and running water, and maybe even taste it. Place her in the tub, and add water until it barely covers her feet. If this is too much, just splash a little on her feet and quit. Let her out when she's calm. She may try to jump out, but restrain her until she calms down and then let her out. Work with her over several sessions until she enjoys the water and looks forward to it.

Try to separate bath time from play-in-the-water time. You don't want your puppy chasing the hose and biting at the water while you're trying to shampoo her.

HAPPY PUPPY

A Lab probably doesn't need a full bath, just a good rinsing, especially at this age. If that's the case, quit while you're ahead and introduce shampoo some other time. It'll be easier on both of you.

When it's time for an actual bath, put cotton balls in your Lab's ears, but don't wet her face or head until later because she'll want to shake. Wet her coat, starting at her tail end and gradually moving forward. Hold the nozzle close to her skin so it penetrates her thick coat and she gets thoroughly wet.

Using a shampoo specifically made for dogs, dilute the shampoo before you apply it so you don't have all the soap concentrated in one place. Massage it into her coat, taking care to get her belly and armpits, too. The hair on her neck and throat is especially thick, so add water as you wash. If she's really dirty or shedding heavily, massage her soapy coat with a rubber curry, which will bring soil and loose hair to the surface.

Lastly, put some diluted shampoo in your hand or on a washcloth and wash her face. You may want to put eye lubricant around her eyes to help keep out the soap. Rinse her face with a wet cloth or a gentle stream of water. Wipe out her ears, too, but avoid getting water in them.

Rinse her thoroughly, including between her toes, under her belly, and between her legs, until all the dirt and bubbles disappear—which will probably take longer than the washing step. When all the shampoo is washed out, the water will run clear. If you leave any soap residue in her coat, it will irritate her skin, so rinse, rinse, rinse! And then stand back and let her shake!

Labs don't generally need a coat conditioner unless they have skin issues. If you like, you can add white vinegar to the final rinse to make her coat shiny. Rinse well so she won't smell like vinegar when you're done.

Now that everyone is soaked, move her someplace dry and towel off the excess moisture. Remove the cotton balls, and thoroughly dry her ears. If you want to salvage a clean Lab out of this project, put her in her crate with some dry towels and a chew toy until her coat dries. Otherwise, she'll head straight for the backyard and roll in the dirt. If she got water in her ears, she'll rub her head along the ground. If you let her loose in the house, she'll rub along the walls and against the couch.

You might want to use a hair dryer to speed up the drying process, especially during winter or shedding season. The dryer also helps blow out any remaining loose coat. Turn the dryer on the lowest possible setting because a dog's skin burns easily. Your puppy may bite at the air or be afraid of the noise, so start by holding the dryer at arm's length away from her. Never blow the dryer directly in her face, and don't put her in her crate with a dryer blowing on her. She can't move away from the heat if it gets too hot.

Shedding: Dealing with Lab Hair

For a short-coated dog, Labs sure shed a lot. A deep, thorough brushing at least once a week makes for a healthy dog and a cleaner house, but it's not enough to prevent shedding and the accompanying mess. Some preventive measures makes housecleaning chores less time-consuming.

You'll probably get used to the dog hair and barely notice it after a while. But you'll cringe when Aunt Charlotte comes to visit and sits on the couch. When she stands up, her entire backside will be covered in fur. Invest in washable furniture covers to protect the furniture. When company comes, uncover the sofa and pretend it always looks this good.

You could teach your Lab puppy never to get on the furniture, but that wouldn't be any fun. Besides, when she lies on the floor in her favorite spot up against the couch, it will still get dirty and hairy. If you really have to keep a room pristine, limit her access with pet gates. For example, let her nap on the sofa in the family room, but the living room is off limits. A healthy coat doesn't shed as much. If you're feeding a discount or grocery store brand of dog food, you may see a marked difference in your dog's coat when you switch to a premium food.

Don't forget to wash your Lab's bedding regularly, too. Besides getting rid of excess hair, your house also will smell fresher. A clean dog who sleeps on a dirty bed won't stay clean and sweet-smelling for long.

Social Skills

A well-socialized Labrador is friendly, confident, and well behaved everywhere she goes. This is no small achievement, and it doesn't happen by accident. It takes ongoing training, and this month is no exception.

Dealing with a Jumping Lab: "Off" and "Sit to Greet"

Puppies jump up because they want to be near your face and smell your breath to identify you. A cute little 20-pound Lab puppy might not be such a bother when she jumps, but a 60-pound jumping Lab quickly becomes a nuisance. You might let her jump on you sometimes, but she can't tell the difference between your Sunday best suit and your Saturday sweats, so she needs to learn not to jump up unless invited.

"Off" is the command for four on the floor. Don't use "Down," because you've already taught her that "Down" means something else—"Lie down on the floor." You want your Lab puppy to learn that "Off" means "Get off me." Off is not punishment; it's an instruction.

To teach "Off," you'll first teach her to jump up on command. Pat your chest with both hands and say "Up" just as she starts to jump. Praise her, and as she backs off, say "Off." Add a hand signal: your flat palm toward her with spread fingers.

Meanwhile, as she's learning "Up" and "Off," don't give your puppy any attention when she's jumping—no eye contact, no touching, no talking. Look away, stand up straight, fold your arms, and turn your back to her. Stand still and wait her out. As soon as she stops jumping, even for a second, praise her and say "Good off." If she immediately jumps back up, ignore her again. When she's got all four feet down, stand quietly and praise her calmly.

Jumping up is a sign of over-arousal; you want her to lower her energy level. If you bend over her or make eye contact, this invites her back up into your face. Ask her to sit when she hits the floor so she has an alternative behavior to keep her busy. When she's first learning and you do pet her, loop two fingers through her collar to keep her feet on the ground. Look away and pet her chest so she's more likely to stay in position.

If she doesn't back off when you ignore her, attach a leash to her collar. When you give the off command, give the leash a quick snap to remind her. You can also stand on the leash so she corrects herself when she jumps. If you drag her off you with the leash or use your hands to push her to the floor, she's not learning anything except that you'll do the work for her. Your hands reward her for jumping up, and even though you think it's a correction, she thinks it's a game.

"Off" is a command you'll use often with your excited Lab. When she can alternate up and off on command, she understands the exercise. Practice often around the house and outdoors, and have every family member teach her to respond.

Your puppy is tall enough to begin playing a Labrador's favorite sport: counter surfing. "Off" is useful for objects as well as people. Hook a leash to her collar, and let her drag it in the house. When her paws hit the counter, grab the leash and tell her "Off." A quick tug will get her attention. As soon as she looks at you, praise her and call her to you. Remember, don't drag her off the counter; she must decide to remove her paws on her own.

> ### TIPS AND TAILS
>
> Clear the counters! Anything that remotely smells like food should be in a cupboard or on top of the refrigerator. Scrape dishes and fill the dishwasher as soon as you've finished eating. One successful scavenging operation rewards her for counter surfing, and she'll try again and again.

Your puppy will happily claim the couch or king-size bed for her own, and the family will be left sleeping on the floor if you allow this behavior. To fix it, use the same method you used for the counters. Let her drag a leash, give the command "Off," and lure her off the couch with a treat. Praise her as soon as she starts to get off. After some practice, hide the treat and don't produce it until she gets off the couch completely.

Invite her up on the bed or couch if you want to. Some dogs will get possessive of their favorite spot (usually at about 1 or 1½ yrs old) and won't want to move, so be sure she willingly gets down when you tell her.

Once she learns "Off," put it to good use. When your puppy charges full speed at you, hold up your palm in the "Off" position and rush at her. Spread your fingers, put your palm right in her face, and immediately ask for a sit. As she gets the idea, use a less-dramatic hand signal and just lean toward her to remind her to stay off and sit. Eventually, she'll decide "Off" is a two-part command—off and sit—and she'll sit every time.

Sometimes a rambunctious puppy doesn't listen, so you need to use stronger measures. Fill a squirt bottle with water, and keep it handy. When she starts to jump up or is charging at you, squirt her in the face or chest. She'll quickly learn to veer off or refrain from jumping as soon as she sees you holding the bottle. Or because she's a Lab, she'll decide the water bottle is a lot of fun, and you'll have to come up with another method.

When Puppy is bouncing up in your face or in front of you, hold a metal dog dish in one hand at waist level. When she starts to jump up, let her bop her head on the bottom of the dish. You aren't hitting her; she's correcting herself by banging into the dish. This method has an added benefit at feeding time. She'll see the dish, avoid it, and learn not to jump at you while you're carrying her food.

> ### TIPS AND TAILS
>
> You may read somewhere to knee your puppy in the chest when she jumps on you. *Don't.* This could injure her, either breaking her breastbone or hurting her when she falls. Another recommendation you may hear is to grab her paws and hold on until she struggles to get down. Again, *don't.* This may teach her to bite at your hands or be unwilling to let you handle her feet in other situations, like when you want to trim her toenails. Neither method builds a good relationship with your puppy.

A polite puppy greets people she meets with a sit. Once she understands how not to jump on you, expand her lesson and teach her not to jump on anyone else, a.k.a. "Sit and greet." This is an entirely different exercise in your puppy's mind. Now she's looking away from you rather than approaching you.

Enlist family or friends to help you. Have them ignore your puppy and make no eye contact. Don't let them greet or pet her until she sits quietly. Once she does this consistently, use this same method when your Lab puppy meets people out in public. People will be amazed at your training skills!

Add "Sit to greet" to front-door greetings at home. Hang a leash on the doorknob, and hook her up as soon as the doorbell rings. Ask her to sit and stay before you open the door. If she starts to get up, shut the door and have her return to the sit. This will take several tries before she remains sitting. When the person comes in the door, you'll have to start all over, asking her to sit and stay. Remember to touch her and say "Okay" when she's allowed to stand up.

When the visitor moves away from the door, walk her quietly to the person to say hello and sit for petting. If she just can't settle down at the door, put her in her crate and let her out on leash after your guest has entered and everything is calmer.

If you see your Lab think about jumping but then think better of it, praise her to the skies because she is definitely the smartest puppy on the planet. She'll remember how happy you are and try to do as well the next time she's tempted.

Going Many Different Places

Continue to take your Lab new places this month. Also return to places you've previously visited so she'll remember them.

In preparation for the adolescent crazies, practice her obedience skills everywhere you go. Bring along a chew bone and have her lie quietly at your feet while you relax on a park bench. For a new sensation under her feet, take her to a harbor if you have one nearby and let her walk on the floating docks. Walk her across a bridge or over a freeway.

If you have a beach nearby, take her there, too. Although you've introduced your Lab to water at home, and she probably loves it, the family pool and garden hose are a far cry from a lake or beach. Waves crashing on the shore, birds running along the water's edge, the smell of the ocean and seaweed—these are all new, exciting, and potentially scary to your Lab puppy. Bring fresh water with you for her to drink; you don't want her gulping salty seawater, which will quickly dehydrate her.

Consider bringing another dog along for your puppy's first beach expedition. Start by allowing your pup to drag a long line. Many dogs are afraid of the approaching water and spook when a wave splashes on their feet. When she sees another dog having fun, she'll be more likely to try it. Start by walking her along the water's edge and letting her get used to the feel of the wet sand. Don't force her into deep water or throw her in.

Bring a ball she can fetch on the beach. Don't throw it out in the water until she's happily playing in the shallow waves. Then just toss it a foot or two and let her chase it out on a receding wave. When she's comfortable, you don't want her swimming to China, so keep her close enough that you can grab the long line.

When you bring her home, you'll be glad you've been practicing her grooming skills as you hose her down to get the saltwater and sand out of her coat.

Teenage Labs and retractable leashes are a dangerous combination. The farther away from you she goes, the less control you have. Many of these leashes extend as far as 26 feet, and when she's that far away, she may ignore your call because she isn't used to responding from a distance yet. And one good, hard jerk when she sees another dog a few hundred yards away and zoom … she's gone, the leash ripped from your hand and bouncing along behind her. If the handle retracts quickly, it could break a bone when it hits your Lab. Please, wait until your Lab is at least 3 or 4 years old before trying retractable leashes.

Behavior

The training and socialization you have worked so hard on up to this point won't completely prevent your puppy from his madcap adolescent activities, but you do have an excellent head start and may avoid some typical teenage behavior problems. But just in case, here are some areas to work on this month.

The Age of Distraction

At 6 months, your Lab puppy is ready to take on the world and sometimes considers that human being at the other end of her leash a hindrance to her plans. Expect a lot of overenthusiasm and pulling in every direction when she's out in public. Be ready with calm and consistent training and rule enforcement. This month, you may have to stop what you're doing and invest a few minutes to get her attention so she'll listen to you. She's strong and determined, and you must be equally so. Your Lab isn't mad at you; she's a preteen.

She'll use as many tricks as she can to get out of obeying you. You'll ask for a sit, and she'll paw at your leg. When she lies down, she'll roll on her back like she has a tremendous itch that just won't wait. She'll whimper, snort, and wrap herself around your legs. She'll creep forward as soon as your attention wanders. Just patiently use the leash to put her back in position, and release her when you're ready. Repeat the exercise until she does it correctly, but set her up for success and ask for a shorter stay next time. If you give up and quit when she's goofing around, she wins and will try to distract you every time you ask her to do something.

Use your body language to keep your dog calm and focused. Speak softly, stand up straight, and use the leash instead of your hands to correct her or put her back in position.

Digging in the Yard

Labs dig for many reasons, but the most common is that it's fun! Digging rewards her with interesting smells, chewy roots, and other garden delights. You can't train your dog *not* to dig, so the solution includes management and prevention. Conduct a regular perimeter patrol to find and fix any loose boards in wood fencing or broken tension wires at the bottom of chain-link fencing. A determined Lab can and will tear apart a chain-link fence.

Boredom and separation anxiety cause many dogs to take up recreational digging. A young dog left out in the yard all day gets restless and needs something to do, so she makes her own entertainment. She may have seen you working in the garden, so she digs up a spot that still has your scent. If you use bone meal or blood meal when you plant, she could be attracted to that smell. She may dig to bury a bone or toy, or to make a cool resting place under a large bush. Remember, a young Lab needs lots of exercise. Tire her out before you leave her in the yard alone. And then leave food-dispensing toys that will occupy her for an hour or more.

Consider providing your Lab with her own digging pit. Set aside a small area and fill it with sand (which is easier to rinse off your puppy than dirt). Bury treat-filled toys, bones, balls, and other prizes in the sand for her to find. When you first introduce her to the pit, leave a few goodies sticking out of the sand so she gets the idea.

Of course, some dogs refuse to use your chosen spot, and this is where management comes into play. Make other holes less attractive. For example, fill holes with dog feces and cover them. Put a balloon in a hole so it will pop when she digs and scare her. Place a piece of chicken wire about 4 inches down in the hole and bury it. She won't like snagging her toenails on the wire.

If you have gophers, moles, or other underground pests, your Lab will do some serious excavating to try to find them. The easiest solution is to get rid of the critters. Rodent poisons usually contain molasses or bran, so they'll also attract your dog and could kill her. Even if the bait is placed underground, your Lab may get to it. Check with the local garden center for dog-friendly methods to eliminate pests.

Your dog may dig because she sees other people and dogs walking past your house. She is frustrated and wants to join them, so she digs under the fence. To solve this problem, you could put up a solid fence (this also reduces nuisance barking). Or line the bottom of the fence with concrete blocks or large rocks. You could also attach a 2-foot-wide strip of chicken wire or hardware cloth along the bottom of the fence. Place it so 12 inches is attached to the fence, and the bottom 12 inches bends out into the yard. Cover the part on the ground with rocks and dirt.

When all else fails, keep your Lab indoors or build a dog run for her to stay in when you aren't there to supervise her activities.

Iron Jaws, Soft Mouth

A Labrador Retriever is supposed to gently pick up a fallen bird and deliver it to the hunter in pristine condition—she's not supposed to eat it. She should hold the bird gingerly so she doesn't tear it up, crush it, or otherwise render it inedible. Keep in mind that this is the same dog who can turn a tree branch into toothpicks. Retrievers should have soft mouths, but they aren't usually born that way.

Sometimes people accidentally train their dogs to grab and bite down hard. They worry that she'll bite their fingers as she takes a treat or toy, so they snatch their hands away as the puppy reaches for it. Or they toss the treat on the ground, which encourages the dog to lunge for it. Dogs who are aroused and excited grab in the heat of a game. Competition from other dogs also causes a puppy to grab.

It's important to teach your Lab to take a treat nicely. Introduce this treat-taking lesson separately from other exercises you're teaching your puppy. If you're asking her to sit or down and then correct her for snatching at the treat, she'll get confused.

First, choose a word to use to remind her to be gentle. *Nicely, gentle, easy,* or *softly* are all good choices because they are soft, two-syllable words, which are easier for you to say in a calming way.

If your puppy is a real shark, wear garden gloves. Put a tiny dab of peanut butter on the palm of your hand, and offer it to your puppy. If she grabs, simply close your hand over the goodie. She needs to lick this treat, not bite at it.

Try again. If puppy lunges at your hand, quickly push your hand at her about an inch. This will slow her down. As she licks the treat, use your word, "Nicely," and praise her quietly. Say "Nicely" in a calm and friendly voice while she's eating the treat. This isn't a command or a warning.

When she's taking the peanut butter off your palm politely, try it with a piece of her kibble. Hold your thumb over the treat and let her chew it out of your grasp. Correct her with the word "Ack" if she bites your fingers, but don't snatch away your hand.

Next, switch to holding treats between your fingertips. As she reaches in for the treat, push the treat about an inch into her mouth. She'll feel your hand coming at her and back off slightly. Also hand-feed your puppy her meals (or even a portion of her meal) for a few days, practicing her new manners. Then incorporate "Nicely" into your daily routine and training sessions.

A puppy who grabs treats probably also grabs toys and holds them in an iron grip. Avoid teaching your dog to bite hard. As she grows up and gets stronger, you won't be able to out-muscle her. Don't play tug-of-war games where you encourage her to hang on and not let go. Don't pull toys from her mouth; her natural reflex is to bite down and resist. Trade her for a treat or another toy instead.

"Give" comes in handy around the house. You'll have a much easier time wrestling Grandma's dentures and other contraband from her mouth using this command than trying to pry something from her grip.

This lesson is easier to introduce at eye level. Attach a leash and present your pup with a toy you know she'll want; use something you can take without sticking your fingers in her mouth. A tennis ball, for example, may be too small, so choose a stick or retrieving *bumper* instead. Use "Nicely" to encourage her to take it gently, just like she did with food. When she has it in her mouth, show her a treat or another highly desirable toy, and say "Give" as she lets go of the first toy. Your puppy may drop the toy or release it into your hand. Praise her and repeat several times. Once she gets the idea, introduce the command "Take it" as you present the toy.

> ### DOG TALK
>
> A **bumper** is a long, narrow rubber or canvas retrieving toy used for training hunting dogs. Due to their length, they stick out of either side of a dog's mouth so you can take them easily. Rubber bumpers are covered with raised knobs that prevent the bumper from sliding around in your Lab's mouth, which would encourage her to chomp down and hold it even more tightly. Canvas bumpers are usually filled with hard foam and sometimes contain weights. Take bumpers away from your Lab when you aren't using them, because she'll shred them easily.

Labs love to retrieve, and they love games. To get a really fast release when you say "Give," throw the other toy for her to retrieve as a reward for giving up what she has in her mouth.

Training

Diligent training is your goal for this month. Your Lab is capable of performing at least 10 obedience commands by the time she's 6 months old. She'll be easily distracted so give her plenty of reminders. With practice, she should be able to do a 1-minute sit-stay and a 1- or 2-minute down-stay by the end of this month.

Keep your training lessons interesting and fun by teaching your Lab new skills and polishing old ones.

Basic Obedience Review and Hand Signals

Your puppy should have learned the following commands so far:

"Sit": Put your rear end on the floor and don't move. Hand signal: scoop one hand upward, palm up.

"Down": Lie down, roll on one hip, and don't move. Hand signal: sweep your flat hand, palm down, toward the ground.

"Okay": You are finished; relax. This command releases your dog from whatever she's doing. Hand signal: toss your hands upward happily, palms up.

"Come": Stop what you're doing and come here. Signal: wide open, welcoming arms.

"Let's go" or "Walk": Pay attention, we're going for a walk. Signal: step off on your left foot (when she's at your left side).

"Stay": Don't move until I come back and touch you. Hand signal: flat palm in front of the puppy's nose as you step off on your right foot.

"Off": Put all four feet on the floor. Hand signal: flat palm, fingers spread, pushing toward the dog.

"Leave it": Turn away from what you're looking at and look at me. No hand signal.

"Take it": Take an item, like a toy, that I present to you. No hand signal.

"Give": Open your mouth and release an item. Hand signal: flat open hand (like a plate) in front of her mouth.

> **TIPS AND TAILS**
>
> Because dogs are so visually oriented, they read your body language before they pay attention to what you say. A hand signal or other cue from you helps your dog understand what you want. You can use the ones mentioned here or make up your own.

Training Problems

She was doing so well with her training, and now she seems to have fallen completely apart. Who is this disobedient puppy? When you lose mental control of your distracted preteen puppy, retain physical control by keeping her on a leash. Insist that she comply with every instruction, even when she gives you a "Wha? [...] to me?" attitude. Training problems may actually be attention problems ra[...] willful disobedience.

If you slack off and let her respond slowly or get away with not responding at all, you will slowly lose control over your dog, just when you need it most. That should be enough to motivate you to work through any training issues you're encountering. Don't reward your puppy if you have to ask twice or physically force her to do what you've asked. Show her the treat but then put it away.

Do, however, reward every sincere try. You're not angry at your puppy; you're teaching her. Her behavior right now is part of the learning process.

> ### HAPPY PUPPY

It takes at least three repetitions before your dog starts to understand what you're teaching her. Stick to numerous 2-minute practice sessions over several days instead of one ½-hour session every day. A puppy gets tired and loses interest after a few minutes. She's most likely to remember the last thing you worked on and nothing else.

Dole out your praise and treat rewards according to her response. When she's done especially well, give her several treats and big, happy praise. When she responds slowly or late, give her mild praise with a small token treat. She'll soon learn by your reaction which responses earn treats and exuberant praise, and her performance will improve.

Why is your Lab testing your patience this month? It could be for a few reasons. For example, your puppy has reached a learning plateau. It takes about 6 weeks before a dog's brain converts a behavior from short-term to long-term memory and it becomes a habit. As she's processing the change, she may act like she's forgotten a simple command. Just keep reviewing, and she'll catch up.

She might also be confused. Take a step back in her training and treat her like she's learning it for the first time. Remember, she'll get mixed up if you ask her to do something in a new place or if someone new asks her to do it. Even a simple sit might befuddle her. What's more, if she's uncertain, and that makes you uncertain, she senses your confusion and delays her response. When you're sure she understands what you're asking, act like you expect her to respond.

Or she might be testing you. You'll see her offer avoidance behaviors—refusing to look at you, barking at you, or bouncing around—if this is the case. Call her bluff, persevere, and reward her when she gives in.

For example, if your puppy sits but pops right back up, wait a second, and if she doesn't settle back into the sit, walk her around you and ask again. Take a few steps and command "Sit" again. Don't give her a treat until she sits promptly the first time you ask her.

If she rolls around and paws at your feet when you tell her "Down," don't touch her, and do not offer any praise, treats, or comments. Remain calm and firm, and repeat "Down" until she responds. Praise her and then quit.

If she won't come when she's called, attach a long line and reel her in. Be sure she complies every time; don't call her if you can't enforce it. Always praise her when she gets to you.

More Obedience Classes

Your Lab graduated with honors from puppy kindergarten. She's learning all these things you've been teaching her, and she's growing into a beautiful, well-behaved young dog. Why invest time and money in another obedience class? Beginning obedience may appear to be a review of the things she already knows, but it offers other benefits as well.

You may be ahead of the curve this month, but adolescence approaches, and your puppy still has a lot to learn about self-control and good behavior. Obedience classes give her the opportunity to socialize and hone her skills in a controlled environment with new dogs and people of all ages.

The structure of a class motivates you, and the rest of your family, to continue practicing with your puppy. You'll have the opportunity to ask questions and try different methods if something you're doing isn't working. No one training method is the best for every dog. There's probably going to be at least one other Lab in your class, so you'll be able to watch how other owners deal with the same challenges you've encountered. Watching other sporting breeds, who also mature late and are very active, will give you insight to your own dog's personality.

Plus, your puppy gets the opportunity to practice things she knows in a new place, and you'll discover if she really understands what you've taught her so far. The instructor will offer new and different distractions to challenge her, too.

Once basic class is completed, you can move up to the next level, where you prepare your Lab for off-leash control.

The Automatic Sit

While walking your Lab, tell her to sit every time you come to a stop. Pretty soon, she'll automatically sit for you. As always, when she's first learning this skill, give her a treat and praise as soon as she sits. As she gets the hang of it, you can continue to praise and *fade* the treats. Ultimately, you won't have to say "Sit" when you stop walking but she'll still take a seat.

> ## DOG TALK
>
> When teaching a new behavior, you reward with a treat every time your puppy complies. When she knows a skill, you can wean her off—or **fade**—the treats by skipping an occasional treat reward while still using verbal praise. As you produce a treat even less often, she'll get one only once in a while for her best effort. If her response isn't reliable, you may be reducing the number of treats too quickly.

Teach "Leave It"

The "Leave it" command is different from "Off." With this command, you want your puppy to turn her attention to you and away from whatever she's interested in. The idea is to prevent her from doing something before she gets too involved with it. You'll use this command in many situations, such as when you drop a cupcake on the floor, when she focuses on the cat across the street, or when she thinks about rolling in horse manure.

To teach "Leave it," put her on a leash and walk her past a treat or toy on the floor. As soon as she notices the item, say "Leave it," turn sharply, and walk away while making happy talk and luring her attention back to you. If she gets the item before you can say "Leave it," you're too close, so walk by the item farther away next time.

When she focuses on you instead of the item, praise her and give her a treat from your hand. Don't let her have the treat or toy on the floor. Practice several times, and she'll soon look at you for a treat as soon as you command, "Leave it." She'll be more motivated if the treat in your hand is one she likes better than the one on the floor.

Practice several times a day and with many different items. When she's reliably looking to you, try the same exercise without turning away. Just keep on walking while saying "Leave it." When she responds to your command, give her something else to do, like come or sit. If you release her, she'll just dive for the toy.

You and Your Puppy

Raising a Lab puppy shouldn't be all work and no play. Teach her to enjoy fun sports like swimming, but remember to also enjoy some quiet time together. Your Lab is ready and willing to do whatever you have in mind.

Fun in the Pool

Labs are born water dogs. Their webbed feet and water-resistant coat makes them naturals at a pool party. But wait! There's one detail you may not be aware of: puppies, even Labs, are not born knowing how to swim. You have to teach them. Once your Lab gets the hang of swimming, you'll have hours of fun together splashing and fetching.

> ### TIPS AND TAILS
>
> Never give your puppy access to a pool until she can swim the length of the pool and knows how to get out on her own. Even then, you should always be present. If you have a pool cover, don't let your puppy play on or under it. And don't throw your puppy in the pool. It will not force her to swim, but instead, she'll sink like a rock and drown. Your dog may never enjoy the water again, which is a tragedy for a Lab.

Start by letting your Lab play in water up to her chest in the bathtub or a kiddie pool. If she's been to the lake or ocean, this will speed up the process. Keep lessons short—maybe only 5 to 10 minutes the first day. Swimming is tiring, and it will likely frighten her at first.

First and most important, teach your Lab how to get out of the pool. Get in the pool with your puppy. Have her on a leash if you need to, and if you have a puppy lifejacket, put it on her. Sit on the step and hold her while letting her stand on the step. Pat the edge of the pool, and use a few treats to encourage her to jump out. Repeat until she starts to understand how to get in and out of the pool.

Now take your pup a foot or two away from the edge and hold her up in the water with your arms under her belly. Most pups start paddling with their front feet immediately, like they're trying to walk. If you don't hold her up, she'll be vertical, rear feet and tail deep in the water, pawing with her front feet as she tries to get out of the pool. She can't swim until she learns to level herself and get her rear up as high as her front.

Continue to hold her stomach up and let her paddle to the steps and get out. If she's willing, take her back in the water and do it again. Always turn her so she's swimming to the steps. You want her to think that's the only direction to swim. After a few tries, give her front end less support as she paddles. Pretty soon, you'll notice she's holding up her front end, and her rear feet are paddling, too. You'll gradually be able to give her stomach less and less support as she learns to hold herself up.

The process may take 1 day or it may take 5. Be sure swimming stays fun and not frightening.

Wait until she's completely comfortable swimming and getting in and out of the pool on her own before you let her jump off the edge into the water. Practice with other people in the pool and a lot of commotion around her, too.

Enjoying Quiet Time Together

You probably have fantasies of spending a cold winter's night in front of a roaring fireplace, reading a good book while your devoted Lab sleeps curled up on the rug at your feet.

It's probably hard to reconcile that picture with the active Lab puppy you have today. Even a puppy needs some down time, and so do you. Once she understands the nightly routine, she'll happily comply. Evenings are also a perfect time for her to keep the kids company while they do homework or watch television.

Your puppy should be able to lie at your feet without being crated or tethered all the time. As with everything else, practice makes perfect. The first few tries may be more training than relaxation, but she can learn it. If she's restless, be patient. It may take her a few minutes to settle down. Or start by having her on leash at your feet for just a few minutes each night.

She needs to learn that life goes on around her and she doesn't need to be in the middle of everything that happens. On the other hand, if you respond every time your little tornado asks for attention, she'll just pester you more and more.

A balance of training, play, and quiet companionship marks the beginning of the partnership you and your Labrador buddy will enjoy for years to come.

Socialization in public

Adult teeth are in—chewing continues

Enroll in basic obedience class

Moderate growth

Sexual maturity

Do you remember junior high school? Every day was full of drama and excitement. You weren't quite a teenager, but you weren't a little kid anymore either. Your body was changing, and you practiced acting like an adult, unsure about this new role.

Think of your Lab puppy going through this same experience. At 6 or 7 months old, he has the emotional maturity of a 12-year-old child, but his physical maturity is dawning. He'll be reckless and uninhibited while he's also insecure and clingy. Most of all, he'll be a whole lot of fun.

Physical Development

Although your puppy may not be fully sexually mature this month, the related hormones are developing. Soon you'll recognize changes in your Lab's appearance and behavior.

Female Sexual Maturity

Female Labs can mature anywhere from 6 to 18 months of age, but most have their first *heat* between 10 to 14 months. The heat cycle is a clear signal of sexual maturity. (In males the onset of puberty is much more uncertain.) A female dog goes into heat twice a year until she's spayed. During this time, you must keep her away from *intact* males to prevent pregnancy. An unneutered male will travel several miles to get to a female in season.

Heat is the period when a female dog is receptive to breeding and capable of getting pregnant. Also referred to as "in season," the cycle lasts 18 to 21 days. **Intact** refers to an unneutered male or unspayed female dog.

But before you start thinking you'll breed your Lab puppy now, know that a teenage dog is too young to breed. She's not yet emotionally mature enough to deal with a litter, and she may harm or abandon her puppies. In addition, the health testing she should have before being bred doesn't provide accurate results until she is 2 years old.

Now, back to her heat cycle. The first stage is called proestrus and lasts about 9 days. She will emit an odor that attracts males but reject any who come near her. Her vulva swells, and there's a slight bloody discharge. The first hint you may have that she's in heat is the gang of male dogs hanging out in your front yard.

The second stage is estrus, when the discharge increases and is pink in color. This period lasts about 7 days, and during this time, she'll accept a male for breeding. This is when she can get pregnant, and keeping her confined is critical. A chain-link fence isn't enough. A determined dog will breed *through* a fence. Keep her safely indoors.

Diestrus is the final stage of active heat, and it starts about the fourteenth day but may be as late as 20 days. The discharge is redder, the vulva returns to normal size, and she no longer accepts a male's advances. Diestrus lasts 60 to 90 days or until the female gives birth, approximately 63 days after conception. When the discharge and swelling have ended, the heat cycle is complete.

A Lab's heat cycle gets messy. Doggie diapers and pads are available to protect your house, but you should also wipe away the discharge regularly, and during the height of her heat you may want to clean her twice a day. Besides keeping your house cleaner, it will prevent skin irritation from excess moisture. She may also get cranky, mount other dogs, or try to escape and breed.

Estrogen is the primary female sex hormone. It maintains the female's sex organs and contributes to the development of a feminine appearance. Because of her estrogen, she'll have finer bone structure, be shorter, and weigh less than most males.

Male Sexual Maturity

Over the past several months, your male Lab's testicles have developed and begun to produce sperm, and soon he'll be capable of siring puppies. Male dogs have an increase in testosterone levels at 4 or 5 months, reaching a peak at 8 to 10 months. His testosterone levels taper off to normal adult levels at around 18 months.

Males don't have heat cycles like female dogs do. Once they reach maturity, they're always fertile. However, like a 6-month-old female, he's too young to be bred now. He doesn't have to raise a litter, but he's not old enough to have health clearances that ensure he won't pass on genetic defects to his offspring.

A sure sign of puberty in the male dog is when he starts lifting his leg while urinating. He may be more aggressive with other dogs and mount them during play.

An intact male will develop distinctly male physical characteristics as he matures. He'll have heavier bones than a female; a bigger, blockier head; and more muscle.

> **TIPS AND TAILS**
>
> To calm down an intact male dog when an in-heat female is near, dab a bit of pure vanilla extract (natural, not synthetic) or Vicks VapoRub around his nose to interfere with his ability to smell. To help mask the smell of a female in heat, put some Vicks on the fur around her tail. You can also give her one chlorophyll tablet twice a day beginning at the start of the heat cycle and continuing for the duration.

Health

Pet Labradors should be spayed (females) or neutered (males). Like any issue regarding your dog's health, you should understand why and when it should be done so you can make an educated decision.

In this section, we also take a look at some more external parasites that might plague your Lab, along with some genetically inherited Lab health issues.

Spaying and Neutering

There are many reasons to spay or neuter your dog and very few reasons to keep him or her intact. The main reason to spay or neuter is pet overpopulation. Shelters and Labrador Retriever rescue groups have hundreds of wonderful Labs available for adoption, sometimes even puppies. Even if you don't purposely breed your Lab, mixed-breed puppies from an accidental breeding have a slim chance of successfully remaining in the same home throughout their lives.

As you saw in previous chapters, being a responsible breeder is expensive and time-consuming. A breeder must ensure both parents have health exams and genetic tests and then spends weeks caring for the mother and her puppies. If something goes wrong, the costs can be huge. The breeder also keeps in touch with the new owners, answers their questions, and takes back a puppy any time during his life if the owner can no longer keep him.

Your breeder probably sold you your puppy on a limited registration, which means any puppies your Lab produces cannot be registered. Labs are the most popular breed in the United States and have been for the past 20 years. The AKC reports more than 100,000 Labs per year—and that just counts the ones who are registered. A lot of study goes into breeding dogs, and only the best of the best should be bred.

Besides the social issues, a spayed or neutered (altered) dog is simply much easier to live with. Your Lab will be more focused on you and less on other dogs. On the practical side, most dog day cares and many kennels won't accept unaltered dogs.

As sex hormones develop in your male Lab, they affect his behavior. He'll be easily distracted, less focused on you, harder to handle out in public, more likely to *mark* indiscriminately, and may not get along as well with other dogs. He will try to escape and roam when he senses a female in heat, even if she's miles away. An unneutered male is also more susceptible to several kinds of canine cancer.

> ### DOG TALK
>
> A mature dog **marks,** or deposits urine, so other dogs can identify him or her and determine his age or readiness to breed. Marking also establishes territorial boundaries.

Although a neutered male will still mark, he won't do it as often or in as many inappropriate places as an intact dog. Neutered males are less of a threat to other male dogs and therefore aren't challenged as often as they would be if they were intact.

Neutering a male dog consists of surgical removal of both testicles. Unless the testicles have been retained in the abdomen, it's a simple procedure and your Lab may go home the same day. The vet will use surgical glue or sutures to close the incision, and your Lab will have to wear an Elizabethan collar (head cone) for a few days to prevent him from chewing at and ripping open the incision. The testicular pouch usually remains and shrinks up into the abdomen.

Most dogs are able to resume normal activity the next day, but don't allow him to exercise too hard. Watch the incision to check for swelling, discharge, discoloration, or odors, which may indicate an infection. It will take several weeks for the testosterone level in his system to decrease.

TIPS AND TAILS

Spaying and neutering affects your Lab's sexual behavior, not his ability to learn. He'll still be able to hunt, compete in obedience, or participate in any other activities you choose. In fact, he'll perform *better* because his raging hormones won't distract him.

Female dogs also behave differently when they're intact. They're more likely to be aggressive toward other dogs, especially females. When in heat, a female is easily distracted, will try to escape, and will mark more to advertise her availability, bringing intact male dogs from miles around to your house. As her heat ends, she'll be aggressive to males. Her housetraining may lapse during this time, too.

When a female is in heat, she undergoes physical and emotional stress and a complete upset to her usual personality and health. She may not be able to participate in her regular activities like hunting, service, or therapy work.

Intact females are susceptible to more health problems than spayed females. They're prone to mammary cancer, pyometra (uterine infection), and other maladies caused by excess amounts of estrogen in their systems.

A spayed female's personality doesn't fluctuate wildly when she doesn't have the seasonal upset of heat cycles. One health issue that occurs in a few spayed females is urinary incontinence. She will leak a little urine while she sleeps. This condition is easily managed by inexpensive medication.

Spaying a female dog involves an abdominal incision to remove the ovaries and uterus, so it is more invasive than neutering a male. She will probably have sutures, which need to be removed after 10 to 14 days. She also will need an Elizabethan collar to prevent her from tearing out her stitches while they heal. Her activity should be restricted for the first few days.

Some vets advocate removing just the ovaries. This is a relatively new method of spaying, and some feel it leaves the dog in a more natural state. The surgery is also less physically traumatic. The risk of pyometra should be very low in a dog spayed this way.

The lack of estrogen after spaying does increase some dogs' appetites, so the old wives' tale about altered dogs getting fat is partially true. Regular exercise and monitoring her weight should keep her as trim as she needs to be with no problem.

For the past 20 years, animal shelter veterinarians have performed spay/neuter surgeries on dogs as young as 8 weeks old. Their motivation is clear: to prevent pet overpopulation. You shouldn't alter your Lab at such a young age. When considering when to alter your dog, long-term health effects of the surgery play an important role.

For years, veterinarians recommended that dogs be altered before puberty, meaning before a female's first heat or before a male starts lifting his leg. Today it's believed there are some benefits to waiting. Weigh these against your Lab's behavior and the inconvenience of having an unaltered dog before you make your decision. Discuss the risks and benefits with your veterinarian.

In both sexes, early spay/neuter surgery may cause a dog to grow taller than if he or she was allowed to mature. During puberty, the *growth plates* of your dog's limb bones grow quickly, and he gets taller. After puberty, the cartilage in the growth plates turns to bone, no new cartilage forms, and your dog stops growing. After the bones reach their full adult length, they expand and become wider, denser, and better able to support the weight of the adult dog. A Lab is usually full height by 8 or 9 months old, but the growth plates don't close until 10 to 14 months.

> ### DOG TALK
>
> **Growth plates** are discs at the end of each limb composed of soft cartilage. Growth plates are located in the hips, knees, elbows, and wrist bones. Older cartilage is eventually replaced by bone as your Lab grows.

Spay/neuter surgery removes the source of hormones that cause the growth plates in your dog's long bones to stop growing. If these hormones are removed, his bones continue to grow. So a dog neutered early will grow taller and lankier than he would if he was neutered later. In most dogs, this doesn't matter. But the growth plates in a dog's body close at different rates. If some close before your dog is altered and some afterward, he may develop odd proportions that impact the functioning of his joints long term.

In males, early neutering prevents some of the male sex characteristics from developing. A mature, unneutered male Lab will have heavier bones and shoulders and a blockier head than a neutered male. Females aren't going to develop these characteristics anyway, so it isn't a consideration. Early spaying in females slightly increases the risk of genital problems like vaginitis, due to the incomplete development of their external sex organs.

Other concerns regarding spay/neuter surgery before sexual maturity include the risk of bone cancer, the effect on the development of hip dysplasia, and reduced bone mass in the spine. All these risks are very small, and some have no effect on your dog's long-term health. If you're having behavioral issues with your intact Lab, spay or neuter now.

Mites and Mange

During month 7, your Lab puppy might have some pests you have to deal with. Although your Lab can be affected by some of them at any time during his life, this is the age when you may encounter these parasites for the first time.

Demodectic mange (demodicosis): The *Demodex canis* mite is present on all dogs. It doesn't cause problems unless the dog has a weak or compromised immune system, and it's not all that common to Labrador Retrievers. The mother passes the mites on to her puppies during the first few days of life. An active case is caused by abnormally large numbers of mites or by stress, which weakens the immune system. It most often shows up in puppies, who go through a tremendous number of changes in their early months: teething, vaccines, moving to a new home, hormonal changes, neutering, spaying, worming, and more.

Localized demodex is concentrated on the face and forelegs. It involves scaly reddened skin, hair loss, pustules, and plugged hair follicles. Symptoms often resolve and disappear on their own by 6 or 7 months of age.

Generalized demodex is much more rare in dogs, but it's much more serious. It develops from localized demodex and usually appears before 18 months of age. Symptoms include patchy hair loss, inflamed skin, enlarged lymph nodes, and severe itching, especially on the feet. Infected dogs are at risk of developing secondary bacterial infections.

Your vet diagnoses demodex by taking a skin scraping and examining it under a microscope. Sometimes the mites are difficult to find, and a skin biopsy is necessary for diagnosis. Treatment of generalized demodicosis includes miticidal dips and oral medication. Your vet will prescribe antibiotics for secondary skin infections.

Canine scabies (*Sarcoptes scabei*): Also called sarcoptic mange, these mites burrow under your dog's skin and cause intense itching. This highly contagious parasite affects young dogs more often than mature canines. Direct contact with an infected dog or infected wildlife transmits the mite to your puppy, where it immediately burrows into the outer layer of skin and lays eggs.

In addition to constant, intense itching, your dog will develop crusty pustules and hair loss, particularly on the elbows, tummy, edges of the ears, and front legs. Severe scratching and biting also cause infection.

Sarcoptic mites are much harder to see under a microscope, so diagnosis often is based on symptoms. Some oral flea and heartworm medications kill mites on your dog before an active infestation can occur. Treatment includes medicated shampoos, miticidal dips, and a course of ivermectin. Your vet may prescribe anti-inflammatories as well to make your Lab more comfortable.

Sarcoptic mange is a zoonotic disease humans can get from their dogs. In people, the mites die out on their own and no treatment is necessary.

Cheylethiellosis (*Cheyletiella yasguri*): These mites are most often seen on young and adolescent puppies. Infection is easy to prevent because the same insecticides that kill fleas work on these pests. The mites live on the skin's surface, and the main symptom is dandruff (scaling and crusting) along the dog's back. They can also cause itching and enlargement of the lymph nodes.

Cheylethiellosis mites are diagnosed by examining a skin scraping. Your vet will prescribe shampoos and miticidal dips. Other dogs and cats in the family should also be treated.

Ear mites (*Otodectes cynotis*): Ear mites cause a buildup of a reddish, waxy-looking substance in the ear. It can become so severe that the ear is blocked with debris. Symptoms of ear mites are similar to those of an ear infection: head shaking, scratching, and tilting his head. Even a small number of mites can set the stage for yeast or bacterial infections.

Once your veterinarian diagnoses ear mites, your dog will need a miticide to kill the mites and a prescription antibiotic or anti-inflammatory ointment to cure any resulting infections. The vet may also prescribe an ear wash. Your Lab's ears may be painful, and he'll resist letting you touch them. Some dogs are in so much pain, muzzling is necessary so you can administer the medication.

Lab Health Challenges

In recent years, researchers have made great strides identifying the genetic components of inherited diseases in Labrador Retrievers. You may have received copies of health clearances for the parents of your puppy from your breeder (see Months 1 and 2), so you know your own Lab has a lower risk of developing some of these conditions. If you didn't get clearances, here are the diseases, their symptoms, and their treatments.

Hip dysplasia: Widespread in Labradors, hip dysplasia develops as the dog matures and the head of the femur (ball) no longer fits properly into the hip socket. Symptoms can appear as early as 6 months of age, when a dog may show lameness in his hind legs, possibly caused by overactive play. When a vet manipulates the rear legs, the dog will show evidence of joint pain. X-rays are used to confirm the diagnosis. The vet will prescribe crate rest and analgesic drugs, but the pain and lameness will reoccur as soon as the puppy is active again.

Hip dysplasia ranges from mild to severe. Some dogs never show symptoms, even though they're mildly affected. Others develop symptoms as they age because the hip joints develop osteoarthritis.

In a young dog, 8 to 14 months old, surgery might be an option. A triple pelvic osteotomy (TPO) is a procedure where the surgeon cuts the hipbone in three places and rotates it so it will heal in a better position, supporting the ball of the femur. As long as arthritis hasn't already developed, most dogs can return to normal activity. This is major surgery, and the recovery time is several months; your dog must remain inactive for long periods, working back up to normal exercise slowly.

For an older dog, total hip replacement surgery is an option. The ball and socket are removed and replaced with metal and plastic, similar to the same procedure in humans. This option also involves a long recovery period.

For dogs who aren't candidates for surgery, owners can take steps to make their Labs more comfortable, like avoiding high-impact activities like jogging or anything else painful for the dog. Low-impact exercise like walking and swimming help build muscle mass, and anti-inflammatory drugs ease the pain. These dogs shouldn't be allowed to carry extra weight because obesity is hard on joints. Many people give their dogs supplements like glucosamine and chondroitin to lubricate joints and to ease the arthritic symptoms.

A responsible breeder waits to breed until her dogs are 2 years old and have been x-rayed and cleared to minimize the possibility of producing puppies with hip dysplasia. However, there is a slight chance two parents who are clear can still produce hip dysplasia.

Elbow dysplasia: This inherited disease is also far too common in Labradors. It's caused by abnormal development of the three bones that make up the elbow joint, which leads to formation of bone chips and areas of loose cartilage. You won't know your dog has elbow dysplasia until you notice front lameness, usually after exercise. He may also move with an unusual gait in front, throwing his elbows slightly out.

Although symptoms can start as early as 4 months, most Labs don't show signs of hip or elbow dysplasia until they're older and the condition causes arthritis in the joints. If your puppy has symptoms, have your veterinarian examine him to correctly diagnose any problems.

Treatment of elbow dysplasia is similar to that for hip dysplasia. Walking, swimming, and other non–weight-bearing exercise, and keeping your Lab at a lean weight reduces pressure on the joints and helps build muscle strength. Anti-inflammatory medications ease the pain. Joint supplements may also help.

Arthroscopic surgery can remove the bone chips in the elbows to make your Lab more comfortable. As with hip dysplasia, breeding dogs should be x-rayed at 2 years of age and not bred if they show signs of the disease.

Exercise-induced collapse (EIC): Young adult Labs of field breeding seem to be the most common victims of EIC, but it has also been seen in show-bred Labs. Although it can happen as young as 4 months, most dogs are at least a year old when the first episode occurs. This often coincides with the beginning of intense hunting training.

An affected Lab in the midst of exercise will suddenly have an uneven gait or appear uncoordinated and eventually completely collapse. The dog will still be conscious and may try to get up and continue running but will appear confused and disoriented. Symptoms worsen for 3 to 5 minutes. The dog does not appear to be in pain, and he usually recovers within 5 to 25 minutes. Some dogs have died during an episode when they were allowed to continue exercising. Dogs seem to be more likely to suffer an episode during hot and humid weather. People sometimes think their Lab is suffering from heatstroke, but the symptoms are different. (See Month 8 to learn about recognizing and treating heatstroke.)

Labs with intense drive and excitable personalities seem to be more likely to be affected by EIC. If they're prevented from excessive exercise and excitement, they can live an otherwise normal life. There's no cure for EIC, but a genetic test is available, and dogs used for breeding should be screened for this disease.

Progressive retinal atrophy (PRA): A disease of the retina that affects many breeds of dogs, PRA is especially prevalent in Labs. The cells of the retina die and eventually cause blindness. First, night vision decreases and then daytime vision diminishes, and ultimately the dog's eyesight fails completely. Labs don't usually show symptoms until they're middle-aged, at about 5 to 8 years old. Dogs adapt well to blindness, and you may not notice your dog is affected until you move the furniture or take him somewhere where he's unfamiliar with the room layout.

An ophthalmologist can diagnose PRA in a puppy or adult, but there is no treatment. Fortunately, the genes causing PRA have recently been discovered and a test is available to identify dogs who carry or are affected with the disease long before they show any symptoms.

Retinal dysplasia: Another genetically inherited eye disorder, retinal dysplasia is caused by abnormal development of the retina. There is no treatment or cure. Responsible breeders take the entire litter of puppies in to be checked by an ophthalmologist at 7 or 8 weeks old. Puppies who are at risk for retinal dysplasia may have retinal folds visible at this age.

Mildly affected dogs may never show obvious symptoms, while other dogs will be completely blind if the retina is completely detached. Affected dogs may also suffer from cataracts or glaucoma. There is no genetic test at this time, so breeders must have their dogs checked annually for signs of the disease.

Tricuspid valve dysplasia (TVD): A defect on the right side of the heart, TVD is the most common type of heart disease in Labrador Retrievers. This malformation causes blood to leak back into the right atrium and causes the heart to work harder. TVD varies in severity, and a mildly affected dog can live a long, normal life. In severe cases, it causes congestive heart failure and death.

Symptoms include excess fluid buildup in the abdomen, which might make you think your dog is getting fat. An affected dog also tires easily and is not as active. Symptoms can develop when your Lab is a puppy or not until years later when signs of heart failure develop. To diagnose, your veterinarian may first listen for a heart murmur. Chest x-rays and heart ultrasound provide confirmation of the disease.

Treatment includes limiting your dog's exercise and feeding a low-salt diet. Occasionally, it may be necessary to remove excess fluid from the abdominal cavity. Some dogs respond to cardiac medications, too.

A genetic test is not yet available to identify TVD, but responsible breeders have their dogs examined by a cardiologist to be sure they are clear of the disease.

TIPS AND TAILS

This list of genetically inherited conditions sounds scary, but don't panic. Labs are generally healthy. By learning about these diseases, you'll recognize any symptoms that show up in your puppy and be able to get an affected dog treated before he becomes seriously ill.

Nutrition

As you look at the many choices available in the pet-food aisle, choosing the right food for your Lab can seem like playing blind man's bluff. Just close your eyes and point. How can you possibly figure out the differences between brands or decipher the tiny type on the labels? With a little education, you can make an informed decision.

All dogs have the same basic nutritional needs: protein, fiber, moisture, vitamins, minerals, carbohydrates, and fats (see Month 2). And that's where the similarity in dog foods ends. Any one food on the market will not meet the needs of every dog. The following sections outline some basic facts to help guide you through the dog-food maze.

Who's in Charge of Pet Foods?

Pet-food companies are required to list ingredients and meet manufacturing standards regulated by several federal organizations. Individual states get in on the act, too.

The Food and Drug Administration (FDA), through its Center for Veterinary Medicine, regulates which ingredients are allowed in pet food, the manufacturing process, and what health claims a manufacturer can legally make. The FDA, working with the U.S. Department of Agriculture (USDA), defines the exact requirements for terminology used on labels. (The USDA is also involved in establishing regulations for identification and approval of pet-food ingredients.) The FDA, along with state and local agencies, also inspects manufacturing plants to ensure compliance with labeling laws. The actual food itself does not have to be preapproved by the FDA.

The American Association of Feed Control Officials (AAFCO) is comprised of officials from local, state, and federal agencies who enforce laws regarding production, labeling, distribution, and/or sale of pet foods. AAFCO specifies the minimum and maximum percentages of nutrients that must appear in a food to be considered "complete and balanced." It also designates requirements regarding product names, flavor designations, and ingredient names that appear on the label. AAFCO also publishes testing requirements manufacturers must follow to meet safety and nutritional standards.

The FDA, USDA, and AAFCO are the heavy hitters, but a few other groups are also involved. The Federal Trade Commission (FTC) works to prevent misleading advertising by requiring manufacturers to conform to truth-in-advertising standards. The Pet Food Institute is a lobbying group that represents pet-food manufacturers.

What's on a Label?

With so many regulators involved, the information that appears on the label can be hard to understand at first glance. A dog-food bag is primarily a marketing tool, with the secondary function of accurately disclosing any information required by law.

When you see pretty pictures of raw beef, colorful carrots, peas, and corn in an attractive arrangement on the bag, the graphics are designed to convince you, the consumer, to buy that brand. The wording, however, is strictly regulated.

The product name: Several rules exist regarding the name:

🐾 A product can only be named "chicken" if it contains at least 95 percent chicken.

🐾 A product labeled "beef dinner for dogs" must contain at least 25 percent beef (excluding water sufficient for processing).

🐾 If the name is "beef formula" (or "recipe," "platter," "entrée"), the product is only required to contain 3 percent of the named ingredient.

🐾 If the label states "with beef," it is required to have at least 3 percent beef.

🐾 A product labeled "beef flavor" must have enough beef to make it taste beefy. Manufacturers are allowed to use artificial flavoring or a small quantity of extract from beef tissues. There may be no beef at all.

Guaranteed analysis: This list states the minimum percentages of protein and fat and the maximum percentages of fiber and moisture in the food. These are not exact numbers, so you're getting only a rough idea of the percentages. Companies are not required to list the percentage of carbohydrates, and the guarantee says nothing about the quality or digestibility of the ingredients that make up the food.

Complete and balanced: Besides percentages, in order to declare a food is complete and balanced, manufacturers must show their food meets the nutrient requirements in one of three ways:

🐾 Through actual feeding trials. This may sound like the best method, but there's debate over how realistic this testing is. Dogs eat the tested food for a period of time, and their health is then measured.

🐾 By formulating the food to meet AAFCO's minimum and maximum standards, confirmed by laboratory testing.

🐾 By stating the food is a "family member" of another of the company's foods that has passed feeding trials or met formulation standards.

Life stages: A dog food is labeled either complete and balanced "for all life stages," "growth," or "maintenance." There is no designation for senior foods.

> **TIPS AND TAILS**
>
> Some foods are not meant to be fed as a complete diet but instead are suggested for supplemental feeding. The label will state "complete and balanced" if the food is formulated for complete nutrition.

Miscellaneous: The company's name and address are required. Many also include their phone number, email address, and website address so consumers can contact them with questions. The bag is also printed with the disclaimer that it contains dog food, not food meant for people, along with the net weight of the contents.

Expiration date: The "best by" date is a stamped or printed code that tells you the latest date food should be used. Some companies include the manufacture date so you can estimate the food's shelf life. Naturally preserved foods don't last as long as those that contain artificial preservatives. Most foods are safe if used within 1 year of manufacture. If a food is close to its "best by" date, you know it has been sitting somewhere for a while.

Ingredients list: This is the most important part of a dog-food label. Like human food, dog-food ingredients are listed in order by volume, from the most to the least included in the food. It can be tricky to decipher what you're actually reading here. The first six ingredients are by far the most meaningful, but there are some other key things you should look for, too.

Understanding Ingredients

The first ingredient listed on your dog's food should be an animal protein source. *Meat* could mean cows, pigs, goats, or sheep. You could also find poultry, venison, bison, and fish listed. Ideally, you want to know what kind of animal the protein source is from.

The meat used in dog food has had much of the water cooked out. Meat meal (or chicken meal, etc.), on the other hand, is made of meat, bone, skin, fat, and connective tissue from which the water has been removed, so it contains more protein per pound than just meat. If meat meal isn't listed first, look for it as a second or third ingredient. Meat makes the food taste good; meat meal boosts the animal protein content. Animal by-products are less desirable and can include things like heads, feet, hooves, hide trimmings, and more.

Another source of protein is plant proteins, which are less expensive. When you see corn or wheat *gluten* on a label, that's a plant protein source. These may be harder for your dog to digest.

> **DOG TALK**
>
> **Gluten** is a mixture of two proteins found in processed grains like wheat or barley. Derived from the Latin term for "glue," gluten literally helps dog food stick together and adds a chewy texture.

When you look at the first three or four ingredients on a dog-food label, you might see chicken, corn gluten, wheat gluten, etc. Although chicken is listed first, the combination of the second two may contribute a larger percentage of protein than the chicken.

Also look for whole vegetables, fruits, and grains, which contain vitamins, enzymes, and antioxidants that haven't been stripped by processing. Dogs are carnivores, but they eat both plants and animals. They've been eating grains for as long as commercial dog food has been around, and grains are a source of carbohydrates as well as protein. Cereal grain–based carbohydrates are fine for many dogs, while others may have trouble digesting them. Whole grains are more digestible than processed grains like wheat flour or rice flour. Additional healthy carbohydrate sources include beans, sweet potatoes, and apples.

Farther down the list, you'll find the preservatives. Preservatives extend the shelf life of food, preventing vitamin loss and rancidity from the fats. Natural preservatives like vitamin C and mixed tocopherols are more desirable than synthetic preservatives like BHA, BHT, and ethoxyquin.

When you see little green things that look like peas and orange bits of so-called carrots in your dog's food, don't be fooled. Those bits of kibble aren't necessarily peas or carrots. Manufacturers add dyes and binders to make it look like vegetables to attract *you,* not your dog. If vegetables are included, they're either part of the mixture that makes up the kibble, or mixed into the food after the kibble is made.

Grooming

Continue your Lab puppy's education this month by teaching him to allow you to brush his teeth—a critical chore that has major health consequences if neglected. You want your puppy to enjoy, or at least tolerate, having his teeth brushed because you're going to be doing it every week (or more often) for the rest of his life.

And because your Lab is pretty inquisitive as a teenager, we also help you prepare for the most obnoxious grooming chore ever: bathing a skunked Lab.

Brushing Those Pearly Whites

Now that your puppy's adult teeth are in, they need regular attention, just like your own teeth do. Many dogs have gum disease by the time they're 3 years old, so early care is essential. Though some wear and tear is inevitable as your puppy ages, you can hold off gum disease by practicing good brushing habits early.

Although Labs chew a lot and that removes some *dental plaque*, it's not enough. Chewing on hard surfaces like bones only cleans the exposed areas of the teeth. Chewing also is the main cause of broken teeth, which can get infected. A Lab who chews throughout his life will completely wear down his teeth to the gum line and expose the nerves. Even chewing tennis balls is bad. They seem soft, but constant chewing can still wear down his teeth.

> ### DOG TALK
>
> **Dental plaque** is a buildup of bacteria on your dog's teeth that, if allowed to remain and harden, discolors and turns into tartar.

Gum disease causes severe pain and infection, which spreads through your Lab's system into his body, causing kidney or heart disease. If his gums aren't healthy, they recede, causing pockets to form at the base of his teeth where bacteria collect and cause infection. You'll notice that his gums are red, inflamed, and bleed easily. Bad breath can also be a sign of infection or gum disease. To keep his gums healthy, massage them with the toothbrush while you brush his teeth.

Besides cleaning his teeth and massaging his gums, regular brushing gives you the opportunity to inspect your Lab's mouth for broken teeth and tumors. He may also have a bit of bone, a sliver of a stick, or dog food stuck between his teeth. If your dog seems to have trouble eating, suspect a broken tooth or gum problems. Dogs don't usually get cavities like humans do because they don't eat as many sugary treats.

Although your Lab will need a professional teeth cleaning at some point, it will take much less time and be less painful for him if you practice regular dental care at home. The doctor will anesthetize your dog, remove the tartar, and polish his teeth, while cleaning thoroughly beneath the gum line. The doctor will also remove cracked or loose teeth and check for abnormalities.

Your Lab won't automatically allow you to mess with his mouth, especially in this new, unfamiliar way. But you can get him used to it with some muzzle-touching lessons. If you've been practicing handling him since he was a baby, you're way ahead of the game. But still, he'll probably try to turn it into a play session.

Put your hand gently over his muzzle from the top. Just touch it for a moment and release so he won't have a chance to struggle. Don't clamp your hand on his muzzle at first. It's normal for him to resist; this is a move his mother used to discipline him. Feed him a treat with your other hand while you're lightly touching him.

As you work up to more pressure and longer time, he may flip his head around. Don't let go. Just follow his head and reward him by releasing when he stops. Ultimately, you want to put your fingers behind his upper canines and open his mouth.

This lesson also makes life easier for your vet when he needs to examine your Lab's mouth. You'll also use it later if he has a run-in with a porcupine or gets something stuck in his mouth.

To brush your Lab's teeth, you'll need to use a toothbrush made for humans, a fingertip brush, or even a piece of gauze wrapped around your finger. Human toothpaste can cause a serious stomach upset if your Lab swallows it, so purchase meat-flavored doggie toothpaste. You can also use baking soda mixed with water to form a paste.

HAPPY PUPPY

Let your Lab hold a ball or big chew toy in his mouth while you brush his back teeth.

Begin by massaging your puppy's mouth with your finger so he'll get used to the sensation. Next, add some doggie toothpaste so he'll learn to enjoy the taste. Gradually transition to using a toothbrush instead of your finger. Brush along his front gum line using small circles, covering both his teeth and gums. Hold the bristles at a slight angle so it isn't abrasive on his gums.

Brush his back teeth, holding the brush at an angle while using back-and-forth strokes. Concentrate on the molars in the back, where food gets stuck between his teeth and cheek. The inside of his molars won't have as much plaque buildup because his tongue washes away excess food. Do a portion of his mouth each day until he's used to the routine and accepts it.

Skunked!

Is there anything worse than the smell of a freshly skunked dog? You let him out for a last pee of the night, and when he comes back in … ack! Run for the tomato juice!

There are more effective ways to remove the skunk smell than tomato juice. Bathe your dog in the following mixture:

> 1 quart 3 percent hydrogen peroxide
>
> ¼ cup baking soda
>
> 2 teaspoons Dawn dish detergent

Mix the ingredients just before using, and lather your Lab's *dry* coat thoroughly, down to the skin, and rinse well. Be sure to keep the mixture out of his eyes because the hydrogen peroxide will burn. Use a soapy washcloth around his head, and rinse his face carefully.

You'll know immediately if the smell is dissipating. You may have to repeat this treatment several times, so be prepared to make more of the mixture.

Social Skills

As your Lab speeds toward sexual maturity, he needs to continue meeting and interacting with other dogs. He is changing, and others will sense that difference and treat him differently, and he'll need to adjust his behavior accordingly. A dog who stays in the backyard for the next few months will be in for a rude awakening when he finally ventures out in public.

Dog Day Care

Dog day care is a great place for your Lab to have supervised interaction with other friendly dogs. If you select a facility staffed by conscientious professionals, he'll have fun, burn off endless energy, and polish his dog manners. Regular attendance 2 or 3 days a week is easier on your dog and less disruptive for the facility because the dogs all know each other and don't have to get reacquainted each time they visit.

There is no legal requirement that dog day care facilities be certified in any way or that employees demonstrate dog-handling skills. No national oversight organization exists, either. Anyone can hang out a sign and offer doggie day care. The local health department usually monitors cleanliness and hazardous materials compliance, and sometimes local animal control will require a kennel license, which specifies standards for the facility, not the staff.

When you contact the dog day care, expect to fill out an application and attend a get-acquainted visit with your dog. The facility will require up-to-date shot records for DHPP, rabies, and bordetella (kennel cough). They may also require proof of a clear fecal test from your vet, showing your dog is free of internal parasites. Your Lab should also be on a regular flea and tick preventative. Most dog day cares require your dog be spayed or neutered after a designated age.

While the manager is busy checking out you and your Lab, ask some questions of your own. You may not be allowed to enter the doggie playroom. Don't take that as a red flag; a stranger walking into a room full of dogs can cause an uproar, and scuffles or fights may break out. You won't be able to see the dogs at normal play firsthand. Instead, many day cares have a doggie webcam or a one-way mirror so you can see the dog playroom.

Here are some points to consider when checking out doggie day cares:

🐾 How many dogs does the facility allow per day?

🐾 Are there separate groups for high-energy and low-energy dogs?

🐾 Are small dogs separated?

🐾 What is the staff-to-dogs ratio?

🐾 What training have employees had regarding dog handling and behavior?

🐾 What are the hours? Are there limited drop-off and pickup times? What about Saturdays?

🐾 Are there special pricing packages? Are ½-day rates offered?

🐾 Do the dogs play all day, or is there a specified nap time?

If you can, watch the employees; are they paying attention to the dogs or in the corner, texting on their cell phones?

No facility, and no dog, is perfect. Accidents can happen, and occasionally a dog is injured by an accidental bite during play or a scuffle. Who is responsible for the vet bill when an accident happens? How do they decide if the offending dog will be allowed to come back?

If you choose carefully, dog day care can be a rewarding experience for you and your Lab.

Teaching "Wait"

"Wait" helps your Lab puppy refine his manners. Ask him to wait before he goes through a doorway, before he eats dinner, and before he jumps out of the car. "Wait" means he's not allowed to move forward until he gets an okay from you. He doesn't have to sit; he doesn't have to lie down. Different from "Stay," with "Wait" he doesn't have to remain in place until you touch him. This is a temporary pause, not a stay.

Teach this skill with your Lab on a leash. Start in a doorway. As the two of you start through, your Lab will undoubtedly try to rush ahead. Say "Wait," and give him the hand signal you use for stay—an open palm in front of his nose. Walk through the door, and if doesn't try to follow, tell him "Okay," and let him walk through after you. If he does try to follow you, body block him with your hip and turn to face him. Continue to block his way through the door until he stops trying and is still, whether standing or sitting. He'll probably look at you, which is what you want. Now tell him "Okay," give him a treat while he's still on the other side of the doorway, and let him walk through.

Practice this many times in many different doorways. Practice in the car, both getting in and getting out. He'll try to read your body language for a signal he can move. Practice moving around a little without letting him through so he learns he has to wait for your "Okay" release word.

It's tempting to say "Wait … wait … no … stay … WAIT!" while you're teaching this command. That will just confuse him. Is he staying or waiting? Dogs really do learn the difference. When you give the command multiple times, he anxiously watches you instead of relaxing and waiting for the release word.

The learning curve may be long and trying for this lesson. It's an advanced concept, but he's old enough to understand it now.

Introducing a New Animal

When your Lab was just a pup, you introduced him to the cat, the rabbit, the pet snake, and any other animals in the house. He should continue to meet different species so he remembers and is able to deal with any new animal he encounters throughout his life.

If you have the opportunity, visit a place where he can meet some really big "dogs." Donkeys, sheep, goats, ponies, peacocks, or geese are all critters he can get to know. (Be sure to have someone restrain the other animal so he can't run away or attack.) Terry's own Lab grew up with horses but he was fascinated the first time he met a miniature horse. It was an entirely new creature to him.

Use your jolly routine, treats, and patience while your puppy checks out the animal, such as a horse, from a short distance. Don't approach until your pup is calm. Barking, lunging, and raised hackles will only scare the animal. Have the owner move the other animal around a little so your Lab sees it walking and realizes it is a living being.

When he's ready to approach, keep the leash loose so he doesn't feel trapped. If he lunges, turn away and keep trying until he can restrain himself. This may be all you can do on the first encounter. If so, practice with a number of animals so he learns this is the proper way to respond to a new animal.

A friendly horse will put her nose down and say hi to your Lab. They'll sniff each other's breath. Don't let your puppy jump up against the fence or the horse, though. When you're done, praise your pup and walk away.

> **TIPS AND TAILS**

If the horse is frightened, keep your distance. A scared horse will strike out with her front feet. It could be that the horse is learning, too.

Playing Too Rough

Your preteen Lab loves to play, and you love to play with him. But even though you're just playing games, he's learning which behaviors are allowed and which aren't. Be careful what you teach him. Between 6 and 7 months, your puppy is figuring out how strong he is, and he'll naturally try to use his body in his dealings with others. If he's allowed to roughhouse, he'll decide it's okay.

In his childish enthusiasm, your Lab forgets himself, bowling over smaller or weaker dogs and body blocking his way across the playing field. His newly raging hormones encourage him to try a new behavior: mounting. Play that was fine in a 12-week-old puppy is now too much for many of his peers. His playmates will tell him when he's played too roughly; they'll growl, snap at him, and chase him away. This helps him learn to mind his manners. Watch these interactions closely, and intervene if your puppy isn't getting the message. You want other dogs to discipline him, but you don't want an all-out fight.

It's one thing to roughhouse with his buddies, but he also needs limits when he plays with you and your family. At this age, he'll jump on you, crash into you while he runs around the yard, slam into your legs, and grab your arms. You may enjoy the game, but when he crashes into someone else, it won't be so cute. He could injure someone, or he could be injured, too. He could land wrong and tear a ligament, crack immature bones, or tear muscles.

Once a 6-month-old Lab clipped the back of Terry's knees in the driveway, popped her up in the air, and dropped her down on her head. She spent 5 days in the hospital with a fractured skull and a month recovering. It can happen to you, too.

Interrupt active games with some control exercises. Have him sit before he retrieves the ball, and practice "Off." When kids are playing, slow everyone down, introduce some structured games, or quit when things get overly rough.

Before we leave this section, we want to say a word about tug-of-war. Playing tug-of-war teaches your Lab all the wrong things. He learns to growl aggressively at you, and he's rewarded for holding on and refusing to let go. Tug-of-war makes a pushy dog pushier and encourages grabbing, biting hard, and jumping. Labs are blissfully happy when they can retrieve all day; they don't need over-the-top aggressive games.

Behavior

Be patient. This month your Lab puppy will have moments where he seems to have forgotten everything you've so diligently taught him. He may not come when he's called, or he may not fetch because his teeth hurt. Just remember that this, too, will pass.

Teenage Regression in Behavior

What looks like a regression in behavior to you is more like a new awakening on your puppy's part. Seemingly overnight, your previously well-behaved and adoring pup has deteriorated into a wild child. His interactions with other dogs may have also deteriorated as he has practiced new ways of dealing with others.

Problem aggression and anxieties may develop during this time, but they also recede as your puppy finds his way. Spaying or neutering makes a huge difference in his behavior, lessening fighting, marking, and bullying among dogs.

Because he's distracted by his adolescence, your puppy's obedience skills may falter, and you'll be required to use a stronger hand to control and redirect his behavior. This is the age when many Labs are relegated to the backyard because of their overly boisterous behavior.

Adolescence may last until your Lab is 2 or 3 years old. It may be small comfort to know he'll get over it, but if you continue to work with your Lab, he'll get through this period, and so will you.

Here are some of the behaviors you may see:

🐾 Shyness or fearfulness

🐾 Destructive, acting-out behavior to satisfy his endless energy

🐾 Housetraining relapse, marking

🐾 Aggression

🐾 Overexuberance

🐾 Bossy, rude, always testing the rules

🐾 Ignores your commands, distracted

🐾 No self-control or ability to resist temptation

🐾 Overprotective

We help you deal with all these issues in this and upcoming chapters.

A Second Fear Period

The fear imprint period that was so important during your puppy's first 2 or 3 months may come back to haunt your dog this month. If your Lab had a bad experience in a particular room when he was 8 weeks old, he may seem to suddenly remember that event now, months later.

The adolescent fear period starts between 6 and 14 months, and can last anywhere from a few days to several weeks. He's going through major physiological and psychological changes now. The fear period seems to correspond to growth spurts, and his anxiety may vary from day to day. He may spook or bark aggressively at something he's seen a thousand times, like the mailbox at the curb. Don't overreact. In most cases, you can ignore the behavior. As you did when he was a baby, let him approach scary things when he's ready, and don't force him into a situation where he feels overwhelmed.

A well-socialized dog will get through this period much more quickly than a dog who has been kept at home and isolated. Your normal, happy, friendly Lab will grow out of it with less trouble than some other hypersensitive breeds. Be sure to keep him on leash in public in case something frightens him.

Still Chewing

By 6½ months, your Lab's adult teeth are in, but they won't completely set in the jawbones until 8 or 9 months. So until then, he'll continue to be a chewing machine. And because he's bigger and stronger now, he'll be more destructive.

Labs especially enjoy chewing on wood. Stair rails, 2×4s, fence posts, shingles, and other things you'd never imagine he'd eat are all fair game. Invest in some chew-repellent products at your local pet-supply store, or make some of your own with red pepper sauce in a bottle of water.

Chew toys are as important now as they've ever been, and diligent supervision on your part will protect your more vulnerable household treasures. Provide a variety of chewables: stuffed frozen Kongs, tire toys, and heavy nylon bones. You'll have to keep an eye on him and remove toys that don't withstand his chainsaw molars. He may lose interest in a certain toy. Put it away for a week or two, and it will be exciting when you bring it out again.

When you give your Lab something new to chew on, supervise him to be sure he isn't going to immediately destroy it and swallow pieces. You can offer some softer toys, like retrieving bumpers, and then put them away when you can't watch him.

Marking

You know your Lab has reached adolescence when he starts lifting his leg. Testosterone levels start to rise as young as 4 or 5 months old. But it isn't just the boys; females mark, too, just not as often or as obviously.

A male Lab will hike up his rear leg so his hip is perpendicular to the ground, while a female will usually lift one rear leg forward while still squatting. Both may kick the ground with their rear legs to spread the scent of their urine. By doing this, your dog is announcing his sexual maturity and laying claim to that territory, whether at home or away.

When your puppy starts marking, the scent of his or her urine has changed, and any other dog who smells it will know there's a new sexually mature dog in town. No longer can he roll over on his back and leak a little urine to get the big boys to back off. Other adult males will know he's an adolescent, and his permission to misbehave is immediately revoked. Many male adults will put a teenage dog in his place before he gets too full of himself and tries to challenge the older dogs.

On walks, your male dog will mark repeatedly and often in unacceptable places, like on the neighbor's car. You'll catch him marking over where another dog has just urinated, too. His motives are not just territorial. Dogs read each other's urine like we read the daily newspaper—comedian Dave Barry called it "yellow journalism." They learn who's been to this spot, when, and the other dog's age and sexual maturity. Then your Lab leaves his own calling card. A dog often releases just a tiny bit of urine, like he's saving up so he has enough for the entire excursion.

There's no reason to let him get away with impolite marking behavior. Correct him and move on; don't just stop and wait while he has a good sniff and lines up to pee. Once excessive marking becomes a habit, it's a hard one to break. Most dogs continue marking after they're neutered, although not as often.

Sexual maturity can also mean a sudden lapse in housetraining. It's not really a housetraining issue; it's marking. Males will lift their leg indoors and out, on any vertical surface they can reach. Females will mark indoors, too.

Treat it like any other accident. Interrupt your dog with a loud "No!" or "Ack!" and take him out to his assigned potty spot you created when he first came to live with you. Go back to supervising him indoors and crating him when you can't. Deal with the problem like he's on his first day of housetraining as an 8-week-old puppy. You can't stop a dog from lifting his leg or marking, but you can teach him where and when he's allowed to go.

> **TIPS AND TAILS**
>
> During this time, you might consider a belly band, which wraps around your dog's belly to absorb the urine. You may have to use this for several months until he gets out of the habit of marking in the house.

Training

Training is a lifelong process, but it doesn't have to be misery. You're investing time raising a well-behaved puppy so you can enjoy years of companionship and fun together. Once you lay the foundation, he'll only need an occasional brush-up to keep his skills sharp and his responses eager.

As he reaches adolescence, a Lab will put your patience to the test. Two or three months now of diligent effort—don't forget to keep it fun!—are worth the payoff.

Practice Makes Perfect

Your Lab may be an obedience champion when you're in the backyard practicing, but does he really understand the commands? And can he perform out in public when you're under stress and really need him to behave?

Dogs depend on body language for much of their communication. What happens if your arms are full of groceries and you can't give him a hand signal along with a command?

Test your dog to see if he really understands "Sit." Face your Lab, ask him to sit, and use your hand signal. He sits. Good. Release him. Now look away, ask him to sit, and stand perfectly still with no body language, eye contact, or hand signal. Did he do it? If not, he still needs some guidance. When he can perform all the commands you've taught him without any visual cues, you know he gets it.

When your dog is doing a solid sit-stay and down-stay, it's time to add some distractions. He'll make mistakes and get up when he's not supposed to; that's how he learns exactly what stay means.

Here's a progression of increasing distractions to help your Lab understand the stay:

- 🐾 Put him in a sit-stay. While you're still holding the leash, start to walk around him. His head will follow you, and his natural response will be to stand up as you leave his field of vision. Touch his muzzle with your hand to remind him to stay in place as you move.

- 🐾 Once he can stay with you circling him while he's on-leash, drop the leash and try it.

- 🐾 Circle in the other direction.

- 🐾 Circle from farther away.

- 🐾 Turn your back on him, and walk away several steps before turning to face him.

- 🐾 Crouch down without saying anything. Don't look at him. You're not trying to lure him out of place; you want to help him succeed.

Every time he stays in place, verbally praise him from a distance. You don't want him to get excited and get up, but you do want him to know he's done it correctly. He also has to learn that praise doesn't mean "We're finished." Always end up at his side, touch him and say "Okay" to release him. Then have a party! When he makes a mistake, just put him back and continue. No scolding. Take plenty of breaks between tries, and quit when he's done something especially well.

The ultimate practice is to make obedience commands part of everyday life, at home and in public. Practice on walks, at the park, and wherever else you take him. At home, he should sit for his dinner, while you brush his teeth or clip his nails, and while you put a leash on him. He should do a down-stay while you do dishes, brush him, or eat dinner.

Your Lab should walk nicely on a leash wherever you take him. He should wait politely at doorways and wait for permission to jump out of the car. Take time to train throughout the day, and pretty soon it won't be training anymore and you'll have a well-behaved Labrador.

Teaching Cooperation, Not Confrontation

A puppy who misbehaves isn't engaging in mutiny, he's just being a teenager. And the only way to respond is with consistent guidance and training. Your dog adores you, but the Lab is a strong-minded breed, and he actually will behave better with discipline and structure. As he challenges you, look for opportunities to build your relationship with your dog.

Reward your dog throughout the day, not just during training sessions. You may not have noticed that perfect sit he offered while you were fixing his dinner, or the way he went to his crate at bedtime without being told. Make a deposit in the bank of goodwill, and praise him when you see he's on his best behavior.

If you correct him or interrupt an unwanted behavior, always give him a chance to do something right and earn rewards. Say "Good boy!" when he stops whatever he was doing that you didn't like. Then ask for sit or down, just so you can praise him. No one, even a dog, likes to be yelled at all the time.

Be fair to your dog. Be sure he understands what you want him to do before you tear out your hair in frustration because he didn't do it. Help and reward him, and always set him up for success. Don't expect him to do something perfectly—like a down-stay—the first time company comes over. Put him in his crate, tether him, or hold on to the leash so he can't make a mistake. He'll try harder for you next time.

Teaching the Retrieve

One day you'll look at down at your Lab pup and find he has dropped a big stick at your feet. His wagging tail gives away the game. "Throw it!" he's saying, his body quivering with excitement. And so it begins; you have a retriever.

For 200 years, Labs have been hard-wired to retrieve. If you've ever watched a hunting dog at work, you can see he loves it: happy and intense, tail wagging, nose to the ground. You don't have to teach a Lab to retrieve; you just have to teach him to bring it back to you.

Control the game—when it starts, when it ends, and who keeps the toy at the end (you). If your Lab gets tired and quits, pick up the ball and put it away until next time. He needs to know it's your toy. This is a subtle message that you're in charge, not him. Although it's a game, you're teaching your dog to cooperate with you and respect your leadership. If you let him decide when to quit and take the ball under a bush for a good chew, he's in charge.

For this example, we'll assume he's retrieving a ball. Labs have endless variations on returning the ball, none of which including giving it to you. Why would he bring it back when you're just going to take it away from him? This makes perfect sense to him. He'll invite you to chase him, he'll stop just out of your reach, and he'll drop the ball and grab it as soon as you reach for it.

Attach a long line—about 20 feet of clotheslines or other light rope—to your dog's collar. When he's running around the yard after picking up the ball, reel him in, take the ball, and throw it again immediately. You don't need treats; throwing the ball is his reward. The longer you hang onto the ball, the less of a reward it is for him, and the less likely he'll be to return it next time. Occasionally, wait a few seconds before you take the ball from him.

Never go to him to get the ball; he just taught you to chase him. If he drops the ball before he gets to you or stops just out of reach, take a few steps backward or turn and run away from him.

And don't keep throwing until he's bored; always leave him wanting more. Keep track of how many throws he retrieves before he gets tired. Quit before you get to that point next time.

You taught your Lab "Give" separately (see Month 6), and fetching is a good time to use that skill. If you're going to hunt with your Lab or compete in formal obedience, you'll want him to release the ball directly into your hand rather than drop it. If you don't care, it's fine if he drops it instead.

When he won't give up the ball, show him another ball. He'll usually give up the one he has and take off after the new one. Don't throw it until he drops the first ball, or he'll take it with him.

You and Your Puppy

Don't expect a lot of downtime this month. He's still very young, and he will play hard until he collapses and falls asleep. You can also play brain games to wear him out if he won't run himself tired.

Keep Playing

The games you played with your Lab puppy—hide and seek, find it, and others—will still entertain you both, and you can make them tougher now to challenge him. Teach him to find a person by name. Have the person hide, and you (restraining your dog) tell him to "Find Joe." Have Joe then call your puppy. He'll quickly learn to find multiple people, one after the other.

Your Lab is probably a retrieving maniac by now. This is the perfect time to teach him to retrieve multiple objects, not just a tennis ball or bumper. As you throw the item, name it for him, and soon he'll learn to identify which item you want him to retrieve by name.

Hit a ball with a tennis racket to send it farther, and make him hunt to find it. Toss a stick in a creek, and watch him search and bring back the right one. Swimming is excellent and tiring exercise.

Learning Easy Tricks

When training seems like a chore, switch to teaching him tricks and bring the fun back into your time with your puppy. The whole family can participate.

"Shake" and "Roll over" are two easy tricks you or anyone else in your family can teach your puppy.

For "Shake," get down on the floor with your pup and have him sit. Don't say anything; just reach out and tickle the back of your puppy's foot just above the floor. He'll lift the foot off the ground. Say "Good," and reward him with a treat. After a few tries (always reaching toward the same foot), he'll lift his foot when he sees your hand coming. Fantastic!

Now give it a name; it doesn't have to be "Shake." You could say "High five" or "Go team" or anything you want to call it. As he lifts his paw, say your word and take hold of his paw. Give him a treat from your other hand while you're still touching him, and release. Work up to where he'll let you shake his paw.

When he's really good at shake, you can teach him variations. You can teach him to put his paw in your open hand or lift his other paw to shake. Give these new behaviors a different name and hand signal. For instance, use a different hand when you want him to shake with the other foot. Use an open hand when you want a high five.

Teach just one behavior at a time until he understands it completely. Later, you can alternate which behavior you ask for.

For "Roll over," have your puppy lie down and roll on one hip, like he's going to do a down-stay. Put a treat in front of his nose, and move it back and toward his spine so he twists his head as he follows the treat. Pull the treat far enough back that he has to put his head on the ground to follow it. As he lies flat on the ground, roll his legs up and over with your other hand and give him the treat. He'll quickly get the idea after a few repetitions. Add the word you choose for the command.

Both of these tricks are easy for your Lab to learn in just a few days. Alternate tricks with obedience commands to keep training time fun and interesting for both of you.

| Month 7 | Month 8 | Month 9 |

Socialization in public

Adult teeth are in—chewing continues

Enroll in basic obedience class

Moderate growth

Sexual maturity

The race is on. Your Lab is anxious to grow up, and you're scrambling to keep up with her. Between 7 and 8 months, you'll have moments when you feel like you've got a new dog you've never seen before. Her personality changes as she inches toward adulthood and finds she has to deal with other dogs differently from when she was a puppy. She'll temporarily forget a lot of what you've taught her, too. Most of her behavior is typical teenage mischief and not a cause for major concern, as long as you deal with it and don't let it become a habit.

All is not lost, however. The training you've done up to this point gives you the tools to handle her behavior. Basic obedience practice solves many seemingly un-related difficulties, and you'll spend a lot of time reinforcing her training and teaching her self-control and manners.

Her teenage exuberance will provide hours of fun and laughs for you and your family, and you'll enjoy even the most challenging times with your Lab puppy.

Physical Development

Her body is ahead of itself this month, and she can't figure out where those long legs came from. Her behavior strays into uncharted territory, and she often leaps before she looks. Be prepared for lots of action!

What Is Adolescence in Dogs?

In Labs, adolescence lasts from about 7 months until 2 to 2½ years of age. With that kind of time span, it's not a phase you can just wait out. But if you're prepared to deal with it, you'll emerge at the other end with a well-behaved adult dog. Enjoy her youthful enthusiasm and energy now, though. She loves to do things and will thrive on the attention you give her.

Hormones play a big role in a Lab's adolescent behavior. This is the time when your dog's sexual maturity is way ahead of her mental and emotional maturity. If your dog has already been spayed or neutered, you're not completely off the hook because brain development also plays a role. Like human teenagers, she doesn't have enough experience yet to make mature choices, and she doesn't understand the consequences of her changing body. But of course, she wants to be all grown up and do what the big dogs do, so she plays the role of an adult and learns from her mistakes.

The first thing you may notice is she'll assert her independence. She "forgets" her name, takes off, ignores you at the park, and refuses to obey obedience commands. She'll grab your shoe and play keep away to get out of doing what you've told her to do. Treats don't always work anymore, and her appetite fluctuates from day to day.

Your Lab has had 7 months to learn to read your body language and facial expressions. She knows if you mean it when you say something to her, and she's at the stage where she'll call your bluff. To deal with this, use authoritative posture—stand tall and straight when you're dealing with her. That will help her understand that you mean it.

You'll find your dog bossy-barking at you when she wants something or urine-marking your belongings. She's trying out new behaviors—bullying, marking, mounting, and maybe some aggression. She'll take teenage rebellion to new extremes, becoming possessive of her toys or growling at you when you tell her to get off the couch. She's suddenly overprotective of her territory and barks at every car driving by or person coming to the door.

Your Lab is conflicted. She's trying to balance teenage insecurity with her endless energy. She still depends on you but needs to rebel. She still knows what you've taught her, but she'll need to be reminded that there are consequences when she misbehaves. Purely positive training may not be enough to keep her attention. Firm but kind discipline has its place this month. What works today may not work tomorrow, so keep trying different things.

Helping Your Puppy Gain Coordination

An adolescent Lab doesn't know she has hind legs, and when she remembers, she trips over them. She runs with her front legs, and her back end just kind of follows. To improve her overall coordination, put together some activities that require her to concentrate on her feet and legs when she moves. You'll be surprised how hard it is for her.

The ladder walk: For this exercise, place a ladder flat on the ground. Put your Lab on leash and have her walk through the ladder to the other end. She'll be impatient and want to leave, so you might need someone on her other side to keep her from jumping out of the ladder and walking beside it. Encourage her with treats in front of her nose. She'll practice lifting up her feet to go over the rungs. After a few tries, she'll be pretty good at it.

Cavalettis: Place some pieces of 2×4 lumber on the ground about as far apart as her stride, and walk her over the boards. She'll stumble at first, unaware that the boards are even there. Adjust the distance apart so she can comfortably trot over the boards. When she's mastered the task at ground level, put them up on bricks, about 3 inches off the ground, and try again.

The platform: Place a 2×2-foot piece of plywood up on blocks. Have her jump up, guide her with a treat to turn around in a circle once, and sit.

Fast and Fearless

Teenage Labradors are big, strong puppies, and they know how to use their strength. Rather than dig under a fence, they'll chew through it. They're pushy and impulsive at this age, and they have no maturity to hold them back. Your little bull in the china shop isn't intentionally torturing you. She's just testing out her age, and when you're frustrated, she'll do her best to make you laugh.

The same adolescent Lab who reacts fearfully to fireworks will be strangely oblivious when plunging through brush and brambles, icy water, and other physical challenges. Her common sense is on vacation for the next few months, and you'll have to protect her from herself so she doesn't have to learn the hard way that some things, like ice-covered lakes, are actually dangerous.

Health

From dangerous weather conditions to holiday safety hazards, your Lab puppy needs to be protected from an assortment of seasonal mishaps. By educating yourself and taking precautions each season, you'll keep your canine buddy safe.

Spring Safety Hazards

'Tis the season to begin hiking, camping, and enjoying outdoor activities. Do some shorter conditioning hikes with your pup before you head out for long expeditions to get your and your Lab's muscles in shape. Even then, remember she's still a puppy and don't overdo it. If your Lab will be carrying a backpack, build the weight up gradually, and check with your vet to determine the maximum weight she can safely carry at this age.

Your dog's paw pads are soft and susceptible to cuts and scrapes at the beginning of the season. Walking on asphalt or concrete can cause road-burn, so build up slowly while her feet toughen.

As the weather warms up, fleas, ticks, and poisonous snakes become active. Be prepared for these pests by using preventatives on your Lab puppy. Consider rattlesnake avoidance training and a rattlesnake vaccine for your dog.

> ### TIPS AND TAILS
>
> Snake avoidance training has become popular in many areas of the Southern and Western United States where people and rattlesnakes live in close proximity. Training methods vary but have the same general goals. Dogs are exposed to live snakes whose mouths have been taped shut or are otherwise disabled. The dog is introduced to the sight, sound, and smell of a snake, so she learns to recognize a snake and alert you even if she can't see it. Most trainers use electronic collars during this training.

Mosquitoes are at their worst during humid summer months, and that increases your puppy's risk of contracting heartworm. If she's not already on a preventative, you will need to have her tested for the parasite before you can safely put her on a heartworm prevention program. Take care of this chore by mid- to late spring, or keep her on a preventative year-round.

At Easter time, keep wrapped candy, Easter baskets, fake grass, and chocolate bunnies out of your dog's reach. Most varieties of lily, Easter or otherwise, are toxic. If your Lab eats a petal, leaf, or even just the pollen, it causes an upset stomach, and if she eats enough, kidney damage. Make generous use of your puppy's crate during the holiday to keep her safe and out of trouble.

Springtime means gardening season, when people fertilize their lawns and spray their gardens with pesticides. Anything from weed control to garden mulch can be toxic to your pup. Cocoa mulch, for example, which contains the same poisonous ingredients as chocolate, is particularly deadly. If you fertilize or spray, follow the manufacturer's guidelines carefully, let the grass dry completely before letting your puppy walk on it, and wash her feet if you think she's been exposed. And don't let her eat plants or mulch.

Although you take these precautions to protect your dog at home, public parks and neighborhood homes may have these hazards—sometimes invisible—so always be aware when you're out and about, too.

Summer Health and Safety Hazards

Heat exhaustion is the single-most dangerous summer hazard for your dog, and a dog's body temperature can rise to dangerous levels and result in organ failure. A black or chocolate Lab's dark coat absorbs heat even faster than a yellow Lab's. Dogs have a limited number of sweat glands and perspire mainly through the pads on their feet. They pant to cool themselves.

Owners innocently assume their dog can jog or hike with them on a hot day without consequence, and your Lab will do her best to keep up. But remember that she's still too young for hard running on solid surfaces. Place your hand on the sidewalk, sand, or road where you'll be walking with your Lab. If it's too hot for your hand, it's too hot for your dog's paws. She can be seriously burned. Humidity increases the risk of heat exhaustion, too. Lightly exercise with your dog in the early morning or evening, and keep her indoors during the heat of the day.

When you're out and about, don't leave your pup in a hot car. Any temperature over 70°F is too hot to leave your dog in the car, even if you've parked in the shade with the windows open. The car can heat up to 100°F in 15 min-utes or less. Being left in a hot car is the most common cause of heatstroke in dogs.

> ### HAPPY PUPPY
>
> Always keep cool, fresh water available for your Lab. Consider putting out two water bowls in case she dumps one during the day, or tie a full bucket to a fence so she can't drag it around and play with it. Many puppies love an ice cube treat on a hot day, so add crushed ice or ice cubes to her bowl. Leave a faucet dripping into her bowl so she can get water even if she runs out. Be sure she has access to cool shade if she's outdoors and it's too hot in the garage or doghouse. It doesn't have to be fancy; a beach umbrella is sufficient. A kiddie pool filled with a couple inches of water gives her a cool spot to beat the heat.

It's important that you learn to recognize and treat heatstroke. A tired and overheated dog will usually try to stop and rest. Don't force her to keep going. Find some shade, give her a drink of water, and wet her paw pads to bring down her body temperature. A dog in serious distress will pant heavily, drool thick saliva, have bright red gums and tongue, have an increased heart rate, and may stagger drunkenly or appear disoriented. As symptoms progress, she may vomit or have diarrhea (with or without blood in it), collapse, go into shock, and fall unconscious. In advanced stages, her gums will turn pale gray or blue.

Your first priority is to safely cool your puppy. Lay her on a cool floor, and turn on a fan if possible. Wet her body with cool water from a garden hose. Or place cool (not cold) wet towels on the dog's head, neck, tummy, and feet. Let her drink if she's able. If you can take her temperature, do so. Anything over 104°F is an emergency, so take her to the vet immediately, even if she appears to recover. This is a life-threatening situation. Dogs who have previously suffered from heatstroke are at increased risk for a second occurrence.

More dogs are lost, killed, or injured on the fourth of July than any other day of the year. And it's not just one day. People shoot off fireworks for a week or more before and after the holiday. A panic-stricken dog will do things she'd never consider any other time: rip the leash out of your hands, jump a fence, or run into the street. Many dogs don't react until something blows up right in front of them. Protect your Lab puppy by keeping her at home and indoors on the holiday.

If your Lab is frightened by the noise, take steps to relieve her anxiety. Products like Thundershirt or body wraps soothe your dog by putting pressure on acupuncture points. Turn on the stereo to mask the sounds from outdoors. An exceptionally terrified dog may need medication. Plan ahead and visit your vet for a prescription or to find out about the use of melatonin or aromatherapies. Don't use over-the-counter sedatives.

If you live near the local high school, fireworks are part of many halftime shows and homecoming games. New Year's Eve is another noisy, terrifying night for many dogs.

You can desensitize your Lab to the sound of fireworks or thunderstorms. Play a tape of the sounds at low volume, and entertain your Lab with a game or otherwise distract her while it plays in the background. You want her to associate the sound with fun or a chew toy. You may have to start at some distance away from the sounds. When she reaches a point where she recognizes the tape and looks to you for her reward, you can increase the volume slightly and move closer to it.

> ### TIPS AND TAILS
>
> Don't comfort your puppy or try to soothe her when she's frightened of fireworks or thunderstorms. Your anxious tone and body language tells her she really does need to worry. Act happy and confident so your dog will realize nothing is wrong.

Fall Safety Hazards

As cold weather approaches and people winterize their cars, beware of antifreeze in driveways and on the roadways. This greenish liquid's sweet taste is especially attractive to dogs. Your Lab can lick enough off her paws to cause kidney failure and even death. Wash your Lab's feet with Dawn dish detergent or olive oil if you think she's stepped in antifreeze and then call your veterinarian.

Halloween can be a challenge to your pup. Remember when you were socializing your puppy, and you invited your guests to wear big hats and raincoats? For your dog, Halloween is all those scary-looking people—times 10. Trick-or-treaters wear wings and masks, and carry large flapping bags. If your pup barks when the doorbell rings, this is either a great time to practice her obedience or a better time to put her in her crate in the back bedroom.

Burning candles, jack-o-lanterns, and other flammable decorations tempt your Lab to investigate. Costumes for pets and people may include choking hazards like string and ribbons. Wooden sticks from caramel apples, candy wrappers, and gum can cause serious injuries. And poisonous chocolate lurks in those goodie bags.

Winter Safety Hazards

If your puppy must be outside for a few hours in extremely cold weather, be sure she has access to a doghouse or other protection from the cold and dampness. Remember, she's still a puppy. Even if she does have the correct Labrador double coat, she doesn't have enough fat to stay warm.

Even a Lab with her thick double coat can get hypothermia if she gets wet to the skin. The first sign is shivering, a physical reaction that helps her retain heat by elevating her metabolism. Take your puppy indoors immediately and warm her body by drying her and wrapping her in blankets. Take her to the vet immediately.

When a dog is hypothermic, her blood retreats to the main trunk of her body to protect and heat her internal organs. That means her paws, tail, the tips of her ears, and other extremities are susceptible to frostbite. Your dog may limp, and the affected area will be pale and hard to the touch. Dry and warm the area with warm (not hot) compresses. Take her to your veterinarian for further care.

When you exercise with your Lab puppy outside in cold weather, don't overdo it. Cold air and high altitude cause your puppy to burn more calories and get tired faster. Also beware of frozen water and thin ice. Be sure you know where rivers and streams are located, and keep your puppy away from them. Don't go in after your dog if she falls in. Send for help instead. Adult dogs can survive in freezing water longer than humans can. Puppies are more vulnerable.

Monitor your pup when she's outside in cold and snowy weather. Snow hides familiar landmarks, and your Lab may not realize she's left her own yard if you're not there to show her the way. She can't distinguish the curb or driveway, and she may wander into the street. Snowplows have a hard time spotting dogs when they're plowing, and yellow Labs are particularly hard to see in the snow. Also, put your Lab inside when you use the snow blower. She'll want to be where you are, and the hard-thrown snow could injure her.

> ### TIPS AND TAILS
>
> After winter outings, wash your dog's feet to prevent irritation from road salt. Salt dries out your Lab's paws pads and leads to painful, cracked skin. If her feet are really dry and irritated, apply vitamin E oil or a lotion with lanolin.

It may not look pretty, but during the winter holidays, it might be a good idea to deck the halls with exercise pens and pet gates for your puppy's first few years. Don't be shocked if your adolescent male pees on the Christmas tree; after all, it's okay to urinate on trees when he's outdoors. Decorations make fun, crunchy noises when they break in his mouth, and crinkling cellophane sounds like a package of dog treats. Ribbons can tangle in his gut and cut off his circulation. As he makes his way to his favorite spot at the window, he'll get tangled in extension cords and crush the gifts. Decorations look like toys to him, and candles can light his fur on fire when he stands too close.

Food is equally hazardous this time of year. Cakes and candies wrapped under the tree don't fool her; she knows there's food in that box. Chocolate is especially dangerous. When food is set out for guests, block your Lab's access.

Leftover turkey is also tempting. You may want to feed your Lab table scraps, but don't. Fatty meat, skin, and gravy can cause pancreatitis, a potentially fatal disease. Dispose of the carcass where she can't get to it. Remember, poultry bones are brittle and can break in your dog's mouth, throat, or stomach, causing life-threatening injuries. Freeze it until trash pickup day.

Nutrition

You go to a lot of trouble selecting the right food for your Lab puppy, and what does she do? She eats kitty litter!

Continue to adjust her food according to her growth, and be prepared for her to make some unusual diet choices of her own.

Determining How Much Food Your Lab Needs

Although her growth is slowing down, your Lab is still eating more than she will as an adult. When she reaches 75 to 80 percent of her adult weight, she'll still need up to $1\frac{1}{4}$ times the calories she'll need when she's mature.

How much she needs to eat varies by her size and activity level. In spring and summer, when Labs are most active, they'll burn more calories. In the fall, a working hunting dog may need more food than any other time of year. In the winter, dogs burn more calories outside because of the cold; but on the other hand, they spend more time indoors and aren't as active overall.

Labs vary so much in size that it's hard to recommend an absolute amount. Labs are not meant to be large dogs, and they don't need 4 or 5 cups of food a day as an adult. Unless you have a 100-pound dog (which some Labs are), she's going to need between 2 and 3 cups of food a day. The type of food you feed is another factor to consider. Premium foods offer more condensed nutrition, so you don't have to feed as much.

The best way to decide how much food is enough for your puppy is to keep track of her condition and weight. See Appendix B for instructions on how to determine if your Lab is overweight, underweight, or just right. When in doubt, consult with your veterinarian.

Dealing with the Icky Things Labs Eat

Although dogs eat things we think are absolutely disgusting, to a dog, they are delicious. Dogs have been natural scavengers since before they were domesticated, eating waste left behind by the nomadic tribes they followed. Today, when Labs eat cat litter or horse manure—or even their own feces—they're just repeating behavior that has been part of their nature for tens of thousands of years. Because they consider it completely normal, punishment doesn't usually eliminate the problem.

Dogs have fewer taste buds than humans and aren't as discriminating about what they eat. There are nutritional as well as behavioral reasons for why they eat feces. If your Lab isn't digesting all the nutrients in her food, they are passed through the body and out into her stool. The stool then becomes a source of additional nutrition. Feces are also a natural source of digestive enzymes and B vitamins. A mother dog eats her puppies' feces to clean the den, hide their scent, and protect them from predators. Puppies often eat the stool of older dogs and their littermates. It's a natural way to establish their intestinal *microflora*.

Stool-eating is self-rewarding and may become a habit. When dogs don't get enough exercise and live in a relatively boring environment, they may start eating feces. The best defense is to pick up feces as soon as your pup deposits it.

Cat feces have a high protein content that's attractive to dogs. But if a dog ingests clumping kitty litter, it could cause an intestinal blockage. The easiest method to avoid this problem is to use pet gates to block your puppy's access to the litter box.

If you want to use aversion training and make her avoid the feces, use a foul-tasting liquid like bitter apple or pepper sauce. Spray some in your puppy's mouth so she'll recognize the taste and smell and want to avoid it, and then spray it on the feces. If you don't introduce her to the taste beforehand, this method doesn't work very well.

Dogs who eat horse and cattle manure are searching for another type of nutrition. Manure is full of digested vegetable matter, like hay and grass. Alfalfa hay is also a source of protein. Dogs are carnivores, but they do include plants in their diet. Dogs may eat manure if they aren't getting enough plant matter in their diets, or just because it is a natural instinct, just like stool-eating.

Whatever kind of poop your Lab chooses to eat, she runs the risk of picking up intestinal parasites—just one more reason to prevent this nasty activity.

When Your Pup Eats Grass

All dogs eat grass; it's a perfectly normal behavior. Grass provides nutritional value in your dog's diet. It's a source of fiber and roughage that's high in potassium and digestive enzymes. Your only concern should be if your lawn is chemically treated with fertilizers, herbicides, or pesticides that could make her ill.

You may notice that your dog vomits after eating grass. If this happens a few times a year, it isn't anything to worry about. A dog with a tummy ache will occasionally eat grass to make herself throw up whatever is irritating her. This may prevent her from getting seriously ill from something she ate.

If your dog eats grass and vomits every week, there may be a more serious reason. It could mean gastric upset, parasites, nutritional deficit, or food sensitivity. She may be trying to compensate for something that's missing in her diet. Try switching brands or flavors of food. A different protein or carbohydrate source may work better for her. You may also add some lightly steamed vegetables such as carrots, kale, or zucchini to her diet.

Grooming

Many Labs suffer from occasional coat problems, and a hundred different causes could be to blame. Besides adolescent hormonal fluctuations, let's look at some other possible reasons for coat problems and how to treat hot spots.

Addressing Skin and Coat Problems

A healthy coat is a sign of a healthy dog. Your Lab's coat should be shiny and her skin should be clear, with no dandruff, red spots, or scaling.

Most people don't notice when their Lab sheds out her puppy coat and the adult coat comes in, but during the transition, she'll shed quite a bit and her coat may look scruffy. This is more obvious in chocolate Labs. The loose coat appears lighter because it's dry, and the new coat coming in underneath seems darker. In a Lab of any color, the adult outer coat feels a little harsher than her puppy coat.

A dull, dry coat along with dandruff or inflamed skin indicates that more than just the semi-annual shedding is taking place. A health problem like hypothyroidism, poor nutrition, or liver disease could be the issue. Once your veterinarian rules out health concerns, you can look for other problems that may be the cause.

Too many baths can remove natural oils and cause a dry coat. If you need to bathe her often, just rinse her well instead of using shampoo. The Lab is a wash-and-wear breed. Human shampoos dry out the coat more than those made especially made for dogs. Frequent brushing distributes oils, removes dirt, and makes her coat shine. That may be all she needs on a regular basis.

If your dog swims in your pool, chlorine will dry out her coat. Be sure to rinse her thoroughly afterward.

Some problems, like allergies, can be inherited. See Month 12 for more information about allergies and treatments.

Your Lab's food may not have enough of the nutrients she needs to keep her coat healthy. A protein deficiency can cause dryness, excessive shedding, and ear infections. The deficiency may be caused by grain rather than meat as the primary protein source in the diet. Fat or fatty acid deficiency can also cause a dull coat, dry skin, and itching.

External parasites like fleas or sarcoptic mange make your Lab scratch constantly, leaving patches of bare skin. It only takes saliva from one flea to cause an intense reaction in some dogs. Another parasite, demodectic mange, is passed down from the mother to her puppies during the first few days of life and is aggravated by a depressed immune system. It doesn't necessarily cause itching, but it does affect the coat dramatically, causing patches of hair loss and red crusty skin.

> ### TIPS AND TAILS

Cool water relieves itchy skin, while warm or hot water aggravates the itching. Antihistamines like Benadryl also provide some relief. Your veterinarian can tell you the appropriate dose for your Lab. For more serious itching, the vet may temporarily prescribe corticosteroids or prescription antihistamines.

Internal parasites (worms) also affect a coat's condition. Your vet can analyze a stool sample to identify and treat worms.

Dealing with Hot Spots

A hot spot is a moist, inflamed circle of skin your dog licks until it's raw. A hot spot could have one of many causes, such as flea allergy or vaccine reaction. They usually develop in warm weather, and rarely in winter. Common locations on Labs are under the ears or around the ruff on the neck.

A hot spot gets bigger and more irritated as your dog continues to bite at it. You may have to put an Elizabethan collar on her to prevent licking. Chewing and licking the hot spot can cause a secondary infection that must be treated with antibiotics.

To treat the hot spot, apply cool, wet compresses to loosen the crusty outer layer and soothe the skin. If it's not too painful for your pup, trim the hair around the spot and clean twice daily with mild, nonperfumed soap or antiseptic solution.

Here are some more suggestions to relieve hot spots:

❖ Wash with cool green or black brewed tea. Tannic acid in the tea helps dry out the spot so it can heal.

❖ Apply aluminum acetate solution (available from your pharmacy) three times a day using a spray bottle or compresses. It also helps dry out the spot and speed healing.

❖ Hydrocortisone cream relieves itching. Apply just enough to rub in completely. Don't use too much or your Lab will lick it off.

❖ Aloe vera cream or gel also eases pain and helps hot spots heal.

If the hot spot does not respond in a day or two, a visit to your veterinarian is in order.

Social Skills

Socializing your Lab is an ongoing process, and when she reaches adolescence, she goes through some major changes. This is a critical time for your dog's development, and she needs to continue her socialization.

Preventing Desocialization

Socialization was an easily acquired skill when your Lab was a puppy, and most Labs are naturally friendly throughout their lives. But during adolescence, they undergo so many hormonal, physical, and emotional changes, sometimes it's just too much trouble to take them out much in public. Continue taking her out, though, because the consequences of not socializing your dog now are hard to overcome.

If your Lab puppy is isolated during adolescence, she quickly becomes desocialized. She is no longer positively reinforced for friendly encounters with other dogs and people, she has no way of working through her lack of confidence, and she has no way to develop the social skills an adult dog needs to get along in the world.

Your Labrador is developing a healthy sense of caution at this age. It will serve her well in adulthood, when she's learned there are consequences to leaping without thought into every situation. You may think your dog is overly cautious, but she is practicing the art of self-preservation and will grow more confident as she settles into her new role as an adult dog.

Dealing with Dog-to-Dog Aggression

Your Lab's relationship with other dogs changes dramatically as she reaches adolescence. No longer on her "puppy pass," she can't just roar up to other dogs and expect them to love her. She has to learn new methods for interacting with other dogs.

Other dogs will treat her differently once she reaches puberty. Your dog will be more assertive as she tries to establish herself as an equal and no longer a puppy in the group. She will be challenged by older dogs and put in her place. These are natural behaviors, and your dog needs to experience them. If she goes unchallenged, it reinforces any aggressive or pushy tendencies; she never learns she has to restrain herself around other dogs or mind her manners.

For males, it starts with competition for females. He's interested in them in a different way now, and play behavior turns into courtship behavior. She won't put up with it, and the other males aren't going to let her take over their turf. Intact females are the least likely to get along with each other. They also compete, and rather than flirt with males, they'll argue with each other.

Altering prevents some conflicts between dogs. Once a Lab is neutered, he isn't competing with the other males anymore so they don't challenge him. Spayed females no longer provoke competition among themselves, either. You'll still observe marking, mounting, and pushy behavior, even in altered dogs of both sexes. If you start seeing aggressive behavior in your Lab, male or female, consider altering now.

HAPPY PUPPY

Play is important during adolescence and allows your Lab to develop her canine instincts. Stalking, chasing, mounting, and other natural doggie behaviors are all part of puppy play sessions. These activities take on new meaning in adult play. Dogs will trade roles as they play and relearn how to interact. Be sure to supervise so play doesn't get too rough. Adolescent dogs don't know when to stop, and they may not read their playmate's body language correctly in the heat of the moment.

Even the best-socialized dogs can lose their temper and get in a spat. Dogs' personalities vary, and not everyone is meant to be best friends. Puppies who formerly played well together may have an occasional dustup. It's almost inevitable that your Lab will get in a few tussles during adolescence. The question is how serious are these encounters?

Many dogfights are simply arguments, not real fights. Everyone makes lots of noise, but no one has a mark on them when all is said and done. You'll also see some competitive growling and snapping over preferred sleeping spots or a favorite toy. One dog usually gives in and it's over. These are puppies who have learned effective bite inhibition from other puppies.

That doesn't mean fighting is okay. When two dogs clearly don't like each other, there's not much you can do about it, and they should be separated. It's important to continue socializing your dog to other friendly dogs, so don't give up.

You can help prevent dog aggression when your pup meets new dogs. New meetings can be high-stress situations, filled with excitement, anticipation, and frustration. The worst thing you can do is hold the leash taut while the dogs sniff each other. She thinks she's restrained and can't escape. She feels the tension in the leash and assumes you're tense, too, which could trigger a fight. It's hard to make yourself do it, but relax your hold and let the leash hang loose from her neck. Introduce unfamiliar dogs on neutral territory, not at home.

If both people are holding their dogs back, once you let go the dogs will explode at each other. Practice getting your Lab's attention while you're still some distance away and then go for a walk with the person and their dog. Start the dogs far apart and as everyone calms down, walk closer together.

Don't reward an aggressive reaction, and don't comfort your dog, either. Use your jolly routine and treats. Reward her for good behavior and for paying attention to you.

If you feel your Lab is developing a real aggression problem or that it's escalating, work with a trainer or behaviorist. Someone who is experienced in evaluating dog behavior can give you a realistic picture of what's going on, and together you can put together a plan to prevent dog aggression from becoming a habit.

TIPS AND TAILS

Life on a chain is a miserable life for a dog. A dog who spends the day tied up outside gets frustrated. She can see things, but isn't able to get to them. She can't escape if an animal or person comes in the yard, and feels she has to defend herself, which can cause chronic aggression in an otherwise nice dog. A lonely, bored Lab barks all day. She can also get tangled in the chain and strangle herself, get wrapped around a tree, or otherwise get injured. Find another way to confine your Lab.

Hopefully you'll never encounter an aggressive dog, but if you do, you need to know how to handle the situation. When you're out with your Lab, carry treats to toss away from you and distract the aggressor. Speak in a high, happy tone, and yell "Treats! Cookies!" or some other term you hope he'll recognize.

Carry pepper or citronella spray, too. Be careful when you aim at an oncoming dog, though, because you don't want it blowing back in your face.

Pay attention to the dogs in your neighborhood, so you know if any are a threat. Some dogs are territorial and will bark every time you walk past their house. If they're in the front yard, they may be inclined to extend their territory to the sidewalk and street. They may be all bluff and bluster, but they may not. Either way, try to avoid aggressive dogs. Cross the street or turn around.

Speak firmly to the strange dog and tell him to sit. He may stop in his tracks and obey. If he's really agitated, don't run. This encourages him to chase you and triggers his prey drive. Remember how we caught your runaway Lab in Month 5? You ran so he'd chase you. In this case, that ploy works against you.

Stand sideways and don't look the aggressor in the eyes. You'll be much less threatening, and he may go on his way. If your puppy is still small, pick her up. For bigger dogs, drop the leash. This may diffuse the situation because your dog isn't getting signals from tension on the leash. If they're going to fight, you don't want to be tangled up in the middle of it. If a dog does attack you, curl up in a ball and protect your face and neck.

If the worst happens and your dog gets in a fight, think twice before jumping into the fray. Most fights are over in a few seconds, and you don't have to intervene. If the dogs are really fighting, you're risking your own safety if you try to stop it.

In the midst of a fight, instinct takes over, and a dog will bite anything that gets in his way. The worst thing you can do is grab a dog by her collar during a fight. She won't realize it's you and may turn and bite you, thinking another predator is attacking her from behind. Keep your hands and body out of the action.

If you decide to try and stop a fight, here are a few tips that may help you stay safe:

🐾 Bang together two metal dog dishes or cooking pots. By startling the dogs, they may separate long enough for you to intervene and safely remove your dog.

🐾 Avoid screaming or hitting the dogs. They don't hear you or feel the blows. And if they do, it just adds to their arousal.

🐾 Spray water from a garden hose at the face of the attacking dog.

🐾 If you're indoors, wedge a chair or broomstick between the dogs to pull them apart.

🐾 Lift the aggressor by his hind legs to throw him off balance, which may force him to let go. If someone is there to help you, have her do the same with the other dog.

Once the dogs have separated, leash the dogs and take them out of each other's sight. Put the end of the leash through the loop at the end. Make a noose to slip over the dog's neck and tighten. It may not be safe to touch her by the collar yet.

When everyone has calmed down, inspect each dog for injuries. You may be surprised to realize there are no large bite wounds. Still, look carefully around the neck and face. Small puncture wounds are hard to find in dark fur and may not bleed.

If you do find a bite wound, treat it immediately. Puncture wounds close up and trap the bacteria in the wound. A dog's mouth contains a lot of bacteria, and bite wounds usually get infected. Clip the hair around the wound, and wash and rinse the wound thoroughly with water or antiseptic solution. Take your dog to the vet immediately because she will need antibiotics.

Larger bite wounds, even just an inch long, may need stitches to safely heal. Your vet may put a drain in the wound for a few days to allow the bacteria to escape.

Behavior

One day your Lab is a cyclone whirling through the house. The next, she sleeps all day. One day she is the perfect obedience student. The next day she's forgotten everything you've ever taught her. All this is typical for her age. She hasn't forgotten her lessons, but they're submerged under a wave of adolescent distraction.

Although she's testing her limits—and your patience—your Lab needs her family to fall back on when adolescence overwhelms her. The rules and structure in her life are her safety net, and you're there to remind her.

Being Proactive (Rather Than Reactive)

A teenager in the house means something's always happening, and it's a challenge to stay one step ahead of your Lab. By taking a few preventive measures, you'll prevent her from getting into mischief—and save yourself a lot of angst. Limit her freedom to keep her safe and you sane.

Just because she's a teenager, this is not the time to give her the car keys. You have to assume she'll get into mischief. Your Lab is still a puppy, so continue to crate her at night and when you can't supervise her. Look at things from her perspective, and set her up for success. She can't chew up your clothes if you shut the bedroom door, for example. And she can't get into the trash if you keep the wastebasket in a closet.

Continue to reinforce her training because the things she knows will deteriorate if they aren't reinforced during this turbulent period. Enforce household rules, and remind her when she forgets. You've probably relaxed a little because you know she knows what she's supposed to do. She's testing the waters right now, and if you slack off, she'll take advantage of every opportunity. If she discovers she can get away with jumping on you occasionally, for example, then she'll keep trying.

You may just be joining us because you've adopted a young Lab. Congratulations! Labs are adaptable and can love their new family with incredible devotion. This is the age when many Labs change homes because of behavior problems. A teenage Lab is a handful, but she's not a lost cause. Enroll in an obedience class, and read through this book from the beginning like you just adopted a small puppy. Take advantage of this honeymoon period when she's soaking up information about her new surroundings, and teach her house rules from the first day. Your new Lab will be a treasured family pet in no time.

Mounting

Adolescent dogs, both male and female, start mounting each other when they reach sexual maturity. Mounting is normal canine behavior, just like barking, digging, or chewing. It's less acceptable because it embarrasses you when your dog mounts a guest's leg or humps her stuffed animal in the middle of the living room. Owners often assume the reason is sexual, but there are other reasons, too. You need to look at the context of each incident to understand what's really happening.

Anxiety and arousal (excitement, not sexual) contribute to a dog's actions. Mounting is a form of *displacement behavior,* a way of acting out to relieve her energy or stress. If she's uncertain of how to react to a situation, or if she's overly excited about the arrival of guests, mounting relieves her tension.

Displacement behavior is a behavior that occurs out of context in response to an internal emotional conflict such as stress or anxiety.

Sometimes a dog will engage in mounting hours after the exciting event, particularly if she's still anxious after being punished for misbehavior she doesn't understand. For example, you may come home and find she's been emptying the wastebaskets. You're angry, and whether you punish her or not (you shouldn't), she's worried. She needs an outlet to release that anxiety.

Your Lab may learn that mounting works as an attention-getting device. You immediately react and try to stop her, and she learns to use it as means to get you to interact with her.

Try to anticipate when she will mount someone or something, and step in to avoid the behavior. If your dog is mounting people, direct her to her toy or pillow instead. Attach a leash to her when company comes. Spaying or neutering your dog will decrease mounting behavior but not eliminate it completely.

The Importance of Exercise

Labradors were bred to be workers, but dogs today spend long hours at home alone. They don't get enough stimulation, either mental or physical, and have no outlet for their energy. Your canine athlete needs daily exercise to develop her muscles and her mind.

Don't forget to give her short breaks during exercise. She will run until she collapses just to please you, so quit while she still wants more. Take it easy during hot, humid weather because she will get tired quickly. Also remember that repetitive pounding on hard pavement or jumping on hard surfaces may injure her.

If you can find a large, fenced field with plenty of interesting smells, she'll entertain herself tracking rabbits, birds, and other scents. Free-ranging exercise is not as stressful on young bones and joints.

At the same time, too much exercise can come back to haunt you. As your Lab puppy builds stamina, she'll need even more exercise to tire her out. If she doesn't get what she needs, you may suddenly have an obsessive retriever, for example, who just can't seem to get enough. For a dog like this, a 15-minute aerobic session followed by calmer problem-solving games works best.

Training

While you train your Labrador during the coming months, you'll develop the fine skill of infinite patience. She'll challenge your skills and creativity as you endure her endless puppy antics. Have a good laugh and keep training because she's learning even when she's not listening very carefully.

Working with a Hyper Lab

Owners of adolescent Labs often decide their dog is abnormally hyperactive. A adolescent male fidgets, can't relax, and is *always* moving. It seems like he can't concentrate, has trouble learning, and doesn't remember what you taught him from one day to the next. Females aren't exempt from hyperactive behavior.

Labs don't completely mature until they're 2 or 3 years old. Within the breed, there's a huge variation in energy level, so you can't predict how your Lab will behave. Other factors also contribute to a hyperactive personality. Her environment, health, socialization, training, and the amount of exercise she gets all play a part in her activity level.

> **TIPS AND TAILS**
>
> Someone, someday, will tell you chocolate Labs are hyper and harder to train than black or yellow Labs. Don't believe it. All three colors can be born into the same litter, and no research exists to prove behavior is a color-linked genetic characteristic.

Spay/neuter surgery helps reduce a dog's frenzied behavior. Once the sex organs and the accompanying hormones are removed, she's not as distracted or constantly on the lookout for intact dogs.

If your Lab is counter-surfing and raiding the trash, lunging at everyone and everything while on walks, and too excited to even notice you are giving her commands, ask yourself some questions:

🐾 Are you accidentally rewarding her with attention when she misbehaves? Even yelling is attention.

🐾 Did you encourage exuberant greetings and wild play when she was little? If so, she's just doing what she was taught.

🐾 Is she getting adequate exercise every day?

The absence of bad behavior is hard to recognize sometimes. Pay attention so you catch her doing something right. She'll learn what behaviors get attention when you consistently reward her for good behavior.

Teaching Self-Control

When the adolescent crazies hit, this is the time some owners give up on their puppies. What was previously cute is no fun anymore. Your Lab is wild in the house, dragging you on walks, and rudely jumping on everyone she meets. She's too much trouble to deal with. The less you take her out in public or allow her indoors, the more her behavior declines. She ends up in the backyard or, worse, a shelter.

Self-control is a developed skill, similar to when you build muscle memory by practicing a sport. Your Lab is in react-first, think-later mode, and she needs to learn to think first, even when she's excited. Help her make correct decisions rather than trying to control her behavior by manhandling her. An excited dog needs calm handling. Most owners instinctively react by yelling and grabbing their dog, which just fires her up more. She learns that you will stop her; she doesn't learn to stop herself. By moving slowly and speaking quietly, you communicate there is no reason to act wild. That advice is easy to give, but hard for almost everyone to do. Rather than try to defuse a situation in the heat of the moment, practice when you're not in the midst of a crisis.

At home, practice sit and down dozens of times a day with food treats. It doesn't have to be a stay. You just want her to respond and have enough self-control to stay put for a few seconds. Down is more difficult for the dog, but she'll get better as you practice. Put her dinner kibble in your pockets and spend the evening doling it out. You'll get her attention. In fact, she'll soon be following you around offering sits and downs when you didn't ask for them.

Practice sit and down while on your walks, so she starts to expect you'll occasionally ask her to do something. When you take her out—which you should do every day no matter how hard it is—watch for opportunities to practice her self-control. You may not go more than a block, but it doesn't matter.

For example, you see someone walking toward you. Focus your Lab's attention on you by asking for a sit and rewarding her before she notices the oncoming person. Start your routine far enough away that your dog can be successful. Once she gets the idea, start closer on future walks. With enough repetitions, she will see an oncoming person and look to you, an occasion you should mark with a huge jackpot of treats and praise.

▶ TIPS AND TAILS

In the midst of a hyperactive frenzy is not the time to teach your dog a settle-down cue. Practice with your dog in a quieter setting so she can learn it without distractions. It's easy to ignore your Lab when she's quietly sitting or lying at your feet, but this is the behavior you want, so watch for it and reward her when you see it.

Teach your puppy to settle down on command. It's probably easy to get your Lab mildly riled up with a tennis ball or toy. Then simply stop. Hide the toy in your pocket. Don't look at her. Ignore her. Cross your arms. At some point she'll be puzzled and stop jumping around. She might even offer a behavior to get a reaction from you. Ignore her until she sits. Praise her quietly and bring the toy out again. Repeat this sequence several times, and you'll soon discover your Lab sits faster and faster, because that makes you produce the toy.

Give both the active and the quiet phase a name, like "Whoopee" and "Cool it." Gradually extend the settle period to a few seconds and work up to a minute or more. Always praise her for settling, even when you don't have a toy. You can now transfer this behavior to a situation where you need it. She won't be perfect the first time, but with practice, she will learn.

Using Equipment to Control Your Dog

Ideally, you should be able to control your dog with training, rewards, and discipline. But Labs are strong, and if she's out of control to the point where you can't handle her, you might decide to look into some equipment that can help you manage her.

Some of these items, like head halters and no-pull harnesses, may provide a much-needed breakthrough in dealing with your dog. Work with a professional trainer, and use these items while you're teaching your teenager to listen to you. These are tools, not solutions. You can't stop training because you have a new collar. You don't want to have to use special devices throughout her life.

Head halters work on the same principle as a horse's halter. By controlling your dog's head, you control her movement. You can't out-muscle a horse, but a halter gives you the control you need. The same is true for your dog.

The halter's straps go over your dog's muzzle and behind her ears, joined by a ring in the throat area, where you attach the leash. The straps tighten over the muzzle when your Lab pulls, and you can steer her gently. She's unable to drag you. There's often another strap you can hook to your pup's regular collar so she can't escape if she rubs and removes the head halter.

Dogs resist a head halter at first. She'll pull away, dance around, and paw at it. Expect to spend several short sessions working with it before she's accustomed to it. Add a second leash attached to her regular collar to give you more control. Once she accepts the halter, it works well. The halter requires some finesse on your part to use it correctly. If you yank on it or drag your dog, you can twist and injure her neck. Never leave a head halter on your puppy.

There's a downside to using head halters. When you meet a stranger, they'll assume your dog is muzzled. Their next assumption is that she's dangerous and will bite. You may have to educate the people you encounter.

A dog who pulls on the leash will cough and gag from the pressure on her trachea. That leads some owners to try a harness, which relieves neck pressure because the straps lie across her chest and rib cage instead. A traditional harness (like you see on toy poodles) triggers an opposition reflex in a large dog like a Lab, and your dog will instinctively resist the pressure. That's why a sled dog wears a harness; it makes her pull. It actually triggers the same reflex in a small dog, but because the owner is stronger than the dog, it doesn't matter as much.

No-pull harnesses were developed so an owner with less strength or an untrained dog could still walk her dog. Several styles are available. Some attach the leash to a ring on the chest band. Others have straps that go under the legs and fasten behind the shoulders, where the leash attaches. They tighten when the dog pulls and give the owner more control.

Equipment to Avoid

The following sections cover a few devices you *should not* use without a trainer or behaviorist's guidance because they can damage your relationship and actually injure your dog: chain collars, prong collars, and shock collars.

> **TIPS AND TAILS**
>
> Any tool in the hands of an inexperienced person can hurt a dog. If you feel you need special equipment to control your Lab, work with a trainer or behaviorist to evaluate the situation. Learn how to use equipment safely and without ruining your relationship with your Lab.

The chain collar—also called "choke collar," for good reason—has fallen out of favor over the past two decades. The training method of choice since the 1950s was what trainers now refer to as the "jerk-and-pull" method. Owners spent their time in obedience classes learning how to give their dogs a "proper" correction, which entailed a quick, hard jerk on the chain and an equally quick release. The method worked, but owners don't like hurting their dogs, and today, positive training approaches have taken its place.

But many dog owners still use these collars. The collar tightens when your dog pulls, which can choke her or injure her trachea. This collar should *never* be left on a dog for any reason. Your Lab could hang up on a branch or fence and choke to death.

A prong collar is a correction device, not a training tool. The prongs go entirely around the dog's neck, which evens out the pressure applied when the dog pulls or the handler makes a correction. Thus, there isn't as much risk of injuring the trachea as with a chain collar. But if the prong collar is too tight or the owner uses too much force, the prongs can puncture the dog's neck. People without enough strength to control their dog often use a prong collar to give themselves some leverage.

The effect when a handler makes a correction is instant and extreme. It really hurts. A sensitive dog might react aggressively in self-defense or fear. Other dogs become increasingly stressed while wearing one. A prong collar can destroy your relationship or save it. Never use one without expert help.

The manufacturer of electronic or "shock" collars call this a "stimulation" collar, or similar name, to sidestep the negative image of you zapping your dog. But zapping is exactly what it does, and it has its place in certain types of training.

Hunters who train their dogs to take commands from a distance make use of these collars. When a person understands the scientific principles of negative reinforcement and uses the collar correctly, the dog can learn. But if you hit the button at the wrong time, all you've accomplished is confusing and frightening your dog. For pet owners, there is no practical purpose in using these collars.

When You Need Professional Help

Pet owners are not professional dog trainers and shouldn't have to be. A frustrated owner with a frustrated dog won't make much progress. If you just can't handle your wild Labrador yourself, get help from a trainer or behaviorist. Many options are available.

You could sign up for a beyond-the-basics class, and repeat it if you need to. You'll absorb more information now that you've had more real-life experience with your puppy. Agility classes will burn off some of your Lab's energy, although she's too young to do any jumping on hard surfaces. If you're looking for a professional dog trainer, check with the Certification Council for Professional Dog Trainers' (ccpdt. org) or the Association of Pet Dog Trainers (apdt.com).

Private lessons might be necessary. Sometimes it helps to have a trainer come to your home where the problems actually are occurring. You spend time working together on the particular issues you're having with your Lab. The entire family gets individual attention and can try different solutions.

Sending your young Lab to boot camp—a board-and-train program—may seem extreme, but professional trainers will get quicker results from her. If you're an inexperienced dog owner, it will be easier for you to learn to handle your Lab if she's already had some training. Then you both aren't beginners. If you decide to go this route, be sure you will get instruction as well. Ask about training methods and types of equipment used. A puppy does not need to be trained with electronic collars or other harsh devices. Get references from other clients, too.

If you're dealing with aggression or other potentially serious behavior in your Labrador, consult an animal behaviorist or other professional with advanced training in behavior modification. A qualified consultant evaluates your situation and helps you work through your dog's specific issues.

There are several types of consultants, and each has an advanced level of education and experience. Specific organizations train and certify these experts, and they often maintain a database of people you can contact for help. Here are some of the organizations and associations you might hear about:

A member of the International Association of Animal Behavior Consultants (iaabc.org) has been tested and certified in the areas of assessment, counseling skills, and behavioral science. Members also must submit references and case studies demonstrating their skills.

The Association of Companion Animal Behavior Counselors (animalbehaviorcounselors.org/acabc_members) certifies specialists at several levels: Certified Professional Dog Trainer (CDT), Certified Canine Behavior Counselor (CBC), and Board Certified Companion Animal Behaviorist (BCCAB). Each requires increasing levels of education and continued training in the field, along with supervised internships.

A Certified Applied Animal Behaviorist (CAAB; certifiedanimalbehaviorist.com) has an advanced degree (an MS/MA or PhD) in the science of applied animal behavior and has demonstrated expertise and experience in diagnosing and treating behavior problems.

Veterinary behaviorists are board-certified veterinarians who have a specialty in animal behavior and have completed a 1- to 3-year residency program in veterinary behavior. He has conducted research, published his findings in academic journals, and passed a 2-day exam. These are the only behavior specialists who can prescribe medication for your dog. The American College of Veterinary Behaviorists (dacvb.org) maintains a database of behaviorists in the United States. You will need a referral from your veterinarian.

> ### TIPS AND TAILS
>
> No magic pill fixes behavior problems. Before you spend a lot of money on professional advice, commit to working with your dog until her issues have improved to an acceptable level.

Clicker Training

Many methods are available for training your dog. In recent years, positive reinforcement instead of punishment methods have gained favor, and with good reason. It's much more fun for you and your puppy if you're rewarding her for doing something right rather than punishing her all the time for doing something wrong.

With that in mind, you might want to try clicker training, where the handler (you) uses a handheld clicker as a signal to the dog that she has done the right thing. Besides being fun, the training method is based on scientific principles and research developed decades ago with dolphin training. It's based on Pavlov's research between 1901 and 1903 when he rang a bell before feeding a group of dogs. The dogs associated the bell with food and salivated in anticipation.

You can't force a dolphin to do something. You can't lure her or shape her into position to show her what you want. So instead, trainers "marked" the correct behavior with a click, followed immediately by a food reward. (Sound familiar? That's what you're doing when you praise your dog while she's sitting and then give her a treat. The click, or your praise, marks the sit and tells the dog food will follow.) The trainers took a sound that had no meaning to the dolphins, and gave it meaning. The dolphins knew a treat was coming when they heard it. The click is called a conditioned reinforcer.

Timing is critical in clicker training. It's impossible to deliver the praise and food reward at the exact second the correct behavior occurs. You must click as your dog performs the correct behavior so she understands what brought her the food reward.

Dogs love figuring out what will make you click and treat. Your Lab puppy will run through her entire repertoire of behaviors until she finally does the one thing you were waiting for. To use the method effectively, we recommend you find a good book and a trainer to get you started. Any lesson can be broken down into pieces and taught with clicker training, and many owners find it a lot of fun and much easier for teaching their puppy.

You and Your Puppy

When your teenage Lab slows down enough to notice you, seize the opportunity to enjoy her company. Write down the stories of her crazier moments. There's nothing funnier than a bunch of Lab owners getting together and sharing puppy stories. Stock up on chew toys, and settle in for the long haul. Adolescence is just beginning.

Time for a Belly Rub

Teenagers need a lot of rest, and after a frantic day of running and playing, your Lab needs some quiet time, although she might not think so. As long as you'll play, she'll be up for a game, so quit before she exhausts herself.

After an active play session, take her for a quiet walk. If you cut off the activity cold turkey and expect her to settle down, she won't. She's still wound up and ready to go. Give her a belly rub or a massage; it will relax you both at the end of a long, active day.

Dealing with a Lab Teenager

Attitude is everything when you have an adolescent Labrador. Don't take it personally. Remember when you were a teenager? You stayed out late, didn't listen to your parents, had to be doing something with your friends every minute, and thought you were invincible. Well, that's what your puppy is going through. She's full of life and having a blast, so you might as well sit back and enjoy it. When she rips up the couch, take a photo so you can laugh about it later. (By the way, who left her alone with access to the couch? Oops.)

One day Terry looked out the window and saw the shingles from the doghouse roof flying across the backyard. Her 8-month-old Lab was diligently pulling them off one by one and slinging them around the garden. See? You're not alone. Enjoy!

Month 8 > Month 9 > Month 10

Socialization in public

Adult teeth are in—chewing continues

Ready for more advanced training

Moderate growth

Sexual maturity

Between 8 and 9 months, your adolescent Lab is mentally maturing, but he's still very much a teenager. You'll see his attention span improve. He'll be pushy but not as aggressively as some breeds. He's also more watchful and protective of you, and he needs your leadership to maintain his good behavior.

Enjoy his company and the challenges he presents. He's a lot of fun and joyfully delights in his time with you.

Physical Development

You'll see subtle differences in your Labrador's physical appearance between 8 and 9 months. His growth has slowed dramatically, even though he is not yet his full adult height. He may grow an inch in a week and then stop altogether for the next 2 weeks. His coordination also improves.

Internally, his bones are developing and hardening. He might still look light-boned and slightly out of proportion until he's 13 to 18 months old.

His teeth have all broken through the gums, and by next month, most of his teething pain will end as his teeth have set in his jaws.

Males Looking More Masculine

If your Lab is neutered, he'll mature differently from an intact male. A dog of either sex stops growing at some point, and his bones begin to harden and thicken. It's the sex hormones that put the brakes on the height, and if a dog is altered, he'll continue to grow a bit taller and lankier than he would have if left intact. This appears to be more obvious in neutered males because females have naturally lighter bone structure anyway.

Last month, your male dog still looked a little gangly to some extent, and his body might have seemed longer than it should be. He might have appeared as if his back legs were higher than his front legs. He'll start developing more muscle in his rear this month, and as he does, his body will start to look more in proportion. His rib cage fills out and broadens. His head becomes larger as it grows in width and breadth. His neck thickens, and the coat around his neck gets heavier. Again, if your dog is neutered, these changes aren't as dramatic.

Females Looking More Feminine

While males look obviously male, females are harder to define. They don't change dramatically like an intact male does as he reaches maturity. Most of the female characteristics stay the same whether or not they are spayed because it's the absence of testosterone that makes them female. If spayed early, they may get taller like neutered males.

There are coat differences between males and females. These aren't as obvious as on a long-coated dog, but they're still there. The ruff over the shoulders and on the neck isn't quite as thick in females.

Also, females have a feminine head when compared to a male, as well as overall lighter bone structure.

Health

There's a lot going on inside your puppy's body this month as he continues to grow and develop. His energy level may differ wildly from day to day, and you'll need to watch for signs of injury or other limb problems that occur in teenage Labs.

Occasional Lack of Energy

Glucose is the form of sugar found within the bloodstream. It's formed from carbo-hydrates during the digestion of foods and is then used as energy. Puppies digest their food faster than adults, and this sometimes prevents absorption of all the nutrients in their food. A puppy who over-exercises uses up the nutrients in his body faster. The combination of the two can cause low blood sugar (hypoglycemia), which makes him tired.

If your puppy is eating a poor-quality food, the carbohydrates in his diet may not be as easily digestible as they should be. This can affect his ability to produce enough energy to keep up with his needs. If your Lab seems to have a frequent problem with low energy, it's worth a look at his food to see if it might be contributing to the problem.

There are other reasons your young Lab might be tired. During growth spurts, he uses a lot of energy to build muscles and bone, and he might need more food. Don't let him get fat, though. If he looks like he's getting heavy, cut back on the amount you're feeding him. His caloric and energy needs may vary from week to week this month.

Parasites like intestinal worms or heartworm can also contribute to a puppy's lack of energy. Look for other symptoms, like a dull coat or watery eyes.

> **TIPS AND TAILS**
>
> If your puppy seems overly tired all the time, take him to the vet for a checkup to rule out serious disease and treat parasites.

What to Do If Your Puppy's Limping

A puppy might limp for several reasons. He could have slipped and twisted a leg while playing, for example, and the limping might go away in a few hours. Or it could be something more serious. Several conditions can occur in adolescent Labradors. Pay close attention to your dog's symptoms, and make notes about what you see so your veterinarian can make an accurate diagnosis.

Most bones start off as cartilage, a flexible connective tissue that gradually hardens and is replaced by bone. The longest bones in your puppy's body are his limbs. These long bones must grow longer in order for your puppy to get taller. They must also grow wider to physically support his adult weight.

We talked about growth plates in Month 7 and the effect spay/neuter surgery has on the timing of when they close. Here, we want to look at this and other problems that might cause lameness in a young Lab. Some scientists believe that feeding a food too high in calcium or that promotes fast growth could be a contributing factor in any or all of these conditions.

Teenage dogs are especially prone to leg and growth plate fractures because their bones are still soft. A dog should not run or jump on hard ground like asphalt until he is at least 18 months old and his growth plates have closed.

A fractured growth plate must be surgically repaired. The fracture may affect the final length and angle of the bone when your dog matures, and he may permanently move with an uneven gait. He'll also be more susceptible to arthritis in the joint where the fracture occurred and in other joints affected by his off-balance movement.

Another condition your Lab puppy might face is osteochondritis dissecans (OCD). OCD is not an inherited condition; it's often caused by excess trauma to a dog's shoulders. Other causes include genetics, rapid growth, hormone imbalances, and nutrition. Immature cartilage is fractured from the bone and sometimes floats loose in the joint fluid. Young, rapidly growing Labs 4 to 8 months old are especially susceptible. Hard-pounding exercise contributes to the risk. If you have slick floors, put down runners so your young Lab won't slip and injure his fragile bones.

OCD can affect one or both shoulders. Your dog may be stiff and sore or limp after exercise. If untreated, the lameness will become permanent as arthritis sets in. X-rays are used to diagnose the condition. The treatment consists of 4 to 8 weeks of complete crate rest and anti-inflammatory medications. Surgery to remove the loose cartilage is also an option.

Also referred to as "growing pains" or wandering lameness, panosteitis affects the humerus in the front legs and femur in the rear. Common in young, rapidly growing breeds like Labs, it causes lameness that often switches from one leg to the other every few days. It's sometimes misdiagnosed as elbow dysplasia, an inherited condition (see Month 7). At the first stages of pano, your Lab's legs are sore and he may be unwilling to play or appear depressed. He may also not feel like eating and may have a fever. X-rays will show changes in bone density.

Treatment for panosteitis includes restricting your dog's activity, plenty of crate rest, and analgesic drugs. The condition isn't hereditary or caused by injury. Panosteitis usually resolves itself in 4 to 6 weeks. There are no long-term consequences if the dog receives treatment and injuries are prevented.

A torn anterior cruciate ligament (ACL) is a soft tissue injury rather than a bone problem like the previously mentioned conditions. A hard-playing Lab will leap up to catch a ball or flying disc and land wrong, tearing this knee ligament. Other causes are making a sudden turn while running, slipping on a hard surface, or being hit by a car. Overweight dogs are at higher risk because their knee joints are weaker from carrying too much weight. With a torn ACL, your puppy will be in intense pain and limp because the tear allows the tibia and femur to grind against each other.

A partially torn ACL may heal with treatment, including limiting his activity for 8 to 12 weeks, with low-impact exercise like swimming or walking when he's ready to start moving again. Your vet will also prescribe anti-inflammatory medications.

At this time, the only treatment for a completely torn ACL is surgery, which involves a recovery time of 6 to 8 weeks. The dog will be restricted to leash-walking with very limited exercise.

If the injured ACL isn't treated, the dog will usually develop arthritis. Also, because the one leg is injured, the opposite leg bears more weight, which often causes the ACL to rupture on that side, too.

The Nose Knows

Hunting for a fallen bird in heavy cover or water, trailing the scent of a lost person, finding traces of arson after a fire—you'll find Labs in each of these situations, and more. Labs are famous for their keen sense of smell. Scientists estimate that a dog's scenting ability is millions of times more advanced than that of his human companions, and up to one third of his brain is devoted to scenting and analyzing what he smells. And that's something Labs have at birth, so your puppy can already smell thousands of things you can't.

The canine nose is divided into two cavities with a vertical wall of tissue, called the nasal septum, dividing them. The nasal cavity contains a maze of bony structures that, along with the sinuses and nasal septum, communicates with the olfactory nerve, which sends scent information to the brain. Often a dog will "lick" the air with his tongue and bring the scent to his nose to absorb it.

When a scent reaches the brain, it goes to areas that process memory, pleasure, and emotions, making associations between them. As your Lab puppy encounters new smells, he builds up a memory bank of scents and what they mean to him. Just like we remember the smell of Thanksgiving dinner and all the fond memories we associate with that experience, your puppy learns that some smells mean good food, some mean a thing tastes bad, and others signify a memorable experience. But with the ability to process thousands or even millions of scents, by the time he's an adult, he's a virtual encyclopedia of scents!

Your Lab puppy's nose is ideally constructed for poking around in the dirt. When he sniffs, his nostrils dilate and mucus in the nose filters out bacteria, dirt particles, and other matter, which he then exhales.

As if that wasn't amazing enough, a structure called Jacobsen's organ (vomeronasal organ) resides in the nasal cavity. This organ communicates with different parts of the brain and can process "smells" that aren't actually odors but chemical messages passed from one animal to another. It's Jacobsen's organ that makes a newborn puppy able to recognize his mother's milk and enables her to recognize her own puppies. It also enables a dog to recognize the "scent" of fear in humans.

Pheromones play a big part in communication between dogs, and Jacobsen's organ is able to detect and interpret quite a bit of this information. For example, one dog can recognize if another is an adult or puppy, male or female, or whether that dog is altered, or ready to breed.

A **pheromone** is a chemical secreted by an animal. Other animals, usually of the same species, can interpret this chemical.

The length of your Lab's nose also has an effect on his scenting ability. Breeds with longer noses, like Labs, have more scent-reception cells.

Alternative Health Care

Dog owners who want to treat their pets with natural remedies or who find conventional medicine isn't working for their dog may turn to alternative or complementary medicine for treatment. Although your Lab is probably years away from serious illness or age-related disease, some forms of alternative treatment can be used in cases of behavior-related problems or to heal injuries.

Most veterinarians practice Western medicine, and some incorporate complementary therapies into their treatment plans. There are also purely holistic veterinarians and practitioners, who treat patients solely with herbal or other remedies.

Veterinarians have advanced degrees and are licensed and regulated by law. There is no similar system for credentialing alternative practitioners. It's up to the consumer to investigate treatments and the people who supply them to be sure they're getting safe and appropriate care for their dog. Do your research, or ask for recommendations and check references if you're thinking of using an alternative practitioner. Also visit the American Holistic Veterinary Medical Association at ahvma.org for more information.

Acupuncture is an ancient Chinese practice that's been successfully used on animals and people for thousands of years. It strives to correct energy imbalances in the body and promote healing. Acupuncture addresses pain and inflammation from injuries, arthritis, hip or elbow dysplasia, neurological disorders, and digestive disorders.

The practitioner applies fine needles that stimulate predefined acupuncture points. These points lie along meridians, or energy lines, that travel through the dog's body. The meridians contain nerve endings, connective tissue, and blood vessels that release endorphins and other mechanisms to relieve pain and trigger healing. Some acupuncturists add electrical stimulation to the needles.

Your veterinarian may recommend acupuncture in addition to physical therapy or conventional medicine. The treatment usually takes 20 to 30 minutes per visit, and dogs accept it with minimal discomfort. In fact, they tend to relax noticeably during a session. To find a veterinarian who provides acupuncture for dogs, visit the website of the American Academy of Veterinary Acupuncture at aava.org.

Acupressure is similar to acupuncture in that it works the same energy meridians on the body. But instead of needles, the practitioner uses pressure on the acupuncture points, similar to massage, to treat allergies, diarrhea, digestive problems, ear infections, respiratory problems, and more. Your veterinarian may teach you how to use acupressure at home on a daily basis to treat your dog. Most practitioners recommend 5- to 10-minute sessions. If you find your dog resists the pressure, winces in pain, or otherwise tries to avoid the session, stop and consult with your vet.

Chiropractic therapy can improve a dog's movement and relieve pain. The practitioner adjusts the dog's vertebral joints, extremity joints, or head. It's often used to treat injuries, arthritis, and hip and elbow dysplasia.

The American Veterinary Medical Association (AVMA) recommends you have a vet examine your dog before you pursue chiropractic treatment. X-rays and other tests will help you and your Lab's doctors choose an appropriate treatment plan. Opt for a chiropractor who specializes in animals and is a member of the American Veterinary Chiropractic Association (avcadoctors.com).

Massage and other body manipulation techniques are also helpful for some dogs—TTouch in particular. Linda Tellington Jones originally developed this therapy for horses, but it has been used on all species of animals. The practitioner uses circular motions with her fingers, applied to different parts of the body, to promote healing and behavior modification by opening the body's awareness and releasing tension. Owners can learn to use the technique themselves. The movements relax your Lab puppy and can improve problem behaviors when incorporated into training programs. Find out more at ttouch.com.

Traditional massage helps improve circulation, relieve pain and stiffness, improve flexibility and range of motion, and help restore proper functioning to joints and limbs.

Homeopathy is based on the law of similars and the concept of "like produces like." Practitioners use a substance that in undiluted form causes a particular symptom. In a highly diluted homeopathic formula, the same substance relieves the symptom. Some remedies are used to treat a variety of health problems at once. Homeopathic remedies are usually diluted with alcohol or distilled water. Most are administered to your dog in the forms of drops that you put directly in his mouth.

Homeopathic remedies are used to treat a variety of health problems, such as pain, inflammation, fluid in the lungs, bruises and wounds, bleeding, skin problems, respiratory illness, allergies, and more. Practitioners do not claim to cure diseases like cancer or arthritis, but they do strive to help your dog attain the best possible overall health so his immune system can fight these diseases.

> **DOG TALK**

Homeopathy is the practice of using herbs, minerals, and natural compounds to strengthen the body's natural defenses and cure disease.

The Food and Drug Administration (FDA) classifies homeopathic remedies as drugs but does not evaluate them for safety or effectiveness. Do careful research and buy only from a homeopathic practitioner or use a well-known brand name. To find a veterinarian who uses homeopathic techniques, visit the Academy of Veterinary Homeopathy at theavh.org to learn more.

Natural Remedies

Natural remedies make use of plants and other natural substances for healing health and behavioral issues. Although they have been successfully used for centuries, they should not be a substitute for veterinary care.

Although owners generally regard them as safe and effective, always consult with your vet and research potential side effects before giving natural remedies to your dog. The quality and concentration of ingredients varies dramatically from brand to brand, and a remedy may not have the same effect on every dog.

> **TIPS AND TAILS**

Neither the FDA nor any other government authority regulates natural remedies, and manufacturers' claims about their effects have not been scientifically proven.

Glucosamine and chondroitin are compounds found in cartilage and are added to dog food to improve joint health. Dogs with arthritis due to hip dysplasia, injuries, or aging can experience increased mobility due to a decrease in inflammation and pain. If a young dog is diagnosed with hip dysplasia, glucosamine can help prevent cartilage breakdown, while chondroitin contributes to the creation of new cartilage. They are usually added to senior formula dog foods because joint problems usually affect aging dogs. These supplements can cause stomach problems like nausea and diarrhea, so be sure to consult with your vet before giving them to your Lab.

Humans have used herbal remedies for centuries for their healing properties. Practitioners use various parts of the plant—roots, flowers, stems, or leaves— depending on the remedy they need. Many remedies are made using a number of herbs. You can make your own remedies or purchase them in tablets or capsules. The plants are used dry or made into teas, juices, or tinctures. In a tincture, the herbs are combined with alcohol, soaked, and the liquid drained off.

Herbs contain nutrients and chemicals that can aid healing in dogs. They some-times work much more slowly than traditional medicine, and it's not unusual for one to take several months before you see any effects. Some remedies target a specific illness or emotional state; others boost the immune system and overall health.

Thousands of plants contain medicinal properties. Some commonly used herbs include the following:

😺 Chamomile, for its calming effect

😺 Alfalfa, as an anti-inflammatory

😺 Ginger, for carsickness

😺 Echinacea, to boost the immune system

😺 Nettle, as an antihistamine

Remember that some plants are poisonous to animals, so do careful research or work with a veterinary herbalist. Herbal remedies are medicines and can have harmful side effects if used incorrectly. Learn more about herbal remedies from the Veterinary Botanical Medical Association at vbma.org.

Flower remedies, also called essences, are homeopathic remedies made from flowers or parts of flowering plants formulated to treat health and behavioral issues. Probably the most well known is Rescue Remedy, which is used to treat stress and anxiety. Developed by Dr. Edward Bach in the early twentieth century, each Bach Flower Remedy includes several flower essences formulated to treat imbalances in the body and spirit. Rescue Remedy, for example, includes several flower essences, including star of Bethlehem, clematis, impatiens, rock rose, and cherry plum. The remedies were developed for use in people, but many are also used for dogs.

The remedies are administered with an eyedropper, either directly into the dog's mouth or added to his water or food. Because they're homeopathic, they're highly diluted, so you just give your dog a few drops.

Also from the plant kingdom, essential oils are made from roots, leaves, flowers, or seeds. Essential oils are used to heal wounds, repel insects, and treat skin problems. Unlike other remedies, these aren't taken internally; they're applied to your dog's skin or fur. One of the most well known is citronella, which is made from lemongrass and repels mosquitoes. Tea tree oil (from the melaluca tree) is another popular oil known for its antiseptic, antibacterial, and antifungal properties. Some essential oils formulated specifically for animals treat skin irritation and repel ticks and fleas.

> ### TIPS AND TAILS
>
> Investigate essential oils carefully, because many are safe for people but not dogs. Also, some oils that are safe for dogs are not safe for use on cats.

Pheromones are naturally produced chemicals dogs can sense in another animal, usually of the same species. We talked a little bit about their powers earlier in the chapter. Synthetic Dog Appeasing Pheromones (DAP), similar to the pheromones a mother dog releases to calm her newborn puppies, are recommended for fearful or anxious dogs or dogs with aggression issues. DAP is widely available as a spray, collar, or mister.

Nutrition

Dog food can influence your puppy's behavior, as we've mentioned earlier in this chapter, so it's important you know what you're feeding your Lab puppy and serve him the best food possible.

The Links Between Food and Behavior

Puppies who are fed diets high in cereal grain carbohydrates sometimes have signs of hyperactivity, are unable to concentrate, don't retain what they've been taught, and just can't seem to hold still. Although a teenage Lab certainly exhibits all these symptoms regardless of what you feed him, you may see a noticeable improvement in his behavior simply by changing his food.

Protein contributes to the *serotonin* levels in your dog's body. Just like in people, serotonin affects his mood, sensitivity, and sleep cycle. Serotonin is produced by tryptophan (the chemical that makes us sleepy after we eat a big turkey dinner on Thanksgiving), and tryptophan comes from eating meat. When too many carbohydrates replace protein in his diet, it can cause a shortage of serotonin in the body, which results in hyperactivity, aggression, and restless sleep.

The types of carbohydrates in food also play a role in your Lab's behavior. Carbs with a high *glycemic index* raise blood sugar rapidly and cause a "sugar high," a sudden increase in energy followed by a dramatic letdown and sleepiness. Rice and corn are two carbohydrates with a high glycemic index. Both are common ingredients in dog food because they're inexpensive.

> **DOG TALK**
>
> **Serotonin** is a neurotransmitter involved in the transmission of impulses between nerve cells. It's found in the brain, blood platelets, and intestinal tract. The **glycemic index** is a scale that measures the speed at which the body converts carbohydrates into sugars.

Carbohydrates with a lower glycemic index digest slowly and are also easier to digest. This provides a balanced blood sugar level, which evens out your dog's behavior. Oatmeal, apples, barley, and beans are all low–glycemic index foods.

The Debate Over Foods

Lab owners want to give their dogs the best care possible, and feeding a quality food is part of that mission. But it's not easy to know if you're feeding the right food. The choices are endless, and marketing claims and pretty packaging don't always tell the entire story.

If you've chosen to feed your Lab commercially made dog food—which is how most people feed their dogs—it's important that you educate yourself about the food, but be skeptical. Don't believe everything you hear or read. Many passionate people out there fervently believe they know how your dog should be fed. Most of them are not scientists and may not have facts to back up their claims. Consider the source, and make your own decision.

Until the early twentieth century, dogs were fed table scraps or horsemeat from the local butcher. Ken-L Ration introduced the first canned dog food in the 1920s. Quality wasn't much of an issue in these time-saving and convenient foods, and pet food companies didn't invest in much research. Easily available, inexpensive ingredients—like wheat and surplus horse and mule meat—were the basis of most dog foods.

Things soon changed. Horses became scarcer as cars filled the roads. During World War II, tin was scarce, so canned dog foods were less available. By the 1950s, kibble was on the market. Convenient and sold as "better than table scraps," it soon took over the pet-food industry.

Today's dog food manufacturers spend millions of dollars researching ingredients and canine health. They've developed unique protein sources like duck and lamb, as well as veterinary diets that address particular health problems like allergies and kidney disease.

The manufacturing processes used today are a mixed blessing. Although you get a food with quality ingredients, the process used in making the food destroys some nutrients. Most foods today are cooked under pressure. The food is cooked at such a high temperature that it kills some minerals, enzymes, and vitamins. The manufacturer then has to add ingredients like fat and other nutrients back into the food after cooking, along with preservatives to prevent rancidity. They often use synthetic chemicals that are harder for your dog to digest. Artificial flavors and coloring are also added.

Cost is a huge factor in dog food manufacturing. Some companies use less-expensive ingredients like cereal grains, by-products, and meat that's not fit for human consumption. They also use leftover ingredients from processing human foods or from slaughterhouses. Some ingredients are imported from overseas where countries have less-stringent regulations.

Although there had been dog food recalls over the years, the 2007 recalls involving Menu Foods brought the issue of pet-food safety to the public's attention. The Food and Drug Administration (FDA) forced a recall of more than 100 different brand-name products. More than 6,000 pets became ill, and more than 3,000 died because wheat gluten imported from China was contaminated with melamine. Soon after, contaminated corn and rice gluten were also discovered.

> ### TIPS AND TAILS
>
> Since 2007, recalls have affected many brands of dry food, wet food, and treats. The FDA maintains a database of all recalls at fda.gov. Log on and search for dog food recalls to find a complete list sorted by brand name.

Commercial food manufacturers aren't trying to kill our pets with tainted ingredients. Although not all food is made with high-quality ingredients, remember that dog foods must reach minimum nutritional standards set by the American Association of Feed Control Officials (AAFCO) and other federal and state agencies. Price is one factor you can look at, but the quality of the ingredients is the key factor. Grocery store and generic (private label) brands are usually the least expensive and include grains and by-products as their main protein sources. Artificial colors, flavors, and preservatives are often used, too. Many dogs are just fine on these foods, but some develop skin or digestive issues.

Premium foods contain a wide variety of ingredients, and some are better than others. They may still contain synthetic preservatives or other chemicals. The price is higher. Most of these foods are found in pet supply or feed stores.

Super-premium foods fall into this category because they're usually made with the best ingredients. You may still find some artificial additives, but on the whole, these brands strive to use healthy ingredients. Many varieties and mixtures of ingredients are available in this category.

Natural foods cannot claim to be natural if any synthetic chemicals or additives are used during processing. The FDA doesn't regulate the use of the word *natural* but states: "natural can be construed as equivalent to a lack of artificial flavors, artificial colors, or artificial preservatives in the product." AAFCO regulates the use of the term, but their regulations allow a lot of leeway. If a label says, for instance, "Natural, with added vitamins," the vitamins could be synthetic.

Organic foods earn this designation based on the way the plant and animal ingredients were raised. Although the U.S. Department of Agriculture doesn't specifically certify organic food at this time, most companies follow the guidelines for human organic foods. To be labeled organic, the food must contain at least 95 percent organic ingredients. The other 5 percent must consist of approved ingredients. Organic foods must be raised with no fertilizers, pesticides, growth hormones, antibiotics, or genetically modified sources.

> **HAPPY PUPPY**
>
> Feed your Lab twice a day. A dog who eats just once a day can suffer from low blood sugar and hunger, which can contribute to stress, irritability, and aggression.

With all these choices and factors to consider, choose a food based on your budget and your dog's overall health.

Grooming

In addition to your regular grooming routine, that includes brushing his coat, cleaning his teeth, and trimming his toenails, pay attention to your dog's seasonal grooming needs this month.

It's easy to forget that our heavy-duty Labradors need extra TLC during different times of the year, so let's take a look at what your Lab needs each season.

Spring Grooming Needs

Spring is the heavy shedding season for Labs. You may need to brush him every day to keep his fur from taking over your house.

After outings in spring and summer, check your Lab puppy carefully for foxtails, especially if he's been in un-mown grassy areas. One blade of grass lets lose hundreds of tiny barbed seedlings, and dried foxtails are most dangerous because they're sharp and can easily penetrate the skin. Foxtails are so small they're often hard to see, and unfortunately, shorthaired dogs like Labs seem to get just as many as longhaired dogs. The best prevention is to inspect your dog's entire body every day, including his ears, rear end, between his toes, in the folds around his face, and his armpits.

During heavy exercise, the vocal folds that protect your dog's windpipe won't close completely when he exhales, which increases the chances he could inhale foxtails or other foreign bodies. If your Lab puppy suddenly develops an explosive sneeze, suspect a foxtail or other foreign body in his nasal passage. He may also rub or paw at his nose, have a nasal discharge, or get a nosebleed. A foxtail can also penetrate the skin and migrate into the dog's bloodstream, eventually lodging in the lungs, causing an abscess and serious illness. Schedule a vet visit to have the foxtail removed before it causes serious problems.

If your dog has seasonal allergies, he may show signs during the spring when plants and grasses are in bloom. Rinsing him off with cool or distilled water can ease his irritation.

A dog's eyes are vulnerable to seasonal pollens and debris, too. A bit of grass can severely irritate his eye, scratch the cornea, or cause other eye injuries. The conjunctiva are membranes lining the eyelids and protect the eye from dust and other particles. An affected dog will rub at his eye, blink, or squint continuously. If you see a discharge from your puppy's eyes, or they appear excessively watery, inspect them to be sure nothing is under his eyelids. You may be able to remove the offending matter by pulling out his lower eyelid and sweeping it with your finger or a wet cotton swab. Be careful not to scratch the eye itself.

> ### HAPPY PUPPY
>
> Your Lab might love riding with his head out the car window, but that's not a safe idea. He's at increased risk for an eye injury from flying debris.

Use an eye rinse or artificial tears (saline solution) to wash out your Lab puppy's eye to remove small irritants. This washes the surface of the eye as well as the surrounding tissue. Wipe the skin around the eyes with a towel to remove any discharge. If his eyes are still irritated, use a cool, wet compress on one eye at a time. If this doesn't clear up the problem, have your vet examine him to rule out an injury. Eye irritation may also be a symptom of allergies, and your vet can help you determine what the problem is.

> **TIPS AND TAILS**

Your vet may prescribe an antibiotic ointment to heal your puppy's injured eye. To administer the ointment, pull down on your puppy's lower eyelid and apply the ointment on the inner surface of the eyelid, not on the eyeball itself. Rub the eyelid gently over the eyeball to spread the medication.

Fleas and ticks are coming out about now, too, so if you discontinued preventatives during the winter, restart them now.

Summer Grooming Needs

Your Lab is probably quite active during summer months, so he'll need more baths or rinsings to keep him clean and smelling nice. Always rinse him off after he swims in a pool, ocean, or lake. Chlorine and salt water are both extremely drying to his coat, and fresh water carries bacteria and parasites that can make him sick.

During his weekly grooming sessions, check your Lab's mouth to be sure no bits of sticks, seeds, and other debris are stuck between his teeth or lodged in his mouth.

A dog's fur usually protects him from direct skin contact with poison oak or poison ivy, two summertime hazards. Learn what these plants look like, and keep your Lab away from them. The oil in the leaves and branches causes an allergic reaction. If he runs through the woods, gets it on his coat, and you touch him later, you can also be infected. Wear gloves and thoroughly bathe your puppy if you think he's been exposed.

If he does get the oil on his skin, he may get an itchy rash just like you would. Especially vulnerable are areas where the hair isn't as thick, such as the tummy, inner legs, and muzzle. If your dog ingests some of the plant, he can suffer from vomiting or diarrhea, or his airway may swell. If this happens, take him to the vet immediately.

Fall Grooming Needs

Labs shed their summer coat in the fall and grow in a heavier winter coat. He'll need extra brushing for several weeks during this time to remove the loose hair. His coat will pick up more debris during the fall, too, like fallen leaves and dead flowers. You're lucky you have a Lab; these bits and pieces brush off easily.

Fall outings mean he'll also track in mud and dirt. It's easier to brush out of his coat when he's dry, if you can stand to wait. What doesn't easily brush out you can remove with a dry shampoo.

Winter Grooming Needs

If you live where the white stuff falls, your Lab will love romping in the snow. Clean his feet after these chilly outings to remove ice from between his toes and road salt from his paw pads. Don't leave your Lab wet, especially if he's gotten soaked to the skin. Dry him well with towels, and use a hair dryer to finish the job. Set the dryer on low so you don't burn his skin.

Your Lab may get a dry coat from being in a heated house all day. Regular brushing helps distribute the oils in his skin and coat, and a humidifier may also help his dry skin.

Social Skills

Your puppy doesn't look so much like a puppy anymore. Strangers often don't react to an adult dog like they do a puppy, and your Lab needs to learn how to interact with people differently now that he's growing up. Pay attention to how other people greet your dog and ensure his safety and theirs.

When People Don't Like Your Dog

How could anyone not love a Lab? Yellows and chocolates are usually recognized immediately, but black dogs have a public relations problem. It even has a name: black dog syndrome. Shelter workers across the country will tell you they have a much harder time placing black dogs, especially large dogs, because people are afraid of them. Movies portraying black dogs like Dobermans and Rottweilers as aggressive monsters are no help.

Many people won't recognize that your dog is a Lab, especially if he's a heavy-boned dog with a larger, blocky head. They'll ask you if he's a mastiff or pit bull. Reassure them he's a Lab and he's not aggressive. You can help ward off prejudice by putting a bright pink collar on your female. For a male, use a fun cartoon-style collar, a flower on his leash, or even have him wear a bright cape. You'll break down barriers just by having a friendly looking dog.

Some people are afraid of dogs of any color, especially big dogs. A lunging, barking Lab is not a good canine ambassador. You can help put them at ease if your Lab is well behaved and polite when he meets people.

Respect the feelings of others, and don't force your dog on anyone. If someone appears afraid, don't try to talk him out of it; you don't know his history or his reasons. Avoid him and keep your dog at a distance. Let him approach you when and if he chooses to do so.

Meeting New People

How should you introduce your puppy to someone new in order to make both the dog and the person comfortable? So many people, especially children, want to rush up and pet or hug a strange dog. Protect your Lab from their ill-informed enthusiasm. Even the nicest dog likes to take his time to get acquainted. Shield your pup from the onslaught and say, "Let me introduce you."

Always allow the dog to approach the person. A large human looming over a dog is scary (remember the socialization process in Months 2 and 3?). Think of how you'd feel if someone much bigger than you got in your personal space—you'd probably immediately back up until you were comfortable. A dog interprets someone coming straight at him as confrontational. He also interprets someone who looks straight into his eyes and holds the gaze as challenging him. Your Lab may even see it as an attack on you and try to protect you. This is all very noble but still inconvenient if he defends you from the wrong person.

You may find your Lab purposely stands between you and the person you're talking to. He is being protective, and you need to alleviate his fears. If you stand face to face, he may see it as a threat. Walk side by side with a person so your dog sees you are friends.

A person meeting a new dog should never put her face right in the dog's face—which is exactly what a child does when she hugs a dog. As she throws her arms around your dog, he'll feel trapped and unable to leave. Most of our Labs love the attention and are wiggling and kissing their new friend by now, but why take a chance? He may someday decide he doesn't care for the stranger who is mauling him with affection. Or when he doesn't feel well, or the person steps on his toes, pulls his sore ear, or otherwise accidentally hurts him, he might not remember his manners when responding.

When a person wants to ward off the unwelcome attention of an overly assertive dog, have her stand sideways to your dog, which makes her seem smaller and less threatening, and tell her not to make eye contact. To encourage a shy dog to approach someone, have the person crouch on the ground while still facing sideways.

Invite the person to scratch your Lab's chest rather than pat him on the head. Patting is annoying, and stroking is much more pleasant for your pup. And a hand coming at your dog from below is less threatening than a hand approaching his face.

Every outing is an opportunity to practice your Lab's social skills. Continue to incorporate obedience commands into your walks so he'll respond to you when he has the chance to show off for someone new.

Out and About in Nature

A well-socialized city dog may be terrified during his first hike in the woods, or he may love it. The safest way to hike is with your Lab puppy on leash until he knows his way around the area and you're sure no predators are around. Wild animals move silently in their natural environment, and you may never realize they're close. Your dog can sense them, though. Snakes, bears, crocodiles, mountain lions, poisonous toads, and even raccoons can seriously hurt you or your Lab. If he appears anxious or reluctant to go on, listen to him and turn back.

Many parks require that dogs be kept on leash to protect both you and the wildlife. Early in the morning, the scent from all the nocturnal creatures who were out and about the night before will be heavy, and your dog will love absorbing all the new smells … until he encounters a deer. He may react fearfully and bark, or he may get excited and chase. Either way, if he took off running, he could easily get lost. Always keep him on leash until you're sure he's well-enough trained to stay with you.

If he's never seen one, an encounter with something as harmless as a tree stump can cause your dog to approach cautiously until he's familiar with his surroundings. Teach him to climb over logs and cross a stream. Accustom him to carrying a backpack. Soon he'll be an eager companion for days outdoors.

Behavior

As your teenager develops, he'll undoubtedly test your patience and misbehave. If you continue to work to establish a good relationship with your Labrador and pair that with calm and consistent leadership and discipline (not necessarily punishment), your Lab will trust you and behave properly.

How Adult Dogs Show Leadership

Adult dogs earn a puppy's respect and compliance by using gentle but firm discipline. They chastise unruly puppies with just enough aggression to make their point, and no more. A mother will plunk a paw on a pup to stop him from harassing her, put her mouth over the puppy's muzzle, or get up and leave when a puppy bites on her teats too hard. A puppy who oversteps his bounds with other adult dogs will receive a snap and a roar that sends him packing. The adult settles back into her nap, and the pup minds his manners from then on.

When a dog rolls another dog over or pins him to the ground, she's either playing or putting an offender in his place because he was too pushy. A submissive dog rolls over voluntarily and shows his tummy to appease the aggressor; he isn't forced. That's usually the end of the discussion. Pinning a dog to the ground and holding him there or grabbing his neck is likely to start a fight.

We'd do well to follow the example of our canine friends. Discipline misbehavior with the minimum amount of force needed to stop the behavior, and no more.

Is *Dominance* a Dirty Word?

Dog behavior is often compared to that of wolves in a pack. The example given is usually one of a dominant wolf who rules the pack and who forces the others to submit to him in order to retain his position.

In recent years, wolf-pack theory, especially as it relates to dogs, has been disproven. The concept of an alpha wolf who is *dominant,* with the rest of the pack deferring to him, was based on observation of unrelated wolves living in captivity. These wolves were thrown together in an artificial situation and had to establish a social order of some sort in order to get along.

> ### DOG TALK
>
> According to the American Veterinary Society of Animal Behavior, **dominance** is a relationship between two or more individuals established by force and submission in order to gain power over resources.

In the wild, wolves live in family groups with a dynamic entirely different from that of captive wolves. Their relationship is one of cooperation and respect, not aggression and violence. A breeding pair of wolves leads the pack. Youngsters are born, grow, and leave the pack to form their own family units. Oftentimes the pack includes a very young litter of infants and older adolescents who haven't left the pack yet. Leadership shifts among members of the pack all the time, depending on what they're doing. The females are in charge when it comes to caring for the pups. The males are in charge when it's time to forage for food.

The term *dominance* has become controversial in dog training and behavior, and experts debate the meaning and how it applies to our relationship with our pets. You may have been told you have an "alpha," or dominant, dog, and you must be the dominant one or he will take over the household and become aggressive. You might think, *Oh no, we have a problem here that's permanent and can't be fixed.* Not really. What you probably have is a silly adolescent Lab.

Being a Kind and Fair Leader

Rather than think of yourself as having to be dominant, think of yourself as a leader, much like parents act toward their children. A parent leads the family and provides resources: food, clothes, money, and shelter. The child looks to his parents for care, education, and protection, and he respects their authority. That's really what we do for our dogs.

What is a leader, and why does your dog need one? A good leader is respected. His followers listen to him and go along with his example. A leader sets limits, establishes rules, and enforces them consistently and fairly. When your leadership is well established, your dog feels secure and happy because he knows what is expected of him. Your puppy has had rules since he was in the litter with his mother and siblings. He knew what he could and couldn't do.

A dog without a leader feels he has to make decisions for both of you, and they will be doggy decisions, not necessarily what you would choose. Your Lab puppy needs you to step in when you see him taking over a situation. This reassures him that you will protect him and he doesn't have to respond to every little thing.

Dogs thrive on consistency. Your Lab learns how to earn what he wants through good behavior. While you aren't thinking about a being a leader all day, your dog is watching you 24/7, taking mental notes. What do changes in your behavior mean for him? Should he test the boundaries to see if the rules have changed? What should he do?

You love your dog, and it's tempting to spoil him, or at least be lenient when he's misbehaving. After all, he's still a puppy. But spoiled dogs are like spoiled children; they want more and more. The more you cater to your dog, the more he'll demand—to be petted, fed, and entertained constantly. And he'll throw a tantrum or act out when he doesn't get his way.

Leaders love their dogs. They don't need to be overly harsh or dominant. Being a leader doesn't mean you can't pet your Lab or hug him. When you have a problem with a rude, hyper, or misbehaving dog, that's when you have to tighten up the rules and reestablish your authority. Leadership and respect are earned, not a gift.

> ### HAPPY PUPPY
>
> Your household is not a dictatorship. Every member of the family should be a leader in your Lab's eyes. He should respect the children as well as Mom and Dad. He'll also learn who he can manipulate. Avoid conflict by having a family agreement that everyone enforces the rules the same way.

Think of a reestablishing your leadership program as "no free lunch"—a concept introduced by canine behaviorist William E. Campbell decades ago to help owners deal with doggy dictators. Dole out your attention and resources. If he sticks his head under your hand to be petted, ask him to sit first. When he wants to come indoors, have him do a down. Before you put his food dish down, have him perform a trick. Ask for something meaningful so he has to make some effort to respond. Sometimes a sit is just too easy and he'll impatiently offer 20 sits in a row just to say "Get *on* with it, already." Sharpen his skills. Be sure those elbows touch the ground during the down or his rear stays on the floor for more than a nanosecond during the sit.

Be clear when you respond to his behavior. Say "Yes" or "No," and don't ignore him or avoid an issue. Use your body language to show you're confident and in control. Don't beg him to comply, and don't repeat yourself. Tell him; don't ask him. Practice dozens of "Downs," "Sits," "Stays," "Leave its," and "Waits"—all commands you've been working on and he should know. Two minutes once a day and scattered moments throughout will make a big difference in how he responds to you.

Don't get angry at your Lab; it just confuses him and makes him think you're unpredictable. Aggression—hitting, yelling, grabbing, or throwing him down on the floor—is likely to be met with aggression from your dog. He sees it as protecting himself from an irrational attacker.

A good leader does not throw his dog on the ground in an *alpha rollover* to prove he is dominant and that the dog must submit. How would you feel if your boss threw you against the wall when you disagreed with him? That's an exaggeration, of course, but a good example of how your Lab feels if his beloved owner is suddenly aggressive and cruel. There are better ways to earn your puppy's respect.

>DOG TALK

An **alpha rollover** is a punishment that's supposed to mimic how wolves establish their dominance over each other. A person forces his dog to the ground and holds him on his side or back until the puppy "submits" and stops fighting the handler. Don't try this at home, and don't let a "trainer" do this to your dog. Trainers who years ago advocated the alpha rollover now have retracted their endorsement. If you try it, you're more likely to get bitten than your puppy's respect.

Dealing with a Rude Dog

Does your teenage Lab block your path as you try to walk? Does he crash through doors ahead of you? Lean on you? Charge out of his crate? Counter surf? Grab food? If so, he's rude, and he needs to know who the leader is at your house.

When your space invader crowds you, do it right back to him. Lean toward him; don't bend over, just push slightly with your body, and he'll back off. Don't move out of his way or go around him if he blocks you. Shuffle your feet and keep moving forward in short steps to push him out of your way. Don't use your hands; he sees hands as the human version of mouthing and playing. He understands a body block because that's what he does. Remember, he reads your body language before he hears what we say.

>TIPS AND TAILS

Horse trainers have perfected the art of using their bodies to move a horse. By moving toward the horse's back hip, they can move the horse forward. By putting on "pressure," or leaning forward toward the horse, they make him back up. The same type of movement works with dogs.

When you see a full-on body block coming at you full speed, do the same thing to him. Take a couple quick steps toward him, and aggressively push your hands toward him in a "Stop!" motion. This should startle him and make him veer away. You don't want to turn it into a game, so don't reward him or praise him a great deal. Just say "Good dog" and move on to another activity, like asking for a sit. When he's pestering you for attention, stand with your arms folded and ignore him. Tilt your chin up and turn your body away.

Doorways are a big issue for dogs. Fights often start between dogs as they jostle with each other, trying to crowd through the door at the same time. Your puppy's excited to go out or in, and he doesn't want to be left behind. He's impolite and impatient, and as soon as he sees you head for the door, he leaps up and gets there before you.

Teach your Lab puppy that calm behavior gets him what he wants. As soon as he starts to rush the door, stop and walk away. When he comes back in and settles, start again. After a few tries, he'll be watching you carefully. If he runs up behind you, block his way to the door. Herd him back into the room with your body, not your hands or the leash. If you drag him by the leash, he's not learning anything except that you'll do the work. Say nothing. He must figure out that he has to wait behind you. It's not an instant process, but eventually the light will go on and he'll understand.

Here's another exercise you can try. Practice it with your Lab on leash. Open the door, and as he dashes out, shut the door behind him with you still on the inside holding the leash. Whoops! That isn't the result he had in mind! In a few seconds, he'll whimper or scratch at the door. He can't leave because he's still attached to you, but he's not actually with you, either. Let him in and try again. After a few tries, he'll hesitate and look at you. Praise him, walk through the door, and let him follow you. Remember that you taught your lab to wait in Month 7. This is the perfect place to use that command.

If your Lab puppy charges out of his crate the second you open the door, that's the next behavior to address. Never open the crate door for a dog who's whining, scratching, or otherwise demanding to be released. Wait until he's quiet. Ignore him because if he sees he has your attention, he'll continue fussing much longer. When you open the door, don't let him come crashing out. Quickly shut it in his face if he tries to charge. Do this as many times as you need to until he hangs back. Then quietly let him out and calmly go about your business.

Continuing Use of the Crate

This is the age of mischief for your puppy, and the crate is an important tool for preventing trouble during adolescence. Your puppy looks grown up, and he sleeps through the night without incident, so you might be tempted to leave him loose at night or in the house during the day. Don't.

A 9-month-old Lab isn't mature enough to handle the responsibility of entertaining himself for long periods of solitude. By putting him in his crate, he'll feel secure, and he won't feel like he has to investigate every sound. When he's excited in anticipation of your return, he won't be able to act out by tearing up a pillow or blanket that smells like you. If he gets hungry, he can't raid the trash. He realizes he can't act on his adolescent impulses so he gives up and takes a nap. He also learns self-control in the process.

Training

Continue to develop your Labrador's skills this month with more advanced challenges. He's capable of learning more complex concepts because his attention span is no longer that of a little puppy. And he can remember his new lessons much better for the same reason.

Solving Problems with Leash Walking

By 9 months old, your Lab puppy is really strong. You can't drag him or hold him back when he's distracted. And at this age, *everything* distracts him. Walking quietly at your side is not a natural canine behavior. When you don't let him rush off every time he sees something that interests him, he's likely to mutiny and try all kinds of different maneuvers to get out of walking at your side.

Solving this problem requires your full attention. This is not the time to be pushing a baby stroller or talking on your cell phone.

First, use a 4-foot leash, or take up the slack in your 6-foot leash. That way, he doesn't have as much length available for his antics. The clip on the leash should hang down, and the rest of the leash should form a U shape. If you let too much length hang down, he'll walk over it and become tangled. Hold your hands at waist level, where you'll have more control.

If you continually hold the leash tight, you're doing his thinking for him. He assumes the leash is supposed to be that way. He doesn't have to pay attention to you; he's knows right where you are. When he's on a loose leash, he makes mistakes and learns from them, and in the process, he learns self-control. When he's walking at your left side, you're tempted to pull tighter if you hold the leash in your left hand. Take your left hand off the leash, and hold it in your *right* hand at your waist.

When he balks, stands up on his rear legs, or refuses to go forward, start walking in the opposite direction. Turn around and go right past him and keep going. If he still doesn't follow you, walk in a circle around him. If he's still dancing around at the end of the leash, stop and work with him until he will sit. When you start walking, stop after just a few steps and ask him to sit again. Reward him when he does what you ask.

When your pup cuts in front of or behind you, block him with your leg, calmly turn into him, and start walking in another direction. If he runs behind you from the left, pull the leash in front of you to the right so he can't get clear around you. Then do an about-turn and walk into him. This also works if he tangles himself in the leash or wraps it around your legs.

TIPS AND TAILS

When walking your Lab, start calm and end calm. He must sit quietly while you put the leash on and walk politely out the door. If he starts acting wild, you must stay calm or his behavior will escalate. When you get home, he must sit politely while you remove the leash.

Your Lab might take the leash in his mouth because he knows you're going to give him a correction, and he wants to avoid it. Have you jerked on the leash too often? Are you nagging him? The simplest solution is sometimes the best. Let him carry his bumper or other toy in his mouth while you walk.

If that doesn't work, spray the leash with pepper spray or chewing repellent before your walk. Spritz a little in his mouth, too, so he recognizes the taste and smell. If you try to jerk the leash out of his mouth, he'll quickly turn it into tug-of-war. To combat this, you might want to switch to a chain leash, which hurts his teeth when he bites it. Chain leashes are chew-proof but they are also uncomfortable on your hands, so you might want to wear garden gloves. Horse-supply stores have chains for horse leads (called stud chains) that are 12 to 18 inches long. You can attach one to his collar and then attach the leash to it.

Does your pup bump into you as you walk? You might think he doesn't realize he's bumping into you, and sometimes your Lab certainly is oblivious to his own body. But most of the time, he knows exactly what he's doing. Bump him back, but overexaggerate the move. Don't be subtle, either. Bump him to the left or make a hard turn or about-face to the left. Leaning into him will just throw you both off balance. His motivation is similar to pulling on the leash: he keeps track of where you are, but he doesn't have to pay attention. He's also being very pushy and rude!

Your puppy may also lean against you when you're standing still. Again, by doing so, he knows right where you are so he doesn't need to pay attention. He's also invading your space. Step away quickly so he loses his balance. He won't fall all the way to the ground, but he will pay closer attention to you.

Maybe you've seen other Labs dragging their people down the street, or maybe your pup has done this to you. This is the toughest problem to fix, and the most common. While you work on this, your walks may not take you very far from home as you practice your obedience commands: sit, down, and short stays. Do plenty of U-turns so he has to pay attention and see what you're going to do next. As you turn, talk and joke with your Lab, "Hey, you missed it! Where'd you go?" Make it a game. Every once in a while, when you do a sudden turn, pull out his favorite toy or treat and reward him with it.

To prevent pulling, you need to be more interesting than his surroundings. You decide when it's time to stop and sniff, not him. If you see something you know will make him pull, be proactive; turn his attention to you and reward him before he starts pulling. If you need to, lure him with a treat right in front of his nose as you walk past the tempting distraction. You can reward him for his good behavior with "Go sniff!"

If one method isn't working for you, there are other ways to teach your dog to walk nicely. For example, stand still and don't move a muscle when he hits the end of the leash. Hold the leash at your waist, and don't pull back against him. Make no eye contact and ignore him until he looks at you to see what you're doing. Then calmly praise him. If he immediately lunges ahead, stop again.

Or if your dog is pulling ahead, stop and back up slowly. Instead of reaching his goal, he's moving farther away. When he stops pulling, you can start walking forward again.

HAPPY PUPPY

If your wild child just can't settle down for a walk, give him a game of fetch out in the backyard before you set out to take the edge off his energy. A walk by itself doesn't provide adequate exercise for a young, energetic Labrador. You'll benefit from a slightly worn-out pup, and he'll love both the game and the walk with you.

If you're using a no-pull harness or a prong collar, you and your Lab may become dependent on these tools. Practice with a trainer so you both can learn to walk without them. If you have to use severe equipment to control your Lab, you'll never get to the point where you can let him off the leash because he isn't listening to you.

Teaching "Watch Me"

When your Lab is distracted, the "Watch me" command helps him focus on you. Labs don't take much of anything seriously, so this is also an entertaining way for him to learn to pay attention. There are several ways to teach the command. You can use part of his dinner as a teaching tool.

Place treats or kibble in both of your hands, let your dog see them, and then hold your arms out sideways at shoulder level. He'll probably sit in front of you or leap at your hands to get the goodies. Wait. At some point, he'll stop focusing on the goodies and look at you. When he does, praise and deliver a treat immediately. After a few tries, he'll be staring at your face to get those treats, ignoring your hands completely. Now you can use the words "Watch me" just before he makes eye contact and praise him for looking at you.

You could also hold a treat right in front of your dog's eyes. Bring the treat up to your face, saying "Watch me." When his eyes shift from the treat to your eyes, praise and give him the treat. If he looks away before you can give him the treat, don't give it to him. He only gets a treat when he maintains eye contact. Just do this a few times and then quit. You don't want to fill him up on treats.

Once he's paying attention, back up while moving the treat to your nose. This helps him pay attention to you while you're moving. Then you can add zigzags, circles, and other variations.

You can also teach him to watch while he's sitting at your side. He doesn't have to swing in front of you. Then he'll know how to keep his eyes on you when you're out on a walk and you ask for his attention.

Teaching "Stand" and "Stand Stay"

When your veterinarian is examining your dog, wouldn't it be nice if your Lab would stand quietly while being handled? Beginning obedience competition requires a stand for exam exercise where your dog must stand still while the judge runs her hands over him. Advanced competition requires a moving stand, where the dog stops while walking and remains in a stand-stay as you continue moving forward.

To teach your Lab "Stand," kneel facing his side while he's sitting. Tweak his skin where his rear leg meets his belly, and lightly poke him up into a standing position while giving the "Stand" command. He'll quickly learn to stand when you touch that spot.

You can also lure your dog from a sit into a stand. Stand facing him as he sits. Take one step back while holding a treat just out of reach, putting pressure on the leash, and telling him to stand. Once he knows the command, turn the motion of luring him with a treat into a hand signal.

You and Your Puppy

Earlier in this chapter, you learned about your Lab's incredible talent for scentwork. In this section, you learn how to use that talent by developing his brainpower and putting those scenting skills to good use, all while having some fun together.

Challenging Your Lab's Mind

Scientists have shown that dogs can learn up to 300 words. With that potential, your Lab's brain is a Scrabble game of opportunity. Think about what a hunting dog is capable of doing: marking the fall of three different birds, remembering where he saw them, figuring out how to pick them up in the order they fell, and returning the birds to his master. Assistance dogs must learn to turn on lights, pick up keys, alert their owners to the doorbell, and many more specialized skills. Future service dogs already know at least 30 commands by the time they leave their puppy-raiser to go into training. Your Lab is capable of great things and, like a child, he must practice using his brain to develop these skills.

Challenge your Lab with puzzle games. He'll figure out how to slide open a compartment to find a treat in interactive games. He can learn the names of different objects during scenting and retrieving games and the names of specific locations in the house. Surely he recognizes the words *walk* and *dinner* by now. Teach him to go to his bed or crate, to ring a bell hanging from a doorknob to go outside, or to fetch the morning paper.

Challenging Your Lab's Nose

You may not be interested in or ready for competitive sports, but there are many other ways to have fun with a young Lab. Nosework is a way for you both to learn search dog skills in a fun, pressure-free environment.

Nosework, where handlers train their dogs to search for their favorite treats and toys, is an activity you can enjoy together at home, out in public, or in classes and workshops. You don't need a lot of equipment, training, or convoluted rules. All you need is a motivated puppy and his favorite reward, whether it's food or a toy. The goal of nosework is pure fun.

Nosework starts out easy, with your Lab searching for his toy that's hidden under or in one of a group of cardboard boxes. The challenges get progressively harder as your dog builds his skills and learns the game. Your pup gets to burn off energy, build his confidence, and best of all, spend time with you. You learn to read your dog's subtle communication signals and recognize when he realizes he's on the scent. If you decide to move up to tracking or search and rescue work, this is a great way to get started.

> **TIPS AND TAILS**
>
> If you are so inclined, you can check out training workshops and trials where your dog can earn nosework titles. For more information, log on to the National Association of Canine Nosework's website at nacsw.net.

Many young Labs start tracking by the time they are 6 or 7 months old. They're too young to do a lot of strenuous jumping or running at this age, so tracking is a perfect outlet for their energy. Your Lab demonstrates his scenting ability by following human scent and finding "lost" articles, such as gloves, dropped by the tracklayer along the way. The handler (you) has no idea where the track goes, so it's completely up to your lab to find and follow the trail.

Before your Lab competes in an actual test, he must earn a certification to compete. He completes a basic Tracking Dog (TD) track while being observed by an AKC judge. If he completes it successfully, he's eligible to compete in official AKC tracking competitions.

Unlike the other canine sports that require several outings and qualifying scores, a dog earns his AKC title after one successful track. The levels are Tracking Dog (TD), Tracking Dog Excellent (TDX), and Variable Surface Tracking (VST).

For a TD, the dog must follow a track in an open field that is 30 minutes to 2 hours old and 440 to 500 yards long. A flag marks the beginning of the track, and a second flag marks direction of the first leg. The track includes 3 to 5 "legs," or changes in direction. An article such as a glove or wallet is placed at the end of the track. At the beginning of the test, the dog is presented with an article containing the scent he's supposed to track.

When he moves up to TDX level, your Lab must follow a longer and older track: 800 to 1,000 yards long and 3 to 5 hours old. A TDX test includes five to seven changes of direction and two crosstracks made by humans. Four articles are along a TDX track—one at the starting flag, one at the end, and two more along the track itself. No flag indicates the direction of the first leg. While a TD is conducted on an open field, there may be natural and man-made obstacles along the route of a TDX. Obstacles may include gullies, plowed land, woods, vegetation, or streams. Man-made obstacles include fences, bridges, or lightly traveled roads.

In the VST, dogs face a much more difficult challenge. The track is 600 to 800 yards long and presents a varied tracking environment. The dog trails a scent 3 to 5 hours old in an urban setting rather than in the wilderness. He follows the track over at least three types of surfaces, such as concrete, asphalt, gravel, sand, or mulch. Tracks may be laid along the sides of buildings and fences, through buildings with two or more openings, breezeways, shelters, or roofed parking garages. There are no obstacles, as on a TDX track. The four articles used in a VST test are one each of leather, plastic (rigid or semi-rigid), metal, and fabric.

A dog who has earned all three titles becomes a Champion Tracker (CT).

> **TIPS AND TAILS**

You can get started tracking by taking classes offered by local obedience clubs. Your breeder may know of a tracking group in your area, and the AKC website also lists tracking clubs.

Month 9 ⟩	Month 10	⟩ Month 11
	Socialization in public	
	Adult teeth are in—chewing continues	
	Ready for more advanced training	
	Moderate growth	

Your Lab puppy is turning into a dog. Although she's not quite full size between 9 and 10 months old, you'll get a better idea of what she will look like as an adult. It's hard to realize she's still a puppy, but she hasn't lost her sense of fun and teenage mischief. As your puppy participates in more activities, she's prone to injuries, so we introduce some basic first aid in this chapter.

You should be able to control her exuberance better now as she learns more advanced obedience skills and starts to listen to you more consistently. Labs aren't pushovers, though, so we also talk about discipline and preparation for off-leash privileges in this chapter. At this age, she can start preparing for her Canine Good Citizen certificate, so we give you information on that as well as take a look at some activities your Lab and your children can participate in together.

Physical Development

Although there's great variation from dog to dog, there are reasons why Labradors look the way they do. The breed has been developed over two centuries to produce the characteristics we see today in our own beloved puppies. The originators of the breed put a lot of thought into what would, in their minds, make the perfect retrieving gundog.

A Look at the Breed Standard

Breed standards for purebred dogs are written descriptions that define the function, ideal structure, size, proportions, coat characteristics, and temperament for a specific breed of dog and how those features relate to the function of the breed.

In 1916, the English Labrador Retriever Club approved the first written breed standard for Labradors. The American Kennel Club (AKC) recognized the breed in 1917, but the American Labrador Retriever Club wasn't formed until 1931. The club submitted a breed standard to the AKC that same year. Minor changes have been made to the Standard over the years, but the basic descriptions remain the same. The latest version of the Labrador Retriever Standard has been in effect since 1994. As a result, when you purchase a purebred Lab, you have a good idea of what kind of dog you're getting.

Today, after 22 years as the dog with the largest number of annual AKC registrations in the United States, it appears the founders of the breed did a pretty good job. As both a pet and a hunting companion, the Lab reigns supreme.

The Standard describes the features that make a Labrador look like a Labrador. If the dog had a curly tail or upright ears, she wouldn't resemble the Labrador described in the Standard. If she weighed 25 pounds or was white with black spots, she wouldn't look like a Lab, either. The Standard sets the guidelines for breeders to follow.

> ## TIPS AND TAILS

To read the complete Labrador Retriever breed standard, visit The Labrador Retriever Club, Inc., website at thelabradorclub.com.

At dog shows, dogs are judged on how well they conform to the Standard physically and temperamentally. There's no such thing as a perfect Lab (or a perfect dog of any breed), so the dog who wins on a particular day is the one who, in the eyes of the judge, appears the closest to the description of the ideal Labrador Retriever.

Some parts of the breed standard are purposely vague. There can be acceptable variations in the characteristics that define a Labrador Retriever, so the breed standard has to allow for those differences. Although conformation judges look at the total dog, judges may also differ in their priorities regarding the importance of specific points of the Standard. For instance, when evaluating two good examples of Labradors and trying to decide between them, the judge may see that one moves better than the other, so the better mover gets the top award that day. Another judge may put more emphasis on head and coat character.

You may have heard breeders talk about "form follows function." When a judge looks at a Labrador, he evaluates features like the dog's stride, the length of her forearm, and if the angle of the shoulder is correct. Is this Labrador built to work all day over rough terrain? Will her coat protect and insulate her from cold water? Are her jaws strong enough to carry a duck or pheasant? Does she have the correct number of teeth? Is her temperament correct, meaning does she appear to be kind, outgoing, and friendly? The breed standard defines all these characteristics.

Comparing Your Puppy to the Standard

Although your Labrador hasn't yet reached maturity, you can have fun comparing her to the breed standard. Ask your puppy's breeder for a conformation evaluation. Even as puppies go through their awkward growth stages, you can learn about general conformation characteristics—how tall your dog will be and what she'll look like when she's fully grown. Ask if you should consider entering a dog show. Puppies may be shown in AKC-approved conformation events at 6 months old.

Even if your puppy doesn't look like a show prospect, she'll seem just as beautiful as any dog who wins ribbons to you and your family. In the long run, it won't matter much to you if she's too tall or is missing a tooth. In fact, some quirks make your own pet that much more endearing.

Let's explain some of the terms used in the breed standard and what to look for in your Labrador.

This is the first paragraph of the Standard:

General appearance:

> The Labrador Retriever is a strongly built, medium-sized, short-coupled, dog possessing a sound, athletic, well-balanced conformation …

Short-*coupled* refers to the area between the last rib and the point of the hip. Why is this important? A short loin, or short-coupling, provides a strong connection between the front and rear parts of the skeleton and uses less energy for movement, helping to increased stamina (an important characteristic for a retrieving gundog).

> … The typical Labrador possesses style and quality without overrefinement, and substance without lumber or cloddiness.

When the Standard states "substance without lumber," remember that a Labrador Retriever is supposed to be an athletic dog. Although she should have strong, substantial bones that can support her frame, she shouldn't be so big and heavy that she fatigues easily.

Size:

> The height at the withers for a dog is 22½ to 24½ inches; for a bitch is 21½ to 23½ inches. Any variance greater than ½ inch above or below these heights is a disqualification. Approximate weight of dogs and bitches in working condition: dogs 65 to 80 pounds; bitches 55 to 70 pounds.

Although males can be 24 inches tall at the shoulders, you rarely see one that tall in the show ring. You won't often see a Lab who is undersize, but many grow overly tall. Labs are intended to be a medium-size dog. A 100-pound Lab who is 26 inches at the *withers* is extremely large for the breed and would be too heavy to sit comfortably in a duck hunter's boat.

> **DOG TALK**

Withers are the highest point of a dog's shoulders, behind the neck.

Skull:

> The skull should be wide, well developed but without exaggeration.

This is a good example of beauty being in the eye of the beholder. It's one of those statements open to interpretation by different judges because most experienced judges have formed a picture of what the skull should look like.

> The skull and foreface should be on parallel planes and of approximately equal length. There should be a moderate stop—the brow slightly pronounced so that the skull is not absolutely in a straight line with the nose.

Using a profile picture of a Labrador head, if you draw a line from the back of the skull to the dog's nose, you'll see a definite "break" in the line at the eyes, at roughly the center point. This is the Labrador's eyebrow, or "stop"—a transition from the back skull to the foreface. It should be a moderate angle, not a flat, continuous line. It should also not be an abrupt angle that moves the eyes forward on the skull.

Nose:

> The nose should be black on black or yellow dogs, and brown on chocolates. Nose color fading to a lighter shade is not a fault.

A black nose on a yellow Labrador may fade during the winter. Some noses turn back to a deep black in summer, but some don't. Many have some pink on their noses. A nose with no black or brown at all is a disqualification.

Teeth:

> The teeth should be strong and regular with a scissors bite, the lower teeth just behind, but touching the inner side of the upper incisors.

This explains how the teeth meet in the mouth. A "scissors bite" is when the top teeth are in front of the bottom ones, which is correct in the Labrador. If the teeth meet evenly, this is called a "level bite," and the teeth wear faster as the dog ages. An "underbite," where the bottom teeth are in front of the top teeth, impairs a Labrador's ability to carry game.

Ears:

> Ears should not be large and heavy, but in proportion with the skull, and reach to the inside of the eye when pulled forward.

Labrador ears have a distinctive triangular shape. Heredity plays a part in size and ear placement, and some Labradors will appear to have longer, droopy ears, which can be the result of how and where the ears are located on the skull.

> **HAPPY PUPPY**
>
> Just for fun, test your Lab's ears to see if they reach or go past the inside corner of his eyes. Make it a peek-a-boo game!

Tail:

> It should be very thick at the base, gradually tapering toward the tip … clothed thickly all around with the Labrador's short, dense coat, thus having that peculiar rounded appearance that has been described as the "otter" tail.

A Labrador's "otter tail" is a unique characteristic of the breed. It's your Labrador's rudder in the water. When carried straight off the back, it's in a perfect position for swimming. It should be broad at the base and covered with the same thick coat as is on the rest of the body but without feathering.

When your Lab puppy is excited, you'll likely see a "gay" tail, carried in the air higher than her body. But when she's moving naturally, a correct Labrador tail should be carried straight off the rear.

Hindquarters:

> Viewed from the side, the angulation of the rear legs is in balance
> with the front.

When viewing a Labrador in profile, angulation refers to the angles of both the front and back limb bones. In the front, it refers to the angles where the shoulder bone (scapula) meets the humerus (upper arm bone), and to the bones that meet at the front point of the chest from the shoulder and elbow. If both the front and back are nicely balanced with similar angles, the dog moves gracefully and has more stamina. It takes a practiced eye and hands-on examination to recognize correct angulation.

Coat:

> The coat is a distinctive feature of the Labrador Retriever … [It]
> should have a soft, weather-resistant undercoat that provides
> protection from water, cold, and all types of ground cover.

A Lab's thick, water-resistant coat should be heavier over the shoulders and can have a slight wave to it. The proper coat is made of coarse guard hairs and a finer, wooly textured undercoat that insulates your pup.

Temperament:

> True Labrador Retriever temperament is as much a hallmark of the
> breed as the "otter" tail.

This one sentence describes why we all love this breed so much. As wild as yours may be when she's a teenager, we all know the Labrador is a fabulous family dog and companion. They should have added her sense of humor to the Standard. We've never met a Lab who doesn't make us laugh at least once a day.

The Conformation Certificate Program

The Labrador Retriever Club, Inc., offers a Conformation Certificate evaluation that any Labrador, even one who's spayed or neutered, may earn. It's noncompetitive, and any Lab over 1 year old is eligible to be evaluated. To be considered for the certificate, your dog is judged to determine if she possesses the "basic attributes" of a Labrador Retriever. The evaluators aren't looking for a perfect dog; they just want to raise awareness and provide education on correct *breed type*. As the LRC website states:

It is an opportunity for owners of Labrador Retrievers who are not interested and/or familiar with competitive conformation events to have their dogs evaluated and recognized as having basic Labrador Retriever conformation characteristics.

> **DOG TALK**
>
> **Breed type** refers to the qualities that define a Lab and make her different from other dog breeds, as set forth in the breed standard.

Many dogs who wouldn't win in the show ring still have correct Labrador characteristics, and the Conformation Certificate recognizes that. For example, many field trial competition dogs have lighter-weight coats than conformation dogs do. But they still have correct coats and, therefore, would pass that portion of the evaluation.

The evaluation contains nine conformation and temperament categories a judge scores from one to three points each. A dog is required to have a total score of 18 or better and demonstrate, in the judge's mind, a 65 percent likelihood of conforming to the characteristic as described in the Standard. The judge also looks at the following:

- 🐾 Does the dog possess the basic attributes of a Labrador Retriever?
- 🐾 Does the dog exhibit a majority of breed characteristics?
- 🐾 Would the dog be excused for lack of merit?
- 🐾 Does the dog possess any disqualifying characteristics according to the breed standard?

General disqualifications apply, such as freedom from lameness, blindness, deafness, or change by artificial means. Dogs noted to possess a disqualifying fault would not receive a Conformation Certificate.

Conformation Certificate evaluations are held in conjunction with events such as hunt tests, field trials, agility or obedience trials, and during National Specialty Event Week every October. Learn more at thelabradorclub.com.

Health

We covered CPR and life-threatening emergencies in Month 6. Now let's look at some other injuries and health problems you might encounter and how to administer first aid or treat them.

Treating Injuries

When your Lab puppy is injured, it can be easy to panic. But your cool-headedness is important to ensure her safety. Here's what to do:

Bleeding: If a wound is deep or spurting bright red blood, apply direct pressure and take your dog to the vet immediately. This is an emergency. She may have a severed artery, which quickly causes major blood loss. And don't wash the wound; that may prevent clotting. Less drastic wounds bleed slowly, ooze dark red blood, and stop bleeding within 5 minutes.

If possible, elevate the bleeding area above the heart to reduce blood flow. Apply direct pressure with a clean cloth, sanitary pad, nonstick gauze bandage, or paper towels. When the bleeding stops, don't remove the cloth because it may cause the bleeding to resume. If one bandage becomes soaked through, add another bandage on top of it rather than remove the first. If the bleeding doesn't stop, have a second person apply pressure just above the wound. Secure the bandage by wrapping it against the dog's body, and get your dog to the veterinarian.

Bleeding ear: A cut on the ear bleeds a lot, and your Lab may make it worse by shaking her head. The good news is that ear wounds usually look worse than they really are. Place a gauze bandage or small sanitary pad on either side of the ear, and apply pressure for several minutes to stop the bleeding. Without removing the bandage, fold the ear up against your Lab's head, and secure the ear to her head by wrapping a length of gauze or panty hose over her head and ear and under her chin. Don't wrap too tightly or interfere with your Lab's breathing. You should be able to slip two fingers between the bandage and her chin.

Within 24 hours, check the wound, clean it, and apply antibiotic ointment. Take your dog to the vet if you feel it needs more attention or may get infected.

Bleeding tail: If the tail is bleeding at the tip, your Lab may have whacked it against a wall or fence repeatedly. This is a common injury for Labs, and it can make an awful mess. Elevate the tail to minimize blood flow, and apply pressure to the underside of the tail at the base, near the anus. This is a pressure point that helps slow the bleeding.

The hardest part of treating a tail wound is keeping it bandaged so she doesn't break it open again every time she wags her tail. Clip away fur from the open wound, and wash the area with saline solution or antiseptic soap.

> **TIPS AND TAILS**
>
> To make saline solution, add 1 teaspoon salt to 1 quart warm water.

You want to bandage the tail, but not too tightly because you could cut off blood circulation and cause severe injury. Put one long strip of adhesive tape against each side of the tail, extending several inches below the wound and above the wound off the end of the tail. Wrap the tail and the tape with gauze, starting well below the wound and ending just past the end of the tail. Fold the tape back over the bandage, and twist the tape so the sticky side adheres to the bandage and past it, adhering to the hair, too. By sticking the tape to the hair, it helps anchor the bandage so it won't slide off the end of the tail.

Place an elastic bandage (like vet wrap) over the gauze wrapping, making sure the wrap sticks to plenty of hair. To keep your dog from chewing off the bandage, you may have to put an Elizabethan collar on her. If the injury is severe or isn't healing, take her to the vet. Most Labs with tail injuries end up at the vet anyway because it's so hard to keep their tails bandaged.

Bleeding paw pad: The most common foot injury in Labs is stepping on a sharp object like glass. Your puppy's paw pads contain many blood vessels, and they bleed profusely when cut.

Be sure you remove all the glass or other object from the bottom of your puppy's foot (see "Object imbedded in body," later in this section), flush the foot with running water to wash out any remaining debris, wash the area with saline solution or warm water, and dry the foot. Bandage the foot to keep dirt and debris out of the wound, using a similar technique as for bandaging a tail injury. Put one strip of adhesive tape against each side of the foot, extending several inches above and below the foot. Wrap the foot and the tape with gauze, starting at the toes and ending just above the ankle. Fold the tape over the bandage and twist it so the sticky side adheres to the bandage.

Place an elastic bandage (like vet wrap) over the gauze, wrapping from the toes to the ankle, tight enough to stick but not so tight that it cuts off circulation. Check after a few minutes to be sure your pup's toes aren't swollen; if they are, the bandage is too tight. Take your Lab to the vet; she might need antibiotics or further treatment.

Broken limbs: A fracture might mean one or more broken bones, usually to a leg. Suspect a broken bone if your Lab is holding her leg in an abnormal position, she appears to be in extreme pain, or is unable to put weight on the limb.

Before you transport your Lab puppy to the vet, put her in a crate or immobilize the break with a splint. The splint must cover the joints above and below the break to safely protect the limb. If your dog struggles too much, she risks worsening the injury. In that case, forego the splint and transport her to the vet as soon as possible.

When splinting a broken limb, do not reposition the bones. Place a rigid magazine, yardstick, or rolled newspaper on either side of or around the limb to prevent movement. Keep the splint in place using multiple pieces of tape wrapped around the splint and leg. Do not wrap too tightly. If you can't find any splinting material, use the opposite leg to stabilize the fracture, putting a piece of cloth or other pad between the two legs and wrapping the legs together.

If a bone is protruding from the skin, you will need to take additional precautions. Don't move the bone, or you could cause internal damage or bleeding. Wash the area with saline solution, and cover it with a sterile nonstick gauze pad. Secure the pad with a covering of cloth or gauze, and tape it a few inches above and below the exposed bone. Immediately transport your dog to the veterinarian. A broken bone requires professional treatment.

Burns: Cooking accidents or caustic chemicals can cause painful burns and permanent scars. Your dog's fur may mask the seriousness of a burn, so take her to a vet after you've performed first aid, even if the burn seems minor. First-degree burns are the least serious and usually just cause redness and pain. Second-degree burns cause blisters and swelling. Third-degree burns—the most serious—damage the skin, hair, blood vessels, and deeper tissue.

To treat a burn from fire, steam, or hot water, flush the burned area for 5 to 10 minutes with cool water. This reduces the temperature of your Lab's skin and prevents further tissue damage. Don't submerge your dog's entire body in water, or you risk sending her into shock.

Cover the burned area with a nonstick bandage or torn, clean cloth. Don't use any type of material that might stick to the burn, and don't apply any ointments or creams. If the burn is near your dog's neck or head, remove her collar in case the skin swells so it won't restrict her breathing. Seek veterinary attention.

To administer first aid for chemical burns from products like bleach, pool chemicals, battery acid, or weed killers, first protect yourself with rubber gloves, a facemask, eye protection, and protective clothing before you treat your dog. If your dog tries to shake off the chemical and you're not protected, you could be burned, too. Then, restrain your dog and muzzle her so she won't try to lick off the chemical. Remove her collar if the burn is near her neck.

A chemical burn will continue to burn into the tissue long after it makes contact with her skin. Flush the burned area with cool water for at least 20 minutes. If the chemical is oily, add mild dish soap to the rinse. For powder burns, attempt to brush off as much as you can before rinsing. Take your dog to the vet immediately.

To prevent burn injuries, keep your Lab out from underfoot when you're cooking, whether you're in the kitchen or outdoors. The smells entice her to investigate, but you might not see her when you're carrying hot pans. She might also try to stick her nose in an open oven to see what's cooking.

Electrical cord/shock: Even though you puppy-proofed your house, your teenage Lab may have found an unprotected electrical cord. If she collapses, has a seizure, or experiences other severe symptoms as a result of contact with electricity, consider it a life-threatening emergency. If she stops breathing, perform CPR (see Month 6), and take her to your vet immediately.

Most electrical injuries are less severe, and consist of, for example, a mild burn on her lips, tongue, or mouth.

If your dog is still touching the cord, put on rubber gloves and disconnect the power before you touch her. Or move her away from the cord with a broom or wooden chair, or throw the main circuit breaker. Avoid stepping in water, which conducts electricity.

Keep your dog as calm as possible to keep her breathing normally and prevent her from going into shock. Flush burns in her mouth with cool water, and apply an ice pack to burned lips.

Then, take her to the veterinarian immediately. She may have internal damage that isn't immediately apparent.

Insect bites or stings: When a curious puppy approaches something new to her that's buzzing—like a bee, wasp, or hornet—the result is often a sting on the face or nose. Unless she has an allergic reaction or multiple stings, these usually aren't life-threatening.

To treat minor stings, remove the stinger as quickly as possible if it's still embedded in your Lab's skin. Pull it out with tweezers, or scrape it with a credit card (you'll squeeze less venom into the wound this way). Soothe her skin with a paste made of baking soda and water, hydrocortisone cream, aloe Vera gel, or cold compresses.

When you travel, carry a bottle of meat tenderizer in your first-aid kit. You can mix it with water to make a paste to apply to bug bites or stings. (This remedy works great on people, too.)

If the sting is on or near her face and starts to swell dramatically, your puppy could be having an allergic reaction that might interfere with her breathing. Take your dog to the vet immediately.

Object imbedded in body: When your Lab puppy comes running up to you with a stick protruding from her side, do not pull it out. Muzzle your Lab because while she's in pain she could attempt to bite you. Wrap cloth around the base of the object without repositioning it, and tape the cloth into place to stabilize it. Keep your dog calm and as immobile as possible, and take her directly to the vet.

Smaller objects like splinters, thorns, or porcupine quills can be removed with tweezers, a needle, or pliers. If a splinter is completely under the skin, sterilize the tweezers or needle before using them by dipping them in alcohol or running them through a flame. Grasp the object as close to the skin as possible, and slowly pull it out. After you remove the object, soak the area with warm water and Epsom salt for 15 minutes. The Epsom salt, made of magnesium and sulfate, absorbs into the skin and reduces inflammation. Repeat daily until completely healed.

Glass or small sticks might break if you try to remove them, and you will need to have her examined by a vet to be sure there are no pieces remaining in the wound. If your dog has more than a few porcupine quills imbedded, she'll need to go to the vet to have them removed and her wounds thoroughly cleaned.

Fishhook in the skin: Labs will get a fishhook imbedded in their face or lips while tasting bait or fish. Push the hook farther through the skin so the barb is exposed, cut off the barb with wire cutters, and pull out the hook the way it went into the body. If there's no exit wound, take your pup to the vet for removal. Your Lab will probably need antibiotics to prevent infection.

> **TIPS AND TAILS**
>
> Removing a fishhook deserves special attention because pulling out a hook incorrectly can do a lot of damage to your puppy's skin.

Torn dewclaw or toenail: If your dog's nails grow too long, they risk being snagged and torn. The front toenails seem to be more at risk for injury. Dewclaws are loosely attached, so the entire toe is in danger of tearing.

Because the nail quick is comprised of living tissue, a torn nail can be very painful. Your dog may need to be muzzled and restrained while you treat it.

Stop the bleeding by applying pressure with a cloth or your finger. The dead portion of the nail may be split or torn, so trim it off if you can. Then apply styptic powder, cornstarch, or flour to help the blood clot.

If the dewclaw is injured, wash the area, dry completely, apply antibiotic ointment, and tape or wrap it against the leg to keep it from flapping around and reopening the wound.

Wrap the foot and take your dog to the vet for treatment if the tear is deep or involves the flesh on the dewclaw. Your Lab may need antibiotics or stitches to prevent infection and repair the tear. If the dewclaw is badly injured, it may need to be surgically removed.

Treating Symptoms of Illness

When you realize your puppy is not well, you can take steps to treat the problem while you evaluate how serious it is. Some issues, like diarrhea and vomiting, may be minor and respond to treatment quickly. If these conditions don't resolve, or accompany other troublesome symptoms, a vet will need to investigate further. Others, like seizures, may be a symptom of a much more serious problem and require immediate veterinary treatment.

Diarrhea: If your puppy is vomiting at the same time she has diarrhea, she may be seriously ill. If there is blood in the stool, either fresh (bright red) or digested (dark red or black), take her to the vet immediately. Take a stool sample with you for the vet to examine.

At the first onset of diarrhea, you may give your puppy antidiarrheal medication. Check with your vet to find out what brand to use and the proper dosage. To prevent dehydration, be sure your Lab has plenty of water available. A pediatric oral electrolyte solution can replace some of the nutrients and moisture she has lost. You'll find this product in the children's section at your grocery store or pharmacy.

Temporarily switch to a high-fiber or bland diet. You can purchase a prescription diet from your vet or make your own by combining cooked white rice with boneless boiled meat or chicken with the fat drained off. If the diarrhea subsides, slowly switch your puppy back to her regular food. If the diarrhea lasts longer than 48 hours, see the veterinarian for further care.

Seizure: Witnessing your Labrador have a seizure is frightening. Before a seizure, she may seem dazed or anxious. During an active seizure, she may twitch and fall over, lose control of her bowels or bladder, and not recognize you. Afterward, she may appear dazed and disoriented, or she may seem just fine. The length of the seizure can vary dramatically. A seizure lasting longer than 2 minutes is an emergency and can cause high fever or brain damage.

To protect your dog from injury during a seizure, move her away from stairs or furniture so she won't fall or hit anything. Don't disturb or restrain her during the seizure. She won't swallow her tongue, so don't put your hand in her mouth because she could accidentally bite you.

If this is your dog's first seizure, have her examined by a vet immediately. Make a note of how long the seizure lasts, when she last ate a meal, the time of day, and the date.

There are many possible causes for seizures in dogs, including poisoning, a tumor, bacterial infection in the brain, organ failure, diabetes, and epilepsy. If your vet can identify the cause, he may be able to treat the condition and your dog may never have another episode. The cause is often hard to identify, though, as is the case with epilepsy. Some animals will need antiseizure medication for the rest of their lives.

Vomiting: When your Lab eats something yucky (as they so often do), she may vomit to get it out of her system before it makes her sick. She may have a simple gastrointestinal upset, or she might have eaten an inedible object like a toy. If she doesn't pass the object in her stool, she will get increasingly ill. Serious infections like pancreatitis also cause vomiting. If your Lab is lethargic or has a fever, take her to the vet immediately.

Rapid dehydration is the biggest risk when your dog is vomiting over a period of hours. Withhold food, but offer small amounts of water or ice chips if she'll take them. If your Lab seems otherwise healthy, after 12 hours, reintroduce food in small amounts—about ½ cup at a time. If she continues to vomit, she may need to visit the vet for antinausea drugs and fluids.

Nutrition

It might seem like there are a hundred different ways to evaluate dog foods and figure out what's best for your Lab. From ingredients to nutrients to calorie count, there's always another way of approaching the same problem. Try to balance out the information you gather from each method without relying too much on any one absolute formula. As always, the best way to decide if you're feeding correctly is to look at your Lab, not the label.

Counting Calories

As you learned in Month 7, dog food labels are required to include information about ingredients, nutrient percentages, serving sizes, etc. Manufacturers are not required to list the calorie count of their food, but many companies do. That's how so many people keep track of their own diets, so it makes sense to take a look at a Lab's caloric requirements.

When it comes to canine nutrition, the waters are muddied; there is no one correct calorie amount your dog should consume each day. Quality of ingredients, premium or generic brands, your Lab's activity level, and her health all play a part in determining her recommended daily amount.

Recommended calorie counts are based on the measurement—for example, 1 cup = 400 calories. A healthy Lab who weighs 50 pounds and maintains an average activity level needs about 1,000 to 1,400 calories a day. A 70-pound dog needs about 1,400 to 1,800 calories.

In general, most adult or large dog formulas have between 350 and 400 calories per cup. Premium brands have a higher calorie count than other foods, so you should feed less. "Light" or weight-loss formulas vary dramatically. Some have as little as 50 calories less than the regular formula, and some have more than 100 calories less per cup. Nutrient percentages may vary, too, with some containing less fat and more fiber. (For more about treating obesity in Labs, see Month 12.)

You need to know the exact calorie count of the specific formula you're planning to feed. If it's not listed on the bag, call the company or visit its website to see if you can get the information you need.

Choosing Training Treats

For training sessions, most Labs are happy with bits of their regular dry food. But to really motivate your Lab, choose a high-value treat that's especially tasty to her. Look for treats with the highest meat content available and human-grade ingredients.

Dehydrated and freeze-dried treats are convenient and don't make a mess in your pocket. You should be able to cut up the treats so you can feed tiny amounts during training sessions. Remember, treats should make up no more than 5 to 10 percent of your dog's total daily calories. To keep her from gaining weight, use part of her daily food ration for training mixed in with special goodies.

> **HAPPY PUPPY**
>
> Your Lab needs to respond even when you don't have food, so mix up her training rewards with toys and games. The latter are sometimes more valuable to her, anyway.

Grooming

Labs are not dainty dogs who never get their feet muddy. In fact, your puppy probably loves nothing better than a good digging session or a roll in a pungent garbage pile.

So although Labs are a wash-and-wear breed, sometimes a good rinsing just isn't enough.

Determining When Your Lab Needs a Bath

Labs almost never need bathing, and you may go more than a year before you feel like you need to do more than just rinse her off. You may see a dirty spot developing on her favorite chair or couch cushion, but that could be surface dirt from her outer coat. If she's been out in the fields or swimming in a river, you may see a buildup of dirt in her coat when you separate the fur down to the skin. This is obvious even in black Labs because the brownish dirt dulls her coat.

Labs don't get doggy odor from the oils in their skin or coat like a Basset Hound will. During humid weather in the summer, more crud may stick to her coat and she may not smell as clean as usual. If she's had fleas, you definitely want to wash out all the flea dirt. (Don't be alarmed when you see the bath water run red from the blood in the flea droppings.)

Taking all this into consideration, it's really up to you whether your Lab needs regular baths or not. Just be aware that if you bathe her too often—like more than once a month—it will dry out her coat and cause problems rather than solve them. Most owners bathe their Labs once or twice a year with some thorough rinses in between.

Professional Groomers and Dog Washes

You're probably thinking there's no reason anyone would ever need to take a Lab to the groomer, but people do! When your Lab is shedding snowdrifts of hair in the spring, you might consider taking her for a professional bath. Groomers have powerful dryers that blow out more hair than you can at home using a regular hair dryer. Their specialized grooming tools can remove mountains of undercoat, too. If your Lab is unruly and hard to groom, a groomer uses a table and harnesses to restrain her while he works, which might be easier—and cleaner—than you trying to wrestle your pup in the bathtub at home.

Groomers also have shampoos and conditioners that soothe dry skin and coat. If your dog gets skunked, your groomer may be able to remove the odor with a powerful enzymatic cleaner. If your dog gets into something especially disgusting in the middle of winter and you don't want it all over your bathroom, take her to a groomer. If you don't like to or are unable to trim your dog's toenails, a groomer can do the job for you. They usually trim nails à la carte, without requiring a full bath and brush. Some groomers even offer teeth-brushing.

When it's bath time, wash all your Lab's bedding and clean her crate to remove fleas and odor.

Many communities have mobile dog-washing companies that come to your door and bathe your dog in their van. They supply everything, even the water. This is less time-consuming and more convenient for you—and less stressful for your Lab—than spending half a day at a grooming shop with a bunch of poodles.

Do-it-yourself dog washes are another option for stress-free grooming. They supply a wide variety of shampoos, conditioners, and towels, and you have access to the facility's high-powered sprayers, raised tubs, power dryers, and grooming tables to make the job easier.

If you take your dog to the beach, check to see if a DIY dog wash is located nearby. You can clean up your Lab before you take her home. If not a bath, she will need a thorough rinsing.

Social Skills

We each have our own ideas about what makes a well-behaved dog and how we would like her to act in public, but you've probably never written down what a canine good citizen actually means to you. If not, you're in luck: the AKC has created a program to help owners reach their goals for a well-socialized and welcome canine member of the community.

As more and more laws are enacted restricting your dog's access to public places, we have a duty to be sure our dogs aren't part of the problem, but part of the solution.

The Canine Good Citizen Program

The AKC Canine Good Citizen (CGC) program was developed to encourage responsible dog ownership and give owners recognition for their training efforts. It also recognizes dogs who have good manners at home and in the community. For families just starting out with a new puppy, the program gives a clear definition of what makes a well-behaved dog and provides goals for you to strive for when you start training.

The AKC feels that the CGC is the foundation for future activities with your Lab. The idea is that once she's learned the basics, you'll want to continue training her and go on to participate in dog sports and companion activities. While learning the exercises for the CGC, you enjoy time with your Lab, exercise her mind, and forge a deeper bond. The best benefit is that a dog who has passed the CGC exam is a joy to live with.

The CGC is accepted throughout the world as evidence that your dog is well behaved and you are a responsible owner. Carry the certificate with you when you travel to present to hotels and other public facilities. Therapy dogs often must pass the CGC test as part of their certification for visits. Animal-control agencies may require owners and their dogs to earn a CGC certificate when there are issues with the dog's behavior in public. Thirty-four states now have CGC resolutions on the books.

Many obedience instructors use the CGC program as the basis for their beginning obedience classes and incorporate the test into graduation. Check with local trainers to find classes for the CGC test. The AKC website lists evaluators you can contact for more information and posts a schedule of upcoming tests in your area.

The CGC Test

To earn a Canine Good Citizen Certificate, your Lab must demonstrate her training and good manners during a 10-step evaluation by an AKC examiner. At the same time, you sign a pledge to be a responsible dog owner. As you'll see from the following exercises, the test is challenging and requires practice before you both are ready. When the two of you complete the test successfully, you receive a CGC certificate from the AKC. Passing is an achievement you and your Lab should be very proud of.

The test is performed on leash, and dogs are not allowed to wear prong collars, head halters, or no-pull harnesses. You aren't permitted to carry food, treats, or toys. You are asked to bring her brush or comb with you for the grooming portion of the exam. You're encouraged to talk to and praise your dog throughout the test. On any of the greeting exercises, you can tell your Lab to sit and stay.

The CGC test is made up of 10 challenges:

Your Lab accepts a friendly stranger who approaches and speaks to you. The evaluator ignores your dog while greeting you in a friendly manner, shaking hands, and engaging in conversation. Your Lab must not show any shyness or aggression, break position, or try to approach the evaluator.

Your dog must sit politely for petting by a stranger. She must sit at your side and show no aggression or resentment while a stranger pets her on her head and body.

Your Lab accepts grooming and handling by a stranger, and is presented in clean, healthy, and well-groomed condition. Your puppy must permit a veterinarian, groomer, or other person to groom or examine her. This also demonstrates that you provide good care for your Lab. The evaluator examines your dog to determine that she's clean, in good health, and the proper weight for her age and breed. You then supply a brush to the evaluator and he brushes your dog, looks in her ears, and picks up each front foot. You are allowed to talk to your dog, praise her, and give her encouragement throughout the process.

Your dog walks nicely on a leash at your side. This test shows that you can control your dog. She must be attentive to you and respond to your changes in direction. She does not have to be in perfect position or on a particular side. You may talk to your dog, praise her, and give commands in a normal tone of voice. The walk includes a left turn, a right turn, a halt, and an about-turn.

You can walk your dog through a crowd and keep her under control without her showing excessive shyness or resentment around strangers. Your Lab demonstrates that she is under control and polite in public places. She shouldn't jump on anyone or strain on the leash.

Your dog will sit and down on command and stay in place while you walk 20 feet away and return. This exercise demonstrates that your Lab has been trained and will remain in position. You first demonstrate that she will do both a sit and a down. Next, you replace her leash with a 20-foot line and ask her to do either a sit or down (your choice). You can talk to your dog and give a command more than once, but you aren't allowed to force her into position. Your puppy must stay in position until the evaluator instructs you to release her. Unless your Lab is fully trained for competition obedience, the down is probably much easier for her to hold.

Your Lab comes when called. She's still on a long line, and you walk 10 feet away, turn to face your dog, and call her to you. You may encourage your dog to come.

Your Lab demonstrates a polite reaction to another dog while owners greet each other and walk together. Two handlers and their dogs approach each other from about 20 feet away, stop, shake hands, and speak to each other. Both then continue on another 10 feet. The dogs should show no more than casual interest in each other, and neither dog may approach the other dog or his handler.

The dog demonstrates confidence when faced with a distraction she might normally encounter, such as someone dropping a chair or rolling a cart past her. Your Lab may express interest or be startled, but shouldn't panic, try to run away, bark, or show aggression. You may talk to your Lab and praise her during the exercise.

Your Lab tolerates separation from you without becoming overanxious while someone else holds her leash. This test shows that your dog can be left in someone else's care and will maintain her training and good manners. The evaluator takes hold of your dog's leash, and asks you, "Would you like me to watch your dog?" or something similar. You leave and go out of sight for 3 minutes. While you're gone, your Lab shouldn't continually bark, whine, or pace unnecessarily or show anything stronger than mild agitation or nervousness. The evaluator may speak to your dog but not attempt to comfort or control her.

If you successfully complete the test, congratulations! You have a well-trained Labrador.

Think about all the work you have put into raising your Labrador puppy. You deserve recognition for the care and training you provide. The pledge represents the promise you made to your puppy when you added her to your family:

AKC CGC Responsible Dog Owner's Pledge Canine Good Citizen Owner's Commitment to Responsible Dog Ownership

I understand that to truly be a Canine Good Citizen, my dog needs a responsible owner. I agree to maintain my dog's health, safety, and quality of life. By participating in the Canine Good Citizen test, I agree that …

I will be responsible for my dog's health needs:

🐾 Veterinary care, including check-ups and vaccines

🐾 Adequate nutrition through proper diet; clean water at all times

🐾 Daily exercise and regular bathing and grooming

I will be responsible for my dog's safety:

🐾 I will properly control my dog by providing fencing where appropriate, not letting my dog run loose, and using a leash in public.

🐾 I will ensure that my dog has some form of identification (which may include collar tags, tattoos, or microchip ID).

I will not allow my dog to infringe on the rights of others:

🐾 I will not allow my dog to run loose in the neighborhood.

🐾 I will not allow my dog to be a nuisance to others by barking while in the yard, in a hotel room, etc.

🐾 I will pick up and properly dispose of my dog's waste in all public areas, such as on the grounds of hotels, on sidewalks, parks, etc.

🐾 I will pick up and properly dispose of my dog's waste in wilderness areas, on hiking trails, at campgrounds, and in off-leash parks.

I will be responsible for my dog's quality of life:

🐾 I understand that basic training is beneficial to all dogs.

🐾 I will give my dog attention and playtime.

🐾 I understand that owning a dog is a commitment in time and caring.

Owner's signature: _____

Date: _____

Behavior

While your Lab's behavior improves every day, you'll still suffer through moments of regression, when she reminds you she's still an adolescent. As much as you want to use positive methods to train your dog, Labs can be pretty obnoxious and sometimes need a firmer hand to deal with their behavior.

Barking

Problem barking often begins during the teenage months. Your Lab goes through periods of uncertainty, and one way she expresses that concern is to bark. The more socialization she has had up to this point, the less fearful she will be.

Barking is a natural behavior you can never entirely eliminate. But if you can get it under control now, you'll prevent her from becoming a chronic barker later, when she matures and becomes more territorial and protective.

Manage your Lab puppy's surroundings to discourage and prevent excess barking and then figure out what makes her bark. If she barks out in the yard, limit her view. Put up a solid fence instead of chain link. Don't let her out on the upper deck where she can see the neighbor kids playing. Bring her in when kids are walking home from school. If she barks out the living room window, don't let her in the living room, or close the drapes.

> **HAPPY PUPPY**
>
> You may want your Lab to bark occasionally. Check out what she's barking at and then quiet her and redirect her to another activity. She's done her job, and now you've taken over.

Does she bark every time the doorbell rings? Think about how she sees it. You jump up and head for the door, so she does, too. She could be either excited or frightened, but either way, it's a big deal in her eyes. Teach her to sit quietly or go to her crate when the doorbell rings. (This lesson may require a helper.) Put a leash on her before you open the door, and practice her sit-to-greet. Give her a toy. After all, when she has a toy in her mouth, she can't bark!

Does she bark aggressively at the neighbor through the fence or someone at the front door? She is most likely afraid of the person. She's too young to be overprotective (something that happens closer to 18 months old), but this type of barking can turn into an ugly habit. Have the person offer her a treat. After a few treat sessions, she'll be happy to see the person and engage in an entirely different type of barking.

Maybe you have a bossy barker. She wants in, so she barks. She knows it's close to dinnertime, so she barks. She wants to play fetch, so she drops a toy at your feet and barks at you. It's time to wake up, so she stands by the bed and barks. Are you seeing a pattern here? We inadvertently teach our dog to bark at us by responding to her every request. Make her earn your attention. Ask for a sit or a down before you give her what she wants. Down is a subordinate position, and most dogs don't bark while lying down.

You may find she doesn't want to lie down when she's excited and wants something. This is all the more reason to insist on compliance. Don't reward her or let her up until she calms down. Put her on a leash if you have to. Give her a 5-minute time-out in her crate if she's barking at you to do something. If bossy barking is really getting to be a problem, have her do many 1-minute downs throughout the day.

Another tactic is simply to ignore her barking. This is really hard to do, but if you can hold out, she'll give up eventually. The barking will get worse before it gets better, though. She'll give it one last over-the-top burst of effort right before she gives up. This is when most of us cave in and respond; if you do, she'll bark much longer next time. Reward her when she stops barking even for a few seconds.

Some people yell at their dog to be quiet, but she has no idea what that means. She figures you're just barking with her. The more excited you are, the more excited she gets, so stay calm. Teach her to bark on command. Catch her when she's barking and praise her, saying "Good bark!" or whatever word you want to use (*speak, talk*). As soon as she breaks off, say "Good quiet" and reward her. She'll learn to respond to "Bark" and "Quiet."

Try to head off barking binges before they get started. If you see something you know is going to make her bark, call her and get her attention on you. Practice when there are no distractions by rattling a treat shaker (a small container of kibble) and calling her. Once she learns that something good happens and she gets treats, you'll be able to call her away from that exciting thing before she starts barking.

Disciplining Your Lab

While most people agree that physical punishment can destroy your relationship with your dog, what are you supposed to do when positive methods don't work and you need to discipline your dog?

When your Lab was a puppy, it was enough to stop her and redirect her to an acceptable activity. You can still do this, but with a lot more conviction. Stop her by saying, "No!" or "Ack!" Your tone of voice conveys your displeasure, and for some Labs that's enough.

Be sure your dog realizes why she's being disciplined. You must catch her in the act, or she won't understand what she did wrong. Dogs live in the moment. She won't understand a correction for something she did 2 hours, or even 5 minutes, ago. If you come home and find she's destroyed the couch, she'll look guilty because she knows you're mad, not because she knows she did something wrong. To effectively discipline your Lab, use the same methods you use in obedience training. Praise her while she's doing it right, so she understands exactly what action earned the praise. Punish her *during* the misbehavior, so she knows what caused your anger.

Give your Lab an opportunity to earn praise right after you have disciplined her. She'll forgive you instantly. Give her a few obedience commands that she can easily perform.

Consider this example: you are walking with your Lab, and she rudely jumps up on a woman in dressy clothes, frightening and angering her. A voice correction ("Off!" or "No!") is appropriate, but that might not be enough. You may have to give a firm pop on the leash to force her to drop to the ground. Then immediately have her do a down stay. After everyone has calmed down, release her and ask for a few sits and downs so you can praise her for listening. Once she puts her brain back in obedience mode, she'll listen to you better, and you can stop misbehavior before it happens.

One good strong correction is better than nagging. "Puppy, no, honey, come here, sit down, good girl … no …" isn't even going to get your Lab's attention. There are so many contradictions in the previous statement that any dog would be confused. Repeated nagging corrections teach your Lab to ignore you until you get really mad. Then she knows you mean it, and she complies. A correction should last 1 or 2 seconds, and no longer. Make it as firm as it needs to be for the situation, quickly said, done, and over with.

When you need to discipline your Lab, use the *minimum* amount of force necessary to stop the behavior.

Never hit your Lab. Hitting your puppy only makes you look unpredictable. You don't want a relationship based on fear. Even the best-trained dog may at some point decide she has to defend herself, and you don't want her to ever feel she has to bite you or anyone else. When you lose your temper, give yourself a time-out from your dog so you can cool down.

Environmental-correction discipline your dog when you aren't around so she doesn't associate the correction with you. If she puts her paws up on the counter, booby trap it with cans full of pennies. When she hits one, it will fall off the counter and startle her. Some other examples of environmental-correction devices include ultrasonic buzzers that make an unpleasant noise when she barks, a ScatMat or battery-operated mat that gives her a mild shock when she jumps on the couch, and a bitter spray that tastes terrible when she chews a table leg (see Appendix E).

Training

Teaching your Lab self-control continues this month, and although you probably don't dare let her off-leash yet, you'll enjoy teaching her the basic principles so she'll be ready when her brains catch up to her body.

Teaching the Emergency Drop

If your Lab dashes into the street, she could be hit by a car and killed. If she breaks her collar and takes off, you need tools to catch her. When she decides to chase a cyclist down the road or bound into the woods after a bear, your dog needs to respond instantly. A life-saving command, the "emergency down"—sometimes called "Drop"— is a lightning-fast version of "Down." When you give this command, she'll probably be running away from you, so it takes some practice for her to understand it.

Start by speeding up the "Down" exercise. If she can't drop quickly in front of you, she won't be able to drop from a distance. Practice the down where you're in different positions—at her side, in back of her, with her in back of you (use a hand mirror so you can see her comply). Finish the exercise when she drops. Once she understands the concept, you can use the word "Drop." "Drop" has a popping sound on the end of the word, which helps get her attention. When she's confused—and she will be—go to her and put her in the down. Then release her by tossing her a treat.

She can't read your body language to figure out what to do next. She won't have time to look back at you in an emergency. Practice while you're standing and sitting so she doesn't learn to look at you for cues. Always toss a treat behind her to release her. You don't want her to automatically think she's supposed to come to you unless you call her. In an emergency, you'll either call her or go to her, so she needs to learn both scenarios.

Now you're ready to add movement. While walking alongside your Lab, suddenly point to the ground, yell "Down!" and pivot in front of her to stop her forward movement. Use an urgent tone of voice; this is an emergency. Release her by tossing a treat away and let her run to get it. Practice just a few times. Attach her to a long line for the next step. As she's wandering around a few feet from you, give the drop command.

This is very stressful for your Lab, so don't train for more than a few minutes per session. She'll build up a lot of excitement. Take advantage of her energy, and make it a game. Toss treats, let her chase them, and come back to you. Occasionally, on her way back, give the drop command and rush toward her a few steps to encourage her to stop and drop. Then toss a treat behind her and let her go.

Once she can drop coming toward you, she needs to learn to drop from any position. As she's running around chasing treats, occasionally throw in a "Drop!" command. Give her a jackpot once in a while: pull her favorite toy out of your pocket or feed her a full handful of treats.

The emergency drop takes hundreds of repetitions and regular practice for your Lab to be reliable. Use the command often during play sessions and walks to be sure she gets it.

Preparing for Off-Leash Control

A 10-month-old Lab is not ready for the responsibility of being allowed off-leash. Reliable off-leash control takes a long time to develop. Your goal is that when she's mature enough to handle it, she's had the training that makes it possible.

> **TIPS AND TAILS**
>
> If you've completed a beginning obedience course, many trainers offer a beyond-the-basics course that starts teaching owners and their dogs off-leash control. It's a course you can take several times just for the fun of training with your Lab.

Answer these questions before deciding if your Lab is ready for off-leash freedom:

- 🐾 Is her recall ("Come") always perfect and immediate? Does she consider it a positive command?
- 🐾 Does she know and reliably perform the emergency drop?
- 🐾 Is her obedience reliable on-leash? Can she ignore distractions and respond when you ask her to?
- 🐾 Do you have off-leash control in the house? What about in the backyard?

If the answer to any of these questions is "No," or "Most of the time," polish her skills until you can answer "Yes" to all of them.

When your Lab is off-leash, you must pay attention and be ready to intervene before she does something impolite or dangerous. If your Lab is defiant and sometimes purposely ignores your commands, it could be a fatal decision.

You'll need two training tools: a 15- to 20-foot light line and a 6- to 8-inch short leash or line. The 15- or 20-foot line is for outdoor training. The short line is a handle you can quickly grab when you're close to her. It should be so light she doesn't feel the weight. You want her to forget it's there.

You've been working on indoor off-leash control since the day you got her, but now she needs to perfect her responses in anticipation of new and bigger responsibilities. You can let her drag a shorter line, maybe 6 to 8 feet, indoors. If there's no loop at the end, it's less likely to tangle in furniture.

TIPS AND TAILS

For her safety, never leave any kind of training line, collar, or leash on your Lab when you can't supervise her.

Your puppy will be confused at first. She's not used to responding to you from a distance. Tie her loosely with the long line to a tree or fence post in the backyard, and walk about 10 feet away. Give her an easy command, like "Sit." If she doesn't respond, move closer and try again. When she does, praise her and try something else, like "Down." Once she gets the idea, you can try commands at different distances and positions, like you did when teaching the emergency drop.

Untie the line and let your puppy drag it. Walk around the yard and give an occasional command from a distance. Include the "Come" and emergency drop. Use the line to reel her in or detain her if she stops paying attention to you. Teach her to check in with you, similar to when you practice the recall, and drop the line and let her wander. When she's in the midst of something, call her to you and enforce the command. Her reward for coming is that you let her go back to what she was doing. Find fenced areas away from home where you can practice.

When you're comfortable that she doesn't need the long line, attach the 8-inch light line and work with her close to you. You can hold the light line and your Lab won't feel the weight of a leash, so she may try to take off, thinking you can't control her.

You and Your Puppy

Your children are a big part of family life, and there are many ways they can enjoy spending time with their Lab puppy. Organized activities introduce them to dog sports and pet care. At the same time, your kids learn how to be a good pet parent and about the many facets of dog ownership and care. They can even explore careers with dogs.

Boy Scouts, Girl Scouts, and 4-H

Children of all ages can participate in activities with their Labs. Besides organized activities like scouting and 4-H, many animal shelters offer day-camp programs and also offer workshops for groups of kids working on badges and awards.

Boy Scouts have several different badges boys can earn while learning about their pets. To earn the Pets merit badge, a child must care for his dog for 4 months, write a report about it, keep records, and read a book about their breed or other aspect of pet care. He also participates in an activity with his Lab like a dog show or teaching his dog tricks.

The Dog Care merit badge introduces boys to responsible dog ownership. They learn about different breeds and track the care and health of their dogs. They teach obedience commands and learn how to perform pet first aid. The Boy Scout must also visit a shelter or veterinary hospital.

To earn the Veterinary Medicine merit badge, the Boy Scout learns about veterinary care for many different species, observes at an animal hospital, and explores other aspects of veterinary care and careers.

In Girl Scouts, girls can earn animal-related badges at each level, from Brownies up through Senior Girl Scouts. Brownies can earn a Pets merit badge by learning about and practicing pet care skills. Juniors earn the Animal Habitats badge by learning about wild animals and how to protect their habitats. Cadettes earn the

Animal Helpers merit badge, studying how dogs and other animals help people in fields like search and rescue, therapy visits, and as service animals. Senior scouts earn the Voice for Animals badge, where they learn about volunteering and animal welfare.

Your local Cooperative Extension generally offers dog 4-H programs for your county. Kids can participate in Grooming and Handling, Obedience, Rally, and Agility. Some counties offer additional classes such as freestyle—that's dancing with your dog. 4-H'ers learn to keep records about their dog's care and training, develop public presentations, and compete at county and state fairs.

Junior Showmanship

Children between 9 and 18 years old may participate in Junior Showmanship at AKC conformation and performance events. Juniors show their own dog or a relative's Lab. Kids have the opportunity to learn more about dogs and dog shows, develop handling skills, and learn about good sportsmanship while enjoying time with their dogs. In conformation, beginners compete in Novice classes. Once a child has received three first-place ribbons in novice, he or she can move up to Open competition.

Children are judged on their ability to present their dogs in a similar fashion as dogs in the breed ring at a conformation show. The quality of their presentation, not the quality of the dog, is judged. Juniors learn to groom their dogs and present them to a judge, conduct themselves properly, and dress appropriately for judging. Top-winning juniors from around the country travel to the Westminster Kennel Club Show and AKC/Eukanuba National Championship to compete for honors.

Attend some dog shows with your family and watch the junior showmanship competition to learn more about it.

In addition to conformation, the AKC has recently introduced recognition programs for children who compete in performance events like obedience, agility, and tracking. The AKC also offers other activities for juniors, along with extensive educational materials and scholarship programs. Learn more at akc.org/kids_juniors/jr_getting_started.cfm.

Month 10	Month 11	Month 12
	Socialization in public	
	Adult teeth are in—chewing continues	
	Ready for more advanced training	
	Slow growth—reaches adult size	

Once your puppy reaches 10 to 11 months, your Labrador is ready to start practicing canine sports like hunting, agility, and obedience. Labs are incredibly smart and willing to do almost anything you could ask of them, so the choices are endless. He'll relish having a job to do, exercising his mind and body while building his skills.

Meanwhile, prepare yourself for his adventures. Put a disaster preparedness plan into place for your dog. Consider pet health insurance, and introduce him to traveling with his family.

Physical Development

Your Lab puppy may reach his full height this month, but his bones are still growing, so they aren't strong and fully developed yet. Continue to limit his running on hard surfaces, and avoid jumping for a few more months.

His teeth are almost fully erupted and not as painful as they have been. They will continue to develop strength until he's 3 years old, and he'll continue chewing as well.

Now that your Lab is almost full size, so is his tail, and that means it's time to clear the coffee table and protect your valuables. His tail is always wagging, and he has no idea what it's doing back there. When you hear strange thumping sounds in the night, look for the tail.

Your puppy will start looking more coordinated this month, as his proportions even out and he gets comfortable using his adult height and body. He'll dive into activities with great enthusiasm. In fact, he'll be hard to hold back!

Health

Hunting dogs and pet Labs are both at risk for contracting internal parasites, and humans risk contracting these pests from their dogs. Learn to recognize the signs of infestation so you can treat these conditions.

Anal glands are another unpleasant subject, but one that's important to discuss for your puppy's comfort and health.

Also in this section, we show you how to plan ahead for your puppy's care in case of natural disasters, and we investigate pet health insurance to cover major illness or accidents.

Dealing with Internal Parasites

You'll spend a lot of time out in nature with your Lab, swimming and retrieving in lakes, tromping through the woods, and other fun activities. Your Lab will be exposed to internal parasites that could make him ill—and could even infect you, too.

Giardia: A single-celled protozoa, giardia is most often found in contaminated water, like streams, lakes, and rivers, but your Lab can pick it up anywhere. Wild animals such as coyotes, rabbits, raccoons, and beavers carry giardia. In fact, it was originally called "beaver fever." An infected animal carries the cysts in his digestive tract and sheds them in his feces. If your dog ingests the stool, drinks infected water, or steps in it and then licks his paws, he can pick up the parasite. Once giardia is in your dog's system, it attaches to the walls of the intestine and reproduces, forming cysts that he then sheds in his stool.

Giardia is a *zoonotic disease,* meaning the disease can infect people as well as animals, if you remember from earlier chapters. The main symptom of giardia is loose stools or diarrhea. This often goes away in a few days, and the owner assumes the dog just "ate something." A dog can carry the parasite for years with no symptoms.

Long-term effects of giardia include weight loss, damage to the lining of the intestine, and *malabsorption.* Repetitive bouts of diarrhea are the most obvious sign of a problem. You won't see any signs of giardia in your dog's feces, because it is a microscopic organism.

> **DOG TALK**
>
> **Malabsorption** is the inability to process and use nutrients in food.

Your veterinarian will perform a fecal flotation test in the clinic to check for giardia. The giardia cysts are not shed in every stool sample, so it may take more than one test to diagnose. Also, before your veterinarian rules out giardia completely, she may send out a stool sample to a medical laboratory for more extensive testing.

Treatment consists of a simple round of medication, but reinfection is a risk every time you take your Lab out into nature. To protect yourself, take care not to touch your face, and thoroughly wash your hands after outings. Carry drinking water for you and your Lab with you on hikes.

Coccidia: Another single-celled parasite, coccidia most often affects young dogs. It's sometimes found in raw meat, dirty kennel situations, or animal shelters. Livestock are often infected, and a dog can ingest coccidia from manure and grass in pastures. Cockroaches, mice, and flies also can transport and spread coccidia.

As an adult, your dog might carry coccidia in his intestines and shed the cysts in his feces, but if he has a healthy immune system, he can fight off severe symptoms. Stress can trigger symptoms if a dog has coccidia present in his digestive tract. A major infestation can cause damage to the intestines.

The primary symptom of coccidiosis is diarrhea. It may be minor or severe, and it may also contain blood or mucous. The symptoms for coccidia are similar to those of giardia and parvo infection. A fecal flotation test identifies the parasite. Medication stops reproduction of the organisms but does not kill them, so a complete cure takes several weeks. The biggest challenge is protecting your Lab from reinfection. To prevent this parasite from taking hold, practice diligent sanitation, including cleaning with ammonia disinfectants and picking up feces.

Coccidiosis is not a zoonotic disease, so you are not in danger of becoming infected.

> **TIPS AND TAILS**
>
> You can help prevent infestation by giardia and coccidia. Don't allow your dog to eat or lick other animals' feces, and don't let your dog drink from unfiltered sources of water.

Anal Glands

The anal glands (also called anal sacs) are two tiny glands just inside the anus. The fluid in these glands contains pheromones, and when a dog defecates, the pressure of firm stool pressing against the glands expels the fluid. The pheromones enable other dogs to "read" the feces (using Jacobsen's organ located in the nose, which we learned about in Month 6) for information about age, gender, and sexual status.

A problem arises when a dog has soft stool or diarrhea that doesn't force the glands to empty. If the soft stool continues too long, you need to work with your veterinarian to figure out what's causing the bowel problem.

Other problems that cause the anal glands to become impacted include inflammation in the gastrointestinal tract, allergies that cause your dog to scratch and chew at his anus, or infection. A small minority of dogs have improperly positioned anal glands. In some cases, surgical removal is the only option.

If you see your Lab scooting his butt on the ground, biting at his rear, sitting in an odd position, or in obvious discomfort, suspect impacted anal sacs. If his anal glands are impacted, your veterinarian can express them during an office visit. No sedation is needed.

Occasionally, in a highly stressful situation, a dog will suddenly expel the anal sac fluid. You'll know, because the smell is extremely offensive.

A healthy dog doesn't need to have his anal glands emptied for him. In fact, emptying the sacs too often causes trauma to the duct. The anal glands will close and can no longer expel fluid on their own. Don't have the procedure done unless your dog actually needs it.

Disaster Planning

Your family's emergency plans should include provisions for your Lab's health and safety. When disaster hits and you have to evacuate, you may not be allowed back into your neighborhood for days, so always take your dog with you. *Always.* Leaving him in the house or turning him loose could be a death sentence.

Some Red Cross evacuation shelters allow dogs, but most don't. During a crisis, hotels may relax their pet policies, and places that do allow pets will require them to be crated. Make a list of pet-friendly hotels, boarding kennels, and veterinarians within 100 miles of your home. You don't know how far you'll have to travel when you're forced to leave, and it's best to be prepared with locations you know you can go to. Also line up friends who will be able to take your dog in an emergency. Make arrangements with a neighbor to evacuate your dog if disaster strikes while you aren't at home.

> **HAPPY PUPPY**
>
> Your Labrador will adjust better to the stress of emergencies or travel if he's already used to spending time in his crate.

If you live in an area at risk for floods or hurricanes, purchase a neon-colored life vest made especially for dogs. If you get separated from your Lab in a disaster, he will be easier for rescuers to spot if he's wearing such a vest. If you have a two-story home, buy a canine evacuation harness similar to the ones used by search and rescue organizations. Keep it under your bed so if a fire breaks out downstairs, you can lower your dog out the window. Practice putting these devices on your Lab; in a disaster, you'll be fumbling and in a hurry and will appreciate the practice. Be sure they fit and can support his weight.

If you can't evacuate, plan a safe area in your house. If it's a basement or similar room, be sure no hazardous materials are nearby that can harm your dog. As soon as you know a storm is coming, find your Lab, be sure he's wearing his leash and collar, and keep him indoors with you. Frightened animals will often wander away during the commotion and become disoriented. Once the storm has passed, nothing looks or smells the same, and your dog may not be able to find his way home.

During disasters, keep a leash on your Lab, even when he's in the car, and keep him crated as much as possible. He'll be as anxious as you are, he'll feel safer in his crate, and you won't have to worry about keeping track of him. After the crisis passes, keep your dog leashed and with you until you're home and safe.

When planning your disaster kit, include the following:

- Your Lab's microchip and license information, your contact info, emergency caretaker phone numbers, your dog's medical records, a photo of your Lab, and feeding and care instructions, all inside a waterproof bag or container
- Extra leash, trash bags, poop scoop supplies, and towels
- Food and water bowls
- Food and water for 3 days
- His crate, marked with your cell phone number and emergency contact info
- Calming medication or herbal/flower formula, like Rescue Remedy or chamomile tea bags to add to your dog's water
- First-aid kit
- Medications, including heartworm and flea control products

Store your kit in an outdoor shed, near an exit door where it's easily accessible, or in your car.

Pet Health Insurance

Should you purchase health insurance for your puppy? If so, should you buy it now or wait until he's older and more likely to get sick? There are many questions to answer when making the decision whether to spend money on insurance. No one wants to be faced with the horrible decision of euthanizing their dog because they can't afford a procedure that could save his life. Lesser expenses add up, too, and you may decide the expense of coverage is worth it for your peace of mind. By removing financial pressure from the equation, it frees you to make better decisions about your Lab's care.

Insurance companies offer many different types of pet coverage. Depending on what you're willing to pay, almost any type of coverage is available.

The most inexpensive plan is usually a major medical plan that only covers accidents and major illnesses like cancer or heart disease. More comprehensive plans include hereditary diseases and routine care like vaccines, spay/neuter, and teeth cleaning. Most plans do not cover preexisting conditions, or they have a waiting period before a previously cured disease is covered. Behavioral problems, parasites (like heartworm), and special veterinary food are also excluded from most policies.

> ### TIPS AND TAILS
>
> Examine pet insurance plans carefully to be sure you completely understand what is and isn't covered.

In one policy we examined, hip and elbow dysplasia, osteochondritis dissecans, and anterior cruciate ligament injury are specifically *not* covered. This reads like a menu of anything that could ever go wrong with a Lab, so the policy might not be right for you.

The following is a sampling of claims filed by Labrador Retriever owners over the past 3 years with a national pet health insurance company (all of these Labs survived with no lasting effects):

Major, a chocolate male, ran into a large rock while retrieving, broke several teeth, and suffered a concussion.

Stella, a black female, got an open can of green beans stuck on her lower jaw. She had to be anesthetized to remove it.

Gus, a yellow male, ate more than 5 pounds of Christmas cookies and fudge, including the plastic wrap and boxes.

Tobey, a yellow male, drank so much water while playing in the sprinklers he became swollen and ill. His owners were afraid he would bloat.

Ellie, a yellow female, ate a hive's worth of dead bees after an exterminator killed them at her home. She had a major stomach upset but no ill effects from the pesticide or bees themselves.

Rock, a black male, ate 23 packages of Instant Breakfast powder, wrapping and all.

Phoenix, a chocolate male, ran into a stick while fetching it, resulting in a puncture wound that went 2 inches deep under his tongue.

Quincy, a yellow male, imbedded a fishhook with two barbs in his nose.

Marley, a yellow male, retrieved a poisonous sea urchin at the beach.

Note that virtually all these emergencies involved a Lab and something in his or her mouth. Many of these emergencies could have been prevented with better supervision and management. Note, too, that color doesn't seem to be a factor in Labrador mishaps—more proof that chocolates aren't necessarily more mischievous.

TIPS AND TAILS

Although not mentioned on this list, the company reports that ingested socks are the most common emergency requiring surgery. More reason to train your Lab to leave your socks alone! And for you to pick them up!

When researching pet insurance policies, here are some good questions to ask:

- ☙ Is there a deductible?
- ☙ Will the price increase as my dog ages?
- ☙ Will the price increase if he's diagnosed with a chronic disease?
- ☙ What illnesses or injuries are *not* covered? What *is* covered?
- ☙ Are hereditary conditions covered, even if my dog shows no symptoms now?
- ☙ Is there a waiting period before some chronic, hereditary, or preexisting conditions are covered?
- ☙ May I choose my own vet?
- ☙ Are diagnostic tests covered?

With most pet insurance policies, the owner pays the bill, submits a claim and receipts, and is reimbursed by the insurance company. The veterinarian doesn't get involved in billing or receiving payment. Some plans have a set amount they reimburse for each type of illness or injury.

Nutrition

Your Lab may be healthy on a diet of dry food, but other options and supplements are available. As you ponder the multitude of choices at the pet store, you may worry you aren't doing enough for your beloved Lab.

The best advice for pet owners is this: if it works, don't fix it. If your Lab has a healthy shiny coat, clear eyes, and healthy skin; if he's the appropriate weight; and if he enjoys good health, he probably doesn't need anything added to his diet. As he ages, this may change, but most Labs live long, healthy lives by eating a diet based on a quality dry dog food.

Beyond Dry Food

Should you add canned or semimoist foods to your Lab's meals? Or should you feed wet food exclusively? Or maybe you'd like to give him a daily bowl of wet food as a treat. Dogs certainly seem to love it.

Canned dog food contains up to 78 percent water, which helps fill your dog. It's more expensive, so you probably won't want to feed him an exclusively canned diet. Canned food usually includes more protein, fat, and animal-based ingredients than dry dog food. Canned food also contains less grain. So overall, the ingredients are usually better quality than you'll find in most dry foods. Read the ingredients on the label to be sure, and look for named meats and minimal grain.

"Nuggets," "chunks," and other shapes aren't actually meat. They're formed from textured plant proteins or sometimes (although rarely) natural meat tissues. Some foods contain vegetables like carrots and peas. These may be real or artificially colored and shaped.

There are advantages to feeding canned food. If your Lab has kidney problems or is constipated, the extra moisture will be beneficial. If he's ill or dehydrated, he'll need extra moisture, and canned food is one way to provide it. Canned food contains fewer preservatives because the can is an oxygen-free environment, which, when properly sealed, does not allow bacteria to grow. Be sure to refrigerate leftovers to avoid spoilage.

Semimoist foods have lots of additives, particularly sugar, for taste and to solidify the food. These are generally the least-healthy diets you can feed your pup. Although semimoist foods contain more moisture than dry food—about 25 to 30 percent—they are extremely expensive in comparison. Reserve semimoist food for treats, if you use it at all.

Nutritional Supplements

If your Lab puppy is eating a quality dog food and in good health, you don't need to add supplements to his diet. In fact, too much supplementation can throw his system out of balance and cause health problems. Too much of a nutrient is just as bad as too little.

But once in a while, supplements can be beneficial to your dog's health. Owners who feed raw or home-cooked diets need to give their dog supplements to be sure he's getting the vitamins, minerals, and other important nutrients he needs.

Work with your vet or consult a nutritionist to determine when and how to add supplements to your dog's diet. Some can interfere with other medications your dog is taking. And be sure you use products specifically meant for dogs because a dog's nutritional needs are different from a human's.

Nutritional supplements are not subject to evaluation by the Food and Drug Administration for their purity, safety, or ability to improve your dog's health, and not all supplements are necessarily equal or risk free. Purchase only brands you trust. The National Animal Supplement Council (nasc.cc/index.php) certifies manufacturers' products and awards a seal of quality to those that meet their standards of safety, quality, and accuracy.

> ### TIPS AND TAILS
>
> If you feel your Lab needs supplements with his food, consider switching to a different or better-quality food rather than oversupplement. Most of the supplements discussed in this section are already included in commercial dog foods.

Probiotics contain beneficial bacteria that can bolster your Lab's immune response to harmful bacteria in his intestinal tract. Probiotics are an important contributor to your puppy's overall health because 70 percent of a puppy's immune system is found in his digestive tract. When added to your dog's diet, probiotics help return his system to a normal state by restoring the balance between good and bad bacteria.

Many things can affect your dog's gastrointestinal health. Eating a poor-quality diet, consuming unclean water, eating feces or grass, or ingesting fertilizers or pesticides can all introduce bacteria to the gut that throw it off balance and cause problems like diarrhea and incomplete food absorption. Stress caused by a change in routine, such as travel or boarding, can be a factor, too. Diseases like inflammatory bowel disease, colitis, or kidney disease also can affect the balance of bacteria in his body. Antibiotics and cortisone can kill good bacteria as well as bad bacteria. For this reason, some veterinarians prescribe probiotics for your Lab if he's on antibiotics.

Antioxidants such as vitamins A, C, and E; beta-carotene; and other compounds also help support your puppy's immune system and protect him from disease. Antioxidants protect your cells against the effects of free radicals, which cause cellular damage and are produced when the body breaks down food or is exposed to pollution, cigarette smoke, or other environmental factors. Owners may want to add antioxidants to their dog's diet if he is suffering from cancer or heart disease. Always check with your veterinarian first—too much of some items can be toxic, such as vitamin A.

Digestive enzymes are sometimes packaged with probiotics because both affect your Lab's gastrointestinal health. Digestive enzymes break down nutrients in food so the body can absorb them. When commercial dog foods are cooked at high temperatures, these enzymes are killed and must be added back into the food. Dogs also produce their own digestive enzymes in their saliva glands, pancreas, and stomach. Yogurt is an excellent source of digestive enzymes. As always, read the label, and purchase one with live, active cultures.

A dog's production of digestive enzymes is affected by aging, and sometimes older dogs will benefit from their addition to his diet. A young, healthy Lab shouldn't need these.

Bone meal adds calcium to the diet, which is something young Labs don't need. In fact, breeders recommend you do *not* feed puppy food or any dog food high in calcium because it causes orthopedic problems later in life.

Vitamin and mineral supplements are necessary for dogs eating home-cooked or raw food, as mentioned, but they're usually unnecessary for Labs eating a commercially made food. If you do feel you need to give your dog additional vitamins and minerals, choose those made especially for dogs. And don't oversupplement any vitamins or minerals because they can have toxic effects.

Fatty acids must be added back to dry dog food after cooking. If your Lab has a dry, dull coat, a supplement in the form of fish oil or cod liver oil can provide essential fatty acids (linoleic acid) and vitamins A and D. Flaxseed is also high in beneficial fatty acids. Some of these are high in calories, so be careful not to give your Lab too much.

If you give your Lab whole foods to supplement his diet, you're less likely to overdose him on any specific nutrient because his body expels the excess as it digests the food. Foods such as carrots, cottage cheese, apples, bananas, blueberries, green beans, dandelions, and kelp all provide extra nutrition. Be sure the foods you choose are beneficial and not toxic to dogs (see Appendix C).

Prepackaged whole-food supplements are also available. Missing Link is a well-known brand that has been on the market for several decades. When in doubt, consult your veterinarian and research different product lines before adding a supplement to your Lab's diet.

Glucosamine and chondroitin both exist naturally in the body, but when a dog has arthritis, his body may not make enough of these substances. Glucosamine helps build connective tissue and stimulates the growth of healthy new cartilage. Chondroitin protects joints and slows the breakdown of existing cartilage. The two supplements are usually taken together and are often added to senior formula dog foods. It takes several weeks to see the effects, but many dogs enjoy greater mobility and less pain when on these two supplements.

Grooming

Most dog owners are more tolerant of the mess their dogs make than are the immaculate housekeepers we all wish we were. By keeping your Lab and his bedding clean, a guest shouldn't be able to smell a dog in your house.

Along with odor-busting tips, in this section we look at an often-neglected grooming (and health-care) chore: caring for your dog's paws.

Dealing with Doggie Odor

Some of us are more sensitive to doggie odor than others, but Labs shouldn't smell bad by anyone's standards. Strong odors can be caused by health problems such as ear infections, tooth decay, gum disease, skin disease, or kidney problems.

If your puppy rolls in something disgusting, swims in foul water, or just generally makes a stinky mess of himself, add vinegar to your rinse water when you bathe him, or purchase an enzymatic odor-removing shampoo, like Nature's Miracle. The skunk bath described in Month 7 also works very well.

Caring for Your Lab's Paws

Your Lab puppy's feet are exposed to extreme heat, pesticides, fertilizers, and uneven surfaces that could bruise his paw pads. His feet are constantly getting wet as he runs through mud, streams, grass, and leaves. Mud can accumulate between his toes and dry into clumps. In the summer, dogs sweat through their paws, which creates the perfect environment for bacteria to grow. If he's licking his paws constantly, something is irritating them. The best way to prevent problems is to keep his paws clean and dry.

Hot asphalt or newly blacktopped streets can burn your pup's delicate paw pads. He can also get road-burn–the bottoms of his feet are rubbed raw—from running on hard surfaces. Treat raw feet with a foot soak and antibiotic ointment or aloe vera gel. You'll need to bandage the feet to keep him from licking off the ointment. Place a gauze pad on the bottom of the foot, and tape it in place. Put an old cotton sock over the foot, and tape the top to his fur.

Labs can also get dry, cracked skin and calluses on their paw pads. After a foot soak, apply a small amount of vitamin E oil to help heal his skin. To keep him from licking it off, put it on his feet just before mealtime, so he'll be occupied long enough for it to soak in. Don't apply too much because it will stain your carpet if he walks on it. You also don't want his feet getting too soft because that will make it easier for them to be reinjured.

If you need to wash chemicals, antifreeze, road salt, or cleaners off your puppy's feet, use liquid dish detergent or vegetable oil to completely remove it. Then rinse and dry thoroughly.

> ### TIPS AND TAILS
>
> Be careful when removing goo from between your Lab puppy's toes. Don't use scissors to trim the goo from his fur. Labs have webbed feet, and you can easily cut him accidentally.

Do your Lab puppy's paws smell like corn chips? You read that right—corn chips. If so, that means he has yeast growing between his toes. Wash his feet in Betadine solution. Betadine is a 10 percent iodine-povidone antiseptic that kills bacteria and prevents skin infections. You can purchase it at a pharmacy.

For general paw relief or for a Betadine treatment, teach your Lab to love a foot soak. Add an inch or two of water to a kiddie pool or plastic tub, and add the solution. Soaking penetrates all the nooks and crannies of his feet better than washing with a cloth. Have him stand in the tub for a minute or two and then rinse and dry his paws with a towel.

Another remedy you can add to a foot soak is green tea, either bags or brewed tea. The antioxidants in the tea soothe his skin. Chamomile tea also has soothing properties. Apple cider vinegar is another topical disinfectant. Between foot soaks, rinse his feet with cool water to remove the irritants, and be sure to thoroughly dry them afterward.

Removing Sticky Stuff

Just like children get chewing gum in their hair, puppies get tree sap, tar, or other sticky things in their fur. Home remedies such as vegetable oil, peanut butter, and mayonnaise all have enough oil to break down the gummy texture so you can scrape or comb out the gunk. They also won't irritate his skin. Commercial products like Simple Green and some orange oil cleaners are nontoxic for use on pet fur.

If your Lab has gum in his fur, put an ice cube on the gum to harden it enough that you can chip it off. Tar and tree sap or pitch may be tough to remove. Apply vegetable oil, and let it soak on the area for 24 hours. You might want to put a T-shirt or Elizabethan collar on your Lab so he won't lick it.

Paint is easier to remove if you let it dry and harden and then clip it off.

Sometimes you just can't lubricate, wash, or soak the crud out of your Lab's coat, and you'll have to cut out the offending substance. Use blunt-pointed scissors or grooming clippers, and be very careful. His coat is so short, you might cut him with regular scissors.

> ### TIPS AND TAILS
>
> Never use gasoline, kerosene, turpentine, or solvents on your Lab. These products can severely burn your dog's skin and are toxic if he ingests them.

Social Skills

Your Lab puppy is a member of the family, too, and he'd love to tag along when your family goes on vacation. With a little preparation and planning, your best friend can also get away from the hustle and bustle of everyday. While on vacation, no one has to go to work or school or other activities, and you all have more time to relax with each other and with your puppy.

Most buses and trains won't accept dogs, so to travel with your pup, you must go by car or airline.

Traveling by Car or Flying

Although you might like to let your pup run from open window to open window while you drive, restrain your Lab while he's in the car. A dog who leaps around in the car can cause an accident, hit you in the face with his tail, or knock the gear shift out of gear.

As much as he might love it, don't let your Lab hang his head out the car window. Bugs or flying debris could hit his eyes and injure them. If the window is down far enough, he could jump out and be badly injured.

If you have room for it, the safest place for him is in a crate. Prevent the crate from tipping over when you go around corners by either tying it down or wedging it between your luggage. If your car isn't large enough for a crate, use a seat-belt harness. Special car harnesses are made for pets, or you can make one with a harness and short leash. Let him ride in the back seat so he won't be injured by the airbag if you're in an accident.

> ### HAPPY PUPPY
>
> It gets hot in the back of an SUV or van, even while the car is running. Be sure your Lab is shielded from direct sun and has plenty of air circulation if he's back there. Stop often to give him water and be sure he isn't overheated. You can purchase small battery-operated camping fans to provide extra ventilation.

Most airlines don't allow online reservations for pets, so call the airline directly to schedule your Lab's flight. Shipping a large dog is expensive; your Lab's ticket may cost as much as yours. Make your reservations early because spots for pets are limited, and reconfirm your reservation with the airline 24 to 48 hours before you leave. Your Lab is too large to travel in the cabin, so he'll have to be shipped in the cargo hold. If you're taking an international flight, research the regulations at your destination because there may be a long quarantine period. Hawaii also has strict guidelines when it comes to bringing animals to the islands.

Check the weather forecast before you leave home. When the ground temperature is too high or too low, some airlines refuse to fly with animals (more on this coming up). Try to schedule an overnight or late-night flight if you're traveling in the summer, so you can avoid extreme heat and humidity. Avoid traveling on holidays or weekends, and try to book a nonstop or direct flight so your dog doesn't have to switch planes.

Your Lab's shipping crate must satisfy the airline's regulations and conform to standards developed by the International Air Transport Association (IATA). The crate must be sturdy plastic (not wire), properly ventilated, and large enough that he can stand, turn around, and lie down. Many airlines require metal doors rather than plastic to prevent the dog from chewing and escaping from the crate. In addition to including your name and address on your dog's kennel, you must use arrows or stickers to indicate the top of the kennel.

Airline policies for traveling with pets may vary from company to company, so check with your carrier for its specific requirements. To view the pet policies for specific airlines, visit pettravel.com/airline_rules.cfm.

Fasten empty food and water dishes inside the crate door: they must be accessible from outside. Attach a food and water schedule, and tape a bag of food to the outside of the kennel. The crate must not be locked in case they need to remove your Lab in an emergency, but it must close securely with a latch that can be opened without tools. You cannot leave a leash with the kennel, but be sure to take one with you so you can take your dog out of the crate for a walk. Airline security will inspect your Lab and his belongings like any other passenger's.

Most veterinarians and airlines recommend you do *not* tranquilize your dog before flying. Tranquilizers and sedatives can affect your dog's equilibrium, breathing, and ability to regulate his body temperature. He may also be more likely to have a bad reaction due to the altitude and change in air pressure. A fully awake dog is usually safer.

If you are not traveling with your Lab, he will ship as cargo. You'll deliver him to the freight terminal, which is in a different part of the airport from where passengers go. Because you won't be at the airport to claim him when he arrives, mark the crate with the phone number of a person at your destination who can be contacted about your Lab.

Find out where the freight terminal is at the destination airport so you know where to pick him up. Get the direct phone number at your departure site and any connecting airports so you can confirm your Lab has made all his connections and arrived safely. Most airlines have complete instructions for shipping pets posted on their website.

Staying at Pet-Friendly Accommodations

Plan in advance to stay at pet-friendly hotels and campgrounds. Most major chains accept dogs, but call ahead to be sure. Pet-friendly hotels may have a limited number of rooms available, so make advance reservations. Others designate their smoking rooms as dog friendly. Some hotels charge an extra fee for dogs, require a deposit against damage, or don't accept dogs above a certain size. Many facilities offer extra amenities for dog owners, like dog day care, play yards, dog walkers, and treats.

Some hotels don't allow guests to leave their dogs in their room. Housekeeping personnel will be frightened if a big black dog greets them at the door, and your Lab could escape. If you are allowed to leave your Lab in the room, crate him while you're not there to watch him. Don't leave him alone for too long, especially if he may bark in the crate and disturb other guests. Leave the TV on to keep him company when you go out.

Feed your dog in the bathroom of your hotel room so he doesn't damage or dirty the carpets while he eats.

Don't allow your Lab to relieve himself right outside the door, where the stains and smell will offend other guests. Take him away from the building. Some hotels have designated pet areas or may be able to guide you to nearby dog parks or walking trails.

When investigating dog-friendly campgrounds and RV parks, ask if there are any size restrictions on the dogs allowed or if you have to pay extra fees to bring your pooch. Clarify if your dog is allowed in all parts of the park or if he must stay at your site. Dogs are allowed in most national parks, but they must be kept in your car, on the roadway, or parking lot, and they aren't allowed on hiking trails at all. National forests allow on-leash dogs to hike on the trails. The rules are so different at the various facilities, you should contact each one to confirm that you can bring your Lab.

Research dog-friendly accommodations at petfriendlytravel.com, petswelcome. com, and dogfriendly.com. While you research hotels and campgrounds, you can also find lists of dog-friendly beaches, dog parks, and other activities. Local dog day cares may allow you to leave your Lab temporarily while you spend the day at an amusement park.

Prepare Your Dog

Ensure your dog is healthy and safe for his vacation, and review his doggie manners before you leave. There are some requirements and precautions you should take before you hit the road or fly.

Health certificate: If you take your dog across state lines or fly him anywhere, you must carry a health certificate, which requires a veterinarian to certify that the dog is healthy enough to travel and is current on your state's required vaccines. (All 50 states require a rabies vaccine.) Some airlines also require an acclimation certificate, which states the dog is allowed to travel when the temperature is below 45°F. Both certificates must be signed by a federally accredited veterinarian. There is no acclimation certificate available pertaining to hot weather, although airlines usually don't accept pets for transport in the cargo hold when the temperature is above 84°F.

Identification: Be sure your puppy's tags are securely fastened and that the lettering is legible. Consider adding a tag with your cell phone number and emergency contact information on it, too. If he isn't already microchipped, do so now. Be sure he has a tag that states he's microchipped, so anyone who finds him will know to scan him. Dogs traveling internationally should have a chip that meets ISO standards, an internationally recognized frequency. Check with the microchip registry to be sure your contact information as well as your backup information is up to date.

Heartworm preventative: If your Lab isn't already on heartworm preventative, have him tested and on medication before you leave. In almost any area of the country, he will be exposed to heartworm, especially in the summer, when mosquitoes are common.

Training: You've probably already taught your dog to eliminate on different surfaces, but if he needs more work, do so before your trip. If he's used to going on grass only, he might not want to go in a strange place or on a new surface. Many dogs who stay in kennels don't like to relieve themselves on concrete. They also don't like to go near where they sleep.

Review his other obedience and manners, too. Practice skills like sitting to greet people, leave it, and walking nicely on leash. Refresh his memory so he'll wait to jump out of the car or go through a door. He could be lost if he rushes off in a strange place.

Review his crate training if you haven't been using it much. He may have to spend more time in the crate while you're on vacation: in the car, in a hotel room, on a plane, or at your host's home. He should feel comfortable and safe when crated.

> ### TIPS AND TAILS
>
> Teach your Lab to eliminate on cue. Every time he relieves himself, give it a name, like "Go potty," or "Hurry." Praise and give him a treat when he goes, and he'll soon associate the word with the action and your rest stops will be much shorter.

It's inconvenient, if not impossible, to leave food down for your Lab while traveling. Most owners don't free-feed Labs (leave food down all day for him) or they'd have a 200-pound dog. But if you do, retrain him to eat within 10 minutes. If he doesn't eat, pick up the food and put it away until the next meal. He'll quickly learn to eat when it's put in front of him.

If you'll be using fold-up travel bowls or giving water from a bottle, teach him to use them before you leave home. Many dogs refuse to stick their noses in a canvas bowl or tight spot. Drinking from a water bottle is an acquired skill, and it may take a few days for him to get the hang of it.

What to Pack and Bring

Pack a suitcase for your Lab when you're packing for yourself. If you're traveling by car, you'll be able to bring more supplies with you. Here's what to pack:

Health certificate: If you're flying or crossing state lines, this is required.

Microchip information: Bring the chip number, brand name, and registry contact information.

Photo of your Lab: If your dog gets lost, you'll need a photo to identify him and make posters.

Food and treats: You may not be able to find the same brands, and a diet change could cause a stomach upset.

Water: Water from an unfamiliar place can cause diarrhea. If you can, take some of your own from home.

Leash: Always leash your Lab in public. Bring a regular leash because in most places a retractable leash is impractical and dangerous.

Crate: If you're traveling by air, be sure the crate is airline approved. Familiarize your Lab with the crate before you travel.

Bedding and toys: Things that smell like home will make your Lab more comfortable in strange places.

First-aid kit: Include medication to treat carsickness. Over-the-counter medication for humans that contains the active ingredient meclizine is safe for dogs. Check with your veterinarian to find out brand names and dosage amounts. Ginger (as in gingersnap cookies) also helps prevent motion sickness.

Clean-up supplies: Bring disposable bags and paper towels.

As You Travel

You and your Lab must mind your manners in public places. If you don't see signs prohibiting dogs, that doesn't necessarily mean they are welcome. Keep him under control at all times, and prevent him from jumping on or sniffing strangers. Don't leave him tied up outside a building. He could be stolen or someone might accuse him of biting.

Being left in a hot car can kill a dog, so eat at drive-through restaurants while traveling with your Lab. Stop at public rest areas to use the restroom. Terry once walked two Labs, a collie, and a sheltie into a restroom with her because it was too hot to leave them in the car. They all crowded into the handicapped stall.

Highway rest areas often designate doggie relief areas. Keep your Lab on leash, and clean up after him, even in designated doggie zones. If there's a fenced dog area, patrol the field for scattered food, wrappers, trash, broken glass, and waste left by other dogs before you turn your dog loose. Wild animals often scavenge at rest areas, so be on the lookout for raccoons, possums, rats, mice, and coyotes. Rattlesnakes nap under picnic tables, in the restrooms, or under nearby bushes.

Be a good citizen so dogs continue to be welcome in public places.

When Your Lab Must Stay Home

If your pup can't travel with you, you have several options for dog care while you're gone. You can board him in a kennel, hire a pet sitter, or have family or friends care for him. Wherever you leave him, it will be a stressful time for your puppy, especially if he goes to a place he's never been before.

A young, active Lab should probably be boarded in a kennel for his own safety. If you leave him at home and have someone come in to see him twice a day, that still leaves him with more than 20 hours a day to entertain himself, and by now you know what that entails. After a few days of isolation, a lonely Lab will do things he'd never do when you're home. Although you may leave him alone while you work each day, that's much different from leaving him to his own devices for a full weekend or more.

Kennels provide safety and a choice of amenities for your Lab. Your puppy will be confined or supervised at all times, and you may be able to add extra activities to his daily routine like exercise, walks, doggie playgroups, or swimming. Although there's usually an extra charge for these services, your Lab will adjust better and suffer from less stress if he can get out of the confined kennel each day.

Labs are adaptable and happy dogs who adjust well to almost any situation. But kennels are noisy and stressful places, no matter how well they're operated. Your Lab may come home extremely tired. Some facilities may offer deluxe suites for your Lab that mimic a home environment with a couch, TV, and real walls instead of chain link or plastic panels.

A boarding facility will require you to provide proof of vaccines: DHPP, rabies, and bordatella (kennel cough). The kennel cough vaccine should be given at least 1 week, and not more than 6 months, before you board your Lab. By giving the vaccine a week in advance, your dog has time to absorb the protection of the vaccine into his system.

You will be asked to sign a contract and a liability release in case your Lab bites someone or injures another dog. Also provide your veterinarian's contact information. Be honest about any behavioral problems your Lab has, like separation anxiety or fear of men. They are trained professionals and can take precautions to prevent injuries or extreme stress.

Alert your own veterinarian that you'll be away and authorize them to treat your dog or give information to the kennel, caregiver, or another clinic should the need arise.

Ask for a tour of the facility when you visit so you can see where your Lab will stay. Ask some questions:

🐾 Will he be housed with another dog in the same kennel?

🐾 May you bring his food or a bed that smells like home?

🐾 Is someone onsite 24 hours a day?

🐾 What veterinarian do they use in case of an emergency or illness?

🐾 Are there extra charges for administering medication or feeding your own food?

Boarding your Lab with friends or family puts a lot of responsibility on people who might not be able to handle a big, goofy Lab. If your Lab knows them well, they have another dog he knows, or if he has spent time at their house with you, the arrangement might work out.

Think carefully before you impose on your acquaintances. If something happens to your Lab, it could ruin your relationship. Dogs often escape from private homes. They're in a strange place, anxious, and want to go home. A dog who never digs could dig out of the yard or jump the fence. Your friends don't know your dog or his habits, and their children could inadvertently leave a gate open.

A pet-sitter is a good option for an adult Lab who has matured and settled down. You may already have a sitter who walks your Lab while you're at work. It's less stressful for your Lab to remain at home, as long as you trust him to behave. If you have multiple pets, this is also a less-expensive option than boarding.

A professional pet-sitter will have you sign a contract and liability release. Because she'll be providing more that just a daily walk, ask some in-depth questions:

🐾 How much experience does she have caring for Labs? How does she deal with their activity level and strength?

🐾 Does she have liability and property damage insurance?

🐾 Does she do each visit herself? Does she have employees?

🐾 How long does she stay each visit?

🐾 Are there any extra charges you should know about? Any extra services she may provide?

🐾 Does she provide references? Could you call other Lab owners whose dogs she cares for?

🐾 Does she know pet first aid? Has she completed a pet first-aid course?

🐾 Is she a member of any professional associations?

🐾 How would she handle a personal emergency? Does she have backup help?

Some pet-sitters also board dogs in their home. Owners like that their dog is in a cage-free environment and treated like a member of the family. In-home or cage-free boarding services vary. Some operators take only a few dogs, while others operate more like a doggie day care and crate or kennel all the dogs at night.

A house-sitter is another option for vacation dog care. When interviewing a house-sitter, ask many of the same questions you'd ask a potential pet-sitter, with extra attention given to the house-sitter's personal routine while in your home. Some sitters only stay overnight and still go to another job during the day. Some guarantee they'll stay in your home a certain number of hours each day. Be sure to clarify these details. Also be clear about sleeping arrangements, food, cleaning, and whether the house-sitter can have guests. Some house-sitters treat their time at your house as a personal vacation. Be sure they understand they are there to care for your Lab and spend time with him.

Behavior

Even a well-adjusted, happy-go-lucky Lab will sometimes be anxious or afraid. He may react to new situations and people or something that has frightened him in the past, possibly during one of the fear imprint periods in his youth. The situation may be temporary and easy to deal with, or it could have catastrophic results.

Respect your puppy's stress or fear. Protect him from real danger, and acclimate him to safe situations where he's reacting poorly. Use the socialization methods you've practiced in previous months. In rare situations, medical help or behavior counseling might be necessary to cure symptoms of an emotional nature.

Recognizing Signs of Stress

Stress can be good or bad. Trying to hold a sit-stay may be stressful. Your arrival at the end of the day is stressful in a good way. But low-level chronic stress can cause serious health problems in your Lab. A short burst of stress causes an adrenaline rush (a flood of stress hormones), which results in a temporary, but sometimes extreme, reaction.

Your Lab puppy may exhibit subtle signs of stress that you won't recognize unless you learn to read his behavior:

- ❦ **Ears pinned back:** This is a classic sign your Lab is worried. Watch how his ears perk up when he's interested in something, how they appear when he is resting, and how they fall down and back when he's unsure.

- ❦ **Yawning:** He's not sleepy; yawning is a stress-relieving mechanism.

- ❦ **Licking his nose:** He may be gathering scent and pheromones so he can further evaluate the situation.

- ❦ **Teeth chattering:** This can be a sign of excitement.

- ❦ **Turning his head away:** He refuses to look at the thing that bothers him. Dogs often avoid eye contact to deflect a confrontation with another dog.

- ❦ **Panting:** This isn't his normal panting in hot weather or after exercise. You'll see rapid stress-related panting even in cool weather.

- ❦ **Drooling:** He may also lick his lips or his feet, have sweaty paws, or whine.

- ❦ **Wide, round eyes:** The white haw in the corner of his eye will show (referred to as whale eye), or he'll have dilated pupils.

A dog subjected to chronic stress with no relief will develop physical symptoms:

- ❦ **Stomach upset:** He may vomit or have chronic diarrhea.

- ❦ **Hyperactivity:** He may suffer from an inability to settle down or listen to you, be constantly vigilant, and overreact to everything around him.

- ❦ **Obsessive-compulsive behaviors:** Symptoms include chronic licking or chewing on himself to the point of leaving permanent, open sores; tail chasing; barking; or pacing.

- ❦ **Separation anxiety:** He is destructive when left alone, or he howls or barks the entire time you're gone.

The Fearful Lab

A frightened or extremely anxious dog will respond in one of three ways: freeze, flight, or fight. He'll freeze to evaluate what's happening. He may lie down and refuse to move or appear not to recognize you. Next, he'll flee by either running away or frantically struggling to escape. If he runs away, he's not paying attention to where he's going or what hazards are in his way. He'll fight if he's cornered and feels he has no other options, starting with a warning snap or growl. If that doesn't work, a full-on bite is his next line of defense.

The signs of stress listed in the previous section will tell you he's worried. Don't comfort him if you see him exhibiting these symptoms. For example, his hackles go up and he starts barking as you approach a mailbox he's sure contains something scary. If you pet him and tell him not to be afraid, he could interpret your tone of voice as confirming there really is something to worry about. By petting him, you're also inadvertently praising him for his fearful reaction.

Keep the leash slack so your Lab never feels trapped by a scary thing. Let him observe from a distance and approach only if he wants to. Don't bribe him; he'll endure his terror just to get the treat. Instead, use your jolly routine, and get his attention on you. When he sees you think that scary thing is no big deal, he'll learn to look to you for your reaction before he decides to be afraid.

> **HAPPY PUPPY**
>
> Got a tense puppy? Herbal or flower remedies like Rescue Remedy may help calm him.

If your dog is chronically afraid, you should work with a behaviorist to develop a program to improve the situation. Counter conditioning and desensitization are two options for treating fears. You can't force him to face his fears. He'll only become more and more terrified. You may not think they're rational, but they are very real to your Lab.

Training

Labrador Retrievers are willing to work hard and learn complex tasks. You may have found you enjoy training your dog and would like to try more challenging things together. Competitive obedience and hunting tests make use of your Lab's natural abilities while honing his skills and yours. You'll enjoy training as much as competing and make many like-minded friends along the way—children, adults, seniors, and people with disabilities—who all enjoy training their dogs and competing.

Rally and Obedience Competition

Are you and your Lab puppy enjoying obedience training? The AKC offers two types of competitive obedience for dog owners in which Labs do very well. The sports require dog/handler teamwork and performance skills and use similar obedience exercises in different ways. Rally and obedience both offer novice "A" classes for beginning handlers who have never before entered trials or earned titles with their dog.

You can take classes just for the fun of working with your Labrador. You're not required to enter trials. Although first through fourth place are awarded in each trial class, you and your dog really compete against a perfect score, and if you qualify, you earn a "leg" toward a title. You can earn a title without ever having to beat others in a class. At each level, you must achieve three legs—a qualifying score—to earn a title.

Rally and obedience trials are usually held in conjunction with conformation events. Labrador *specialty shows,* where only Labs are competing, may offer an obedience or rally trial at the same time. Sometimes all breeds may enter a specialty trial, while at other times the trial is for Labs only. To start training or learn more about rally and obedience, find a local obedience club or dog trainer who teaches competition classes.

> ### DOG TALK
>
> A **specialty show** is a conformation dog show for a single breed of dog held by a breed club. In a Labrador Retriever Specialty, the breed club often also conducts obedience, rally, hunting tests, and agility trials.

Rally is a good place for a newcomer to start in competitive obedience because it's less structured than traditional obedience, but it's a step up from the Canine Good Citizen test you read about in Month 10. You and your Lab move at your own pace through the course, completing challenges at individual stations. Each station has a sign with written instructions regarding the skill you are to perform. Scoring is not as precise and rigorous as in regular obedience, and you are encouraged to talk to your dog and have fun while you're going through the course.

A rally course includes 10 to 20 stations, depending on the level of competition, with both stationary and moving exercises. Stationary exercises include those such as halting and sitting your dog. Moving exercises include executing an about-turn and heeling at a face pace.

The levels in rally are Novice, Advanced, and Excellent.

In Rally Novice, there are no more than five stationary exercises, and all exercises are performed on-leash. Dogs earn the Rally Novice (RN) title after three qualifying scores.

In Rally Advanced, all exercises are done off-leash, and there are no more than seven stationary exercises. The exercises are more difficult, and one jump is included. Rally Advanced (RA) is the title for this level.

Rally Excellent exercises include challenges like backing up three steps while the dog stays in the heel position, and a moving stand while the handler walks around the dog. Rally Excellent includes 15 to 20 stations, and no more than 7 stationary exercises. An added challenge in the Excellent class is the honor exercise, where your dog must remain in a sit or down-stay while another competitor navigates the entire course with their dog. This exercise is done on-leash and you are 6 feet away from your Lab. The title earned for this level is Rally Excellent (RE).

▶ HAPPY PUPPY

Both rally and obedience trials test your teamwork as you and your Lab perform obedience exercises together. Rally is less formal, and you can talk to your dog and praise him in the ring. Obedience is more precise and structured, with strict rules that restrict touching or talking to your dog.

Once you've conquered rally, the Novice class in traditional obedience will look easy. Rally was officially accepted as an AKC event in 2005, but obedience competition has been part of the AKC for decades. In fact, the first AKC obedience test in 1933 had only eight entries, and two of them were Labrador Retrievers.

AKC clubs hold all-breed obedience trials and specialty trials, the latter of which are usually held in conjunction with conformation events. When compared to rally, obedience competition requires a more structured and precise performance and much less interaction between dog and handler while in the ring.

The exercises in obedience are the same at each trial, where courses can vary quite a bit in rally. In the Novice class, handlers and their Labs perform on- and off-leash heeling, figure-eight heeling, stand for examination, recall, 1-minute sit-stay, and 3-minute down-stay. When you and your Lab have completed three qualifying rounds, your dog earns the Companion Dog (CD) title.

In the Open class, all the exercises are performed off-leash. These include heeling, figure eight, retrieve a dumbbell, go over a jump and retrieve a dumbbell, drop on recall (a formal version of the emergency drop you have taught your Lab in Month 10), broad jump, 3-minute sit-stay, and 5 minute down-stay. Both stays are performed with the handler out of sight. After three qualifying scores, your dog earns the Companion Dog Excellent (CDX) title.

The Utility class is the most difficult. The dog must respond to hand signals for the stand, stay, down, sit, and come. He must demonstrate scent discrimination by finding an article with his handler's scent on it from a pile of identical articles. In the directed retrieve, the dog must retrieve a glove indicated by the handler. The directed jumping exercise consists of the dog going away from the handler and returning over a specified jump. The moving stand and examination involves the handler moving forward while the dog halts and stays standing. A judge walks up to the dog and runs her hand over him. The dog then must return to the handler on command.

As you see, the Utility class requires a high level of teamwork between you and your dog, and it usually takes much longer to achieve a title than at the other two levels. The Utility Dog (UD) title is given to teams who successfully qualify in three trials. Dogs may continue to compete and earn a Utility Dog Excellent (UDX) title after qualifying in both classes at 10 trials.

In addition to regular classes, obedience clubs and breed clubs often offer nonregular classes at their trials. Nonregular classes don't count toward titles, but they are fun for dogs and their owners. You can enter them for fun or while training for the next level of competition. There are also "optional titling classes": Beginner Novice (BN), Grad Novice (GN), Grad Open (GO), and Versatility (VER).

> ### HAPPY PUPPY
>
> One nonregular class in particular is fun for Lab owners: team obedience. Often offered at Lab specialty shows, a team of four Labs and their handlers perform the novice exercises together in the ring, like a drill team.

Hunting Tests and Field Trials

Plenty of opportunities are available for you to practice hunting skills and compete with your dog, even if you don't want to hunt. The AKC conducts hunting tests and field trials, and the United Kennel Club (UKC) also has a hunting division that conducts tests. You can learn about the UKC Hunting Retriever Club and its levels at hrc-ukc.com. The North American Hunting Retriever Association (NAHRA), nahra. org, also holds competitions. The competitions profiled here are AKC, but all the organizations have similar levels and procedures. To get involved in hunting tests, contact local clubs for a referral to trainers and group practices.

For beginners, the LRC, Inc. (the AKC Labrador Retriever parent breed club) offers a Working Certificate (WC) to test a Lab's natural working ability and retrieving instinct. This gives owners the opportunity to enjoy and experience the work Labs were bred for, without having to spend months training for competition. It's a great way to see if you're interested in pursuing the sport. Your dog only needs to pass the test once to earn his WC. Labs who have earned their conformation championship must also earn a Working Certificate before they can use the champion title.

To earn a Working Certificate, the Lab must do the following:

❧ A single retrieve of 50 yards on land in light cover.

❧ Back-to-back single retrieves in water to prove he's willing to reenter the water.

❧ Drop the bird within the boundaries designated by the judge. (The dog does not have to deliver the bird to hand.)

❧ Not be gun shy.

Local and regional Labrador Retriever clubs hold the tests in conjunction with AKC Hunting Tests or separately if they have enough people entered. You don't have to be a member of a club to enter. Pheasant and ducks are used, or sometimes pigeons and ducks.

Hunting tests are the next step for you and your Lab. Hunting tests are not competitive. If your dog completes the retrieves according to the rules, he qualifies and earns a leg toward his title. The purpose of the tests are to evaluate a retriever's ability as a hunting companion. Natural situations are set up on land and water, and dogs must retrieve any type of game bird. There are three levels: Junior, Senior, and Master Hunter.

In the Junior Hunter tests, your Lab is judged on his ability to mark where the bird falls and remember it, along with his style, perseverance, and hunting ability. Your Lab also must retrieve four single *marks*—two on land and two in the water. Each retrieve is completed one at a time. When he returns one bird, he turns and another bird is thrown. He must stay quietly at his handler's side until sent to retrieve the bird, return it to the handler, and release it "to hand" (not drop it on the ground) when asked. The handler doesn't have to actually shoot a bird. Throwers out in the field throw or shoot for them. Your dog must have a soft mouth and not damage the bird. After your Labrador qualifies in four tests, he earns the Junior Hunter (JH) title.

In a hunting test, a bird is thrown or shot and the dog **marks** it by visually recognizing where it fell and remembering the location.

After the Junior Hunter, dogs and handlers may work toward entering Senior Hunter (SH) and Master Hunter (MH) tests, which include "blind" retrieves, where the dog doesn't see the bird fall. The handler must guide his Lab using signals to find and retrieve the bird. The handler is not allowed to touch his dog, and the dog must remain steady—that is, not leave until sent. Advanced tests also include "doubles" and "triples," where the dog visually marks multiple falls, must remember where each bird is, and retrieve them in the same sequence they fell. Dogs also must "honor" by sitting quietly while another dog retrieves.

Top trainers and serious sportsmen compete in field trials, which are more competitive and difficult. At a field trial, dogs are competing for placements, and only dogs finishing in the top four placements receive points toward their Field Trial Championship. While Hunt Tests strive to mirror realistic hunting situations, dogs in field trials typically retrieve birds shot several hundred yards out in the field—much farther than a hunter could shoot a bird in a realistic hunting situation.

Once the dog achieves a certain number of points in field trials, he earns a Field Champion (FC) or Amateur Field Champion (AFC) titles. The highest honor a Labrador can achieve is Dual Champion, which a dog who has earned a Field Championship and Conformation Championship.

You and Your Puppy

Finding a job for your puppy also means finding a "job" you'll enjoy, too. From dancing to therapy visits, there are many activities you and your Lab can enjoy together.

Competitive Dog Sports

You don't have to be a super-athlete to compete in most canine sports. In fact, people with disabilities perform in a number of AKC-approved activities. You can also train just for fun and never actually enter a competition.

Some of the sports listed in this section offer AKC competitions, others are put on by the sport's parent organization, and some sports have several groups that sponsor events, which gives you access to more trials and training.

For AKC sports (referred to by the AKC as "companion events"), your Lab must either have registration papers or get a PAL (Purebred Alternative Listing) number, which is available to unregistered dogs and mixed breeds. The PAL used to be called ILP (Indefinite Listing Privilege), so you may hear both terms used. Along with the PAL application and registration fee, you must submit two recent and clear color photographs of your Lab, one full front view showing the facial characteristics, and one view showing the full side profile of the dog standing on a flat surface (not grass). Once you've received your PAL number from the AKC, you use that number on the entry forms for events.

Agility: Agility classes are fun and also help your Lab develop his coordination. Similar to jumping competitions in the equestrian world, dogs run an obstacle course and must complete it within a preestablished time frame and without any faults, such as knocking over a jump pole or failing to hit a required contact point on an obstacle.

Although your puppy shouldn't start jumping until his growth plates have closed, he can learn many aspects of agility now. Weave poles, the A-frame, teeter totter, pause table, dog walk, and tunnel are all safe for a young dog's growing bones if you don't overdo it. When he starts jumping, instructors usually set the jumps and A-frame low while your dog learns. When he's fully grown and able to compete, in the AKC, jumps for Labs are set at one of two heights: 20-inch Class for dogs over 18 inches and up to 22 inches at the withers (shoulder); or 24-inch Class for dogs over 22 inches at the withers.

Contact obstacles have painted zones at the ends that the dog must touch with at least one paw in order to qualify. Contact obstacles include A-frame, dog walk, and seesaw. This keeps the dogs from leaping off the top of an obstacle and being injured.

Five organizations in the United States offer agility trials, and your dog can earn dozens of titles. The titles can't be mixed and matched with each other, but your Lab can build an impressive list of initials at the end of his name. The five groups are these:

🐾 American Kennel Club (AKC): akc.org/events/agility

🐾 United States Dog Agility Association, Inc. (USDAA): USDAA.com

🐾 United Kennel Club (UKC): ukcdogs.com/WebSite.nsf/WebPages/DogAgility

🐾 North American Dog Agility Council (NADAC): nadac.com

🐾 Australian Shepherd Club of America (ASCA; accepts all breeds for competition): asca.org/programs/agility

Two newer venues are Companion Performance Events (CPE), k9cpe.com, and Dogs On Course North America (DOCNA), docna.com. Both offer agility events nationwide.

The organizations have similar obstacles, levels of competition, and awards. As an example, the AKC offers three levels: Novice, Open, and Excellent. The minimum time allowed and the number of obstacles to complete increase as the level of difficulty increases. Novice dogs compete over 14 to 16 obstacles, and judging focuses on the owner's handling technique, while scoring any faults.

Open agility, the second level, consists of 16 to 18 obstacles. The obstacles are more difficult than novice and require the handler to use more advanced skills.

Excellent, the highest level for AKC agility, consists of 18 to 20 obstacles. The handler and dog must work as a team and have advanced skills to complete the course. In Excellent B (for dogs who have completed titles), a dog competes for the Master Agility Champion (MACH) title.

The AKC divides the classes into Standard, Jumpers With Weaves (no contact obstacles), FAST (Fifteen and Send), and Time to Beat (T2B). FAST classes add additional challenges so dog and owner can demonstrate speed, handling skill, accuracy, and distance handling. T2B uses obstacles from Jumpers With Weaves, with the option of having one or two contacts included on the course. Each owner has the chance to set the "Time to Beat" for each jump height division.

In addition, trials offer the Preferred Class, which offers longer course times and lower jump heights for the regular classes.

Canine freestyle: Dancing with dogs is fun and increasingly popular. You don't have to be a great dancer to participate with your Labrador. Based on basic obedience training and dressage, musical freestyle adds music, timing, costuming, and showmanship. You and your Lab perform heelwork or dance moves to music. Your Lab dances both at your side and away from you. You select the music and develop your own choreography.

Both men and women enjoy the sport. You can see the dogs are having fun and enjoying the crowd's approval. Once you've developed your routine, you can do demos or compete in freestyle events. For more information about canine freestyle, visit the World Canine Freestyle Organization's website at worldcaninefreestyle.org or The Canine Freestyle Federation's site at canine-freestyle.org.

Dock dogs: This sport must have been invented for Labs, because they *love* it. You may have seen dock dogs at the fair or on television. It's exciting and easy for a beginner to get started. If your Lab loves to chase a retrieving toy and enjoys swimming, you're ready. All you need is a floating toy he loves, a leash, plenty of towels, and a place to practice. There are clubs all over the United States where you can practice and compete.

Dock dogs compete in three types of games:

Big air, a long jump for dogs, is the event you see on TV. Handlers throw their Lab's favorite floating toy in the pool and their dog retrieves it, running the length of a 40-foot dock and jumping into the water to get his toy. His jump length is measured where the base of his tail enters the water. The goal is jump length; he doesn't have to return the toy to earn a score.

Extreme vertical tests a dog's jumping ability. A toy is suspended in the air 8 feet out and $4\frac{1}{2}$ feet up from the edge of the dock. Dogs have two chances to jump and grab the bumper. If they make it, the bumper is raised in 2-inch increments until all the other dogs are eliminated.

Speed retriever is a new game in dock dog sports. You hold your Lab 20 feet back from the edge of the dock, behind an infrared beam that serves as the starting line. A suspended foam duck toy is at the far end of the pool. When you get the green light, you release your Lab to retrieve the duck. He leaps off the end of the dock and swims to the duck. The dog is timed, and when he grabs the duck, the timer stops. He doesn't have to bring the duck back to you. The challenge is finished when the timer stops. To learn about dock dogs and to find local clubs, visit dockdogs.com.

Flyball: Another exciting sport based on speed and retrieving, flyball races have two teams of four dogs who compete against each other in relay races. The course is 51 feet long, with 4 jumps. Each dog jumps the hurdles, catches a ball at the end, and returns. The dog steps on a tennis-ball launcher at the end of the line to release the ball. When he crosses the finish line, the next dog is released to do the same thing. Both teams run at the same time side by side, so competition is fierce and the audience cheers their team on to the finish line. Teams are divided into divisions so they can compete against teams with similar levels of ability.

The hurdle heights are determined by the height of the shortest dog on the team, so you'll often see an odd combo of breeds—for instance three tall dogs like Labs and a short Yorkie. The start line and timing are measured electronically, and the winning team might win by a thousandth of a second. Four experienced dogs can finish a run in less than 20 seconds. The North American Flyball Association has more information available at flyball.org/aboutflyball.html.

Conformation: When you see a televised dog show, like the Eukanuba National Championship or the Westminster Kennel Club Show, that's a conformation event. Dogs are judged against the breed standard, which we talked about earlier in this chapter. In each breed, the judge evaluates dogs in classes separated by male and female dogs and further divisions within each sex. The winners of each class compete against dogs who have their championship for the Best of Breed award.

Dogs earn points based on how may dogs they're shown against, and when they have a certain number of points won against a representative number of dogs for the particular breed, they earn their championship. Champion dogs are considered excellent candidates for breeding because they've proven they have the correct structure and temperament representative of the breed. Once they have their health clearances, these dogs may go on to produce sound, healthy puppies and improve the breed overall.

Breeds are divided into seven groups in AKC competition. Labrador Retrievers are part of the Sporting Group, and the Best of Breed Lab competes against other retrievers, spaniels, pointers, and setters for the Best in Group award. Other breed groups (and some representative breeds) are the Working Group (Rottweilers, Boxers), Herding (Collies, German Shepherds), Toy (Maltese, Toy Poodle), Non-Sporting (Standard Poodle, Keeshound), Terrier (Scottish Terrier, Airedale Terrier), and Hound (Bloodhound, Dachshund). The winner of each group then proceeds to the Best In Show ring, where a judge chooses a winner among the seven top dogs from that day's competition.

If you're interested in conformation, talk to your breeder. Your Lab may or may not be a "show-quality" dog, and an expert will need to go over him to confirm whether he should be shown. Conformation dogs must be intact (not spayed or neutered). You'll need to learn about handling your dog in the ring, grooming, nutrition, conditioning, and pedigrees so you can be competitive. Many breed clubs have fun matches where you can practice and take classes, and some breeders will mentor people who are new to the sport.

Therapy Dogs

Accompanied by their owners, therapy dogs make visits to schools, nursing homes, rehabilitation hospitals, libraries, and other facilities to the cheer patients, staff, and residents. Labrador Retrievers are naturally suited for this kind of work.

Most facilities require that you and your dog be trained and certified through a recognized therapy dog organization, and local and national groups offer training and testing. Therapy Dogs International (tdi-dog.org) and Delta Society (deltasociety.org) both have local chapters that train and certify animal-assisted therapy dogs. Delta Society also offers a home-study course to prepare you and your dog for visits.

Therapy dogs must be immaculately groomed for their visits. For example, their toenails must be cut short so they don't tear the skin of fragile or elderly patients.

They must also be healthy and free of parasites because they will be around patients with compromised immune systems.

Many therapy groups use the Canine Good Citizen test as the basis for certification and expand it to include exposure to wheelchairs and hospital situations. Dogs with more advanced training can participate in animal-assisted therapy, attending actual physical or psychological therapy sessions. For example, a patient in a rehab hospital may learn to use her hands by brushing your Lab, throwing a ball for him, or opening a can of dog food. Your dog might sit next to a child who is undergoing a frightening procedure to calm him. In schools, a child could read to your dog while working on her reading skills.

To find a therapy dog group near you, ask local obedience trainers or hospitals to refer you to a group. Or contact the national organizations and see if there is a local chapter in your area.

Month 12 (and Beyond)

Your Lab Grows Up

Month 11 | Month 12

Socialization in public

Ready for more advanced training
Slow growth—reaches adult size
Annual vaccinations and checkup

Labrador Retrievers have an extended puppyhood, and yours won't settle down much until she is 2½ to 3 years old. Some Labs are quiet and mellow, but most keep their happy-puppy attitude well into old age. You have many years of laughter to look forward to as your pup matures.

Physical Development

Over the next 2 years, your Labrador will continue to physically mature, although the changes will be nowhere nearly as dramatic as those you've seen during her first year.

Changes from 1 Year to Adulthood

Your Lab will continue to look like a teenager until she's about 18 months old. Then she'll fill out and look fully mature and balanced at 2½ to 3 years old. The growth plates in her limbs will close between 10 and 18 months, and her height will stabilize. Her legs will grow stronger and sturdier, and for a male, characteristics like a broader head and chest will develop if he's not yet neutered. Females won't look a lot different when they reach maturity, but they, too, will stop growing and fill out a little.

Your 11-month-old Lab has the maturity of a 15-year-old child. She's still very much a puppy, with a teenager's exuberance and energy level, and she might not have much common sense yet. By the time she's 18 months old, she will have matured a bit. She'll be less frantic, but still very active.

Adult Sizes and Weights

Your Lab puppy probably won't grow more than another inch between now and full maturity. She will add on a few pounds, and she'll eat like a horse, but don't excuse weight gain as "filling out." Continue to check her body condition (see Appendix B) and adjust her food accordingly.

Remember that an adult male should weigh between 65 to 80 pounds when he's 3 years old, so depending on his height and build, he should be less than his expected weight now. A female should be 55 to 70 pounds at 3 years old. When in doubt, keep your Labrador lean rather than heavy.

Health

With a little attention, your Lab should be healthy and active for many years to come. Schedule regular wellness exams and vaccines. Watch for signs of health problems so you can catch them before they get serious.

When Are the Next Vaccinations Due?

Assuming your Lab puppy had her rabies vaccine and final DHPP booster at 4 months, she should need her next inoculations at 16 months, or 1 year later. Consider waiting a week between the DHPP and rabies vaccines to avoid overloading your puppy's immune system. Once this round of vaccines is completed, you shouldn't have to revaccinate your dog for 3 years.

> ### TIPS AND TAILS
>
> In 2003, the American Animal Hospital Association (AAHA) changed its vaccine guidelines, recommending that veterinarians vaccinate dogs only every 3 years. Research has shown that yearly vaccines are unnecessary because most animals retain the immunity from the initial vaccines for many years. There are also indications that overvaccination is potentially harmful. Adverse long-term effects are still being studied, but researchers suspect excessive vaccination may contribute to anaphylaxis, immunosuppression, autoimmune disorders, infections, and other disorders.

You may have given your Lab other noncore vaccines such as those for Lyme disease, coronavirus, or leptospirosis. Discuss optional vaccines and the risk of contracting the diseases in your area with your veterinarian.

If you'll be boarding your dog, the bordetella vaccine is required and must be given on a yearly basis.

If you take your dog to the veterinarian for a suspected illness, and her vaccines are ready to be updated, wait until she has recovered from whatever ails her. Her immune system is compromised when she's ill, and the vaccine might not create the protective immunity the vaccine is supposed to provide.

As your Lab ages, consider her health status before administering vaccines. It's possible that older dogs with diabetes, hypothyroidism, glaucoma, or any other chronic medical condition should no longer be vaccinated. Explore this option with your veterinarian when the time comes.

Titers

An alternative to vaccines is a *titer*. This is a blood test that confirms if a dog has responded to a specific vaccine and still has that immunity. If she does, no further vaccination is necessary. Veterinarians usually test for parvovirus and distemper, because if the dog is protected from these two, it's fairly certain her immunological status in good shape. Titers should be repeated yearly to detect when or if your Lab loses her immunity.

> ### DOG TALK
>
> A **titer** measures the amount of antibodies to a particular disease your Lab is carrying in her body.

Vaccines cost less than running a titer test, but the benefit is that you aren't exposing your dog to unnecessary vaccines.

The Annual Checkup

Even if you don't vaccinate your dog every year, she still needs an annual wellness exam. Dogs age faster than humans, and your Lab changes dramatically between vet visits. Dogs also hide pain well, and your vet may discover something you haven't noticed yet.

The annual exam establishes a history so that when your Lab does have a problem, the veterinarian has a record of her past health status to compare to. This helps him decide if further tests are needed and help him make a diagnosis.

Before you take your Labrador to the vet, make a list of questions about her health, behavior, nutrition, and anything else on your mind. Review your puppy's health record so you know the date of her last vaccines and any other treatments she's had. Bring her treats so you can make the visit a positive experience for your dog. Bring in a stool sample to be checked for worms and other parasites along with any medications or supplements you're giving her.

During your visit, the veterinarian will examine your dog. He will …

🐾 Check your puppy's weight, and assess if it's normal or if she's overweight.

🐾 Conduct a nose-to-tail examination, listening to her heart, lungs, and digestive sounds, and feeling for any abnormalities, lumps, or signs of pain.

🐾 Test your dog's reflexes to be sure they're normal.

🐾 Examine her teeth to see if they're clean and the gums are a healthy color.

🐾 Draw blood for heartworm test and any other tests indicated, such as testing for tick-borne diseases.

🐾 Administer annual bordetella (kennel cough) vaccine if needed. Update any other inoculations as needed.

🐾 Examine her ears to see if they're pink and healthy and free of infection or foreign bodies.

🐾 Renew prescriptions for flea control, heartworm preventative, and any other necessary medications.

If the vet finds a problem, he may order further bloodwork, x-rays, or other testing.

Common Lab Ailments

Like all dogs, Labs are vulnerable to disease as they mature. Some ailments strike young dogs for no apparent reason. Others are preventable if you take sensible precautions.

Allergies: Many Labs suffer from allergies. If yours is licking her paws, scratching for no obvious reason, chewing the base of her tail, or has dander or flaky skin, she may be reacting to an allergen. A Lab's allergies may be caused by food sensitivities, flea allergy, or environmental allergies. Just as people do, she may suffer more during certain times of the year.

We've talked about food, noting your Lab may be sensitive to a particular grain or protein source. Food allergies are actually uncommon in dogs. Careful experimentation with elimination diets may solve this problem, and your vet may prescribe a hypoallergenic food. It can take up to 12 weeks to see a difference in your dog's health if a food allergy is the issue.

Your pup can also be allergic to flea saliva; it only takes one flea to cause an intense itchy reaction. Check her coat for flea dirt, and bathe her if you see evidence of infestation. Keep her on a regular flea preventative. Some preventatives lose their effectiveness because your dog builds up immunity to them, so switch brands if your dog is still suffering from fleas. If your dog is clean and in excellent health, she won't be as attractive to fleas.

Environmental allergies are harder to treat because you usually can't eliminate the allergen. Called *atopic dermatitis*, such allergies often start slowly, with just one or two sensitivities, and your Lab starts reacting to additional substances over time. Many things can affect her, including pollen, grasses, dust mites, feathers, or mold. As your dog continues to suffer, she may develop thick, greasy-looking skin.

Your veterinarian or a veterinary dermatologist can perform skin sensitivity testing and develop injections to desensitize your dog to the offending substances. Unless the allergies are extreme, most owners just take measures to keep their dog comfortable. Veterinarians prescribe antihistamines, antibiotics, and steroids to control symptoms. As your puppy scratches, she'll get secondary yeast and staph infections, which also need treatment.

> ### HAPPY PUPPY
>
> If your Lab has allergies or hot spots, a cool, medicated bath will soothe her skin. Don't use oatmeal shampoo. Although it soothes the itching, it's a grain, and dogs with grain sensitivities may have an additional allergic reaction.

If you think your Lab has environmental allergies, keep her indoors with the windows closed when the pollen count is high. (Check your daily paper for that information.) Also keep her indoors during the peak hayfever times of day—early morning and evening. Rinse her feet and wipe her down with a damp towel when you bring her indoors.

Even if they don't have a food allergy, some dogs with atopic dermatitis improve when switched to a higher-quality dog food. If your Lab is allergic to house dust mites, they often react with grain mites. In that case, your puppy will benefit from a canned food or kibble that has no grain.

Arthritis: Manage your Lab's exercise for life so she won't be crippled by arthritis as she ages. Whenever possible, have her run and play on soft ground. Hard pounding jars her bones and joints. Although arthritis is sometimes caused by hip dysplasia, otherwise healthy dogs can also get it due to a previous injury, tick-borne disease, autoimmune disorder, obesity, or cartilage problems caused by poor diet.

If your veterinarian diagnoses arthritis …

🐾 Manage your Lab's weight and provide gentle exercise to maintain her muscle tone. Swimming and walking are both excellent for dogs with arthritis.

🐾 Give her glucosamine and chondroitin supplements that lubricate her joints and may relieve her pain.

🐾 Consider getting her acupuncture to help relieve symptoms.

🐾 Be sure she has a soft bed that cushions her sore joints.

🐾 Allow your Lab to stay indoors on cold, damp days.

🐾 Raise her food bowl if she has a stiff neck.

🐾 Help her climb stairs and provide a ramp to help her get in and out of the car.

🐾 Ask your vet about pain-relieving medications.

🐾 Put carpet runners on hard floors so she can walk more easily.

Bloat: Gastric dilation volvulus, also known as bloat, most often occurs in large, deep-chested dog breeds. Although Labs are vulnerable, it's not common in the breed. With bloat, the stomach fills with gas and fluid and swells because the dog cannot expel it (gastric dilation). As a result, the stomach twists (volvulus). Symptoms include drooling, unproductive retching, restlessness, biting at her side, a distended abdomen, and signs of shock. Emergency surgery to relieve the twisting could save your dog's life. If your dog's stomach doesn't twist, the veterinarian may relieve the gas by passing a tube into the dog's stomach.

Dogs who have suffered from bloat are very likely to have another occurrence. To prevent bloat …

🐾 Restrict access to water for 1 hour before and after meals.

🐾 Avoid strenuous exercise 1 hour before and after a meal.

🐾 Divide her food into three small meals, spaced well apart.

🐾 Do not feed your Lab from a raised food bowl.

🐾 Avoid feeding dry food that lists fat among the first four ingredients on the label.

🐾 Never let your dog gulp a large amount of water all at once. If she's very thirsty, let her have a quick drink and then wait a minute or so for another one. Repeat as needed to quell her thirst.

> **TIPS AND TAILS**

Bloat is a life-threatening situation, so if your dog shows symptoms, take her to the veterinarian immediately.

Cold tail: Also called "limber tail," cold tail is a painful condition that can affect a Labrador of any age. It occurs most often in hunting dogs, and it also shows up in some other sporting breeds. When moving, a Lab normally carries her tail straight out or at least up off her back legs. An affected dog holds her tail down limply against her rear. The condition has been blamed on hard workouts, heavy hunting, and swimming or bathing in water that's too cold. The tail is not broken; the condition may be associated with muscle or nerve damage to the tail. It most often occurs in male Labs.

Dogs usually recover within a few days, but sometimes it takes as long as week. Warm packs at the base of the tail and analgesics will help ease your Lab's pain.

Gum disease: Caring for your Lab's teeth and gums is crucial to ensuring her lifelong health. By the time your dog is 3 years old, she may need a teeth cleaning to remove tartar and plaque on her teeth and beneath the gum line where the toothbrush can't reach. Without diligent dental care, she could get a serious infection that will spread through her system and shorten her life.

Although her teeth are beautiful and white now, chewing on sticks and tennis balls can wear them down significantly over time. She may also break a tooth that will need to be removed.

Your veterinarian can determine if your Lab needs her teeth cleaned and can show you where plaque has built up or gum disease has started.

Hip and elbow dysplasia: Research has shown that overly rapid growth and obesity, in addition to genetics, play a role in whether your dog will develop these diseases. Dogs suffering from hip or elbow dysplasia develop arthritis, sometimes at a very young age. Puppies don't exercise as hard as adults and don't carry a lot of weight, so symptoms in a severely affected dog may not show up until she reaches her full adult size. Some dogs with hip dysplasia never show symptoms, like gait abnormalities or holding her elbows at an unusual angle, but most develop arthritis in their middle years, between 5 and 8 years old.

One of the keys to slowing the progression of dysplasia is to keep your Lab at a lean weight. Work with your veterinarian to decide what that weight should be. To make your lab more comfortable, follow the same tips as given for arthritis earlier in this chapter.

Arthritis, hip dysplasia, and other ailments can be prevented or at least improved by keeping your Lab slim and trim.

Laryngeal paralysis: A disease that affects primarily older Labrador Retrievers, laryngeal paralysis occurs when a dog's vocal folds, which usually open when the dog inhales, don't open at all or open out of sync with the dog's natural breathing rhythm. Part of a neurological disease process that develops over a long period of time, it can affect one or both vocal folds. A dog who has laryngeal paralysis pants excessively, is overly sensitive to heat, and is easily fatigued. Often the dog's breathing won't return to normal until hours after exercise.

A surgeon can tie back the vocal fold (or folds) to the outer sides of the larynx so the airway will remain open. Although the dog's breathing improves, she is susceptible to aspirating (inhaling) her food. When she eats, she might get food or water in her lungs, which can cause pneumonia.

Lumps and bumps: As Labs age, they often get an assortment of lumps on their bodies. This is perfectly normal, but you'll want your vet to take a look at them to be sure they're not something serious. Sometimes he can tell by how the lump is attached to the body. He may withdraw some fluid or cells from the lump and examine it microscopically to confirm it's harmless. If the lump is benign, there's no need to remove it except for cosmetic reasons, and you can wait until your dog has to go under anesthesia for another procedure, like teeth cleaning, if you want it removed.

If a lump starts to grow or drains fluid, take your Lab to the vet for further testing.

Select a permanent guardian for your Lab to ensure she won't end up in a shelter if something happens to you. In fact, select three people who have agreed to care for your Lab. Then, if someone's situation changes and he's unable to fulfill your wishes, there's still someone available to care for your Lab.

Nutrition

In the previous section, we touched on food allergies. There are other ways your Lab's diet can affect her health, too, and we look at those here. We also explore raw and home-cooked diets, along with their benefits and drawbacks.

The Relationship Between Food and Health

Poor-quality food can cause nutritional deficiencies in your pup and lead to major illness. Now that the pet-food industry does a much better job of manufacturing complete and balanced dog foods, there's a much lower incidence of diseases caused by nutrient imbalances. But even a food label that states "complete and balanced" might not provide the best nutrition for your dog's particular needs.

Here are some examples of what happens when certain nutrients are out of balance:

🐾 Vitamin A toxicity can occur when too much liver, cod liver oil, or vitamin A is added to the diet. It causes lethargy, loss of appetite, and bone and joint pain.

🐾 Vitamin B$_{12}$ deficiency causes anemia.

🐾 Vitamin D toxicity causes excess levels of calcium in the blood and can lead to kidney stones and organ failure.

🐾 Fatty-acid deficiency causes skin and hair disorders, such as a dry, brittle coat and hair loss. It also causes slow healing from injury or illness.

🐾 Zinc deficiency sometimes occurs in dogs fed poor-quality or generic dog foods, or dogs who have been oversupplemented with other minerals like iron, calcium, and copper. A deficiency causes poor growth in puppies. Too much zinc causes calcium and copper deficiencies.

🐾 Protein deficiency causes infections, weakened immune system, slow healing, hormone deficiencies, and skin problems.

TIPS AND TAILS

If you're feeding your Lab a raw or home-cooked diet, you are responsible for ensuring she's getting the proper balance of the nutrients she needs.

Obesity

Too much food can affect your Lab's health if she becomes obese. Labs gain weight very easily. They're active, but they also love to eat and don't seem to know when to stop. If your Lab is 20 percent or more over her ideal weight, then she's not just plump, she's obese. That means an 84-pound dog who should weigh 70 pounds has to lose 14 pounds—that's a lot of dog biscuits. Spayed females are the most likely to gain weight, but all Labs are susceptible.

If your pup develops this problem, you're risking serious future health problems:

🐾 Arthritis

🐾 Heart and respiratory disease

🐾 Hip dysplasia

🐾 Cruciate ligament injury

🐾 Kidney disease

🐾 Cancer

🐾 Pancreatitis

🐾 Decreased life expectancy—up to 2 years less

Once you've established that your Labrador is too heavy, work with your veterinarian to put together a realistic weight-loss plan. Before you start anything, have your vet do a complete physical exam. Health conditions like thyroid disease can cause weight gain.

Helping your Lab lose weight is similar to going on a diet yourself. To say "less food and more exercise" is simple. But you need to do more. Let's look at productive ways to help your Lab maintain a healthy weight:

🐾 Cut back on her food a little bit at a time so she isn't suddenly starving. Her metabolism will slow down to compensate for the decrease in food if you cut back too fast.

🐾 Add beans, pumpkin, and other high-fiber veggies to her meal to help her feel full.

🐾 Switch to a "light" commercial food or a low-calorie, high-fiber prescription diet dog food. The bulk is the same so she doesn't feel deprived.

🐾 Feed your puppy twice a day, and pick up her food in between.

🐾 Soak her food in water before feeding her so it expands in the bowl and makes her feel full as soon as she eats.

🐾 Eliminate coat supplements that might be high in fat and calories.

🐾 Cut back on treats. A big dog doesn't need giant dog biscuits. A little snack will do just fine. Choose less-fattening treats like carrots, rice cakes, or popcorn (if your Lab isn't sensitive to rice or corn). Give her air-popped popcorn, and don't add butter or salt.

🐾 Avoid table scraps. Those calories add up fast.

🐾 Put her meal in a treat-dispensing toy so she'll be entertained and less focused on scarfing down as much food as possible.

Last but never least, begin an exercise program with your Lab. Assuming she's healthy enough to exercise, start with walks and work up to more active games of fetch or other activities when her fitness begins to improve. Daily exercise builds muscle tone, and muscle tone decreases the amount of fat your Lab carries around. Muscle mass also increases metabolism, which helps burn calories.

> **HAPPY PUPPY**

Swimming is excellent exercise, and most Labs enjoy it.

Home-Prepared Foods

Today's dog owners have more options than ever when choosing food for their dog. Instead of commercially manufactured dog foods, many people opt to feed their dogs raw or home-cooked diets. Many of these owners want to provide their puppy optimum nutrition and have control over the quality and ingredients they're feeding, without added dyes, fillers, or preservatives. Others may have lost faith in commercial foods due to a recent food recall. Some want to try a home-prepared diet to see if they can resolve a health problem their Labrador suffers from, like allergies or digestive issues.

There are advantages and disadvantages to home-prepared foods, and you'll find plenty of advice in books and online. When you're researching diets, take into consideration the source of the information. This is a subject people get very passionate about, but they are sometimes long on opinions and short on facts.

A poorly prepared, imbalanced diet can cause more health problems than it solves, as you saw in the previous section about the links between health and nutrition. Unless you're a veterinary nutritionist, consider working with one to be sure you're providing the healthiest possible diet for your Lab.

Dogs are carnivores, so whatever type of diet you choose, it should contain about 75 percent meat. No more than 10 percent should consist of grains, and 15 percent can be vegetables and fruits.

Feeding home-prepared foods is not an all-or-nothing proposition. You can feed a quality commercial food to be sure your Lab is getting sufficient vitamins and minerals and supplement it with raw or home-cooked ingredients.

Monitor your Lab's health to be sure the diet is working for her. Her stools should be smaller because her body is making better use of the nutrients she consumes and she isn't eating too many grains and fillers that are hard to digest efficiently.

Her teeth should be cleaner and her gums healthier. Her skin should be healthy and her coat thick and shiny. Overall, she should appear healthy and happy, with clear eyes and ears and plenty of energy. If you find bits of bone in her stool, she's not chewing them completely. Grind them smaller or discontinue feeding bones.

If your Lab suddenly develops diarrhea, vomiting, gas, or a decrease in appetite, discontinue feeding the diet and consult with your veterinarian. It could be due to a single ingredient, or something else might be wrong.

Raw diets are often referred to as BARF (Bones And Raw Food or Biologically Appropriate Raw Food). The BARF diet was popularized by Dr. Ian Billinghurst, an Australian veterinarian. His premise is that dogs should eat the way their ancestors ate. But considering that dogs have been domesticated for more than 10,000 years, this might not be an appropriate comparison.

Another way of looking at is that wolves still eat this way in the wild. Wolves are much different from dogs, and dogs have changed dramatically since they were first domesticated. Wolves don't necessarily get the nutrients they need for good health, and ancient dogs quickly became dependent on humankind for food.

So although the reasoning may be flawed, there are some advantages to feeding raw, whole foods, along with some disadvantages.

Advantages of a raw diet:

❧ Your dog needs a good balance of calcium and phosphorus in her diet. Raw meat provides phosphorus; raw bones provide calcium.

❧ You have complete control over the ingredients.

❧ You can purchase fresh, whole foods and avoid pesticide-treated, processed foods and meat raised with antibiotics or growth hormones.

❧ You can experiment with different ingredients and take advantage of seasonal produce.

Disadvantages of a raw diet:

🐾 Raw meat must be from healthy animals and handled carefully during processing to prevent spoilage or contamination, especially as it is not cooked, which kills bacteria.

🐾 Ingesting raw meat can give you or your dog E. coli or salmonella if you aren't careful.

🐾 Large, raw bones can break a dog's teeth or perforate her stomach or intestinal tract. Small, softer raw bones, like chicken or turkey necks, are safer. You can also grind raw bones to minimize the risks.

🐾 Raw foods are more expensive than feeding commercial dog food and take a lot of planning and preparation time.

🐾 It's hard to know if you're feeding a proper balance of nutrients, especially vitamins and minerals.

🐾 There's a risk of feeding too much fat, which can cause pancreatitis, a potentially fatal disease.

Home-cooked diets are usually a stew made of meat, grains, and vegetables. You get many of the benefits of a raw diet without as much risk of contamination, although safe handling practices are still necessary.

Table scraps don't provide adequate nutrition for your Lab and usually contain excessive amounts of fat. Cooked bones should be removed and discarded after cooking or ground into small, safe pieces.

> **TIPS AND TAILS**

Make the transition to a new diet gradually to avoid major stomach upsets.

Grooming

You've taught your puppy to enjoy handling and grooming, and now it's time to make good use of those skills and not let her forget them.

Maintaining a Regular Grooming Schedule

Every Sunday night, as she relaxes in front of the television, Terry gets down on the floor with her Lab and has a good grooming session. Her dog is tired after an active weekend and willing to sit still. He looks forward to their time together—as well as the multitude of treats he gets when she trims his toenails.

A weekly grooming is all your Lab should need on a regular basis, except when he's blowing his coat twice a year. You can break up grooming chores into several sessions during the week if you want to. Teeth-brushing Tuesdays, Friday fur-fights—the idea is to be able to look forward to spending this time with your Lab while keeping him clean and healthy.

The more time you spend grooming, the more cooperative he will be. If you slack off for a couple months, maybe in winter, you'll find he gets a case of the wiggle-butts come springtime when you want him to sit still for grooming.

Performing Weekly Health Checks

Don't forget to perform a weekly health check (see Month 4) during your grooming sessions.

Go over your Lab's entire body—skin, feet, mouth, eyes, and ears—to identify grooming needs and health issues before they cause serious problems. As your Lab ages, you'll also want to look for lumps and signs of soreness due to arthritis or other conditions.

Social Skills

You've spent a lot of time and effort raising a well-behaved Labrador, and now it's time to enjoy the fruits of your labor. A backyard dog will quickly forget his manners and social skills, and she'll also develop the behavioral problems you've worked to avoid. Continue socializing her and enjoying your Lab's company.

Enjoying Daily Walks

No matter how old your Lab is, she'll always need some daily activity, both for companionship and exercise. A daily walk helps you unwind and gives her some much-needed exposure to the outside world, and you'll enjoy some nice time together. Once around the block won't be enough to wear her out, though. He needs at least a half hour of active exercise and a long walk. A nightly trip to the dog park or a visit to the neighbor dog for a play date takes care of both.

If you don't keep up with walks and exercise, your Lab will gradually get harder to handle, and her training will deteriorate. The more trouble she is, the less time you'll want to spend with her, and next thing you know, she's spending way too much time alone or in the crate.

Remember, your Lab is still young and needs a lot of exercise, guidance, discipline—and time with you.

Keeping Up with Socialization

As we've said before, dogs quickly become desocialized if they don't get out regularly. Plus, at 12 months, males are reaching an age where they might become more territorial and protective, so he still needs diligent socialization.

Include him in activities when company comes to your house so he continues to welcome people into your home. Be sure he spends time with children if you don't have any of your own.

Your Lab, male or female, needs to continue meeting other friendly dogs of all sizes on a regular basis.

With a little work on your part, his social skills will continue to improve, and he'll remain the friendly outgoing dog a Lab is supposed to be.

Behavior

She may look like an adult, but your Labrador Retriever isn't quite there yet. Give her leeway as she earns it, but don't be afraid to continue with crating and discipline when she needs it.

If her behavior deteriorates, back up a few steps and put her on a puppy boot-camp program around the house. Once her skills have been reviewed, try again to offer her some adult privileges.

Changes as Adulthood Approaches

As a Labrador Retriever encounters adulthood, she'll still be your happy-go-lucky puppy, but she will grow bigger, stronger, and more protective of her territory.

Although Labs aren't particularly good defenders, you may find her sounding the alarm well before your doorbell rings. You shouldn't see any aggression like might appear at this age in other breeds, however, because a typical Labrador is universally friendly to one and all.

You'll find her attention span has improved and she concentrates better. She's not as distracted and impulsive as she once was, and she obeys you more readily and accepts your leadership.

In other words, although she's still a rambunctious youngster, your pup should be developing into a sociable, well-mannered member of society. If you haven't neutered your Lab yet, be sure to plan this in the next few months.

Continue Crating

A 12-month old Labrador is not mature enough to have full run of the house when you're not there to supervise her. It's just too much responsibility.

Continue crating her at night and when you're unable to watch her. She can't resist temptation yet, and like most teenagers, she always needs to be doing something. She may need to be crated at night until she's past 2 years old.

You'll also find her spending time in her crate by her own choice, so don't worry that you're being cruel.

Training

She's still an adolescent, and she will be for many months, so your Lab puppy may suddenly test the rules when you least expect it.

Continue practicing, taking her to classes, and adding new skills to her repertoire. Socialization and training go hand in hand, and the more time you invest in both—while having fun with your Lab—the better companion and pet she will become.

Lifetime Training

When you finished basic obedience class, your work wasn't done. A Lab puppy still has a lot of maturing to do, and her skills need reinforcement on a regular basis. Here are some reminders for how to use training throughout her life and keep her skills fresh.

- ❧ Always ask her to sit when you put on the leash and wait for you before going through doors.
- ❧ Have her sit to greet people.
- ❧ Ask her to do a down-stay while you eat dinner or are out in public.
- ❧ Incorporate obedience commands like "Sit," "Down," and "Stay" into your daily walk routine.
- ❧ Have her sit or do a down before you give her her food bowl.
- ❧ Don't allow her to boss you around, enticing you to play or go for a walk, without asking her to earn her privileges by sitting first.

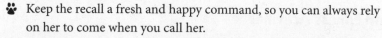

- Practice self-control exercises with your Lab. You don't want her to be rambunctious and out of control when you most need her to behave.

- Keep the recall a fresh and happy command, so you can always rely on her to come when you call her.

- Even when you're playing a game, enforce commands like "Give," "Off," and "Sit." She'll enjoy the challenge.

Search and Rescue

As mentioned earlier, Labs make excellent search-and-rescue dogs and also work with professionals as arson dogs, drug dogs, and in many other capacities. If you've enjoyed tracking and want to volunteer with your Lab, this is an excellent way to give back to your community.

Rescue teams work with law enforcement agencies and must be available to join a search at a moment's notice, day or night. Search dogs must be able to concentrate on a single scent that might be days old while blocking out distractions such as traffic, crowds, food, and other animals.

You and your Lab will undergo extensive training and be certified in various skills such as CPR, canine and human first aid, radio communication, map reading, and crime-scene preservation. Your dog can participate in urban and wilderness searches or human-remains searches or serve as a first responder in case of a national disaster. The National Association for Search and Rescue offers more information on how you can get involved at nasar.org.

You and Your Puppy

Your Labrador Retriever puppy's first year presented a lot of challenges and now your Lab is almost grown. All the time you've invested pays off now. You've built a good foundation for your next decade or more together.

Your Changing Relationship

Your relationship with your puppy will gradually change from one of constant supervision and training to one of friendship and understanding. You've spent a lot of time getting to know each other, and your Lab can read your moods so well sometimes you'll think she's human. And of course, you'll learn to read her, too, especially when she's about to take off with your shoe.

Check in with your breeder at least once a year, and give him an update on your puppy. He'll want to know if she has any health issues you're concerned about, and he'll be thrilled to catch up on her activities.

Social and Fitness Activities

Hiking with your Lab is fun and challenging. Once she has matured, work up slowly to more challenging hikes so she doesn't get overly tired, heated, or injured. Research hiking trails before you go to be sure dogs are welcome.

Here are some things to take along:

- 🐾 A quart of water each for you and your Lab and a portable water bowl for her
- 🐾 Snacks for added energy—peanut butter on dog biscuits provides a quick energy boost for your dog
- 🐾 Waste bags—be a responsible hiker; pick up the poop
- 🐾 A first-aid kit that includes Benadryl, eyewash, tweezers, antibiotic ointment, a large bandana for bandaging, gauze pads, insect repellent, and MSG to put on bites
- 🐾 Leash
- 🐾 Doggie backpack (Be sure you've tested it beforehand and it fits your dog without rubbing.)

Sometimes it's hard to get yourself off the couch to exercise, but your Lab will help you get out the door. You two can participate in one of the multitude of doggy fitness classes nationwide. Walking groups, exercise classes, and even doga—yoga for you and your dog!—offer the opportunity to strengthen the bond between your and your Lab while reaping health benefits for you both.

Meetup groups offer get-togethers for like-minded folks in any number of hobbies and activities, including dogs, and you're sure to find a special Labrador meetup group near you. Go to meetup.com, put in your zip code, and see what's happening near you. Lab owners schedule play dates at local dog parks, beach walks, costume contests, and even "yappy" hours.

Labrador Retriever rescue groups always need more volunteers, and members share a common love for their breed. Even if you can't bear to visit a shelter, you can help out with adoption fairs, transport, fund-raising, and other events. Members often bring their own Labs along, so be sure to take yours, too, if she's well socialized.

Dog Boots, Jackets, and Other Special Gear

Owning an active Lab means outfitting her with her own gear for your adventures together. These products make it easier to take your dog along and ensure her safety. Don't be surprised if she soon has her own closet in your home!

You may need some accessories to take your Labrador out on the town, or at least for camping and hiking activities. Major sporting-goods chains and camping and hunting catalogs carry an array of products especially designed to outfit the well-appointed Labrador Retriever.

You may remember the search-and-rescue dogs who worked after September 11, 2001. A nationwide campaign gathered donations to supply the dogs with protective boots to wear while searching in the hot, dangerous debris after the disaster. Even if your Lab isn't a search-and-rescue dog, she may be more comfortable on your adventures if she's got some boots.

Protective boots come in everyday lightweight styles that provide air circulation while protecting his paw pads from hot pavement. For snowy, cold weather, tall, insulated boots keep snow out while a textured sole prevents her from slipping on ice. Traction sole boots also help your Lab navigate rocky terrain or a slippery boat deck. Whatever your activities together, you're sure to be able to find some appropriate footwear for your pup.

Carrying a backpack gives your Lab a job to do and helps you out, too. She can carry her own gear in the pack, or you can get a special water pack that has two compartments for water—one for yours and one for hers. Start with light loads and get her used to carrying the pack before you take her on a longer trip. Your dog should never carry more than 25 percent of her body weight. For a 70-pound dog, that's 17½ pounds.

If you're boating, kayaking, or hunting from a boat with your Lab, a life vest will help keep her safe. Most life vests are reflective so you can easily see your dog, and they have a handle you can use to lift her out of the water. For larger boats, you can also buy boat ladders made especially for dogs, which are really more like stairs or ramps with rubberized steps for traction. They'll make it easier for your 70-pound wet Lab to get in and out of the boat, and you won't have to pick her up.

Hauling a wet dog in the back of your SUV is no fun, but bench seat covers make it a little easier to do. Removable and washable, they fasten around the seat with straps so they'll stay in place and protect the upright part of the seat as well as the bench.

Here are some other smaller convenience items for Labrador activities you might want to check out:

- 🐾 Reflective, waterproof collars
- 🐾 Safety reflectors to hang from your Lab's leash or collar
- 🐾 Bungee leashes you can attach to your waist and to your dog for use while jogging or hiking
- 🐾 Folding canvas food and water bowls with waterproof inserts
- 🐾 Crate-cooling fans
- 🐾 Heated dog beds
- 🐾 Canvas and rubber bumpers for retrieving

Your Best Friend

The loving companion you envisioned sleeping at your feet in front of the fireplace is well on her way to growing up. During this first year, she's probably given you lots of laughs, made you want to tear out your hair, eaten your prize rosebush, and vomited at the foot of your bed. She's snuggled with the kids and dried your tears with her big, sloppy tongue while knocking over your favorite lamp with her tail. Maybe it's her sense of humor that's made you love her so much, but you can't imagine life without her now, and why would you want to?

We hope you'll enjoy your Lab's youth and exuberance, her maturity and loyal companionship, and her devoted old age. She'll be your best friend through thick and thin, always ready to play, always happy to see you come home. Include her in your life, and allow her to love you. There's something about a Lab that's made her the most popular dog in the United States year after year, and you are lucky enough to find out why.

AAFCO   The American Association of Feed Control Officials, an association of local, state, and federal agencies charged by law to regulate the sale and distribution of animal feeds and animal drug remedies.

alpha rollover   This punishment is supposed to mimic how wolves establish their dominance over each other. A person forces his dog to the ground and holds her on her side or back until the dog "submits" and stops fighting the handler. Don't try this at home, and don't let a "trainer" do this to your dog.

bitch   A female dog.

breed type   The qualities that define a Lab and make him different from other dog breeds as set forth in the breed standard.

bumper   A rubber or canvas retrieving toy. Used for training hunting dogs, bumpers are long and narrow enough that they stick out of either side of the dog's mouth so you can take them easily.

CERF   Canine Eye Registration Foundation. This organization keeps a record of eye exams done on puppies and adult dogs and certifies the dogs to be free of inherited eye diseases, such as Progressive Retinal Atrophy, which is common in Labrador Retrievers.

"come"   The command that means "Quit what you are doing and come here, to me, right now."

dam   The mother of the litter.

displacement behavior   A behavior that occurs out of context in response to an internal emotional conflict.

dog   A term that can mean any dog or specifically refer to a male.

dominance   A relationship between two or more dogs that's established by force and submission to gain power over others.

"down"   The command that means "Lie down, roll on one hip, and don't move." The hand signal is to sweep your flat hand, palm down, toward the ground.

"give"   The command that means "Put that item in my hand." The hand signal is to hold your hand open, palm upward, in front of his face.

glycemic index   A scale that measures the speed at which the body converts carbohydrates into sugars.

growth plates   Discs at the end of each long bone (of the leg, for example) that are composed of soft cartilage. The cartilage is eventually replaced by bone.

intact   An unneutered male or unspayed female dog.

"leave it"   The command that means "Turn away from what you are looking at and look at me."

"let's go" or "walk"   The command that means "Pay attention, we're going for a walk." The hand signal is to step off on your left foot (when she is at your left side).

malabsorption   The body's inability to process and use nutrients in food.

mark   In a hunting test, a bird is thrown or shot and the dog "marks" it by recognizing where it fell and remembering the location.

marking   When a mature dog deposits urine so other dogs can identify him or her and determine the dog's age or readiness to breed. Marking also establishes territorial boundaries.

microflora   Microorganisms that live in the digestive tract of an animal and perform various functions, such as training the immune system, producing vitamins, and preventing growth of harmful bacteria.

neonatal period   The first 2 weeks of a puppy's life, when the puppy sleeps and eats and not much else.

OFA   The Orthopedic Foundation of Animals, a nonprofit group that collects information about the incidence of orthopedic and genetic diseases in dogs. OFA evaluates and grades hip and elbow x-rays of dogs prior to breeding. A breeder provides the rating of your puppy's sire and dam.

"off"   The command that means "Put all four feet on the floor." The hand signal is to push your flat palm toward the dog, fingers spread.

"okay"   The command that releases your dog from whatever he's doing. Okay signifies "You are finished; relax," or "At ease." The hand signal is both hands palms up.

pheromone   A chemical secreted by an animal that another animal, usually of the same species, can interpret.

serotonin   A neurotransmitter involved in the transmission of impulses between nerve cells. It's found in the brain, blood platelets, and intestinal tract.

sire   The father of a litter of puppies.

"sit"   The command that means "Put your rear end on the floor and don't move." The hand signal is to scoop one hand upward, palm up.

socialization period   The period between 3 to 12 weeks of age when your puppy starts to explore her world. During this time, positive or negative experiences will impact her behavior for the rest of her life.

specialty show   A conformation dog show for a single breed of dog, held by a breed club. In a Labrador Retriever Specialty, the breed club often also conducts obedience, rally, hunting tests, and agility trials.

"stay"   The command that means "Do not move a muscle until I come back and touch you." The hand signal is your flat palm in front of the puppy's nose as you step off on your right foot.

"take it"   The command that means "Take this item" as you present it to her, like a toy.

titer   A test that measures the amount of antibodies to a particular disease your Lab is carrying in his body.

transition period   The time between 2 and 3 weeks of age when your puppy starts to be more aware of his environment.

weaning   The process of gradually changing a puppy's diet from mother's milk to solid food.

whelping box   A large nest where the mother gives birth to her puppies. There's often a ledge around the sides, so the mother won't accidentally crush a puppy against the wall.

withers   The highest point of a dog's shoulders, behind the neck.

zoonotic disease   A disease that's transmissible from one species to another, for example, from dogs to humans.

Growth and Body Condition Assessment

It's difficult to predict exactly what a Lab's size and weight should be at any given month during his first year. The most dramatic growth period is from birth to 6 months, when your dog grows to roughly 75 percent of his adult height. After that, growth slows dramatically until he reaches his full height at 10 to 12 months. Although the breed standard states that an adult male Lab should be 22.5 to 24.5 inches at the shoulders (females 1 inch smaller), in reality, some Labs are taller. Labs from field breeding will be taller and leaner than their show-dog brethren.

So when you read the following estimates, take your own Lab's build into consideration. There will be clear differences, even between two 12-week-old puppies. Even within a litter, puppies grow at different rates.

Age, Height, and Weight Estimates

The following numbers are estimates you can compare to, taken from the growth records of Lab puppies:

> *Birth:* 12 to 20 ounces
>
> *8 weeks:* 10 to 12 pounds
>
> *12 weeks (3 months):* 20 to 25 pounds
>
> *16 weeks (4 months):* 32 to 35 pounds; 14 inches at the shoulder
>
> *20 weeks (5 months):* 44 to 48 pounds; 18 to 20 inches at the shoulder
>
> *6 to 12 months:* 55 to 70 pounds; probably won't reach full weight until 2 to 2½ years; mature height is 22½ to 24½ inches

All the heights and weights are approximate. It may be better to look at the percent of increase. For example, weight doubles between 8 and 12 weeks.

Is My Puppy Fat?

Obesity is a common problem in Labs. Our dogs just love to eat, and many Labs do not do the energy-intense work they were bred to do. A family pet doesn't need as many calories as a hunting dog. Even puppies can overeat, and this predisposes them to grow into heavy adults.

Being overweight puts extra stress on bones and joints. And because Labs are prone to arthritis and other joint problems as they mature, a little light is better than a little heavy in our breed.

Don't feed your puppy according to the instructions on a food bag; feed him according to his current size, weight, condition, and overall health.

Body Condition Assessment

Regardless of any charts and estimates, the best way to know if your dog is obese, ideal weight, or too thin, is to do a body condition assessment. At any age, use the following guidelines to check your dog. If you have any doubts about your puppy's weight, consult with your veterinarian or your puppy's breeder for advice.

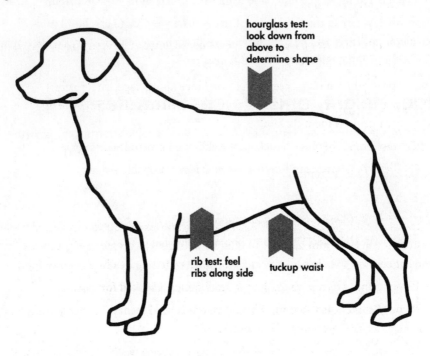

Use this illustration to help determine if your puppy is ideal, too heavy, or too thin.

Have someone help you by holding your puppy in a standing position and keeping him relatively still. Look down on your puppy from above and look at where his rib cage ends. See if he is ...

❧ *Ideal.* There is a slight narrowing behind his rib cage that continues to his rear. He's shaped like an hourglass.

🐾 *Too heavy.* Your puppy is wider or rounder in the back half.

🐾 *Too thin.* He appears dramatically narrower; you may also see his ribs.

The size of his rib cage won't change, but the padding on it will. Run your hands down each side of his rib cage. See if he is …

🐾 *Ideal.* You can find his ribs with little effort. You may barely see them when he's in sunlight.

🐾 *Too heavy.* There's a layer of fat, and that makes it hard to find his ribs.

🐾 *Too thin.* You can see his ribs without feeling for them. You may also easily see his spine.

The bottom outline of your Lab puppy's body should start at his front elbows and tuck up slightly behind his rib cage. See if he is …

🐾 *Ideal.* You can see or feel a slight rise after his rib cage. This varies between show and field Labs, with field-bred dogs sometimes having a more prominent tuckup.

🐾 *Too heavy.* There is no tuckup; the abdomen protrudes or sags.

🐾 *Too thin.* There's a noticeable waist; you can probably see his hipbones.

If you feel your pup is too heavy, cut back *slightly* on the amount you feed him—a drastic cut will leave him hungry. Supplement his meals with some vegetables (like beans or carrots) to help him feel full. Consider switching to a higher-fiber food.

If your puppy has a potbelly, have a stool sample checked for worms.

If your Labrador is too thin, see your veterinarian. He may just need more food, or he may not be digesting his food properly.

Check your puppy's body condition regularly every 2 weeks during the first 18 months. As he grows, his calorie needs will vary. For the first 6 months of dramatic growth, you need to feed him increasing amounts of food. When he reaches full height, you can gradually reduce his daily amount to a normal adult quantity based on his size.

Appendix C Poisonous Plants

Many common landscaping, decorative, and houseplants are potentially hazardous to your dog. Some may cause a contact allergy, such as poison sumac or ivy; others can be potentially fatal. When ingested, castor bean, English ivy, and hemlock, for example, can kill a dog.

If you have any of these plants in your house or yard, either remove them or be sure your dog doesn't have access to them. If you aren't sure of the identity of a specific plant, take a close-up photo of it and ask at your local garden center or nursery.

Flowering Plants

These plants could be in a flower bed or used as potted plants. In some regions, some are also used as houseplants.

- Amaryllis
- Anemone
- Azalea
- Bird of paradise
- Buttercup
- Christmas cactus
- Crocus
- Cyclamen
- Foxglove
- Impatiens
- Jasmine
- Larkspur
- Lilies (including Asian, Day, Easter, Glory, Japanese Snow, and Tiger)
- Lily of the Valley
- Morning glory
- Snapdragon
- Sweet pea
- Verbena

Bulbs, Tubers, and Fungi

For many of these plants, the tuber or bulb contains the toxins, not the flower or green parts of the plant. Unfortunately, many times the bulb or tuber is what dogs are attracted to, especially when the bulb or tuber is planted with mulch or bone or blood meal to nourish the growing plant.

- ❤ Amaryllis
- ❤ Calla lily
- ❤ Daffodil
- ❤ Gladiola
- ❤ Hyacinth
- ❤ Iris
- ❤ Jonquil
- ❤ Lantana
- ❤ Mushrooms and toadstools (many varieties)
- ❤ Tulip

Trees, Decorative Plants, and Shrubs

Some of these plants are used frequently as landscape plants because they're attractive and easy to grow in many regions. Others are more commonly found as potted houseplants.

- ❤ Asparagus fern
- ❤ Bottlebrush
- ❤ Boxwood
- ❤ Caladium
- ❤ Cocoa bark
- ❤ Creeping Charlie
- ❤ Croton
- ❤ Dieffenbachia (all varieties)
- ❤ Dogwood
- ❤ Dracena (most varieties)
- ❤ Elephant ear (all varieties)

🐾 Emerald feather fern

🐾 English Ivy

🐾 Heavenly bamboo

🐾 Hemlock

🐾 Holly

🐾 Horse chestnut

🐾 Hydrangea

🐾 Ivy (including Boston, Glacier, and others)

🐾 Mistletoe

🐾 Nightshade

🐾 Oleander

🐾 Pennyroyal

🐾 Philodendron (all varieties)

🐾 Privet

🐾 Rhododendron

🐾 Sago palm

🐾 Wisteria

🐾 Yew

Vegetables, Fruits, and Nuts

This list contains a variety of plants that have different parts that are dangerous to dogs. If one specific part is dangerous, that's noted. If nothing is noted, the entire plant should be avoided.

🐾 Avocado (leaves, stems, and pit)

🐾 Eggplant

🐾 Grapes (the fruit)

🐾 Macadamia nut (the nut)

🐾 Peach (and other stone fruit seeds/pits)

🐾 Potato (foliage)

🐾 Rhubarb

🐾 Tomato (foliage)

Herbs, Weeds, and Miscellaneous Plants

This category is also a mixed one, with common herbs, noxious weeds, and a variety of other plants. Many, such as jimson weed and locoweed, are also toxic to many animals, including livestock.

- 🐾 Belladonna
- 🐾 Castor bean
- 🐾 Jimson weed
- 🐾 Locoweed
- 🐾 Marijuana
- 🐾 Milkweed
- 🐾 Pokeweed
- 🐾 Poison ivy
- 🐾 Poison oak
- 🐾 Poison sumac
- 🐾 Pokeweed
- 🐾 Sage

 **Appendix D** # Household and Yard Hazards

Puppies, like young children, have no concept of what's good to eat (or play with) and what's dangerous. Never assume your puppy won't touch something. If it's different, out of the ordinary, has a smell, or is within reach, she probably will investigate it.

Problem Foods

A number of foods we normally consume can be a problem for our dogs. Some may cause mild gastrointestinal upset while others are poisonous and potentially toxic. If your puppy consumes any of these foods, call your veterinarian or emergency veterinary clinic right away.

- Alcoholic drinks (of any kind)
- Caffeine
- Chocolate (milk chocolate is the least toxic; dark and baker's chocolate the most toxic)
- Coffee
- Grapes and raisins
- Macadamia nuts
- Onions and onion powder
- Xylitol (including baked goods, gums, or candies that contain it)
- Yeast dough

As a general rule, don't allow your puppy to eat any spicy foods, fatty foods, leftover grease, or spoiled or moldy foods. They may not be toxic, but they're likely to cause gastrointestinal upset.

In the House

A wide variety of potentially hazardous materials are around your house—many of which you might not have realized could be a danger.

- Bug sprays and repellents (including insect traps)
- Cigarettes, cigars, pipes, and tobaccos

🐾 Cleaners and cleansers (including floor, kitchen, bathroom, shower, countertop, and toilet cleaners)

🐾 Craft supplies (including small parts that might be swallowed, like beads, and many paints and glues)

🐾 Holiday decorations (all holidays, including Christmas tree decorations, Halloween, electrical cords, ribbons, tinsel, batteries, and plants)

🐾 Laundry products (including detergents, bleach, and fabric softener sheets)

🐾 Makeup, hair-care products, and nail polish (as well as hair coloring and nail polish remover)

🐾 Mothballs

🐾 Plant-care products for houseplants (including fertilizers and insecticides)

Medicines

Almost all medications, if ingested in quantity, can have a detrimental effect on your puppy. If you believe your puppy has ingested a medication, call your veterinarian or emergency veterinary clinic immediately. Do not wait for a reaction to begin.

Keep all medications out of your pet's reach but especially these:

🐾 Cold remedies (including those with alcohol)

🐾 Pain medications

🐾 Prescription medications (of any kind but especially antidepressants and anticancer drugs)

🐾 Vitamins

In the Garage and Yard

To keep up our homes and yards, we use a number of potentially dangerous substances. We know what they are, and out of habit, we use them with care. But with a puppy in the household, we must be even more cautious.

🐾 Automobile care and maintenance products (gas, oil, antifreeze, cleaning products, waxes, and more)

- 🐾 Home-maintenance supplies (including paints, paint removers, and supplies)
- 🐾 Rodent killers (including traps of all kinds as well as poisons)
- 🐾 Snail and slug poisons
- 🐾 Yard-care supplies (fertilizers, insecticides, herbicides, and fungicides)

Weather-Related Hazards

Some potential problems are only seen during certain seasons. This doesn't make them less of a hazard; in fact, because these products or hazards are only seen occasionally, they can be more attractive to a curious puppy.

- 🐾 Antifreeze
- 🐾 Blue-green algae in ponds (especially during hot weather)
- 🐾 Candles (lit or unlit)
- 🐾 Cocoa mulch (sold commercially as a garden mulch)
- 🐾 Compost piles (with decaying matter)
- 🐾 Frogs and toads
- 🐾 Ice-melting products
- 🐾 Insects (ants, spiders, scorpions, and others)
- 🐾 Potpourri (especially those used over a candle or in a heated container)
- 🐾 Snakes
- 🐾 Swimming-pool supplies

When you need in-depth information or are searching for professionals to help you care for your Lab puppy, refer to the following list. It includes resources for registration information, dog clubs, health care, veterinarians, trainers, dog sports and activities, microchip registries, and pet sitters.

Clubs

American Kennel Club (AKC)
akc.org

Canadian Kennel Club (CKC)
ckc.ca

Labrador Retriever Club, Inc.
(AKC Parent Club for the Labrador Retriever)
thelabradorclub.com

National Disaster Search Dog Foundation (SDF)
searchdogfoundation.org

North American Hunting Retriever Association (NAHRA)
nahra.org

United Kennel Club (UKC)
ukcdogs.com

Performance Sports

DockDogs
dockdogs.com

North American Dog Agility Council (NADAC)
nadac.com

North American Flyball Association (NAFA)
flyball.org

United States Dog Agility Association (USDAA)
usdaa.com

World Canine Freestyle Organization (WCFO)
worldcaninefreestyle.org

Microchip Registries

AKC Companion Animal Recovery (CAR)
akccar.org

American Animal Hospital Association (AAHA) Universal Pet Microchip Lookup
petmicrochiplookup.org

AVID (American Veterinary Identification Devices)
avidid.com

HomeAgain
public.homeagain.com

Pet Sitters

National Association of Professional Pet Sitters (NAPPS)
petsitters.org

Pet Sitters international (PSI)
petsit.com

Therapy Dog Training and Certification

Love on a Leash
loveonaleash.org

Pet Partners (formerly Delta Society)
deltasociety.org

Therapy Dogs, International (TDI)
tdi-dog.org

Therapy Dogs Inc.
therapydogs.com

Training

Association of Pet Dog Trainers (APDT)
apdt.com

International Association of Animal Behavior Consultants (IAABC)
iaabc.org

National Association of Dog Obedience Instructors (NADOI)
nadoi.org

Veterinary

AKC Canine Health Foundation
akcchf.org

American Animal Hospital Association (AAHA)
healthypet.com

American College of Veterinary Ophthalmologists (ACVO)
acvo.org

American Holistic Veterinary Medical Association
ahvma.org

American Veterinary Medical Association (AVMA)
avma.org

ASPCA Pet Health Insurance
aspcapetinsurance.com

ASPCA Poison Control Center
aspca.org/pet-care/poison-control
1-888-426-4435 (North America; fees apply)

Canine Eye Registration Foundation (CERF)
vmdb.org/cerf.html

Orthopedic Foundation for Animals (OFA)
offa.org

PennHIP
research.vet.upenn.edu/pennhip

Pet Poison Helpline
1-800-858-6680 (United States and Canada; fees apply)

Pets Best Insurance
petsbest.com

VPI Pet Insurance
petinsurance.com

Miscellaneous

International Association of Canine Professionals (IACP)
canineprofessionals.com

Jive Media LLC Pet First Aid smart phone app
jive.me/apps/petfirstraid

PetMD Dog First Aid smart phone app
petmd.com/iphone

PetTech PetSaver First Aid smart phone app
pettech.net/app/index.php

Index

D

H

I

T